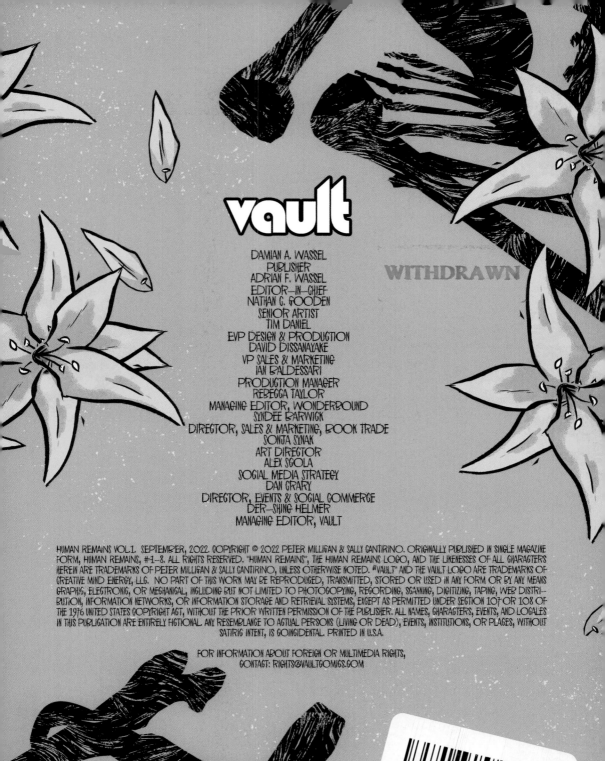

vault

DAMIAN A. WASSEL
PUBLISHER
ADRIAN F. WASSEL
EDITOR-IN-CHIEF
NATHAN C. GOODEN
SENIOR ARTIST
TIM DANIEL
EVP DESIGN & PRODUCTION
DAVID DISSANAYAKE
VP SALES & MARKETING
IAN BALDESSARI
PRODUCTION MANAGER
REBECCA TAYLOR
MANAGING EDITOR, WONDERBOUND
SYNDEE BARWICK
DIRECTOR, SALES & MARKETING, BOOK TRADE
SONJA SYNAK
ART DIRECTOR
ALEX SCOLA
SOCIAL MEDIA STRATEGY
DAN CRARY
DIRECTOR, EVENTS & SOCIAL COMMERCE
DER-SHING HELMER
MANAGING EDITOR, VAULT

FOR INFORMATION ABOUT FOREIGN OR MULTIMEDIA RIGHTS,
CONTACT: RIGHTS@VAULTCOMICS.COM

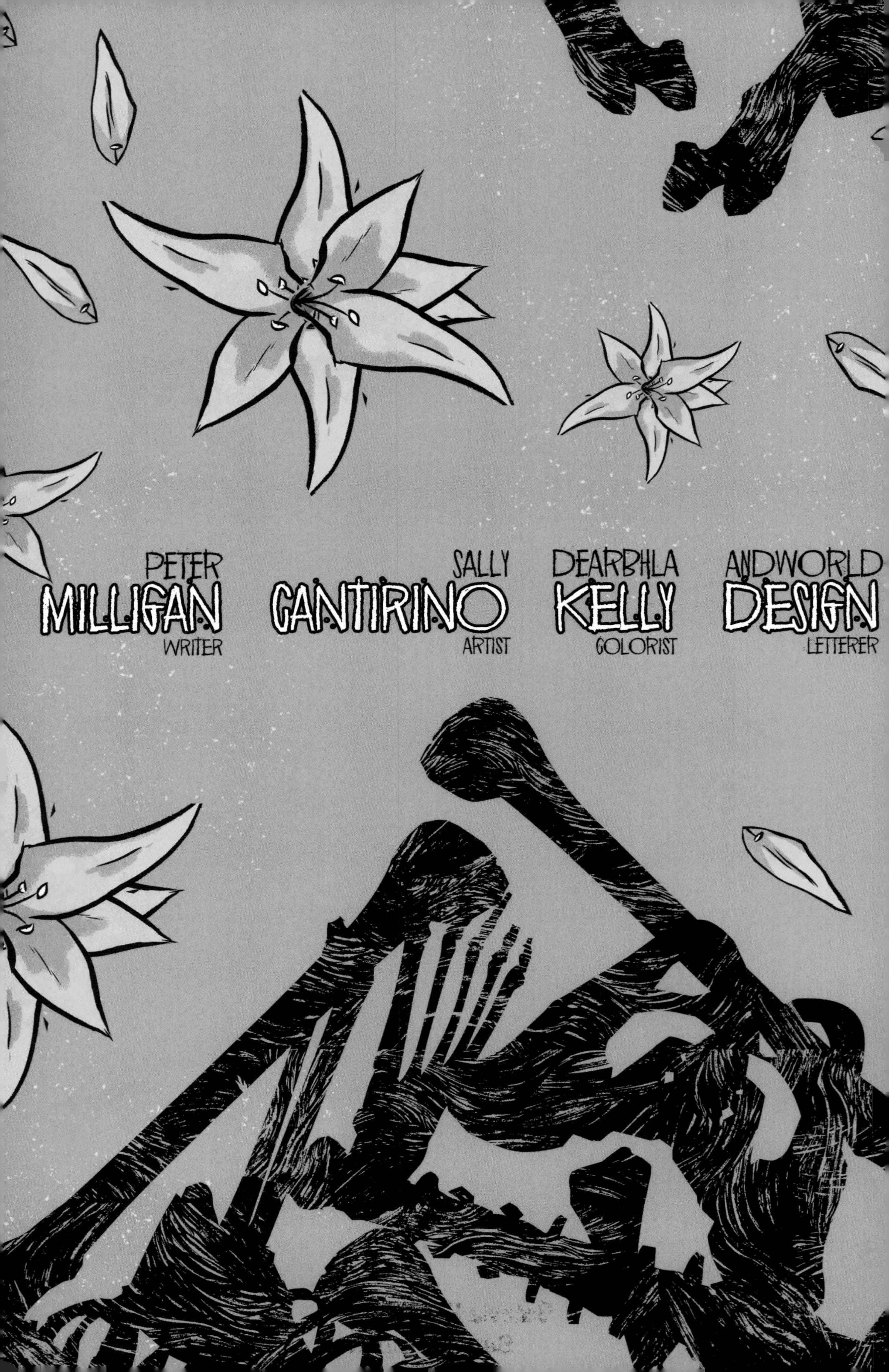
PETER MILLIGAN WRITER
SALLY CANTIRINO ARTIST
DEARBHLA KELLY COLORIST
ANDWORLD DESIGN LETTERER

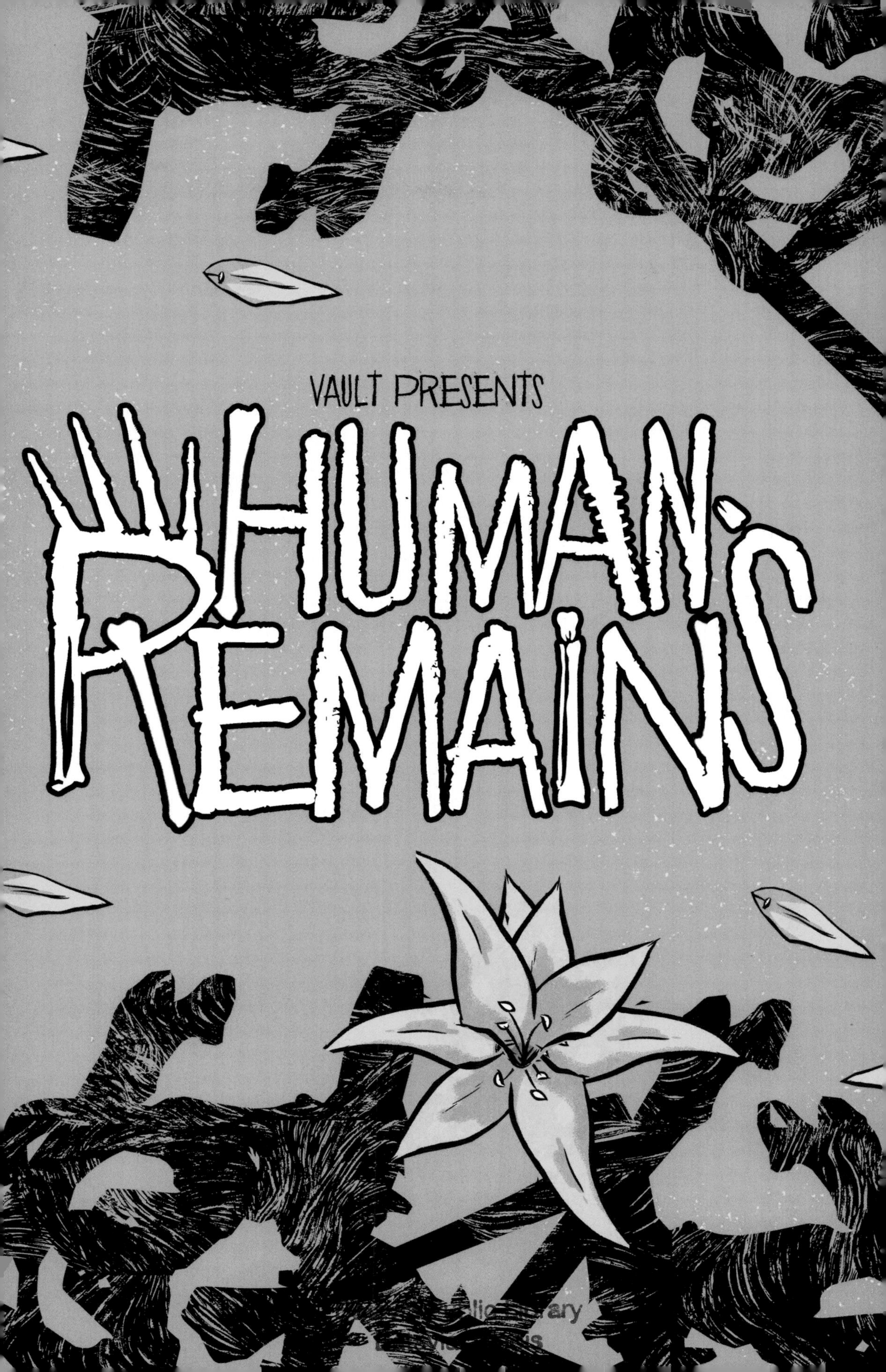
VAULT PRESENTS
HUMAN REMAINS

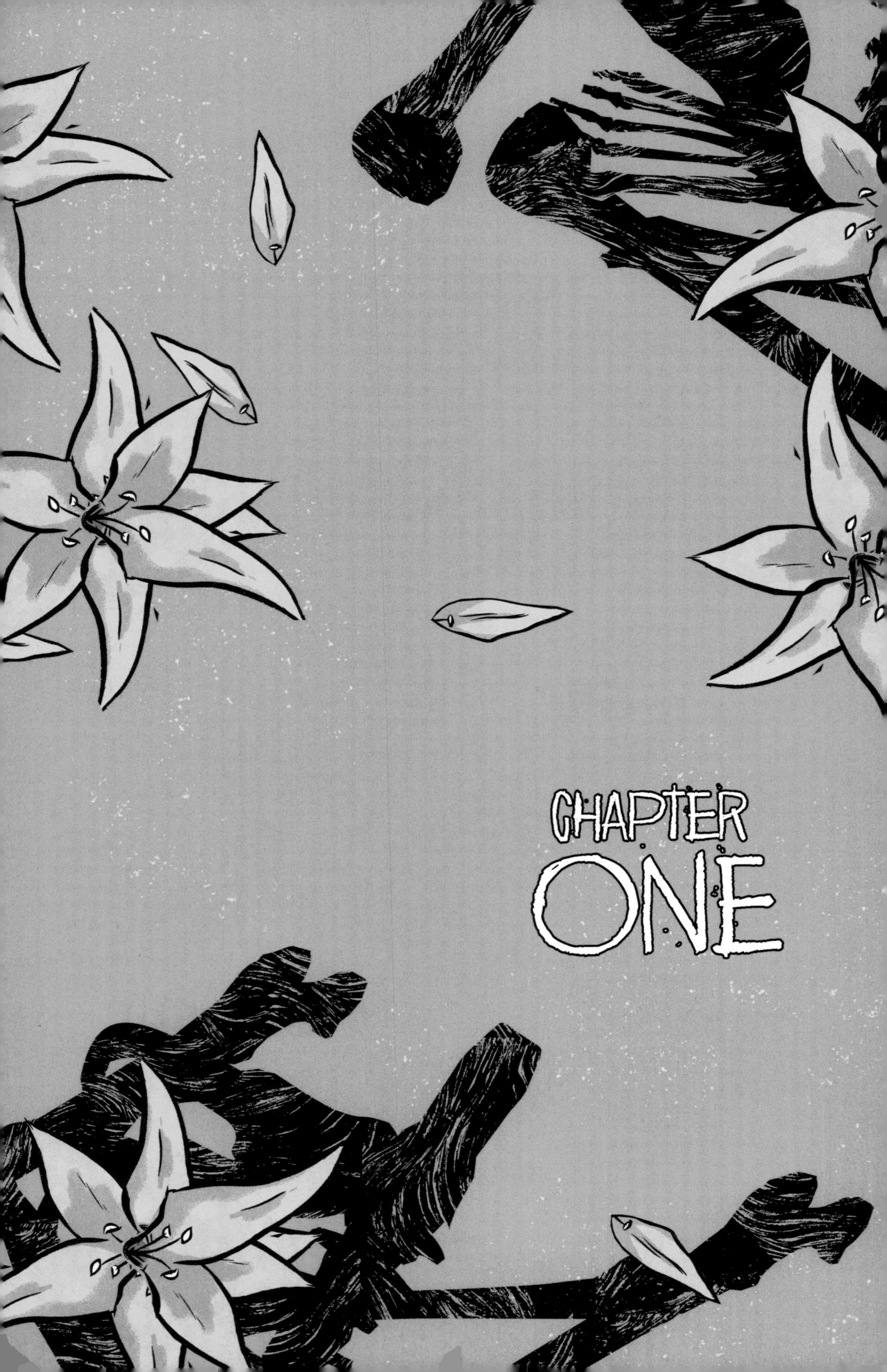
CHAPTER
ONE

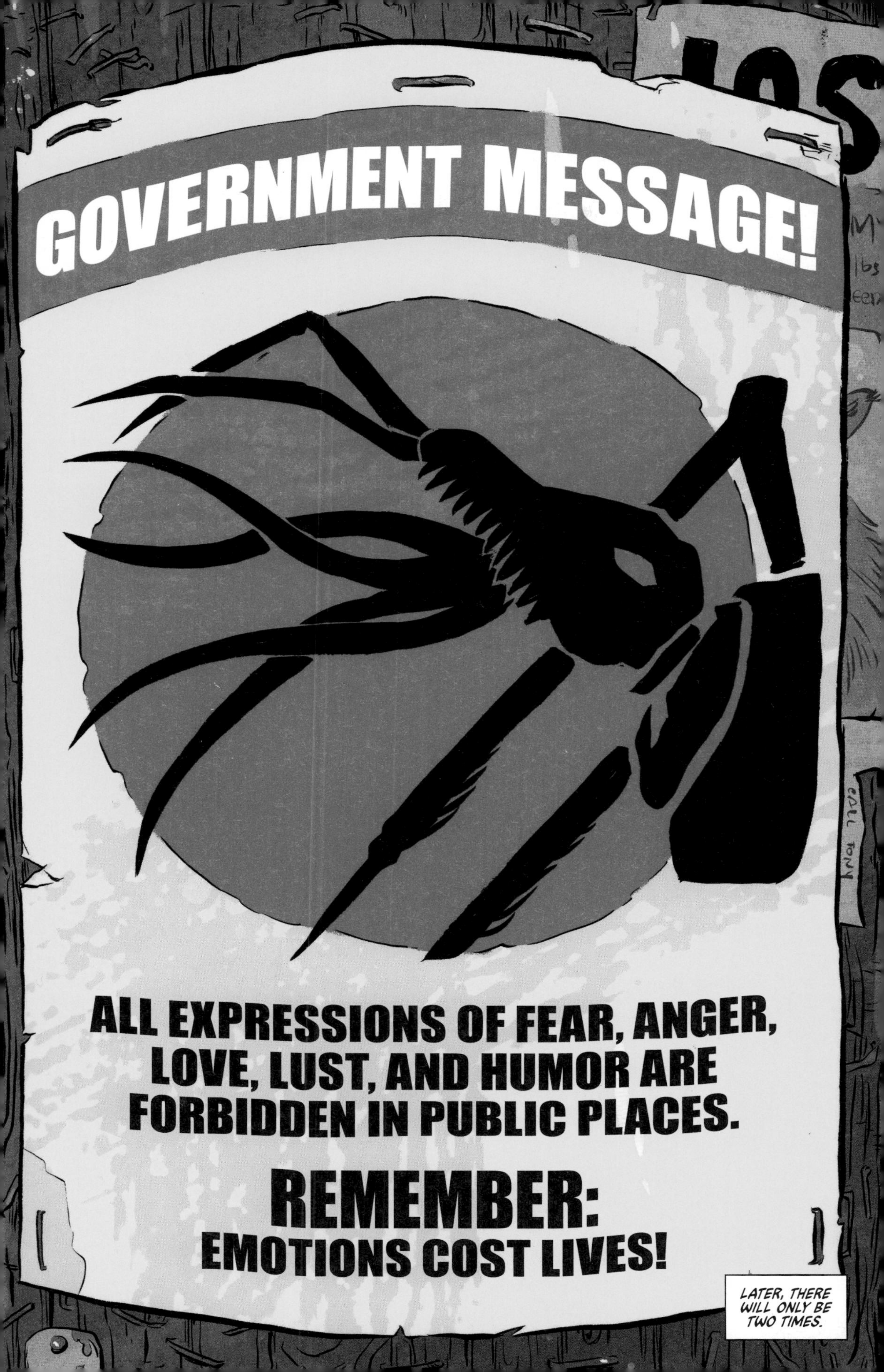
GOVERNMENT MESSAGE!
ALL EXPRESSIONS OF FEAR, ANGER, LOVE, LUST, AND HUMOR ARE FORBIDDEN IN PUBLIC PLACES.
REMEMBER: EMOTIONS COST LIVES!
LATER, THERE WILL ONLY BE TWO TIMES.

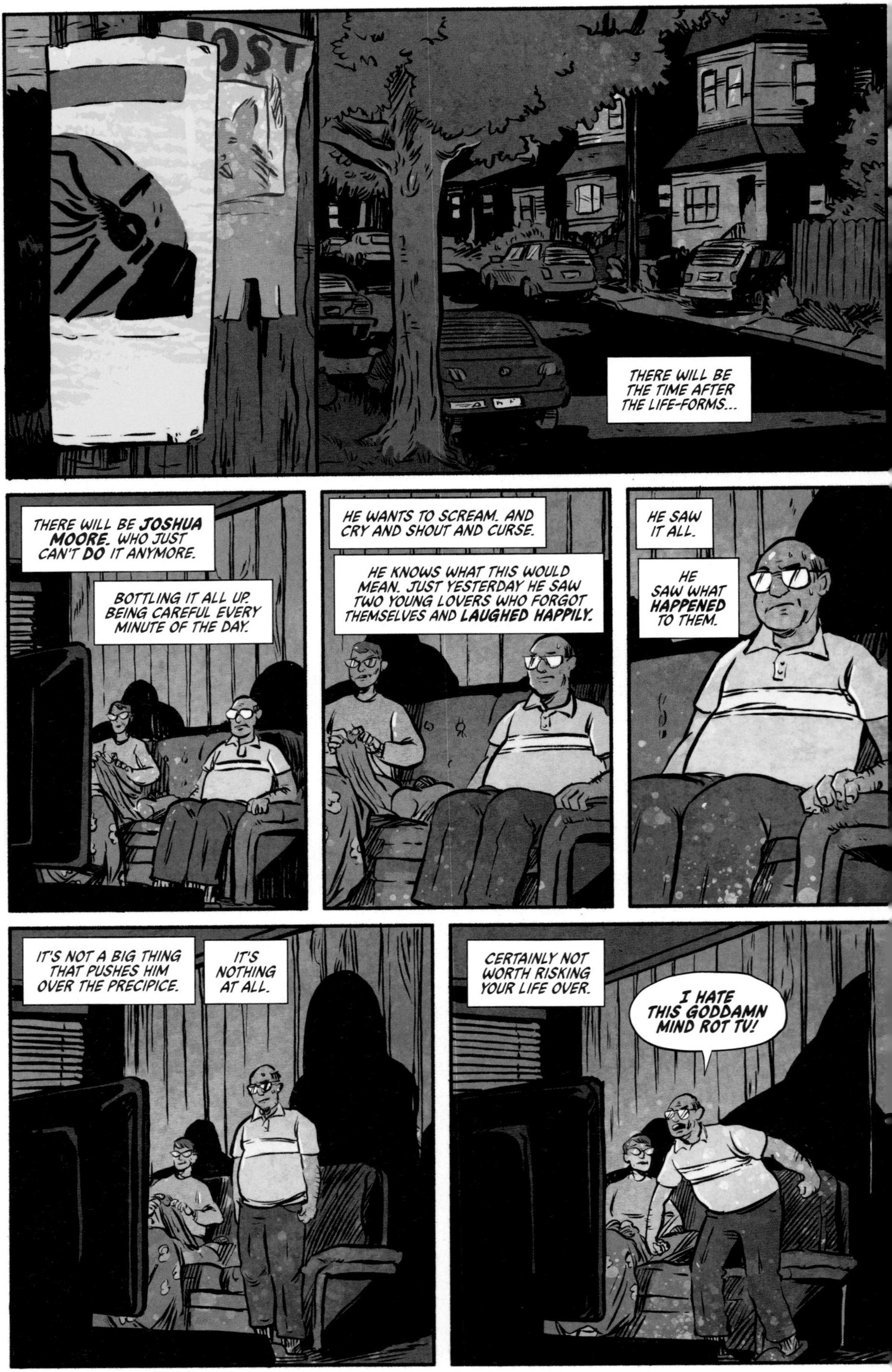

LOST
THERE WILL BE THE TIME AFTER THE LIFE-FORMS...
THERE WILL BE **JOSHUA MOORE.** WHO JUST CAN'T **DO** IT ANYMORE.
BOTTLING IT ALL UP. BEING CAREFUL EVERY MINUTE OF THE DAY.
HE WANTS TO SCREAM. AND CRY AND SHOUT AND CURSE.
HE KNOWS WHAT THIS WOULD MEAN. JUST YESTERDAY HE SAW TWO YOUNG LOVERS WHO FORGOT THEMSELVES AND **LAUGHED HAPPILY.**
HE SAW IT ALL.
HE SAW WHAT **HAPPENED** TO THEM.
IT'S NOT A BIG THING THAT PUSHES HIM OVER THE PRECIPICE.
IT'S NOTHING AT ALL.
CERTAINLY NOT WORTH RISKING YOUR LIFE OVER.
I HATE THIS GODDAMN MIND ROT TV!

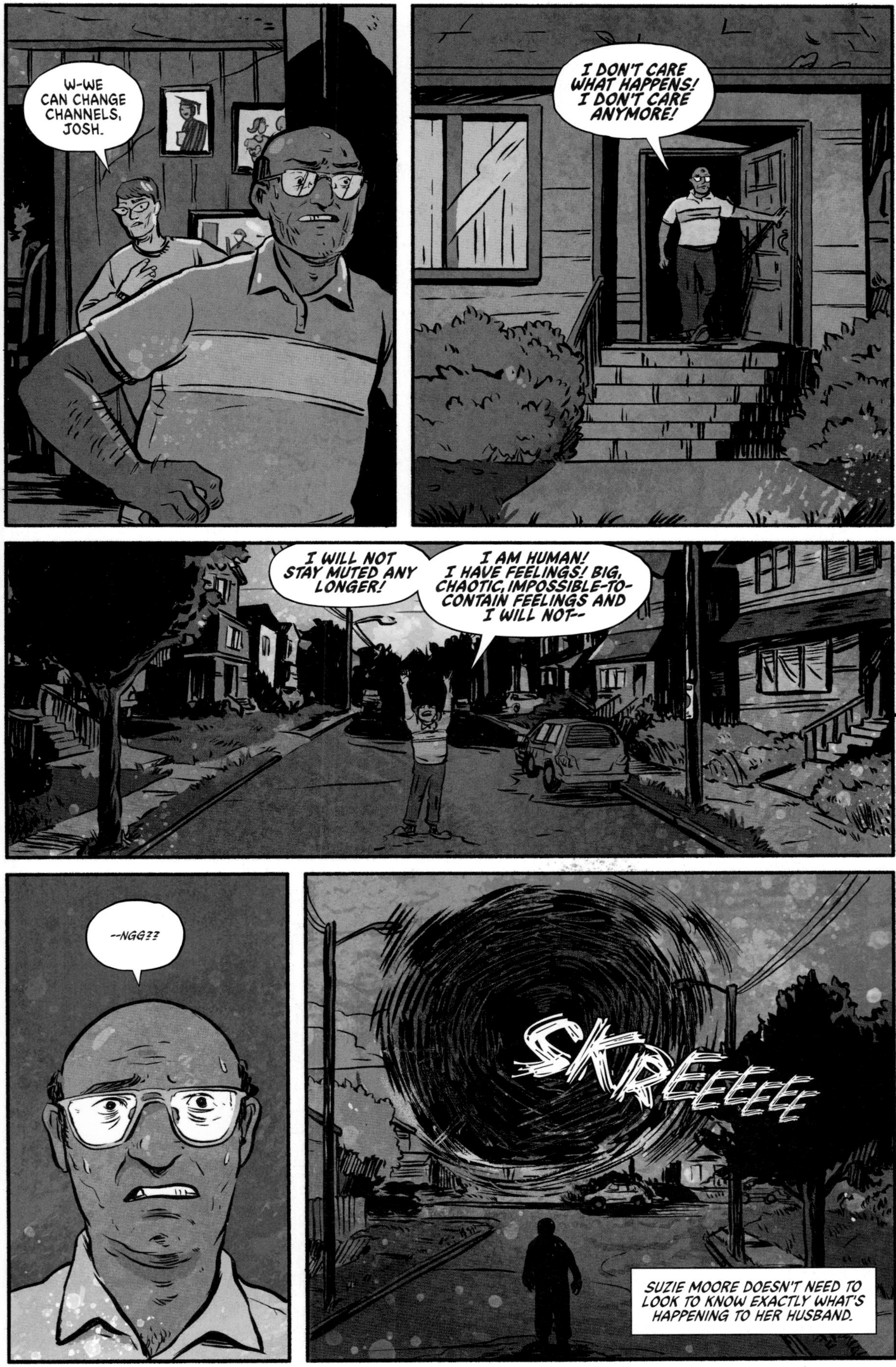
W-WE CAN CHANGE CHANNELS, JOSH.
I DON'T CARE WHAT HAPPENS! I DON'T CARE ANYMORE!
I WILL NOT STAY MUTED ANY LONGER!
I AM HUMAN! I HAVE FEELINGS! BIG, CHAOTIC, IMPOSSIBLE-TO-CONTAIN FEELINGS AND I WILL NOT--
--NGG??
SKREEEEEE
SUZIE MOORE DOESN'T NEED TO LOOK TO KNOW EXACTLY WHAT'S HAPPENING TO HER HUSBAND.

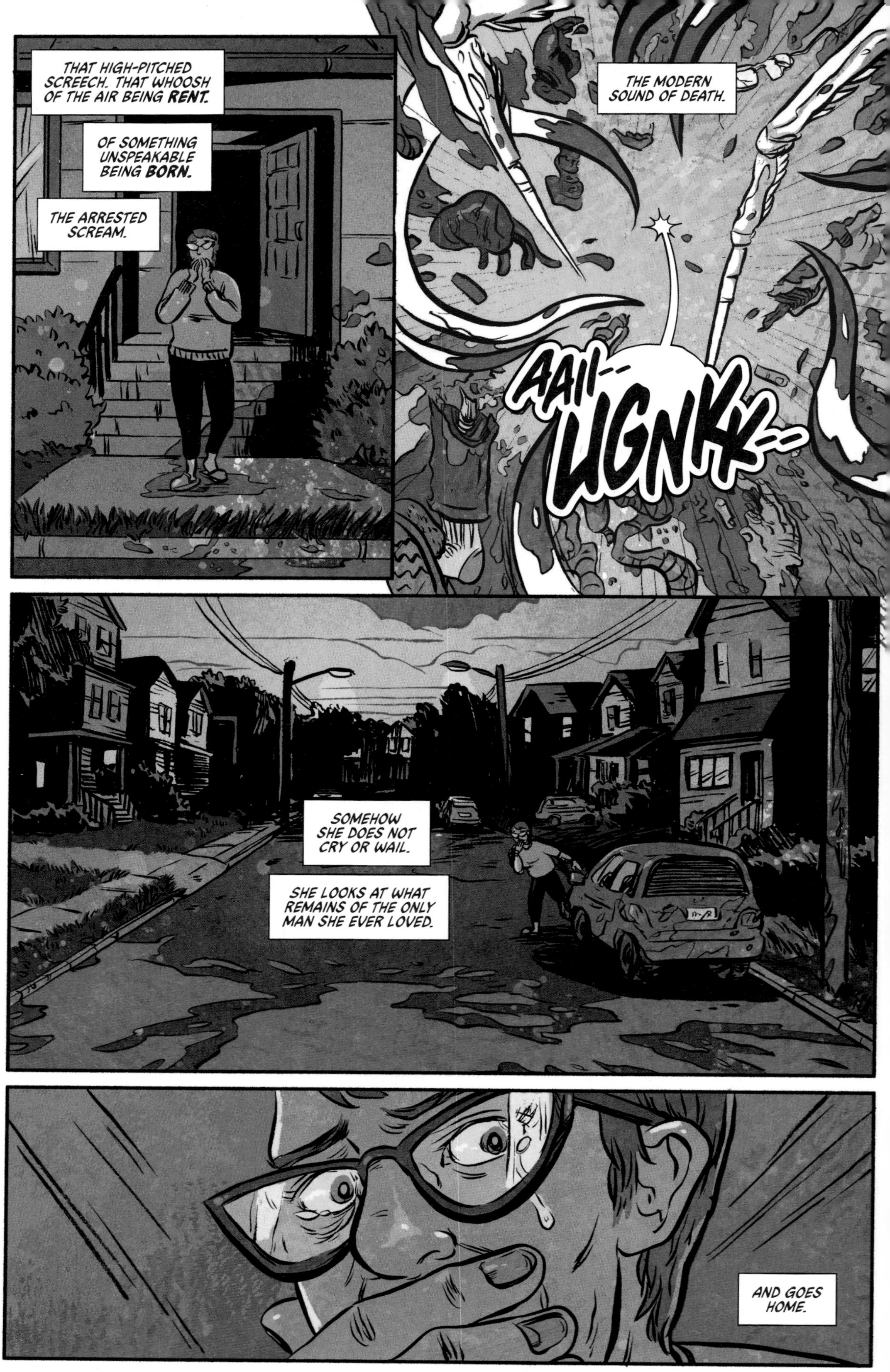
THAT HIGH-PITCHED SCREECH. THAT WHOOSH OF THE AIR BEING **RENT.**
OF SOMETHING UNSPEAKABLE BEING **BORN.**
THE ARRESTED SCREAM.
THE MODERN SOUND OF DEATH.
AAII--UGNKK--
SOMEHOW SHE DOES NOT CRY OR WAIL.
SHE LOOKS AT WHAT REMAINS OF THE ONLY MAN SHE EVER LOVED.
AND GOES HOME.

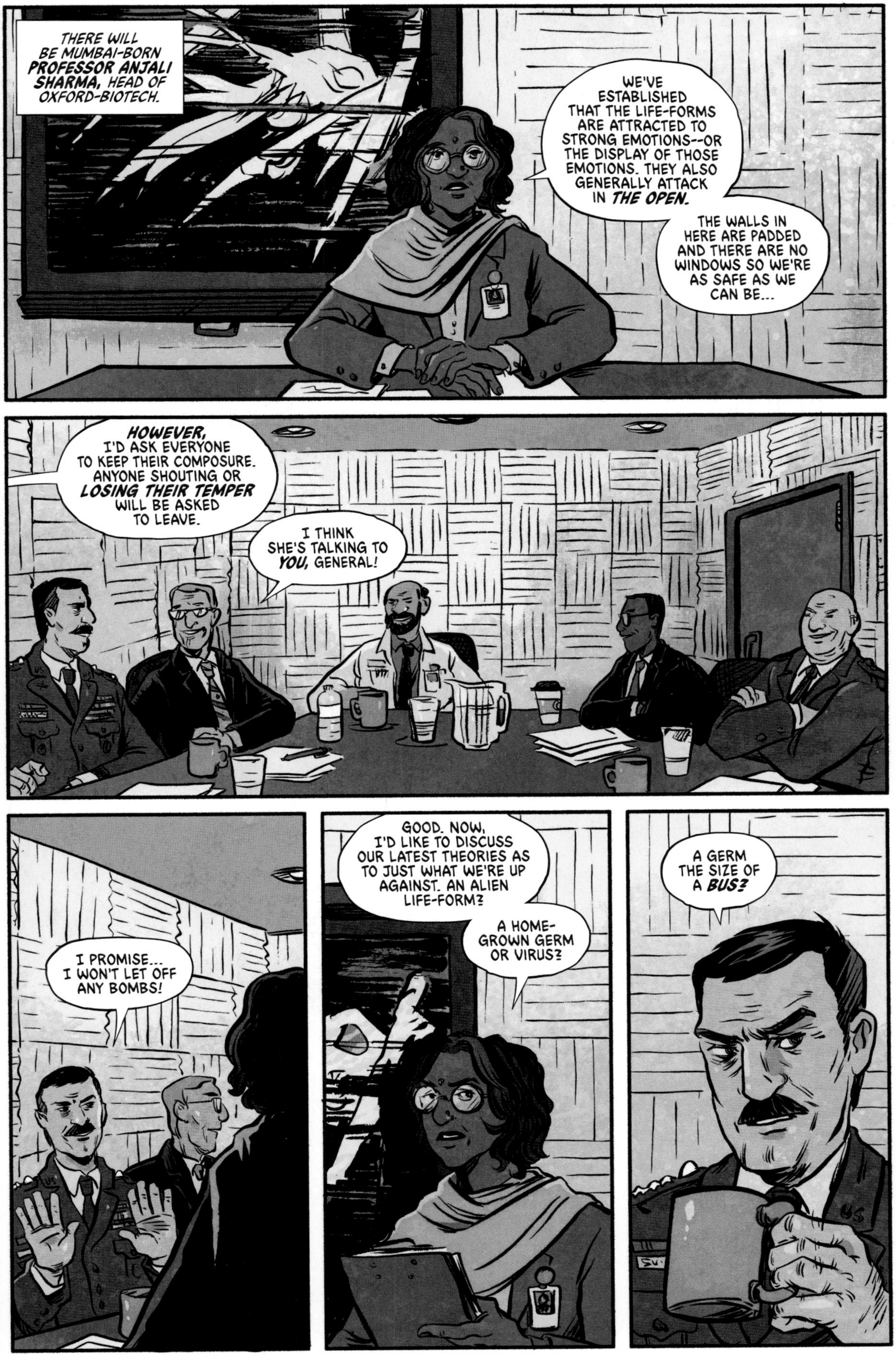
THERE WILL BE MUMBAI-BORN PROFESSOR ANJALI SHARMA, HEAD OF OXFORD-BIOTECH.
WE'VE ESTABLISHED THAT THE LIFE-FORMS ARE ATTRACTED TO STRONG EMOTIONS--OR THE DISPLAY OF THOSE EMOTIONS. THEY ALSO GENERALLY ATTACK IN THE OPEN.
THE WALLS IN HERE ARE PADDED AND THERE ARE NO WINDOWS SO WE'RE AS SAFE AS WE CAN BE...
HOWEVER, I'D ASK EVERYONE TO KEEP THEIR COMPOSURE. ANYONE SHOUTING OR LOSING THEIR TEMPER WILL BE ASKED TO LEAVE.
I THINK SHE'S TALKING TO YOU, GENERAL!
I PROMISE... I WON'T LET OFF ANY BOMBS!
GOOD. NOW, I'D LIKE TO DISCUSS OUR LATEST THEORIES AS TO JUST WHAT WE'RE UP AGAINST. AN ALIEN LIFE-FORM?
A HOME-GROWN GERM OR VIRUS?
A GERM THE SIZE OF A BUS?

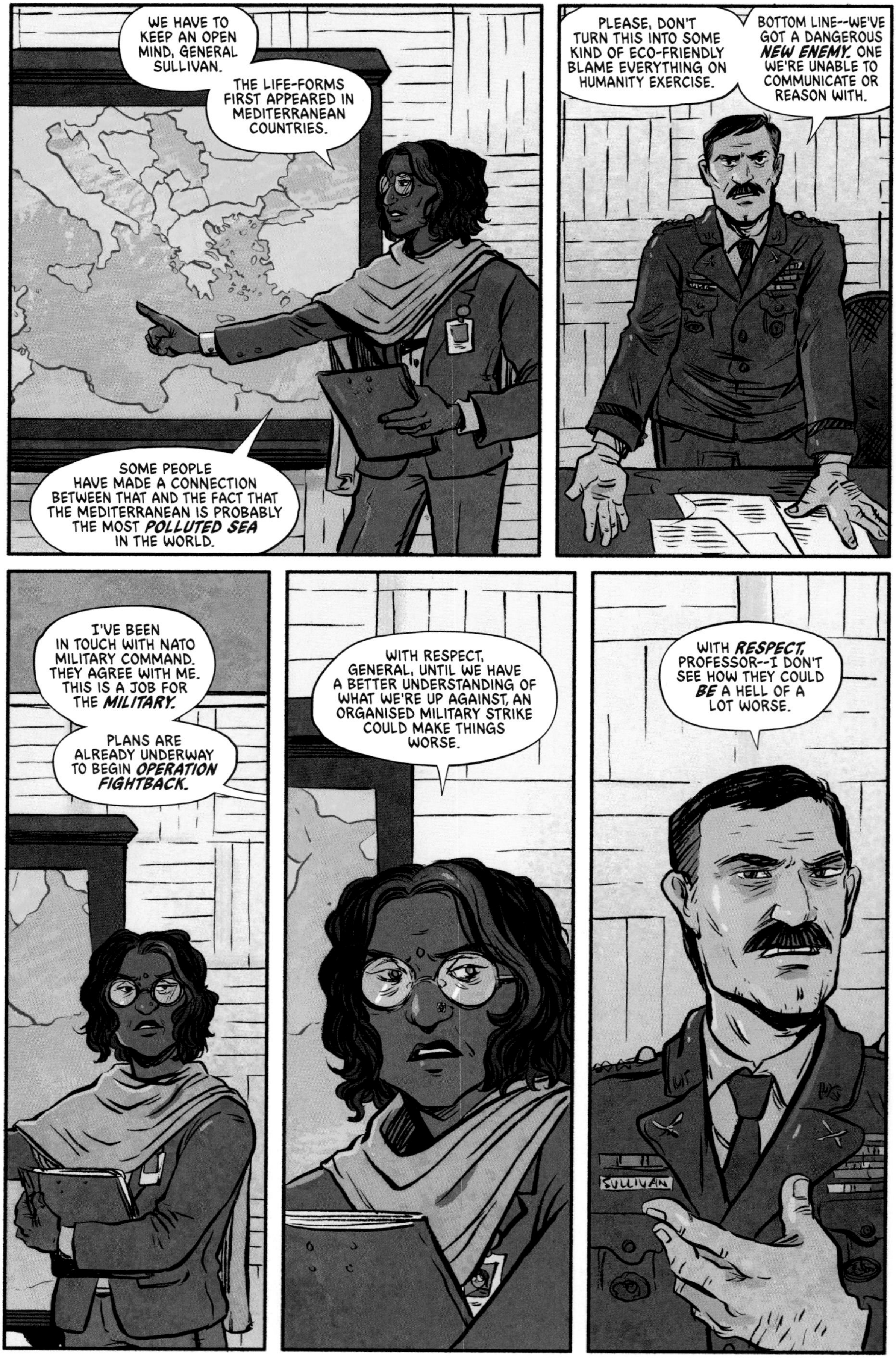
WE HAVE TO KEEP AN OPEN MIND, GENERAL SULLIVAN.
THE LIFE-FORMS FIRST APPEARED IN MEDITERRANEAN COUNTRIES.
SOME PEOPLE HAVE MADE A CONNECTION BETWEEN THAT AND THE FACT THAT THE MEDITERRANEAN IS PROBABLY THE MOST POLLUTED SEA IN THE WORLD.
PLEASE, DON'T TURN THIS INTO SOME KIND OF ECO-FRIENDLY BLAME EVERYTHING ON HUMANITY EXERCISE.
BOTTOM LINE--WE'VE GOT A DANGEROUS NEW ENEMY. ONE WE'RE UNABLE TO COMMUNICATE OR REASON WITH.
I'VE BEEN IN TOUCH WITH NATO MILITARY COMMAND. THEY AGREE WITH ME. THIS IS A JOB FOR THE MILITARY.
PLANS ARE ALREADY UNDERWAY TO BEGIN OPERATION FIGHTBACK.
WITH RESPECT, GENERAL, UNTIL WE HAVE A BETTER UNDERSTANDING OF WHAT WE'RE UP AGAINST, AN ORGANISED MILITARY STRIKE COULD MAKE THINGS WORSE.
WITH RESPECT, PROFESSOR--I DON'T SEE HOW THEY COULD BE A HELL OF A LOT WORSE.
SULLIVAN

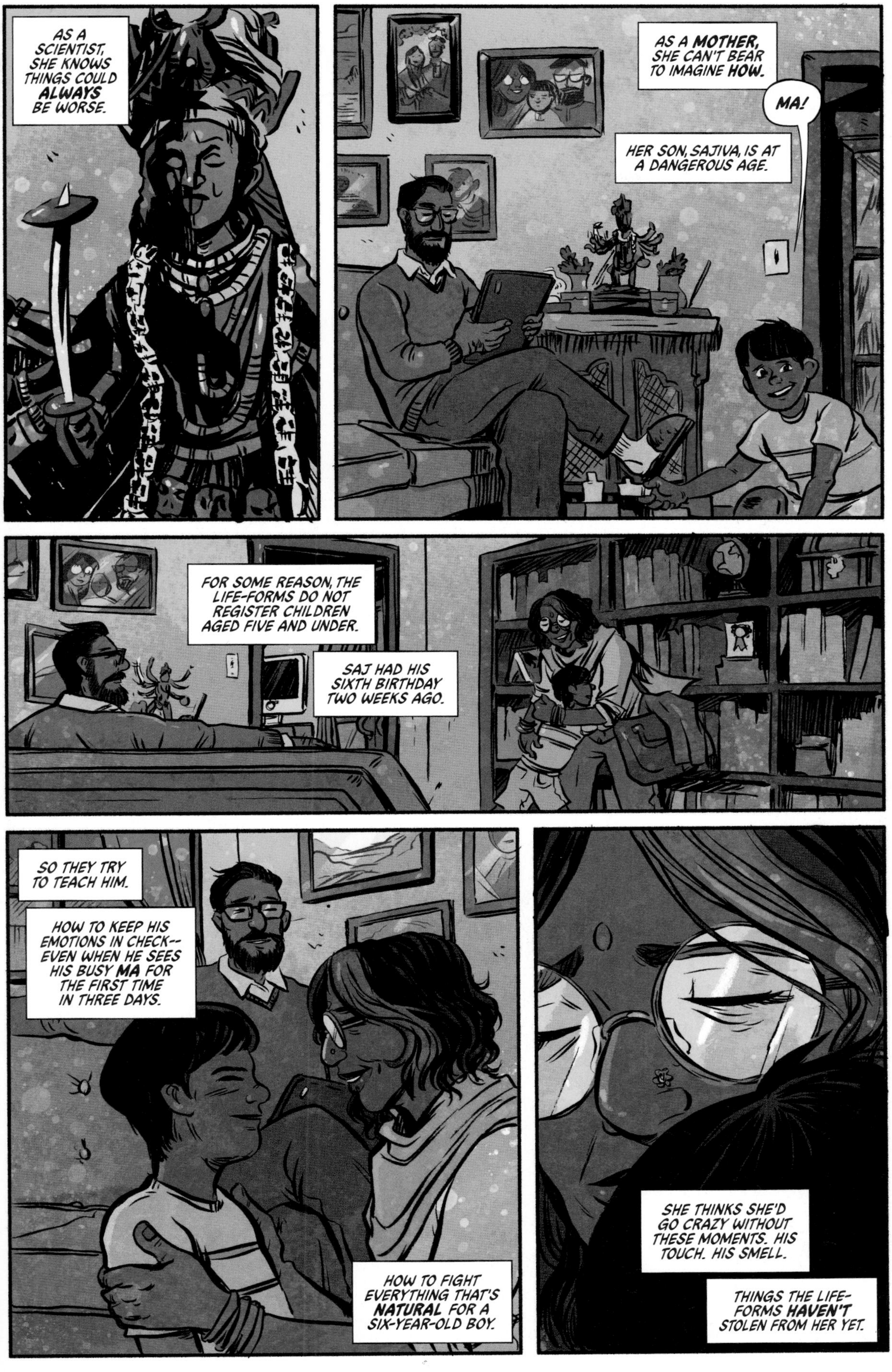
AS A SCIENTIST, SHE KNOWS THINGS COULD ALWAYS BE WORSE.
AS A MOTHER, SHE CAN'T BEAR TO IMAGINE HOW.
MA!
HER SON, SAJIVA, IS AT A DANGEROUS AGE.
FOR SOME REASON, THE LIFE-FORMS DO NOT REGISTER CHILDREN AGED FIVE AND UNDER.
SAJ HAD HIS SIXTH BIRTHDAY TWO WEEKS AGO.
SO THEY TRY TO TEACH HIM.
HOW TO KEEP HIS EMOTIONS IN CHECK-- EVEN WHEN HE SEES HIS BUSY MA FOR THE FIRST TIME IN THREE DAYS.
HOW TO FIGHT EVERYTHING THAT'S NATURAL FOR A SIX-YEAR-OLD BOY.
SHE THINKS SHE'D GO CRAZY WITHOUT THESE MOMENTS. HIS TOUCH. HIS SMELL.
THINGS THE LIFE-FORMS HAVEN'T STOLEN FROM HER YET.

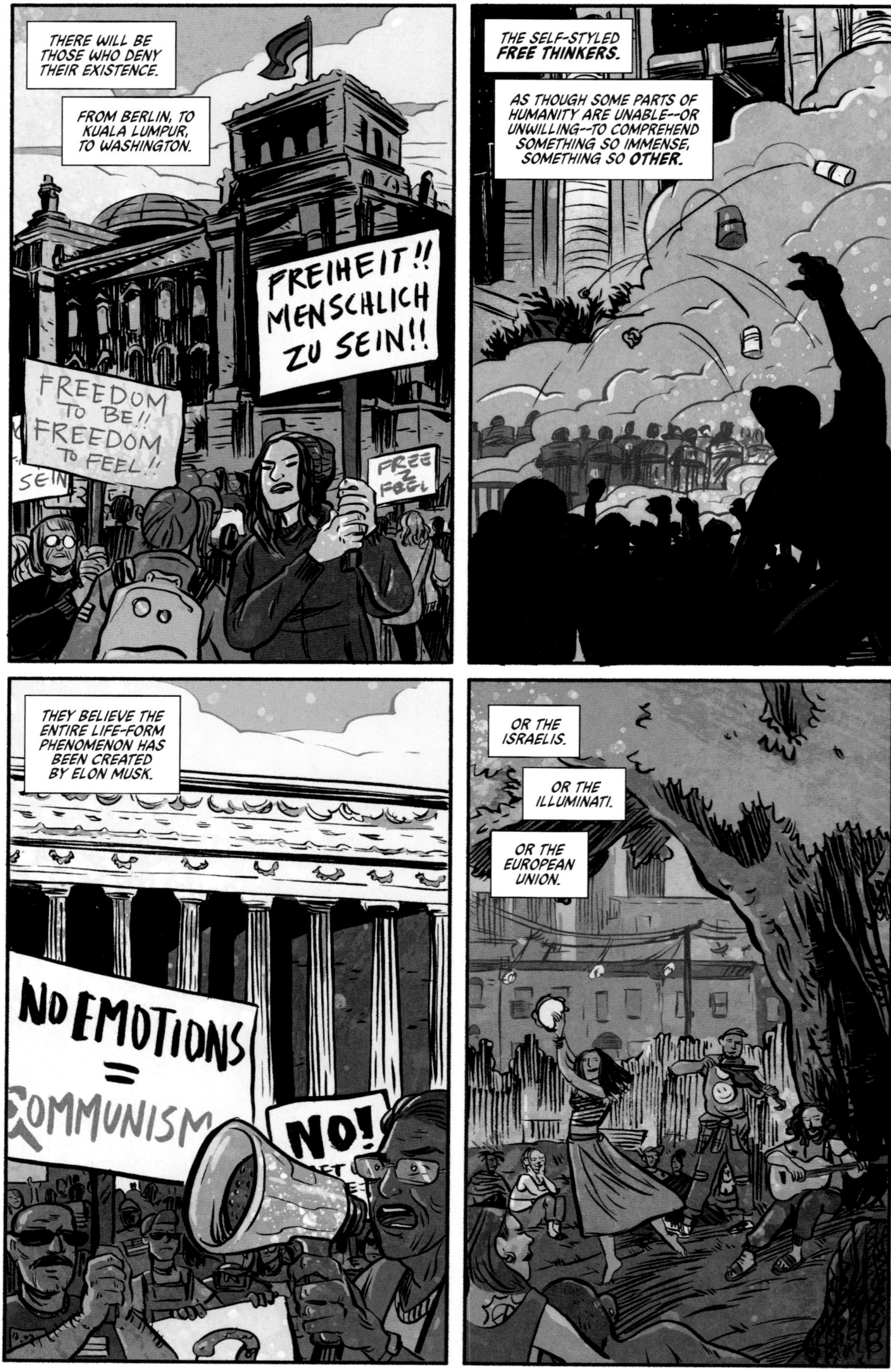
THERE WILL BE THOSE WHO DENY THEIR EXISTENCE.
FROM BERLIN, TO KUALA LUMPUR, TO WASHINGTON.
FREIHEIT!! MENSCHLICH ZU SEIN!!
FREEDOM TO BE!! FREEDOM TO FEEL!!
SEIN
FREE 2 FEEL
THE SELF-STYLED **FREE THINKERS.**
AS THOUGH SOME PARTS OF HUMANITY ARE UNABLE--OR UNWILLING--TO COMPREHEND SOMETHING SO IMMENSE, SOMETHING SO **OTHER.**
THEY BELIEVE THE ENTIRE LIFE-FORM PHENOMENON HAS BEEN CREATED BY ELON MUSK.
NO EMOTIONS = COMMUNISM
NO!
OR THE ISRAELIS.
OR THE ILLUMINATI.
OR THE EUROPEAN UNION.

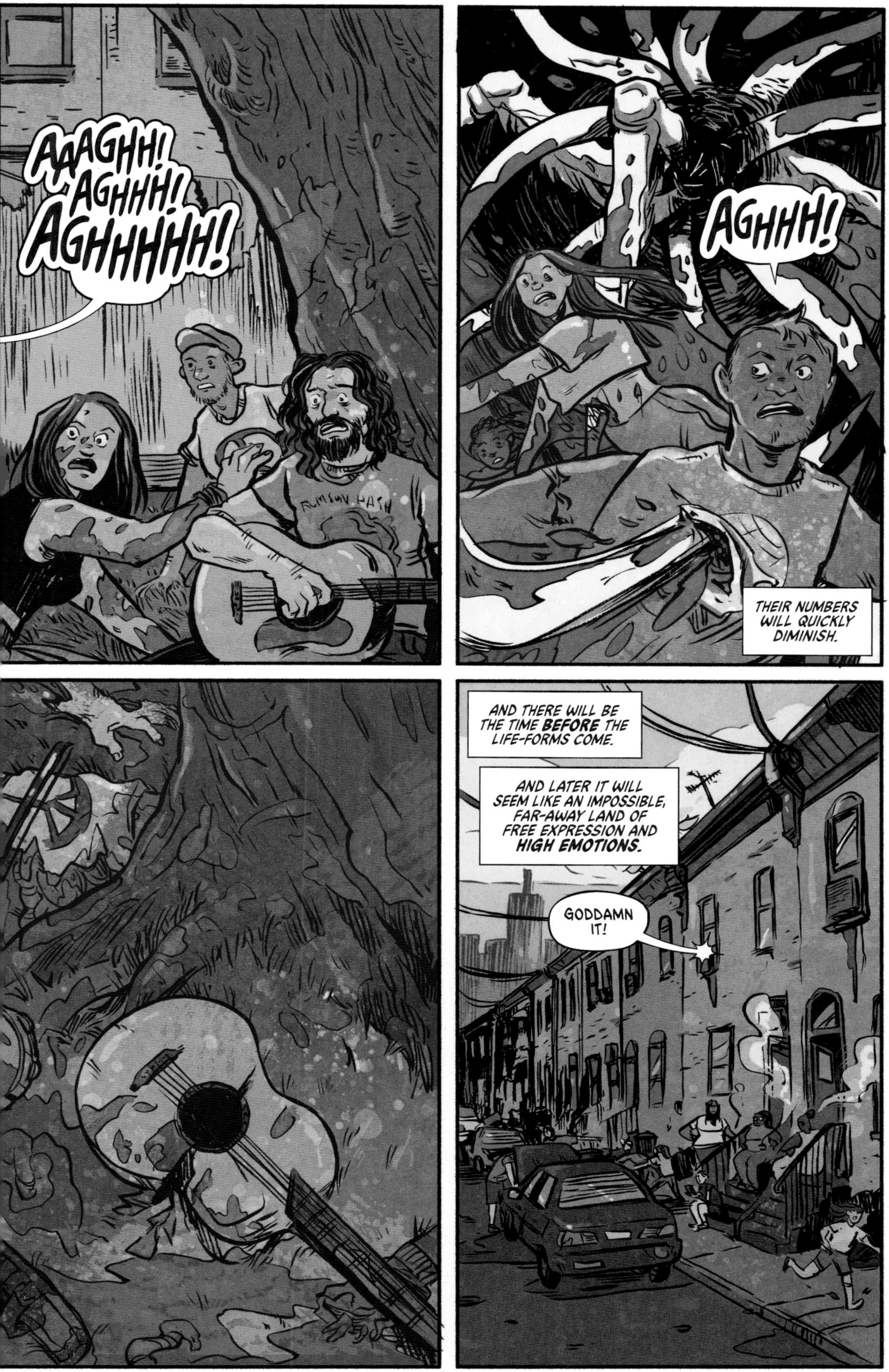
AAAGHH! AGHHH! AGHHHHH!
AGHHH!
THEIR NUMBERS WILL QUICKLY DIMINISH.
AND THERE WILL BE THE TIME **BEFORE** THE LIFE-FORMS COME.
AND LATER IT WILL SEEM LIKE AN IMPOSSIBLE, FAR-AWAY LAND OF FREE EXPRESSION AND **HIGH EMOTIONS.**
GODDAMN IT!

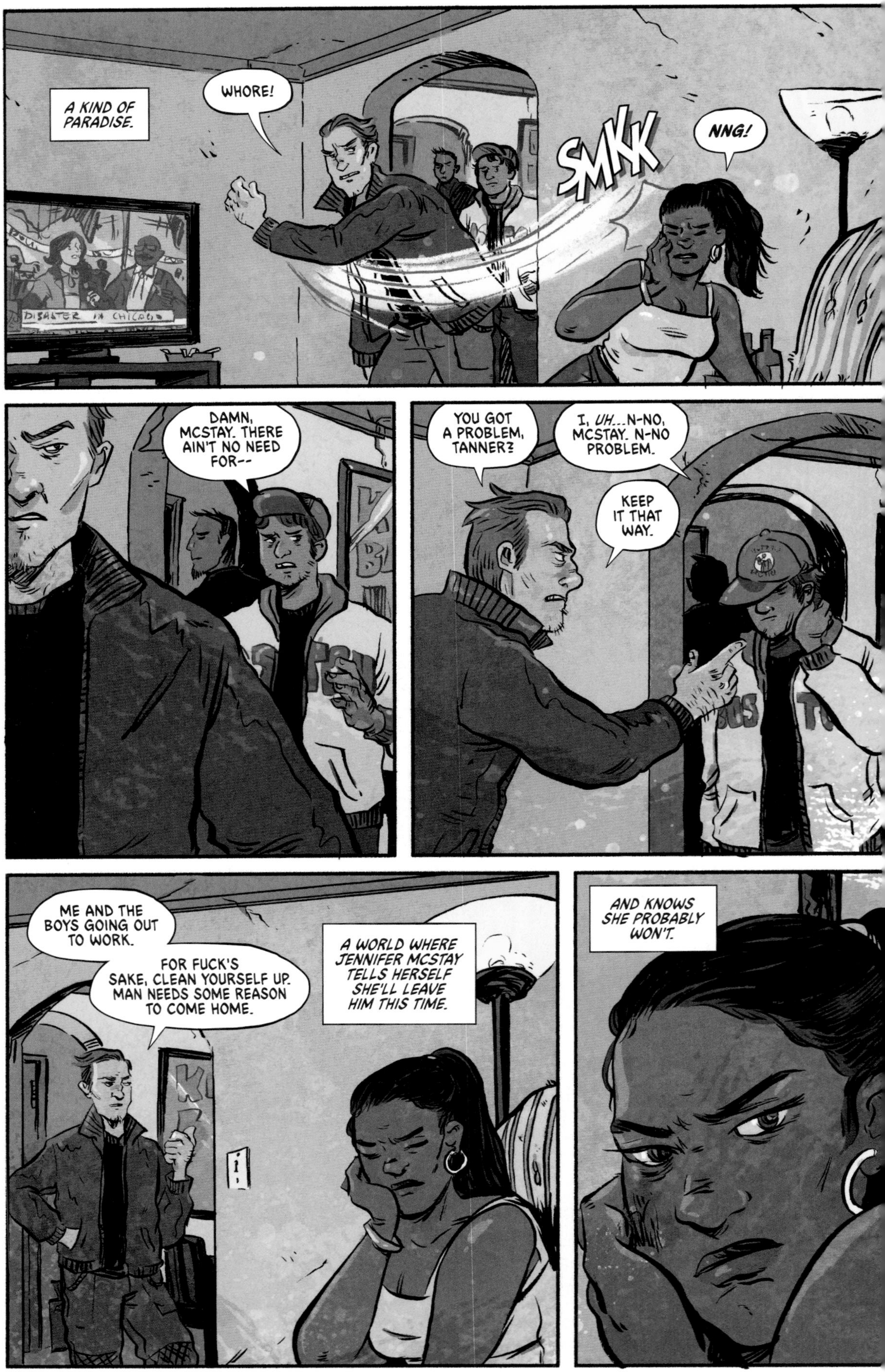

A KIND OF PARADISE.
WHORE!
SMKK
NNG!
DISASTER IN CHICAGO
DAMN, MCSTAY. THERE AIN'T NO NEED FOR--
YOU GOT A PROBLEM, TANNER?
I, UH... N-NO, MCSTAY. N-NO PROBLEM.
KEEP IT THAT WAY.
ME AND THE BOYS GOING OUT TO WORK.
FOR FUCK'S SAKE, CLEAN YOURSELF UP. MAN NEEDS SOME REASON TO COME HOME.
A WORLD WHERE JENNIFER MCSTAY TELLS HERSELF SHE'LL LEAVE HIM THIS TIME.
AND KNOWS SHE PROBABLY WON'T.

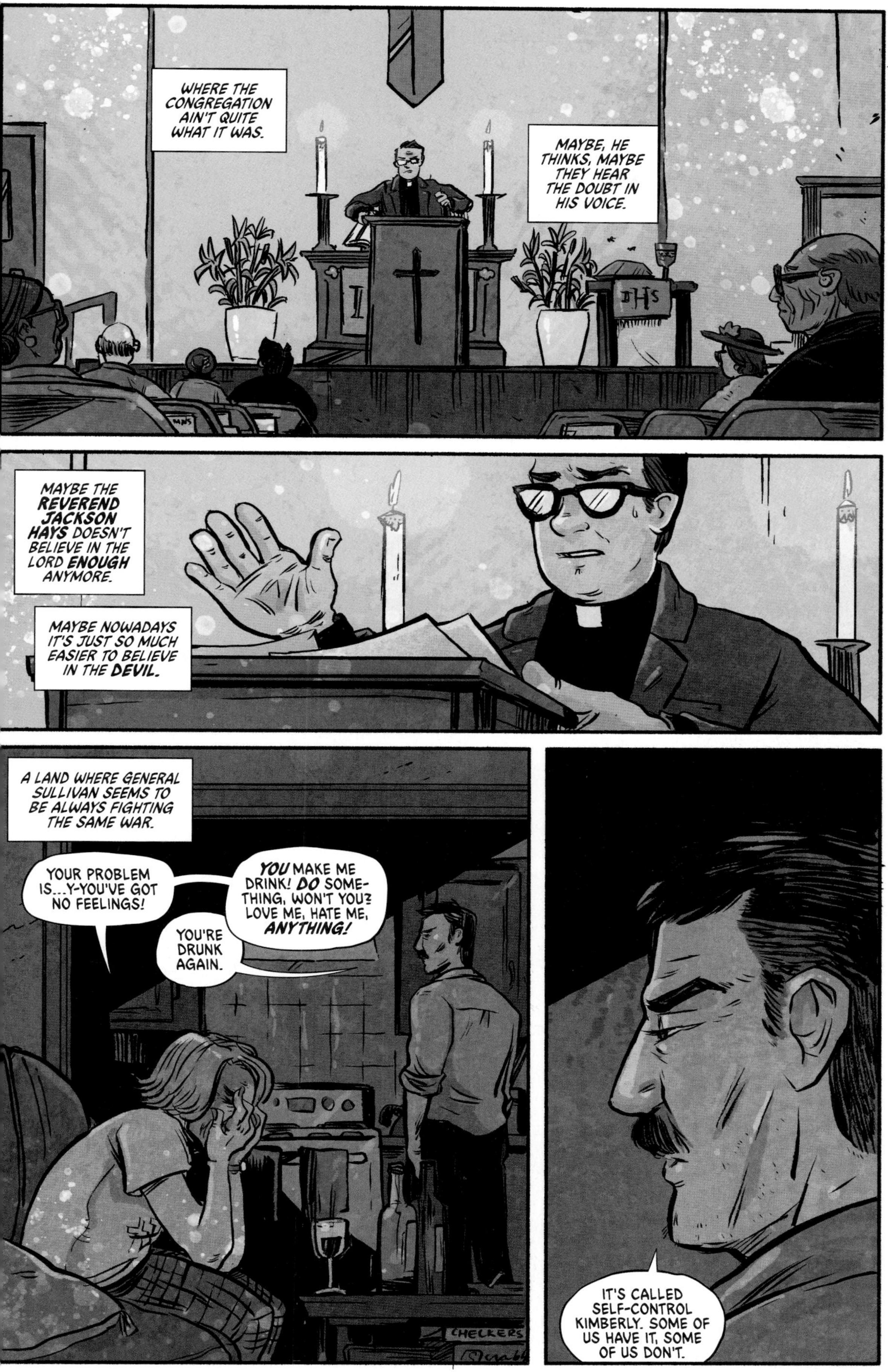
WHERE THE CONGREGATION AIN'T QUITE WHAT IT WAS.
MAYBE, HE THINKS, MAYBE THEY HEAR THE DOUBT IN HIS VOICE.
MAYBE THE **REVEREND JACKSON HAYS** DOESN'T BELIEVE IN THE LORD **ENOUGH** ANYMORE.
MAYBE NOWADAYS IT'S JUST SO MUCH EASIER TO BELIEVE IN THE **DEVIL.**
A LAND WHERE GENERAL SULLIVAN SEEMS TO BE ALWAYS FIGHTING THE SAME WAR.
YOUR PROBLEM IS... Y-YOU'VE GOT NO FEELINGS!
YOU'RE DRUNK AGAIN.
YOU MAKE ME DRINK! ***DO*** SOMETHING, WON'T YOU? LOVE ME, HATE ME, ***ANYTHING!***
IT'S CALLED SELF-CONTROL KIMBERLY. SOME OF US HAVE IT, SOME OF US DON'T.

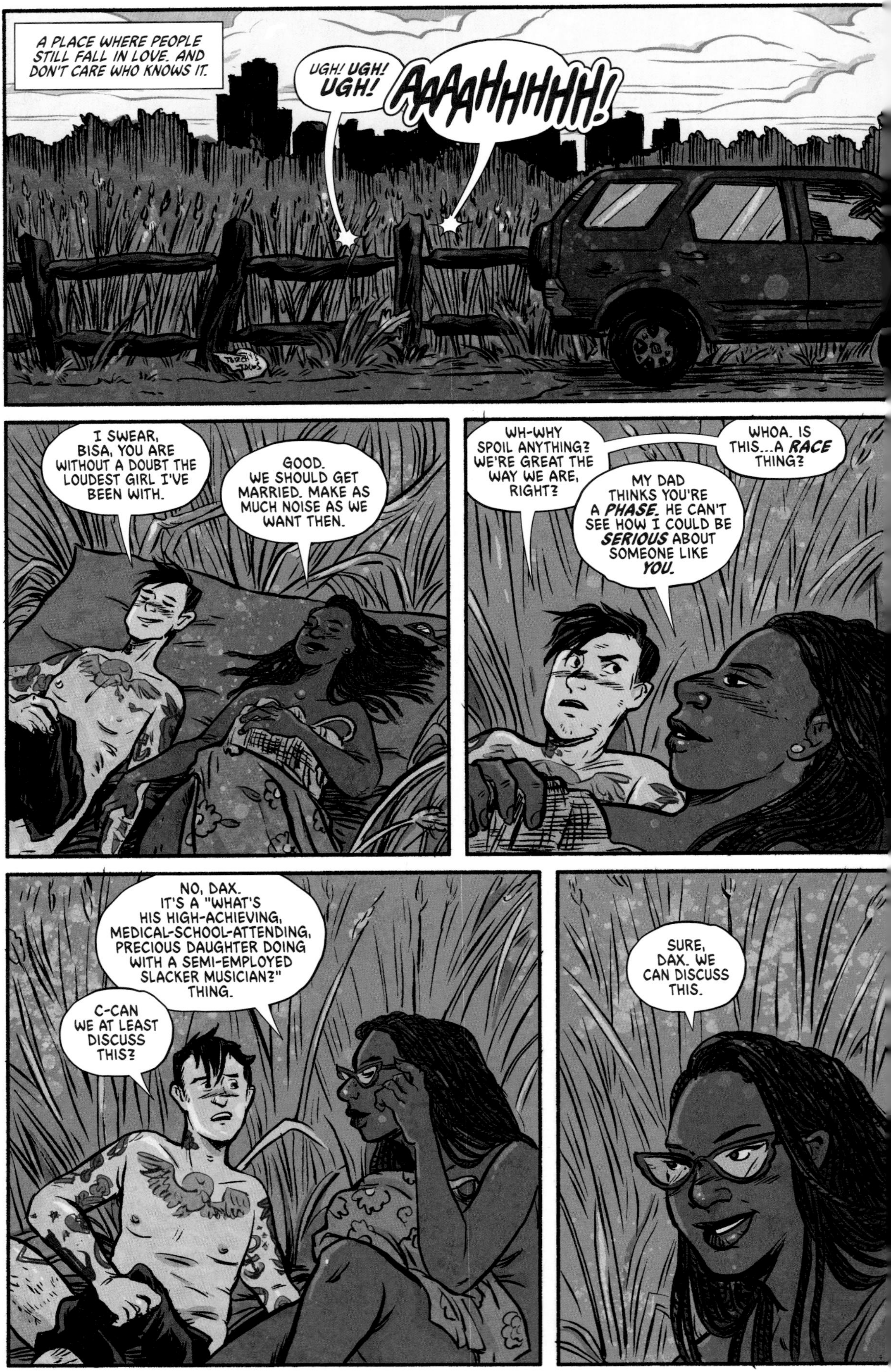
A PLACE WHERE PEOPLE STILL FALL IN LOVE. AND DON'T CARE WHO KNOWS IT.
UGH! UGH! UGH!
AAAAHHHHH!
I SWEAR, BISA, YOU ARE WITHOUT A DOUBT THE LOUDEST GIRL I'VE BEEN WITH.
GOOD. WE SHOULD GET MARRIED. MAKE AS MUCH NOISE AS WE WANT THEN.
WH-WHY SPOIL ANYTHING? WE'RE GREAT THE WAY WE ARE, RIGHT?
MY DAD THINKS YOU'RE A PHASE. HE CAN'T SEE HOW I COULD BE SERIOUS ABOUT SOMEONE LIKE YOU.
WHOA. IS THIS...A RACE THING?
NO, DAX. IT'S A "WHAT'S HIS HIGH-ACHIEVING, MEDICAL-SCHOOL-ATTENDING, PRECIOUS DAUGHTER DOING WITH A SEMI-EMPLOYED SLACKER MUSICIAN?" THING.
C-CAN WE AT LEAST DISCUSS THIS?
SURE, DAX. WE CAN DISCUSS THIS.

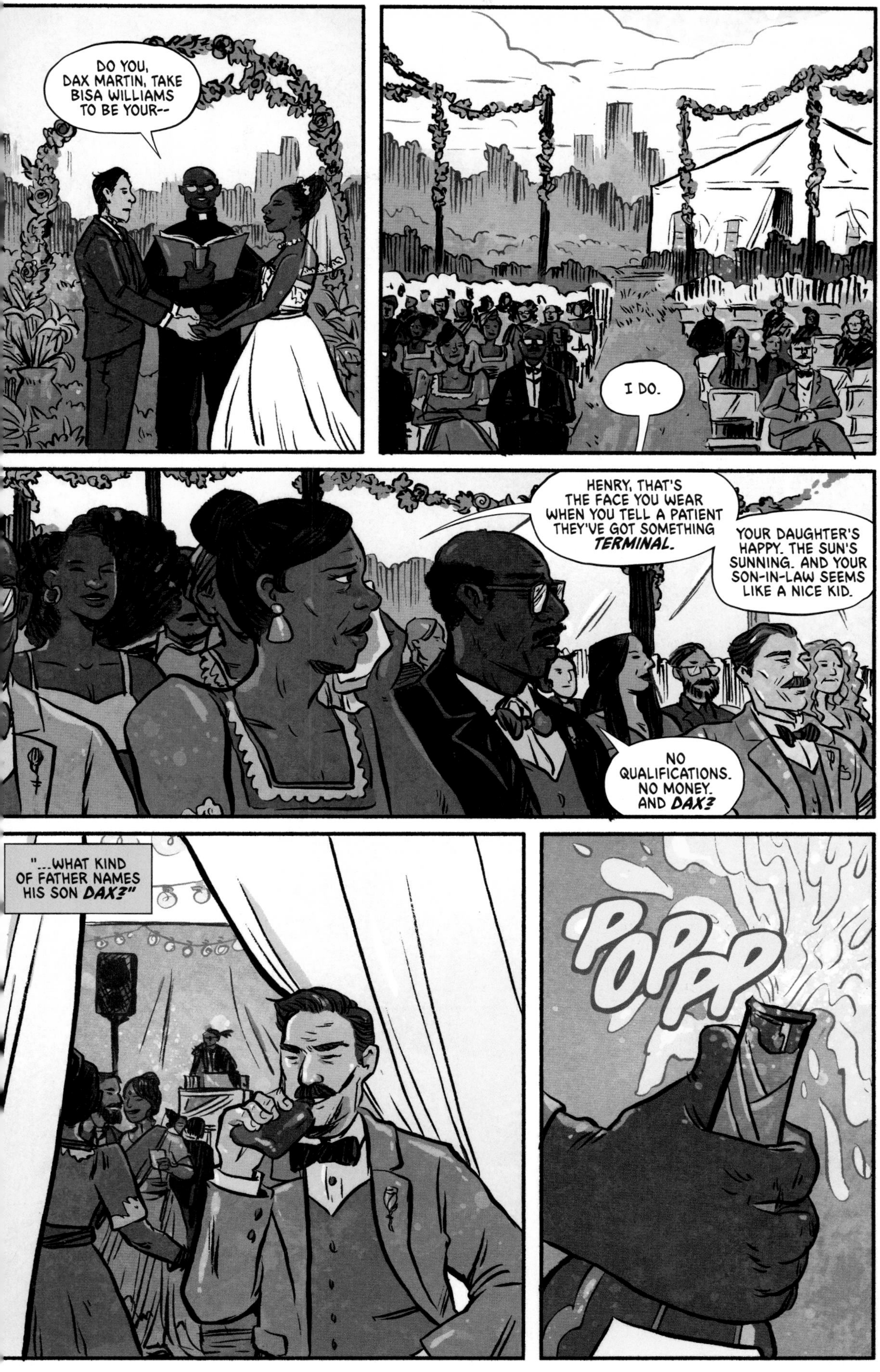
DO YOU, DAX MARTIN, TAKE BISA WILLIAMS TO BE YOUR--
I DO.
HENRY, THAT'S THE FACE YOU WEAR WHEN YOU TELL A PATIENT THEY'VE GOT SOMETHING TERMINAL.
YOUR DAUGHTER'S HAPPY. THE SUN'S SUNNING. AND YOUR SON-IN-LAW SEEMS LIKE A NICE KID.
NO QUALIFICATIONS. NO MONEY. AND DAX?
"...WHAT KIND OF FATHER NAMES HIS SON DAX?"
POPP

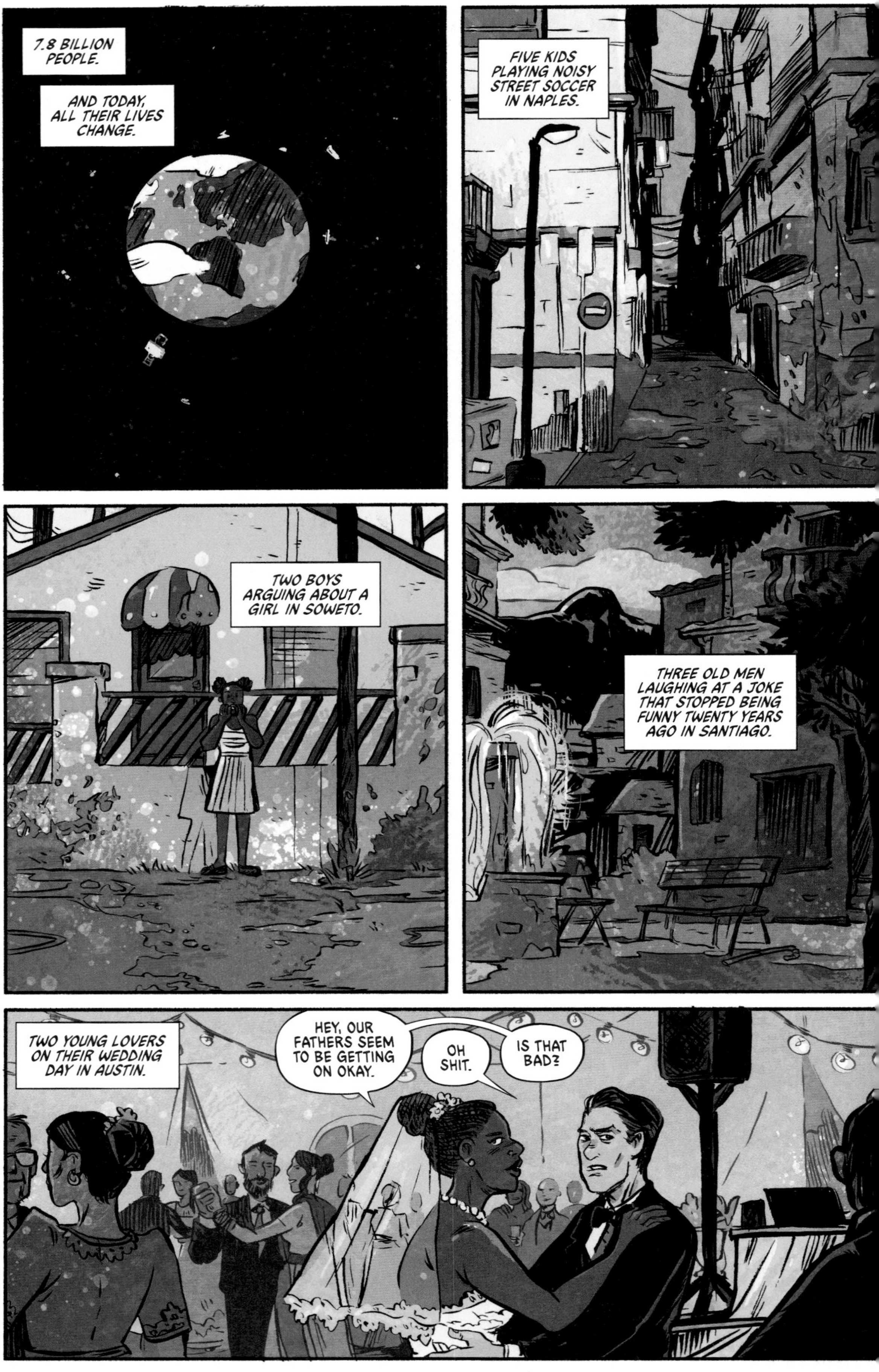
7.8 BILLION PEOPLE.
AND TODAY, ALL THEIR LIVES CHANGE.
FIVE KIDS PLAYING NOISY STREET SOCCER IN NAPLES.
TWO BOYS ARGUING ABOUT A GIRL IN SOWETO.
THREE OLD MEN LAUGHING AT A JOKE THAT STOPPED BEING FUNNY TWENTY YEARS AGO IN SANTIAGO.
TWO YOUNG LOVERS ON THEIR WEDDING DAY IN AUSTIN.
HEY, OUR FATHERS SEEM TO BE GETTING ON OKAY.
OH SHIT.
IS THAT BAD?

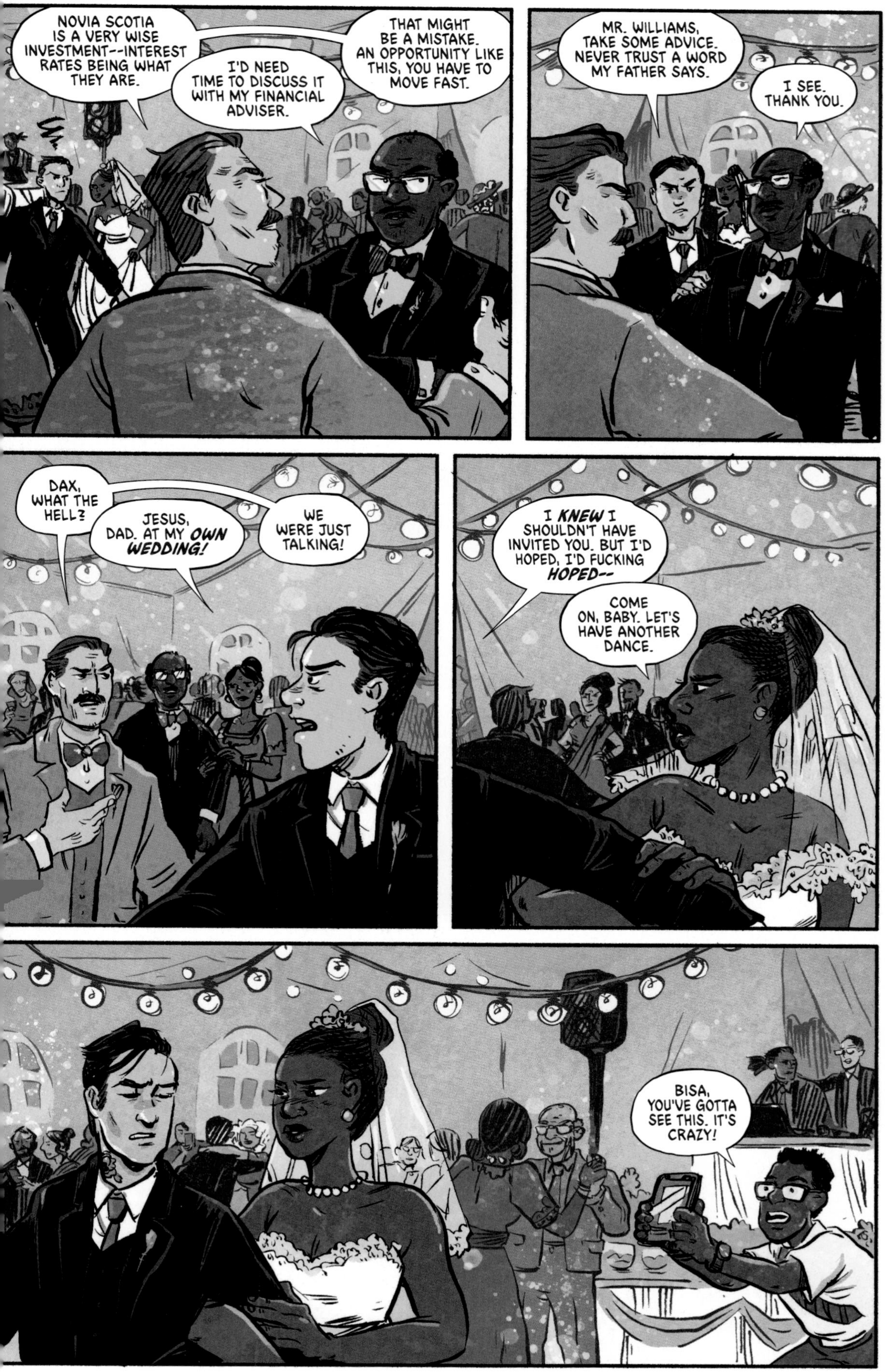
NOVIA SCOTIA IS A VERY WISE INVESTMENT--INTEREST RATES BEING WHAT THEY ARE.
I'D NEED TIME TO DISCUSS IT WITH MY FINANCIAL ADVISER.
THAT MIGHT BE A MISTAKE. AN OPPORTUNITY LIKE THIS, YOU HAVE TO MOVE FAST.
MR. WILLIAMS, TAKE SOME ADVICE. NEVER TRUST A WORD MY FATHER SAYS.
I SEE. THANK YOU.
DAX, WHAT THE HELL?
JESUS, DAD. AT MY OWN WEDDING!
WE WERE JUST TALKING!
I KNEW I SHOULDN'T HAVE INVITED YOU. BUT I'D HOPED, I'D FUCKING HOPED--
COME ON, BABY. LET'S HAVE ANOTHER DANCE.
BISA, YOU'VE GOTTA SEE THIS. IT'S CRAZY!

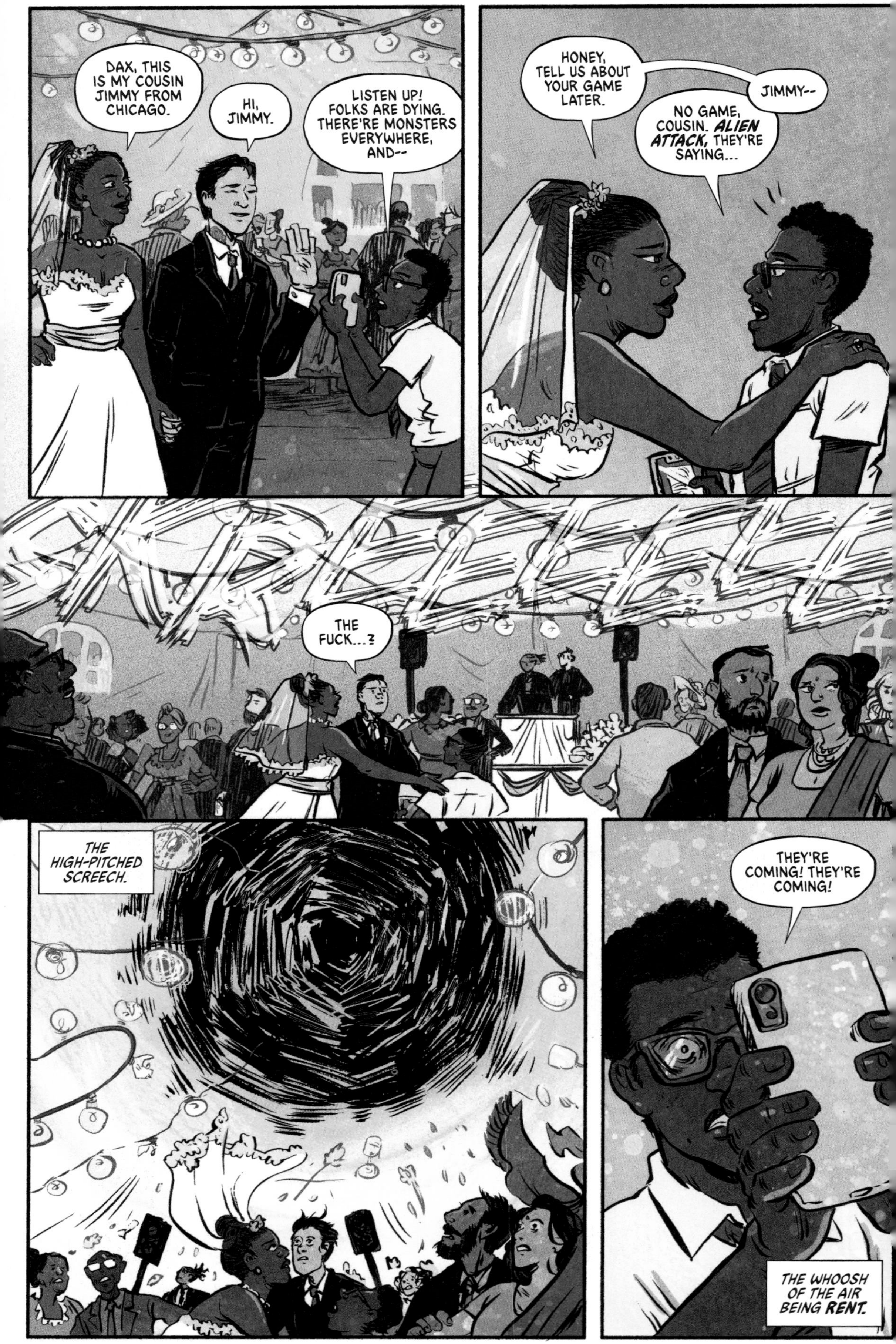
DAX, THIS IS MY COUSIN JIMMY FROM CHICAGO.
HI, JIMMY.
LISTEN UP! FOLKS ARE DYING. THERE'RE MONSTERS EVERYWHERE, AND--
HONEY, TELL US ABOUT YOUR GAME LATER.
JIMMY--
NO GAME, COUSIN. ALIEN ATTACK, THEY'RE SAYING...
THE FUCK...?
THE HIGH-PITCHED SCREECH.
THEY'RE COMING! THEY'RE COMING!
THE WHOOSH OF THE AIR BEING RENT.

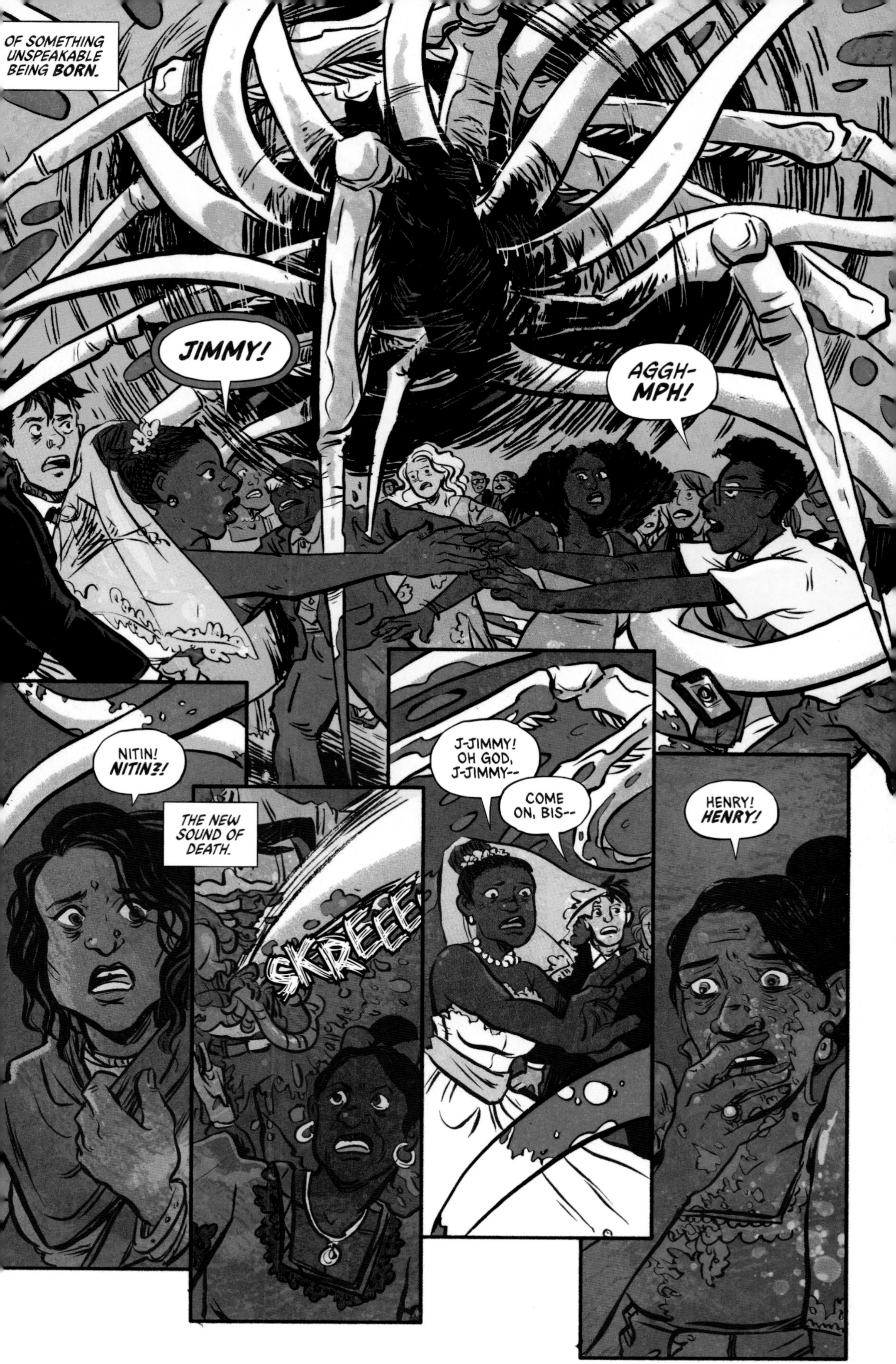
OF SOMETHING UNSPEAKABLE BEING **BORN**.
JIMMY!
AGGH-MPH!
NITIN! **NITIN?!**
THE NEW SOUND OF DEATH.
SKREEE
J-JIMMY! OH GOD, J-JIMMY--
COME ON, BIS--
HENRY! **HENRY!**

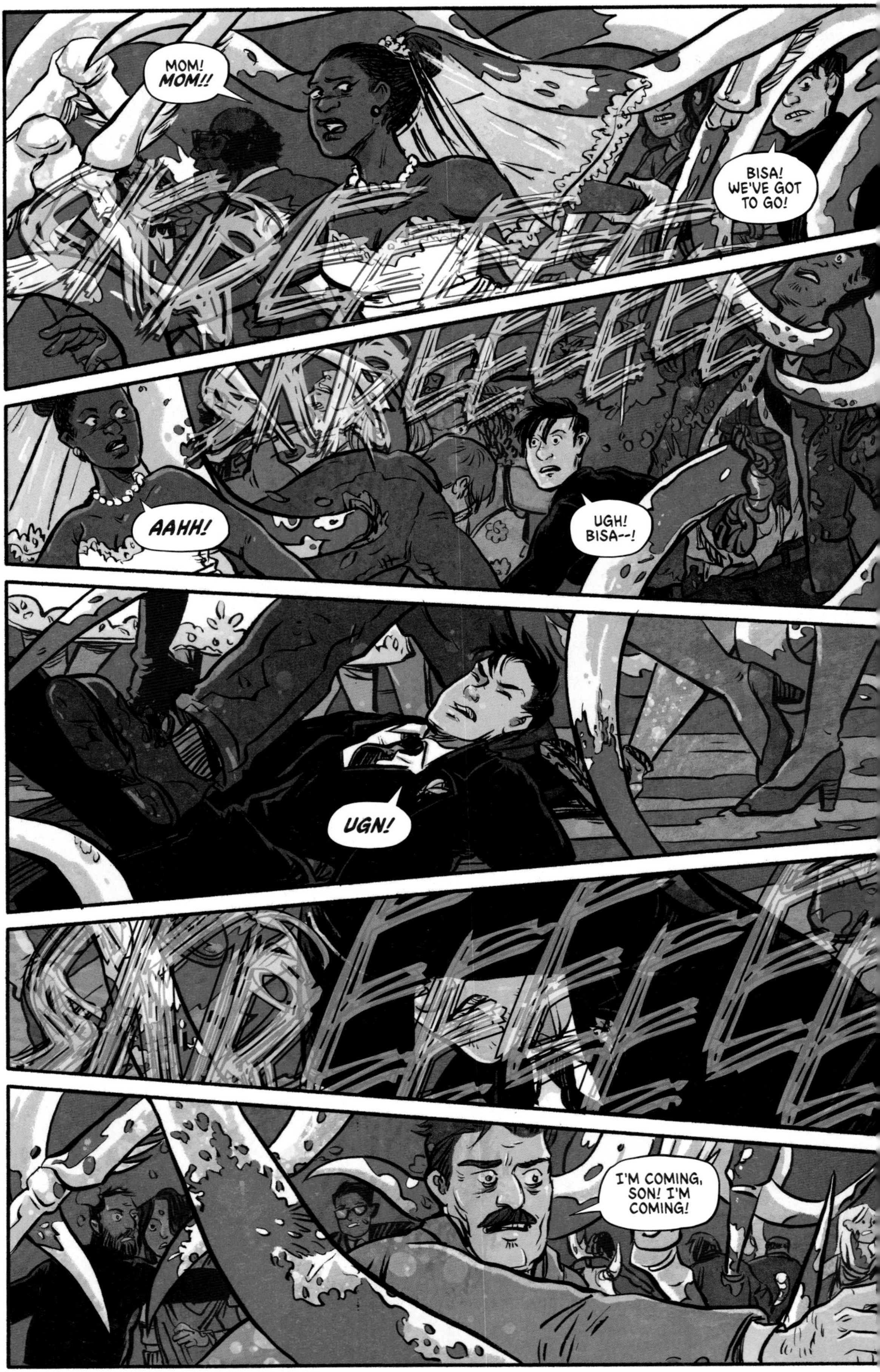
MOM! MOM!!
BISA! WE'VE GOT TO GO!
AAHH!
UGH! BISA--!
UGN!
I'M COMING, SON! I'M COMING!

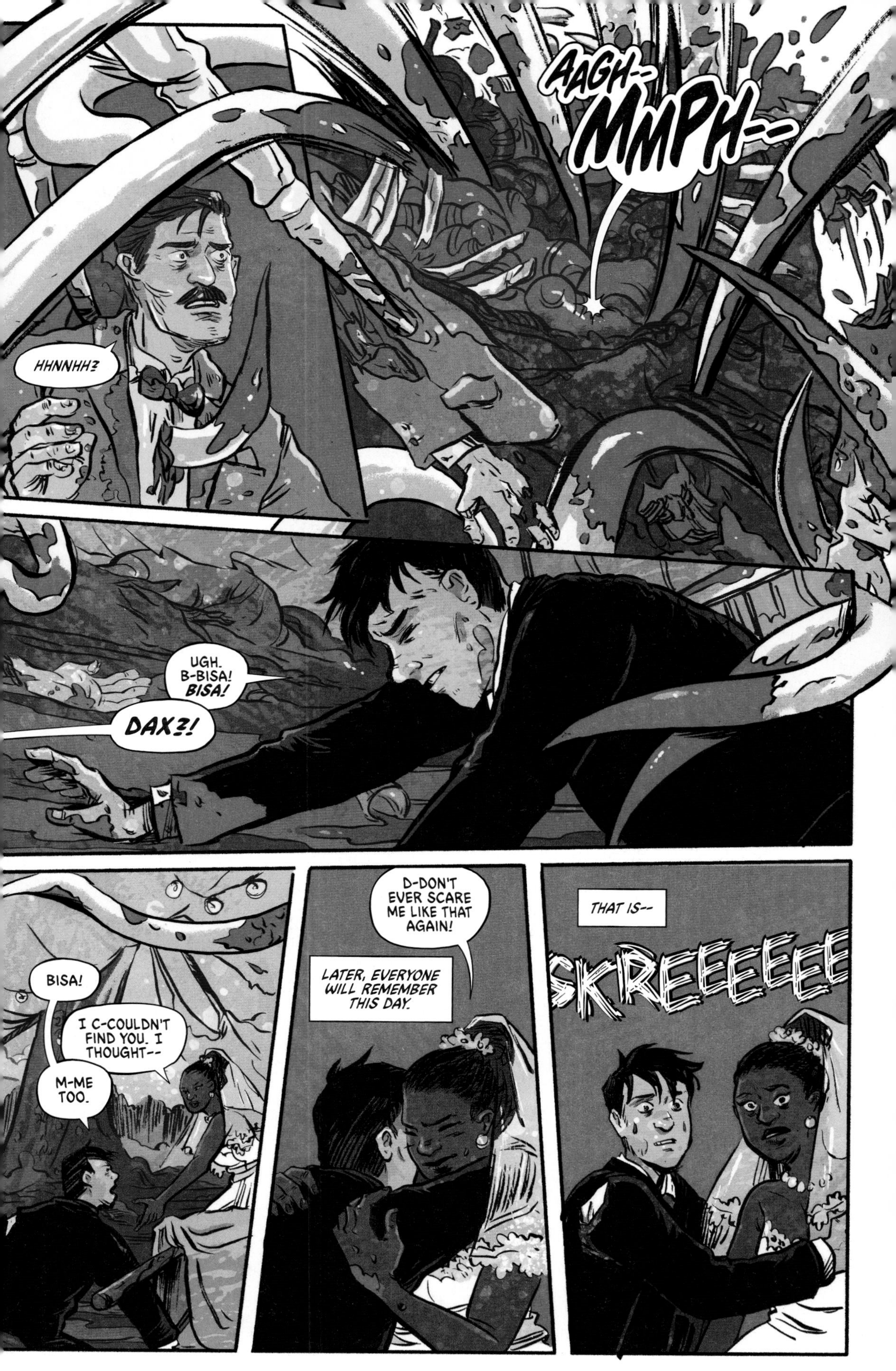
AAGH-
MMPH--
HHNNHH?
UGH.
B-BISA!
BISA!
DAX?!
BISA!
I C-COULDN'T FIND YOU. I THOUGHT--
M-ME TOO.
D-DON'T EVER SCARE ME LIKE THAT AGAIN!
LATER, EVERYONE WILL REMEMBER THIS DAY.
THAT IS--
SKREEEEEEE

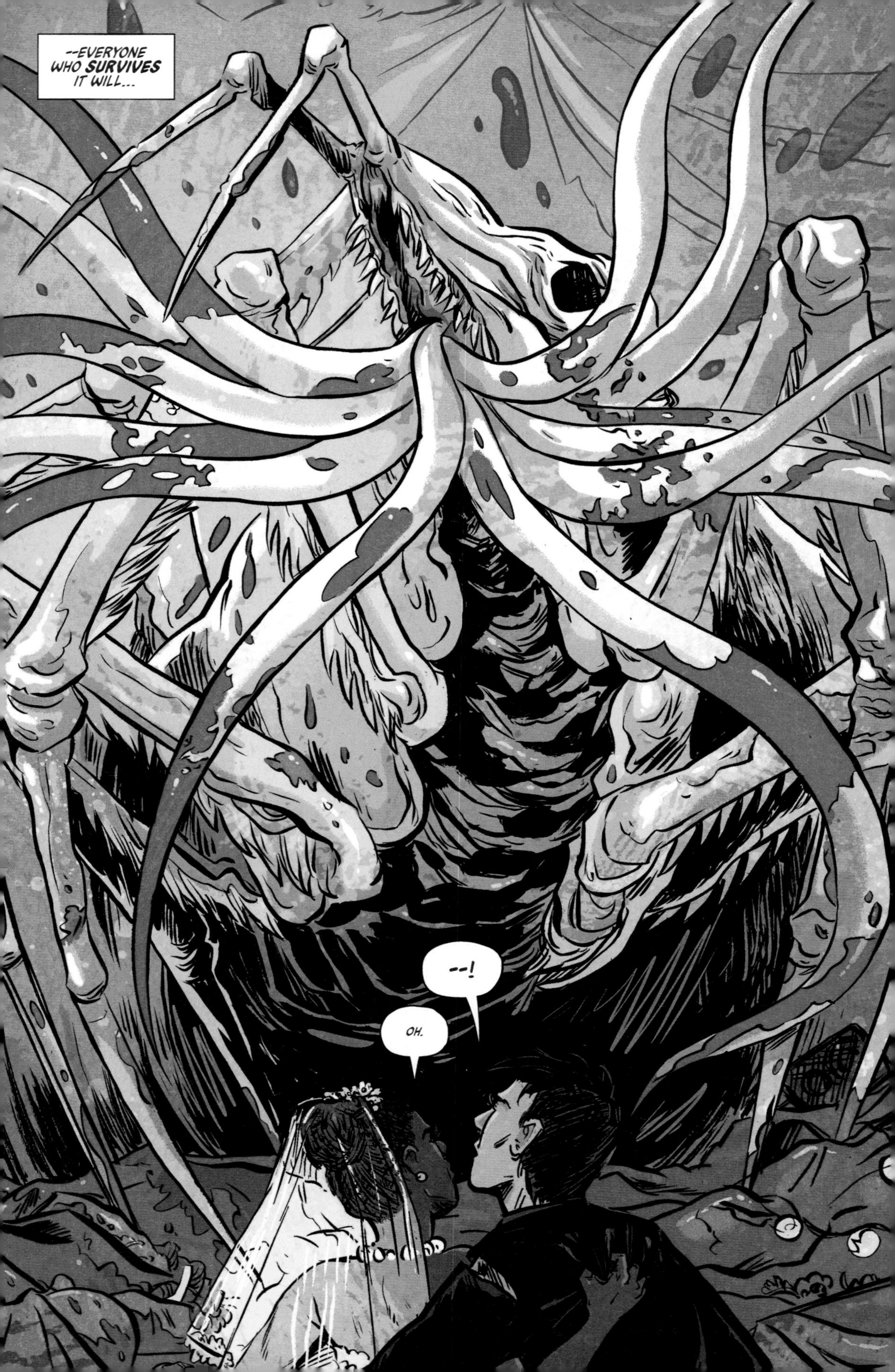
--EVERYONE WHO SURVIVES IT WILL...
--!
OH.

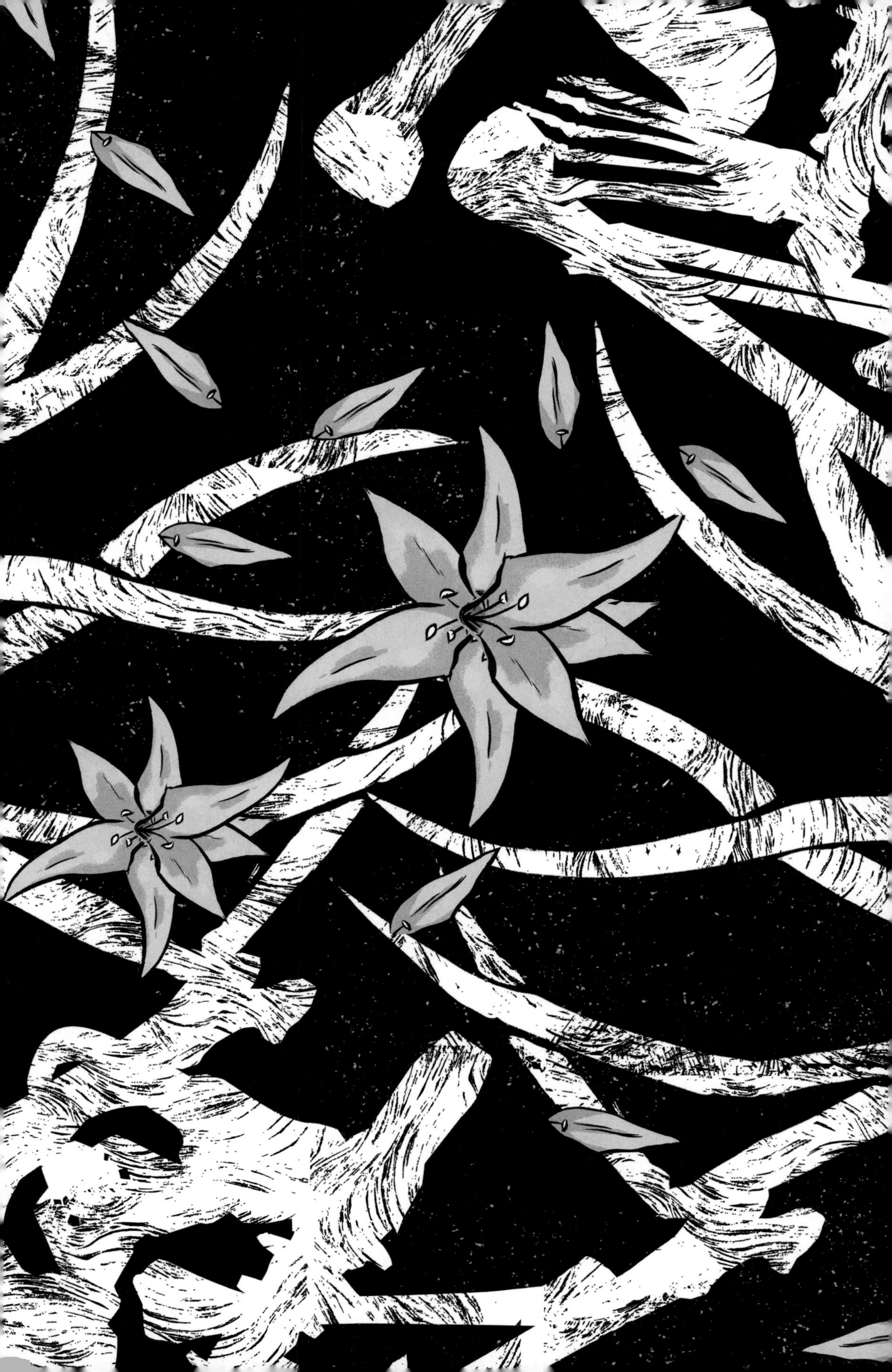

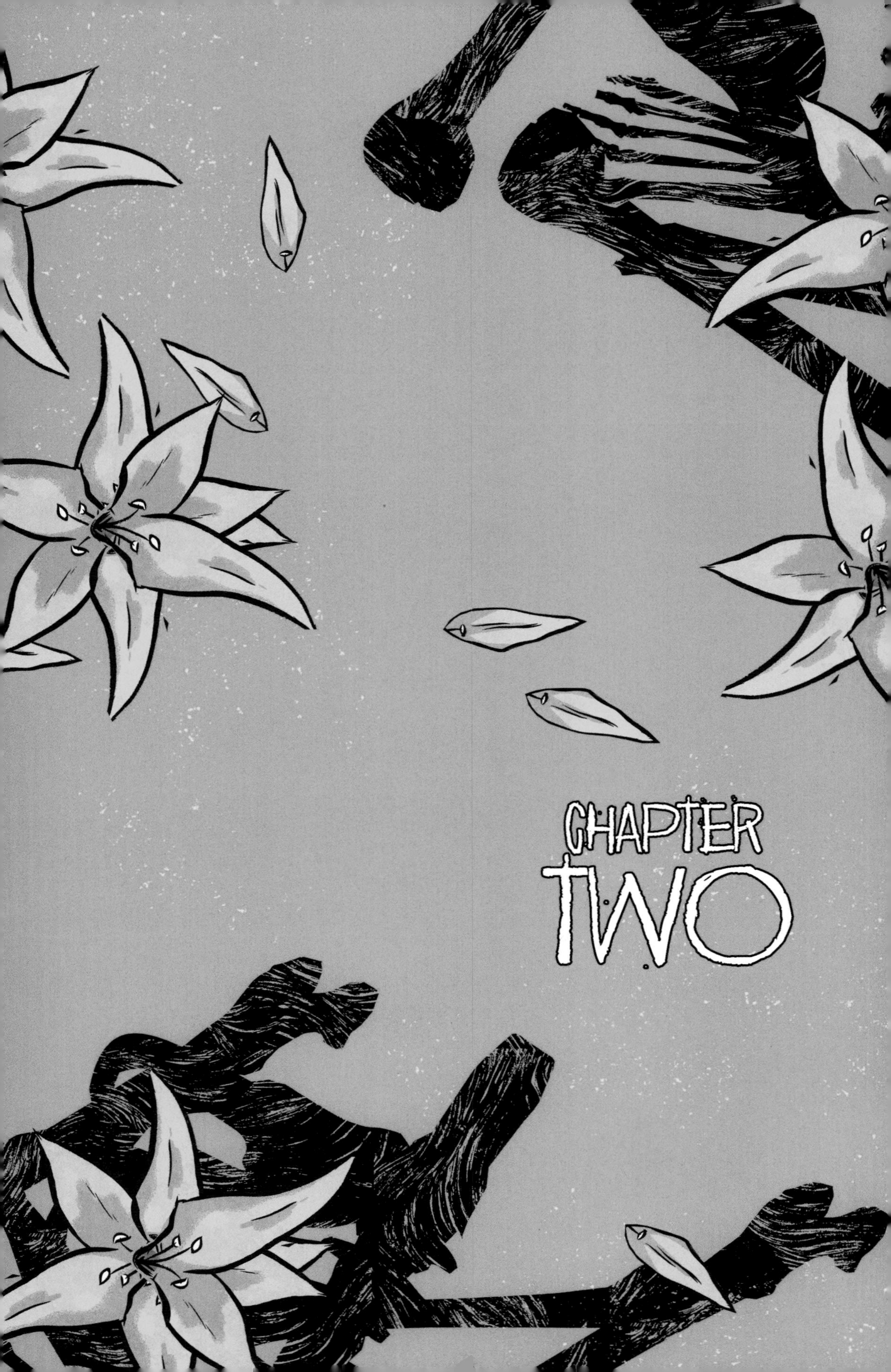
CHAPTER
TWO

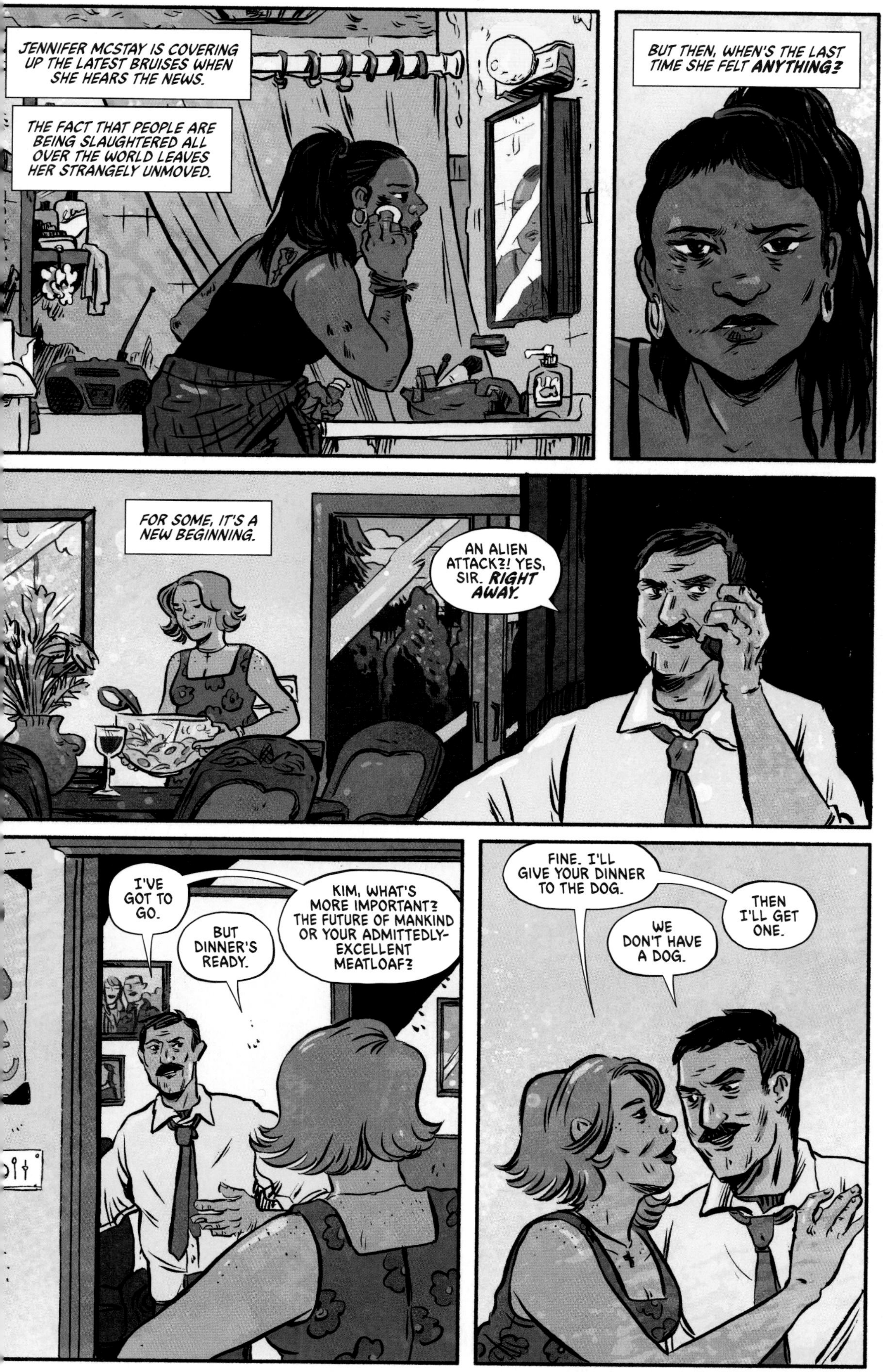
JENNIFER MCSTAY IS COVERING UP THE LATEST BRUISES WHEN SHE HEARS THE NEWS.
THE FACT THAT PEOPLE ARE BEING SLAUGHTERED ALL OVER THE WORLD LEAVES HER STRANGELY UNMOVED.
BUT THEN, WHEN'S THE LAST TIME SHE FELT ANYTHING?
FOR SOME, IT'S A NEW BEGINNING.
AN ALIEN ATTACK?! YES, SIR. RIGHT AWAY.
I'VE GOT TO GO.
BUT DINNER'S READY.
KIM, WHAT'S MORE IMPORTANT? THE FUTURE OF MANKIND OR YOUR ADMITTEDLY-EXCELLENT MEATLOAF?
FINE. I'LL GIVE YOUR DINNER TO THE DOG.
WE DON'T HAVE A DOG.
THEN I'LL GET ONE.

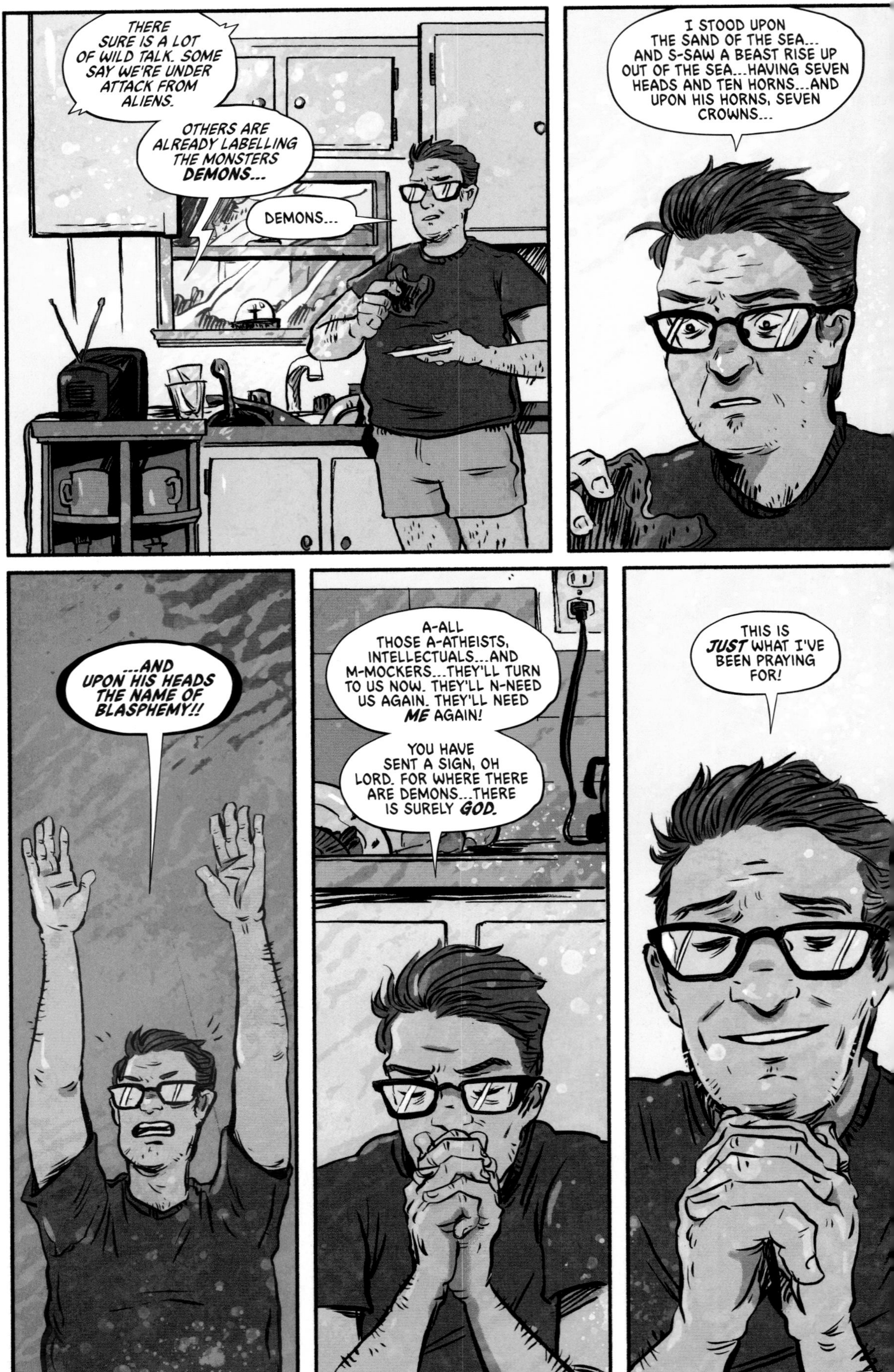
THERE SURE IS A LOT OF WILD TALK. SOME SAY WE'RE UNDER ATTACK FROM ALIENS.
OTHERS ARE ALREADY LABELLING THE MONSTERS DEMONS...
DEMONS...
I STOOD UPON THE SAND OF THE SEA... AND S-SAW A BEAST RISE UP OUT OF THE SEA...HAVING SEVEN HEADS AND TEN HORNS...AND UPON HIS HORNS, SEVEN CROWNS...
...AND UPON HIS HEADS THE NAME OF BLASPHEMY!!
A-ALL THOSE A-ATHEISTS, INTELLECTUALS...AND M-MOCKERS...THEY'LL TURN TO US NOW. THEY'LL N-NEED US AGAIN. THEY'LL NEED ME AGAIN!
YOU HAVE SENT A SIGN, OH LORD. FOR WHERE THERE ARE DEMONS...THERE IS SURELY GOD.
THIS IS JUST WHAT I'VE BEEN PRAYING FOR!

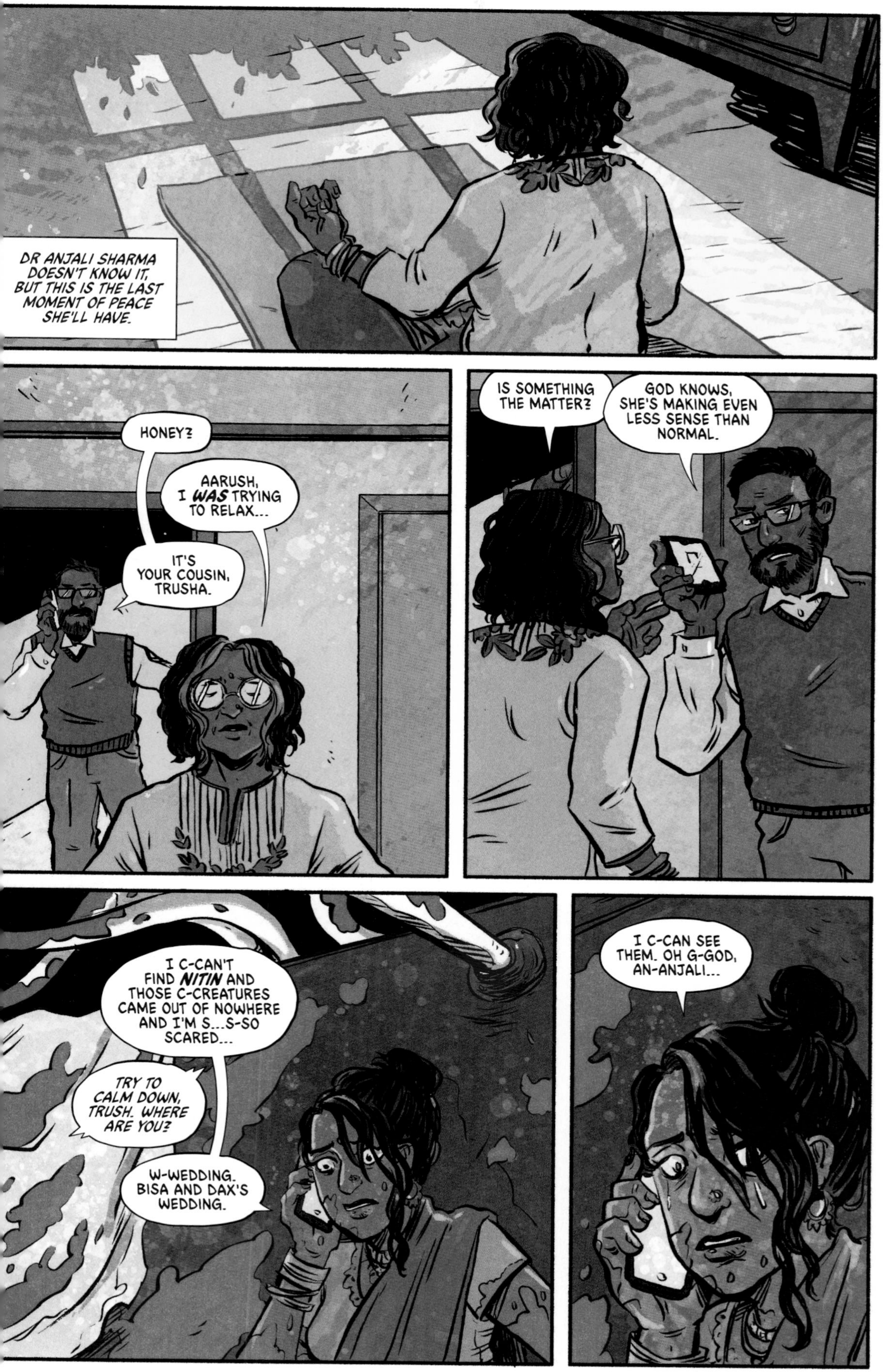
DR ANJALI SHARMA DOESN'T KNOW IT, BUT THIS IS THE LAST MOMENT OF PEACE SHE'LL HAVE.
HONEY?
AARUSH, I WAS TRYING TO RELAX...
IT'S YOUR COUSIN, TRUSHA.
IS SOMETHING THE MATTER?
GOD KNOWS, SHE'S MAKING EVEN LESS SENSE THAN NORMAL.
I C-CAN'T FIND NITIN AND THOSE C-CREATURES CAME OUT OF NOWHERE AND I'M S...S-SO SCARED...
TRY TO CALM DOWN, TRUSH. WHERE ARE YOU?
W-WEDDING. BISA AND DAX'S WEDDING.
I C-CAN SEE THEM. OH G-GOD, AN-ANJALI...

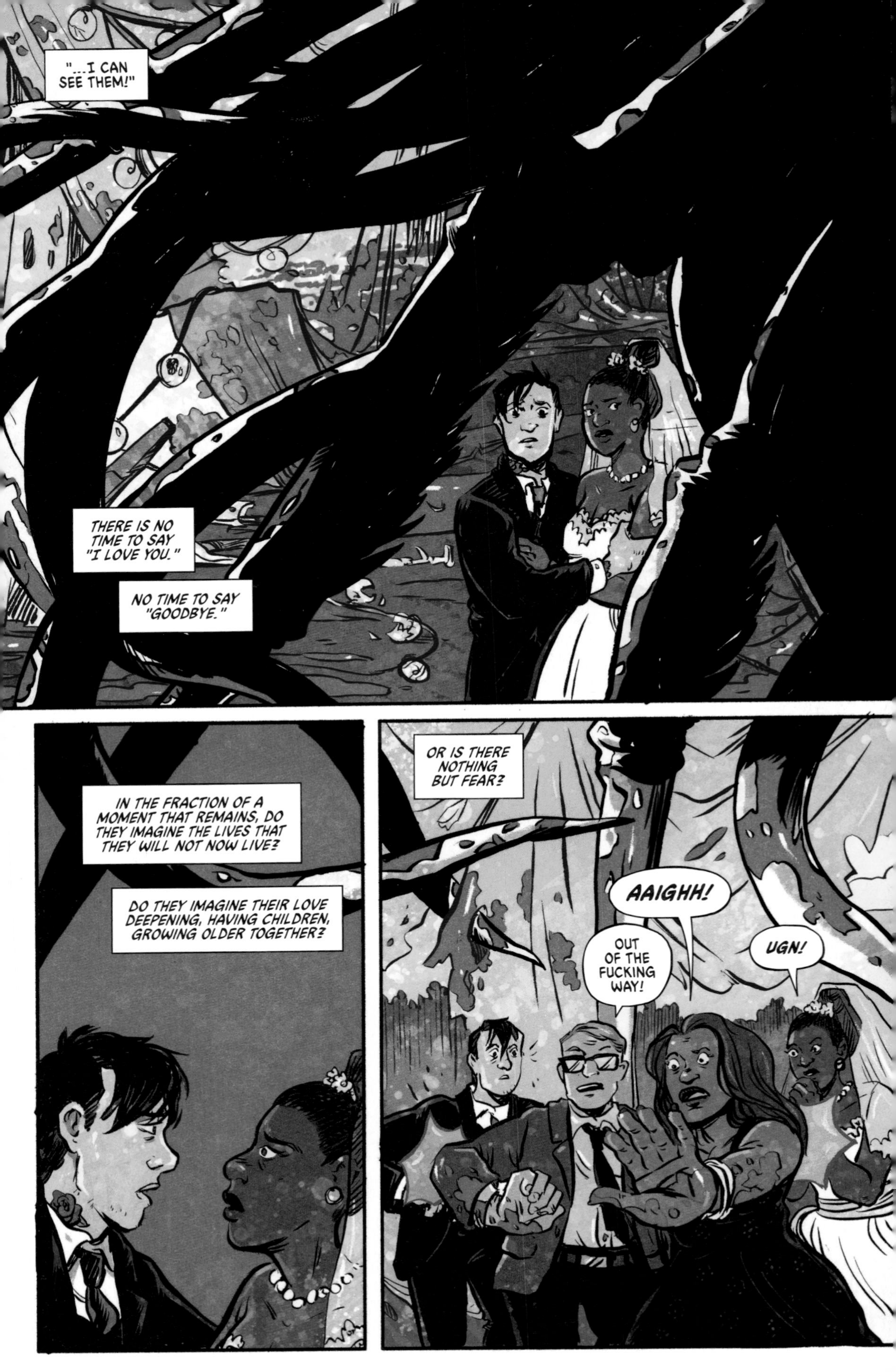

"...I CAN SEE THEM!"
THERE IS NO TIME TO SAY "I LOVE YOU."
NO TIME TO SAY "GOODBYE."
IN THE FRACTION OF A MOMENT THAT REMAINS, DO THEY IMAGINE THE LIVES THAT THEY WILL NOT NOW LIVE?
DO THEY IMAGINE THEIR LOVE DEEPENING, HAVING CHILDREN, GROWING OLDER TOGETHER?
OR IS THERE NOTHING BUT FEAR?
AAIGHH!
OUT OF THE FUCKING WAY!
UGN!

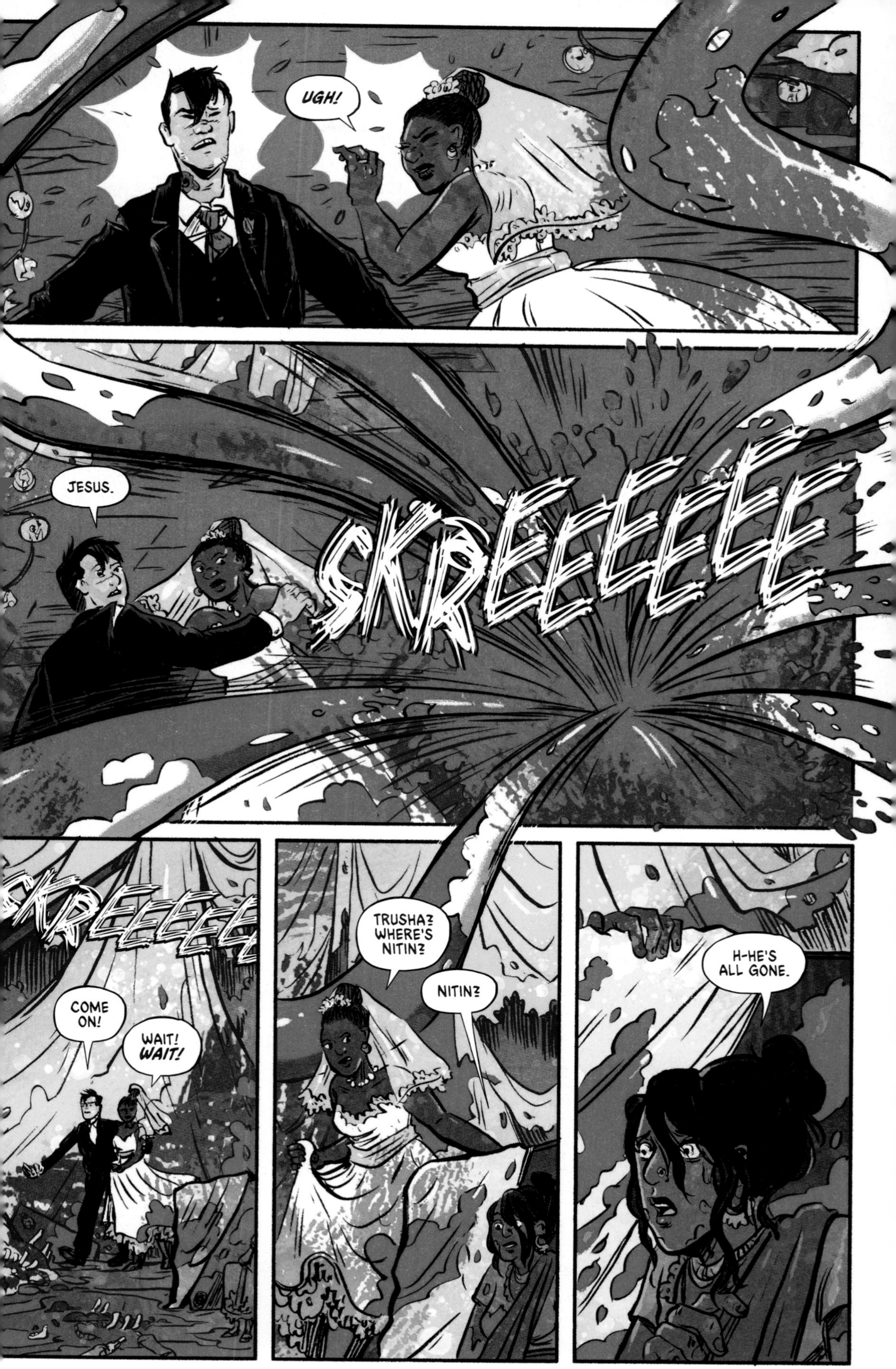
UGH!
JESUS.
SKREEEEEEE
SKREEEEEE
COME ON!
WAIT! WAIT!
TRUSHA? WHERE'S NITIN?
NITIN?
H-HE'S ALL GONE.

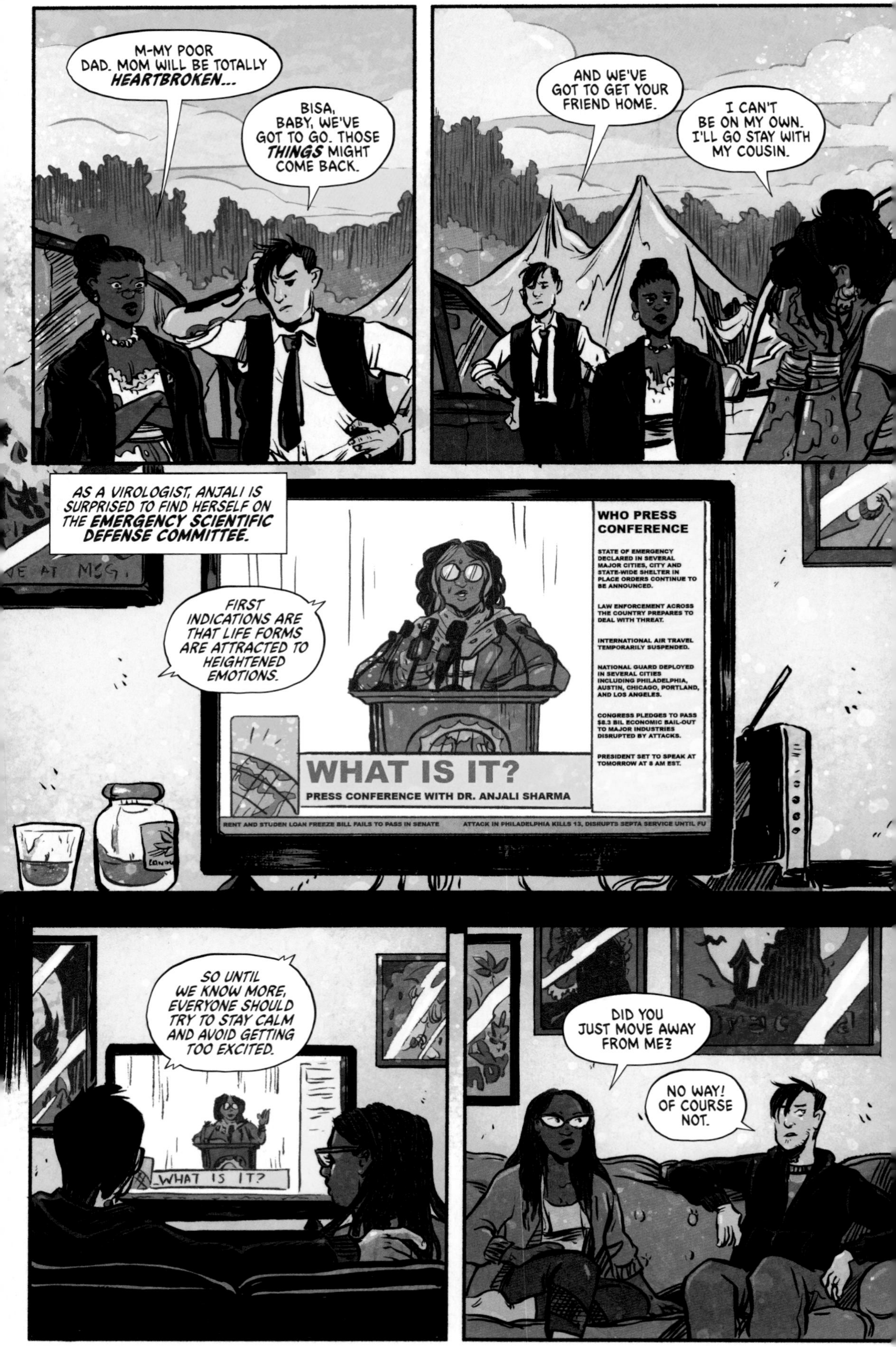
M-MY POOR DAD. MOM WILL BE TOTALLY *HEARTBROKEN...*
BISA, BABY, WE'VE GOT TO GO. THOSE *THINGS* MIGHT COME BACK.
AND WE'VE GOT TO GET YOUR FRIEND HOME.
I CAN'T BE ON MY OWN. I'LL GO STAY WITH MY COUSIN.
AS A VIROLOGIST, ANJALI IS SURPRISED TO FIND HERSELF ON THE **EMERGENCY SCIENTIFIC DEFENSE COMMITTEE.**
WHO PRESS CONFERENCE
STATE OF EMERGENCY DECLARED IN SEVERAL MAJOR CITIES, CITY AND STATE-WIDE SHELTER IN PLACE ORDERS CONTINUE TO BE ANNOUNCED.
LAW ENFORCEMENT ACROSS THE COUNTRY PREPARES TO DEAL WITH THREAT.
INTERNATIONAL AIR TRAVEL TEMPORARILY SUSPENDED.
NATIONAL GUARD DEPLOYED IN SEVERAL CITIES INCLUDING PHILADELPHIA, AUSTIN, CHICAGO, PORTLAND, AND LOS ANGELES.
CONGRESS PLEDGES TO PASS $8.3 BIL ECONOMIC BAIL-OUT TO MAJOR INDUSTRIES DISRUPTED BY ATTACKS.
PRESIDENT SET TO SPEAK AT TOMORROW AT 8 AM EST.
FIRST INDICATIONS ARE THAT LIFE FORMS ARE ATTRACTED TO HEIGHTENED EMOTIONS.
WHAT IS IT?
PRESS CONFERENCE WITH DR. ANJALI SHARMA
RENT AND STUDEN LOAN FREEZE BILL FAILS TO PASS IN SENATE
ATTACK IN PHILADELPHIA KILLS 13, DISRUPTS SEPTA SERVICE UNTIL FU
SO UNTIL WE KNOW MORE, EVERYONE SHOULD TRY TO STAY CALM AND AVOID GETTING TOO EXCITED.
WHAT IS IT?
DID YOU JUST MOVE AWAY FROM ME?
NO WAY! OF COURSE NOT.

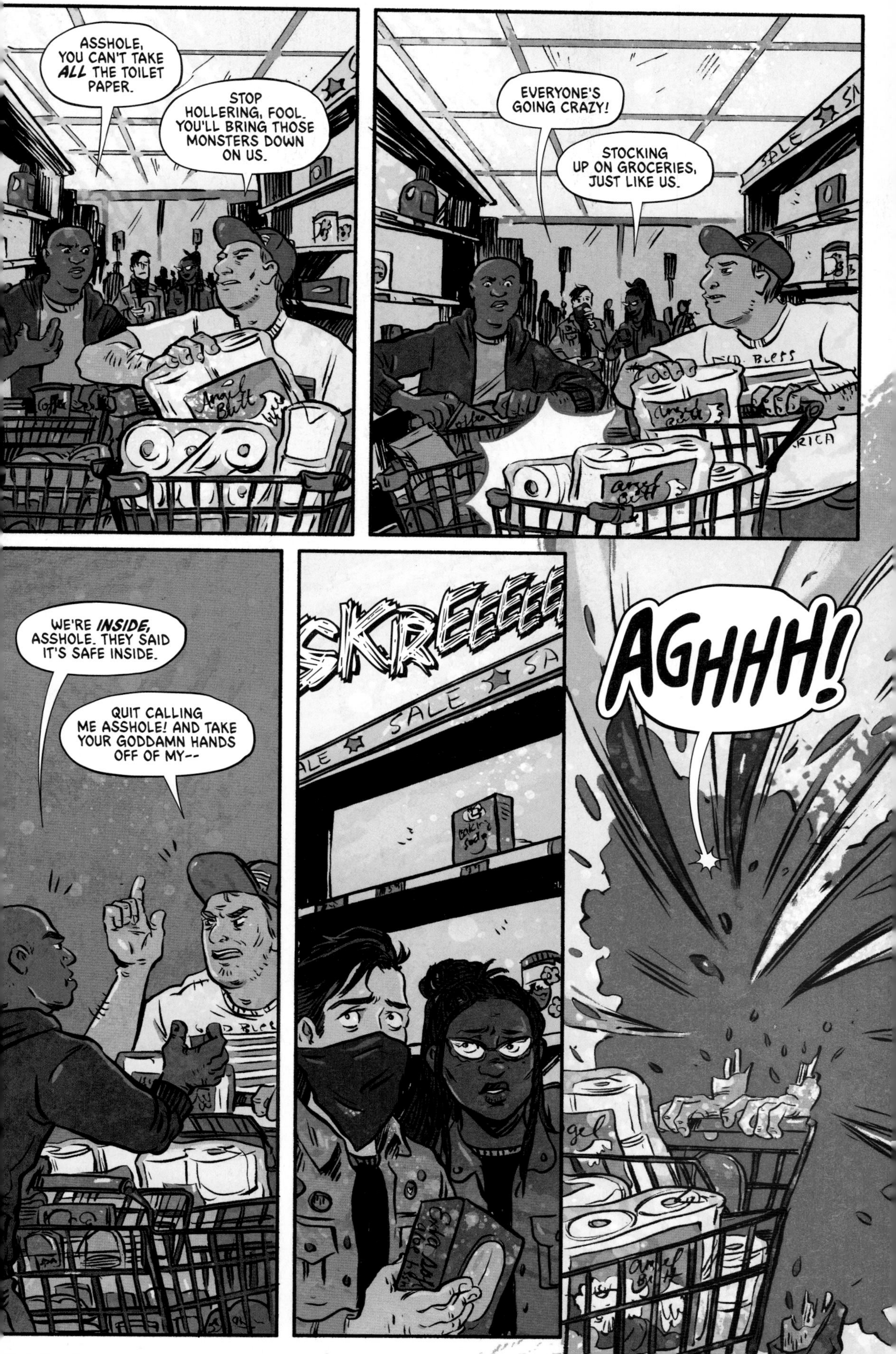
ASSHOLE, YOU CAN'T TAKE *ALL* THE TOILET PAPER.
STOP HOLLERING, FOOL. YOU'LL BRING THOSE MONSTERS DOWN ON US.
EVERYONE'S GOING CRAZY!
STOCKING UP ON GROCERIES, JUST LIKE US.
WE'RE *INSIDE,* ASSHOLE. THEY SAID IT'S SAFE INSIDE.
QUIT CALLING ME ASSHOLE! AND TAKE YOUR GODDAMN HANDS OFF OF MY--
SKREEEEEE
SALE
AGHHH!

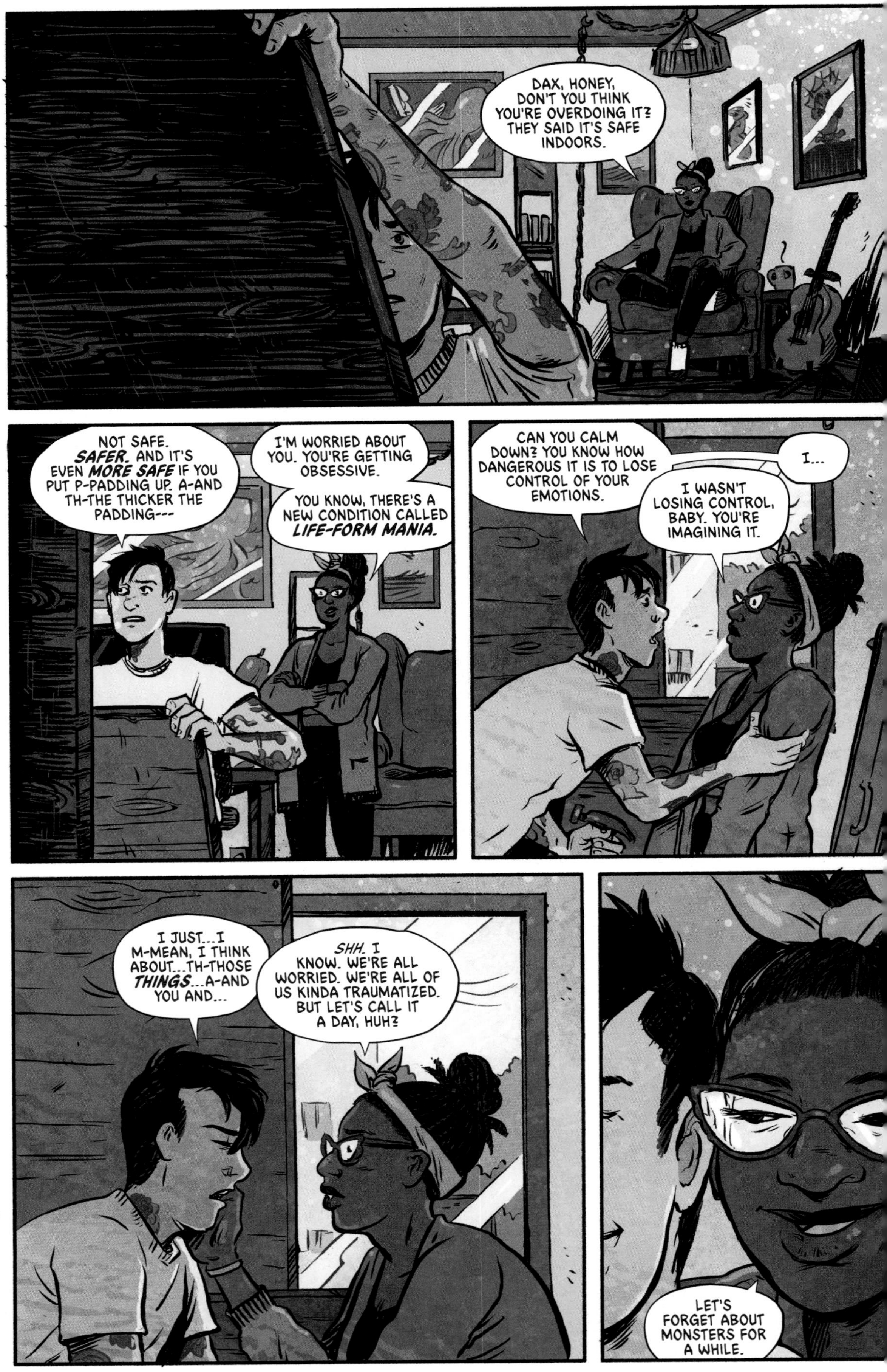
DAX, HONEY, DON'T YOU THINK YOU'RE OVERDOING IT? THEY SAID IT'S SAFE INDOORS.
NOT SAFE. SAFER. AND IT'S EVEN MORE SAFE IF YOU PUT P-PADDING UP. A-AND TH-THE THICKER THE PADDING---
I'M WORRIED ABOUT YOU. YOU'RE GETTING OBSESSIVE.
YOU KNOW, THERE'S A NEW CONDITION CALLED LIFE-FORM MANIA.
CAN YOU CALM DOWN? YOU KNOW HOW DANGEROUS IT IS TO LOSE CONTROL OF YOUR EMOTIONS.
I...
I WASN'T LOSING CONTROL, BABY. YOU'RE IMAGINING IT.
I JUST...I M-MEAN, I THINK ABOUT...TH-THOSE THINGS...A-AND YOU AND...
SHH. I KNOW. WE'RE ALL WORRIED. WE'RE ALL OF US KINDA TRAUMATIZED. BUT LET'S CALL IT A DAY, HUH?
LET'S FORGET ABOUT MONSTERS FOR A WHILE.

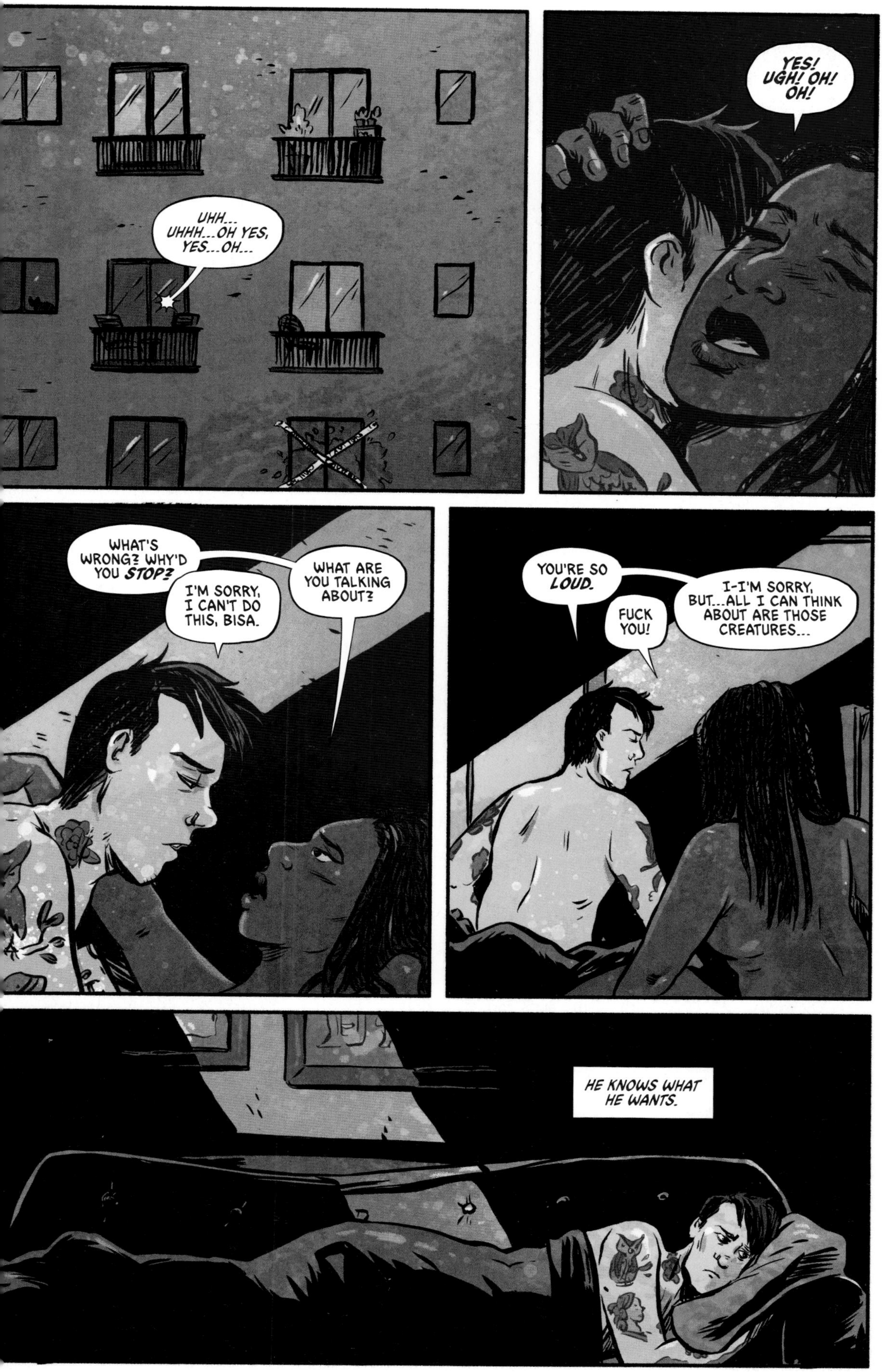
UHH... UHHH...OH YES, YES...OH...
YES! UGH! OH! OH!
WHAT'S WRONG? WHY'D YOU STOP?
I'M SORRY, I CAN'T DO THIS, BISA.
WHAT ARE YOU TALKING ABOUT?
YOU'RE SO LOUD.
FUCK YOU!
I-I'M SORRY, BUT...ALL I CAN THINK ABOUT ARE THOSE CREATURES...
HE KNOWS WHAT HE WANTS.

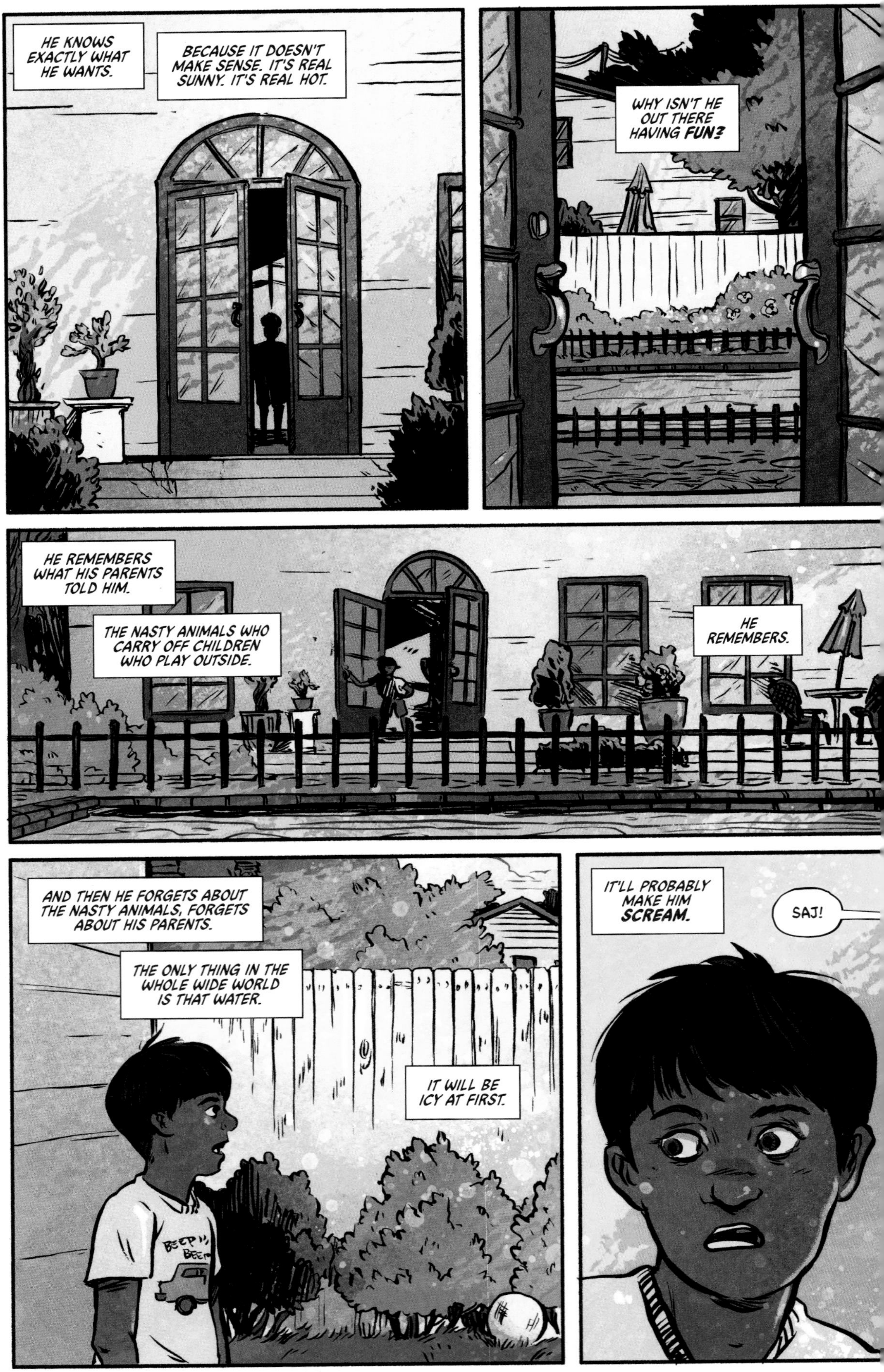
HE KNOWS EXACTLY WHAT HE WANTS.
BECAUSE IT DOESN'T MAKE SENSE. IT'S REAL SUNNY. IT'S REAL HOT.
WHY ISN'T HE OUT THERE HAVING FUN?
HE REMEMBERS WHAT HIS PARENTS TOLD HIM.
THE NASTY ANIMALS WHO CARRY OFF CHILDREN WHO PLAY OUTSIDE.
HE REMEMBERS.
AND THEN HE FORGETS ABOUT THE NASTY ANIMALS, FORGETS ABOUT HIS PARENTS.
THE ONLY THING IN THE WHOLE WIDE WORLD IS THAT WATER.
IT WILL BE ICY AT FIRST.
IT'LL PROBABLY MAKE HIM SCREAM.
SAJ!

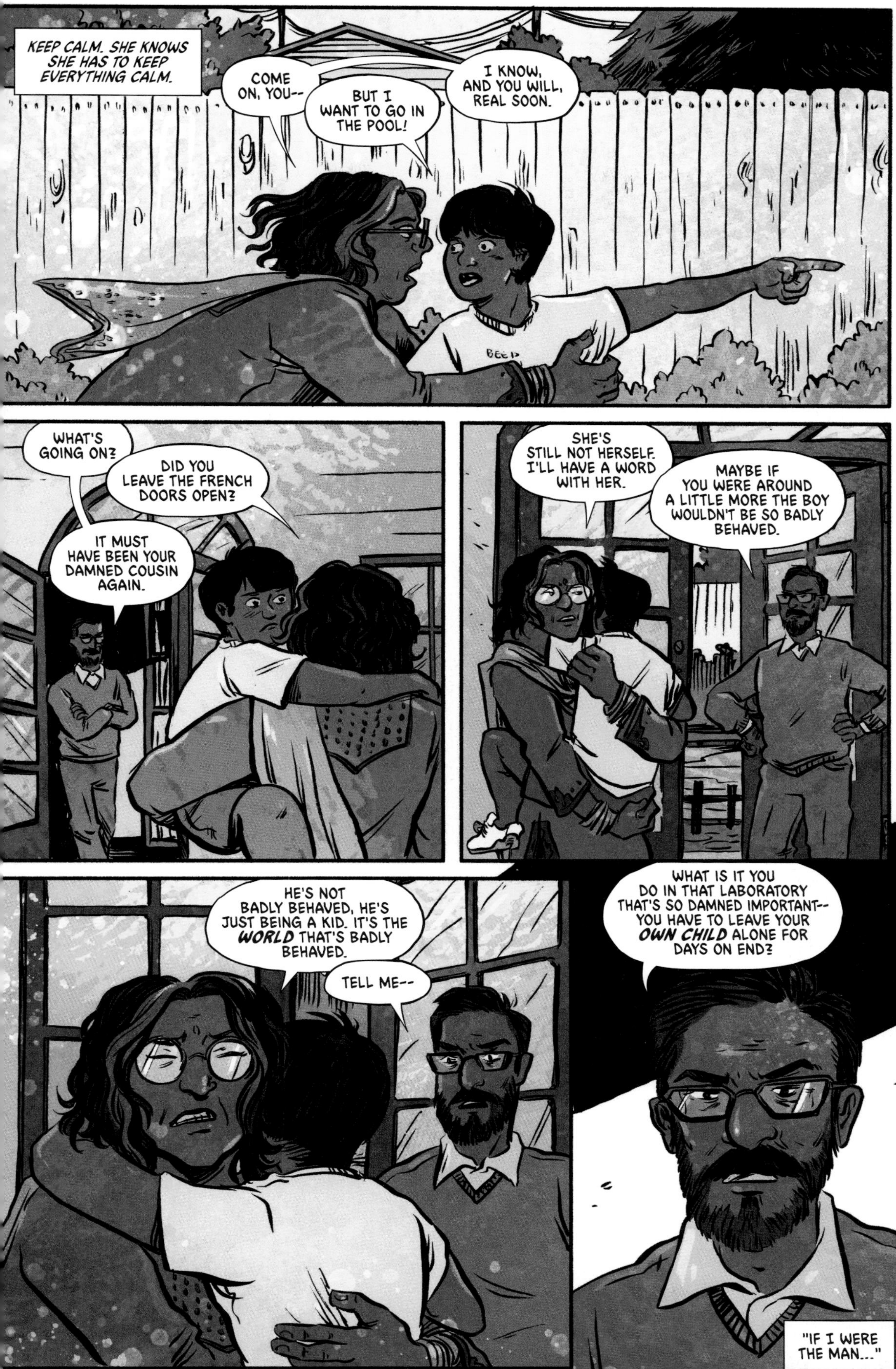

KEEP CALM. SHE KNOWS SHE HAS TO KEEP EVERYTHING CALM.
COME ON, YOU--
BUT I WANT TO GO IN THE POOL!
I KNOW, AND YOU WILL, REAL SOON.
BEEP
WHAT'S GOING ON?
DID YOU LEAVE THE FRENCH DOORS OPEN?
IT MUST HAVE BEEN YOUR DAMNED COUSIN AGAIN.
SHE'S STILL NOT HERSELF. I'LL HAVE A WORD WITH HER.
MAYBE IF YOU WERE AROUND A LITTLE MORE THE BOY WOULDN'T BE SO BADLY BEHAVED.
HE'S NOT BADLY BEHAVED, HE'S JUST BEING A KID. IT'S THE *WORLD* THAT'S BADLY BEHAVED.
TELL ME--
WHAT IS IT YOU DO IN THAT LABORATORY THAT'S SO DAMNED IMPORTANT-- YOU HAVE TO LEAVE YOUR *OWN CHILD* ALONE FOR DAYS ON END?
"IF I WERE THE MAN..."

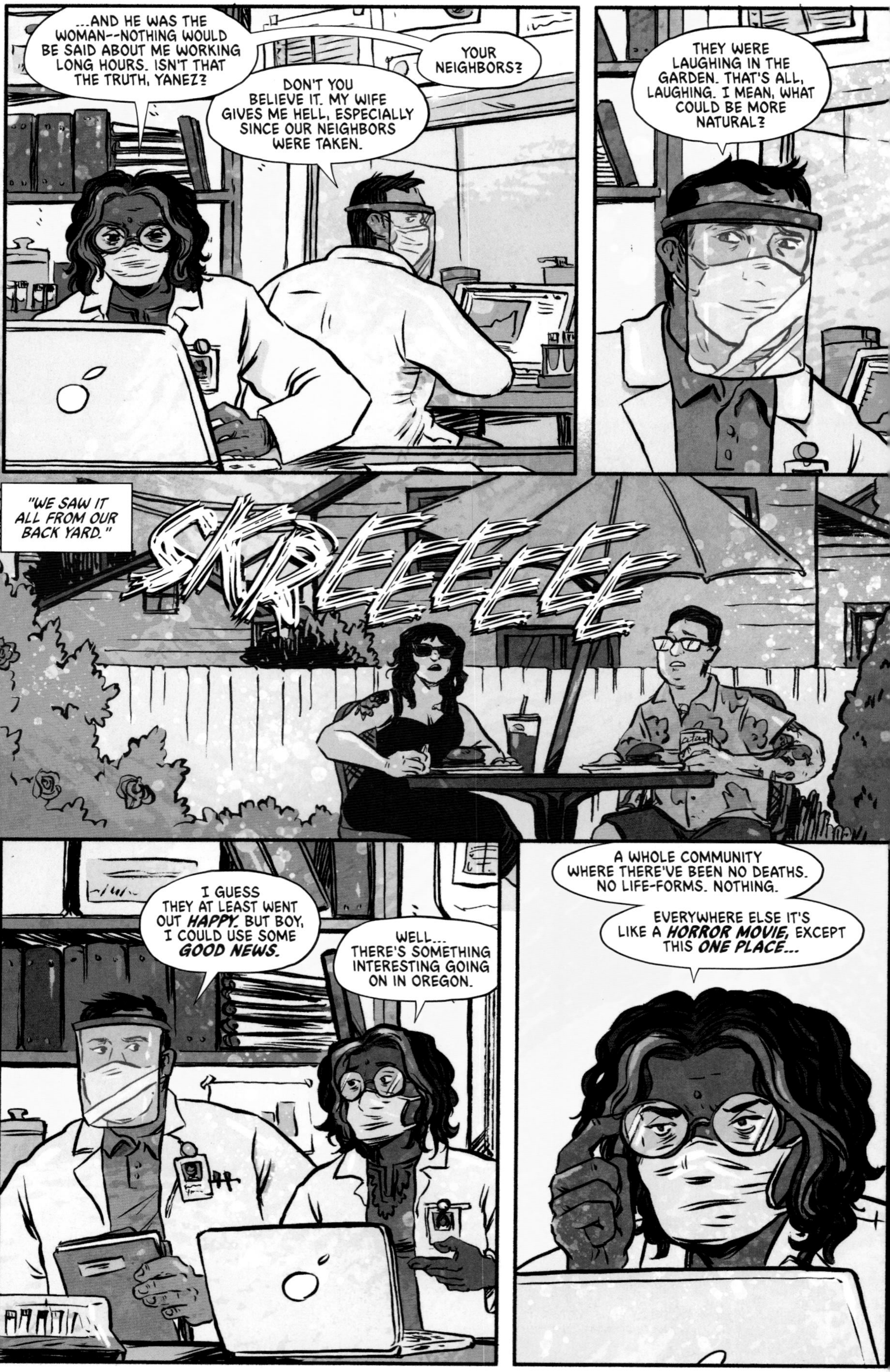
...AND HE WAS THE WOMAN--NOTHING WOULD BE SAID ABOUT ME WORKING LONG HOURS. ISN'T THAT THE TRUTH, YANEZ?
DON'T YOU BELIEVE IT. MY WIFE GIVES ME HELL, ESPECIALLY SINCE OUR NEIGHBORS WERE TAKEN.
YOUR NEIGHBORS?
THEY WERE LAUGHING IN THE GARDEN. THAT'S ALL, LAUGHING. I MEAN, WHAT COULD BE MORE NATURAL?
"WE SAW IT ALL FROM OUR BACK YARD."
SKREEEEEEE
I GUESS THEY AT LEAST WENT OUT *HAPPY.* BUT BOY, I COULD USE SOME *GOOD NEWS.*
WELL... THERE'S SOMETHING INTERESTING GOING ON IN OREGON.
A WHOLE COMMUNITY WHERE THERE'VE BEEN NO DEATHS. NO LIFE-FORMS. NOTHING.
EVERYWHERE ELSE IT'S LIKE A *HORROR MOVIE,* EXCEPT THIS *ONE PLACE...*

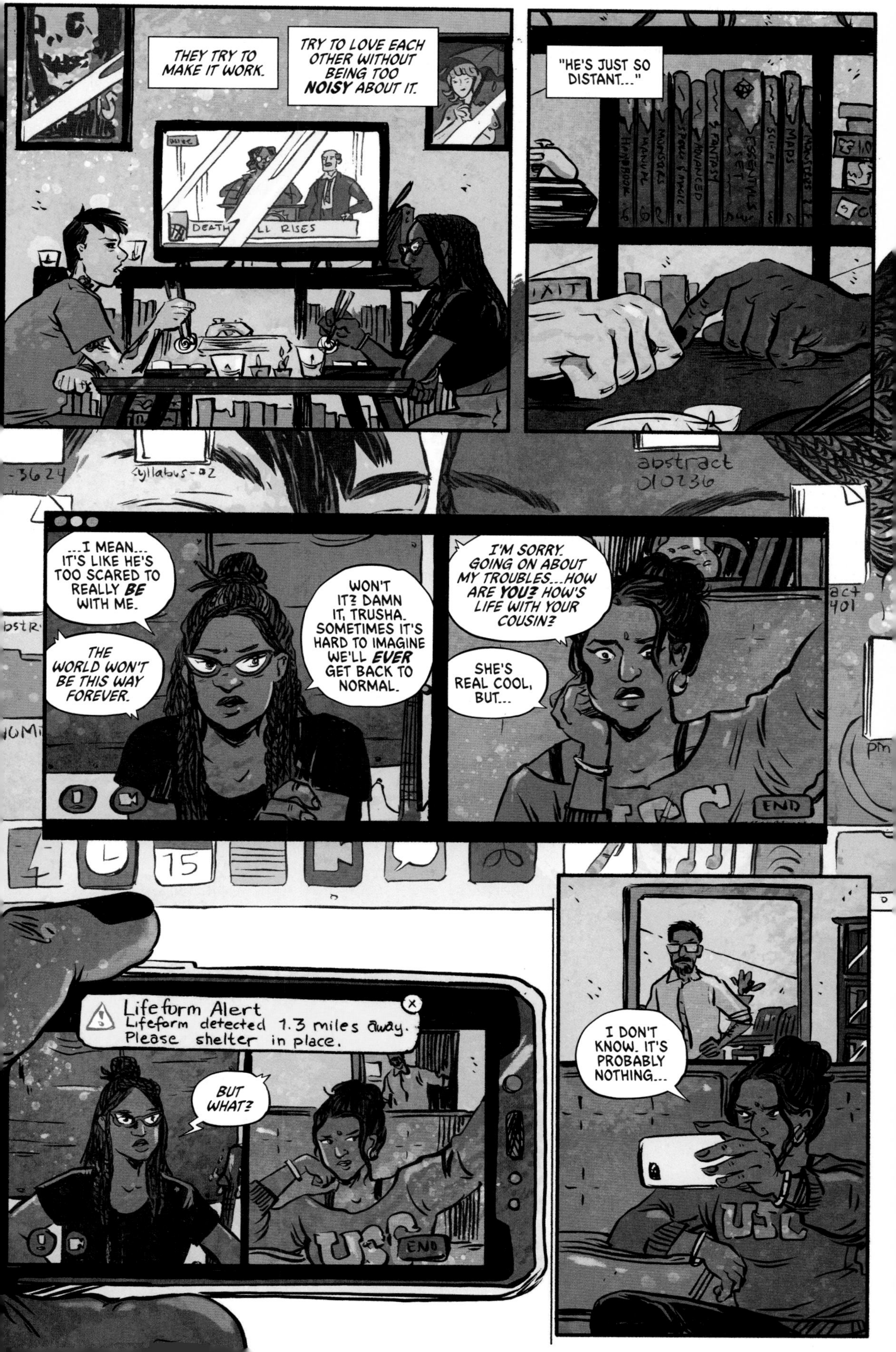

THEY TRY TO MAKE IT WORK.
TRY TO LOVE EACH OTHER WITHOUT BEING TOO NOISY ABOUT IT.
DEATH LL RISES
"HE'S JUST SO DISTANT..."
...I MEAN... IT'S LIKE HE'S TOO SCARED TO REALLY BE WITH ME.
THE WORLD WON'T BE THIS WAY FOREVER.
WON'T IT? DAMN IT, TRUSHA. SOMETIMES IT'S HARD TO IMAGINE WE'LL EVER GET BACK TO NORMAL.
I'M SORRY. GOING ON ABOUT MY TROUBLES... HOW ARE YOU? HOW'S LIFE WITH YOUR COUSIN?
SHE'S REAL COOL, BUT...
END
Lifeform Alert
Lifeform detected 1.3 miles away.
Please shelter in place.
BUT WHAT?
END
I DON'T KNOW. IT'S PROBABLY NOTHING...

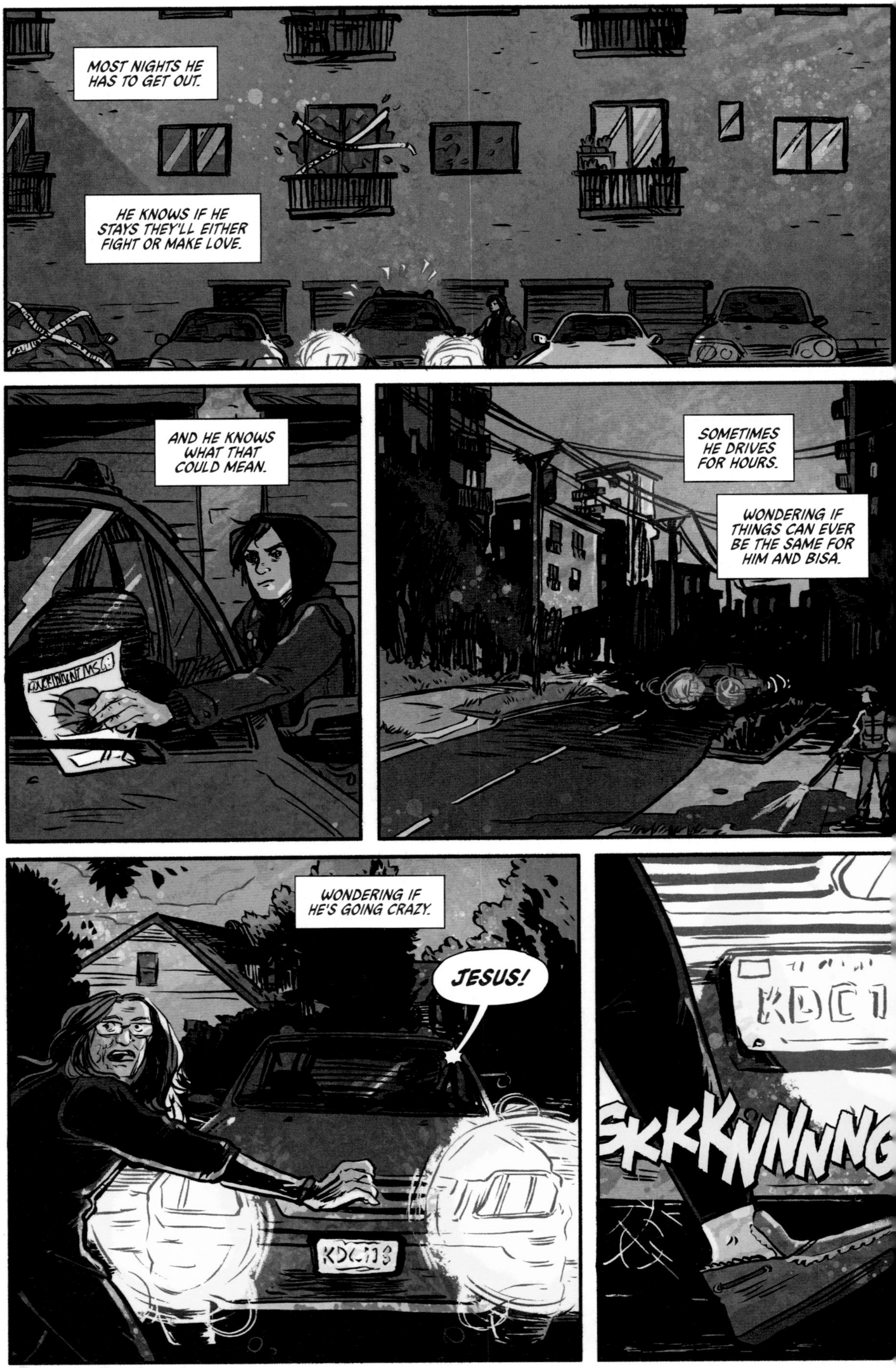

MOST NIGHTS HE HAS TO GET OUT.
HE KNOWS IF HE STAYS THEY'LL EITHER FIGHT OR MAKE LOVE.
AND HE KNOWS WHAT THAT COULD MEAN.
SOMETIMES HE DRIVES FOR HOURS.
WONDERING IF THINGS CAN EVER BE THE SAME FOR HIM AND BISA.
WONDERING IF HE'S GOING CRAZY.
JESUS!
SKKKNNNNG

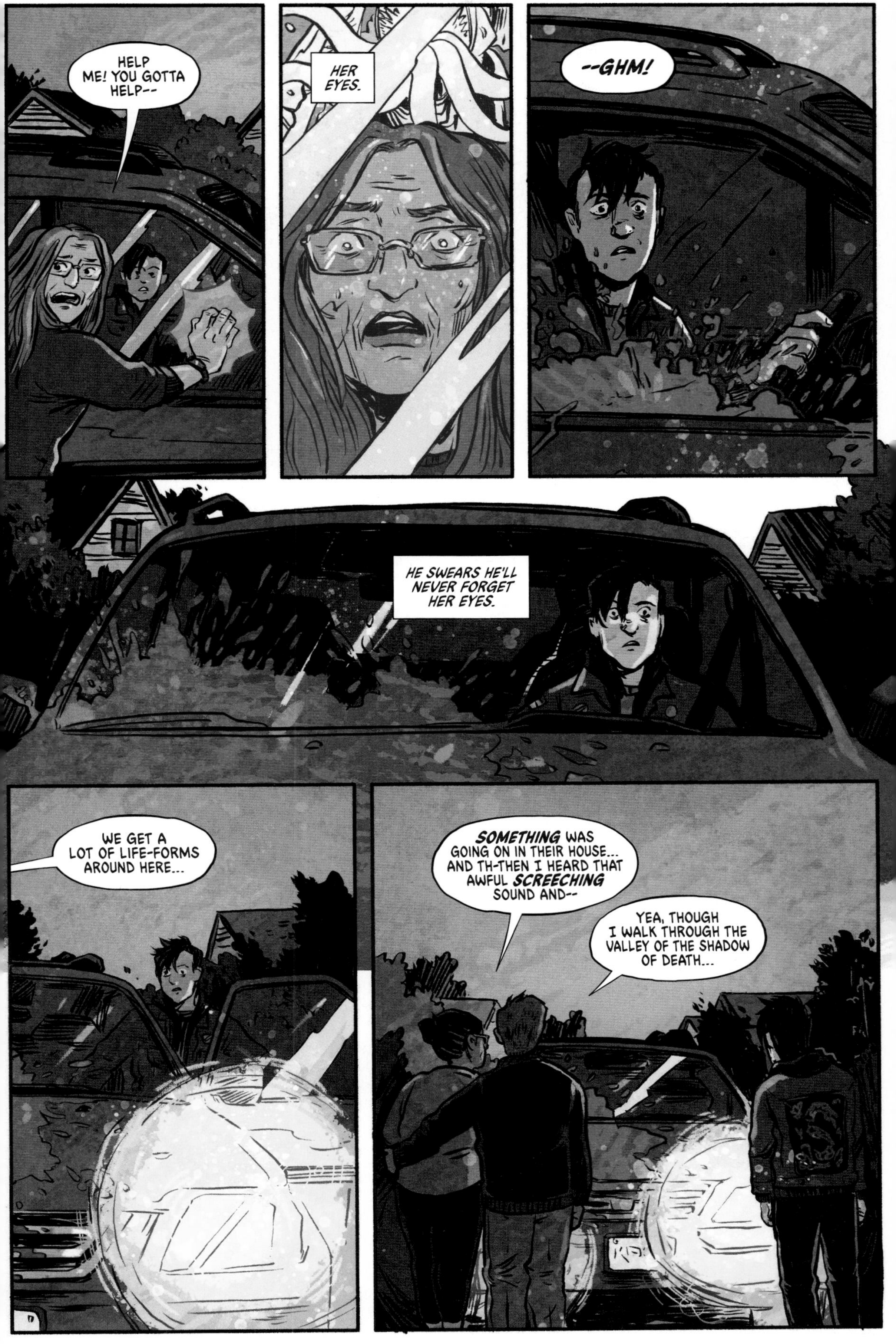
HELP ME! YOU GOTTA HELP--
HER EYES.
--GHM!
HE SWEARS HE'LL NEVER FORGET HER EYES.
WE GET A LOT OF LIFE-FORMS AROUND HERE...
SOMETHING WAS GOING ON IN THEIR HOUSE... AND TH-THEN I HEARD THAT AWFUL SCREECHING SOUND AND--
YEA, THOUGH I WALK THROUGH THE VALLEY OF THE SHADOW OF DEATH...

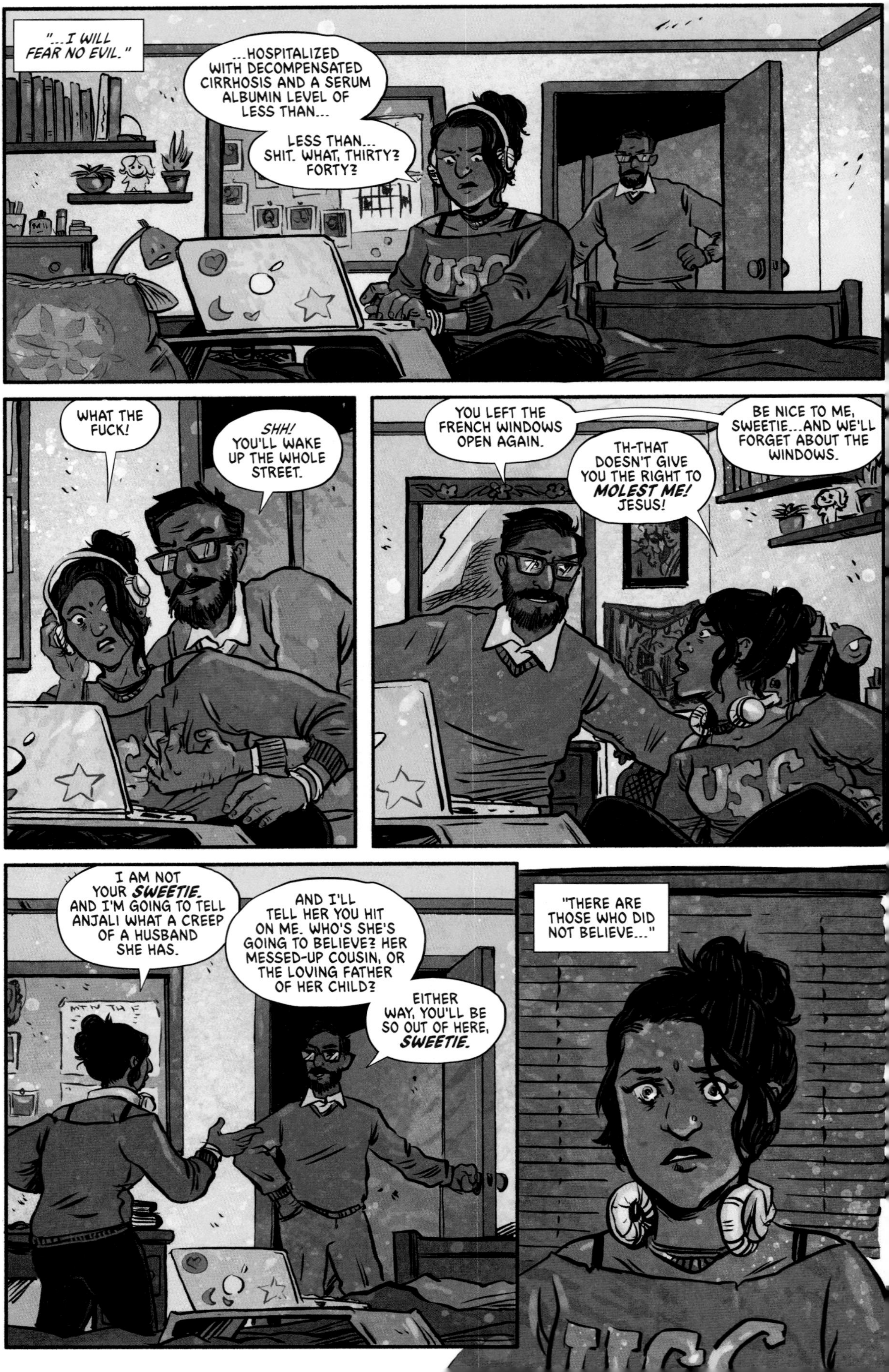
"...I WILL FEAR NO EVIL."
...HOSPITALIZED WITH DECOMPENSATED CIRRHOSIS AND A SERUM ALBUMIN LEVEL OF LESS THAN...
LESS THAN... SHIT. WHAT, THIRTY? FORTY?
WHAT THE FUCK!
SHH! YOU'LL WAKE UP THE WHOLE STREET.
YOU LEFT THE FRENCH WINDOWS OPEN AGAIN.
TH-THAT DOESN'T GIVE YOU THE RIGHT TO MOLEST ME! JESUS!
BE NICE TO ME, SWEETIE...AND WE'LL FORGET ABOUT THE WINDOWS.
I AM NOT YOUR SWEETIE. AND I'M GOING TO TELL ANJALI WHAT A CREEP OF A HUSBAND SHE HAS.
AND I'LL TELL HER YOU HIT ON ME. WHO'S SHE'S GOING TO BELIEVE? HER MESSED-UP COUSIN, OR THE LOVING FATHER OF HER CHILD?
EITHER WAY, YOU'LL BE SO OUT OF HERE, SWEETIE.
"THERE ARE THOSE WHO DID NOT BELIEVE..."

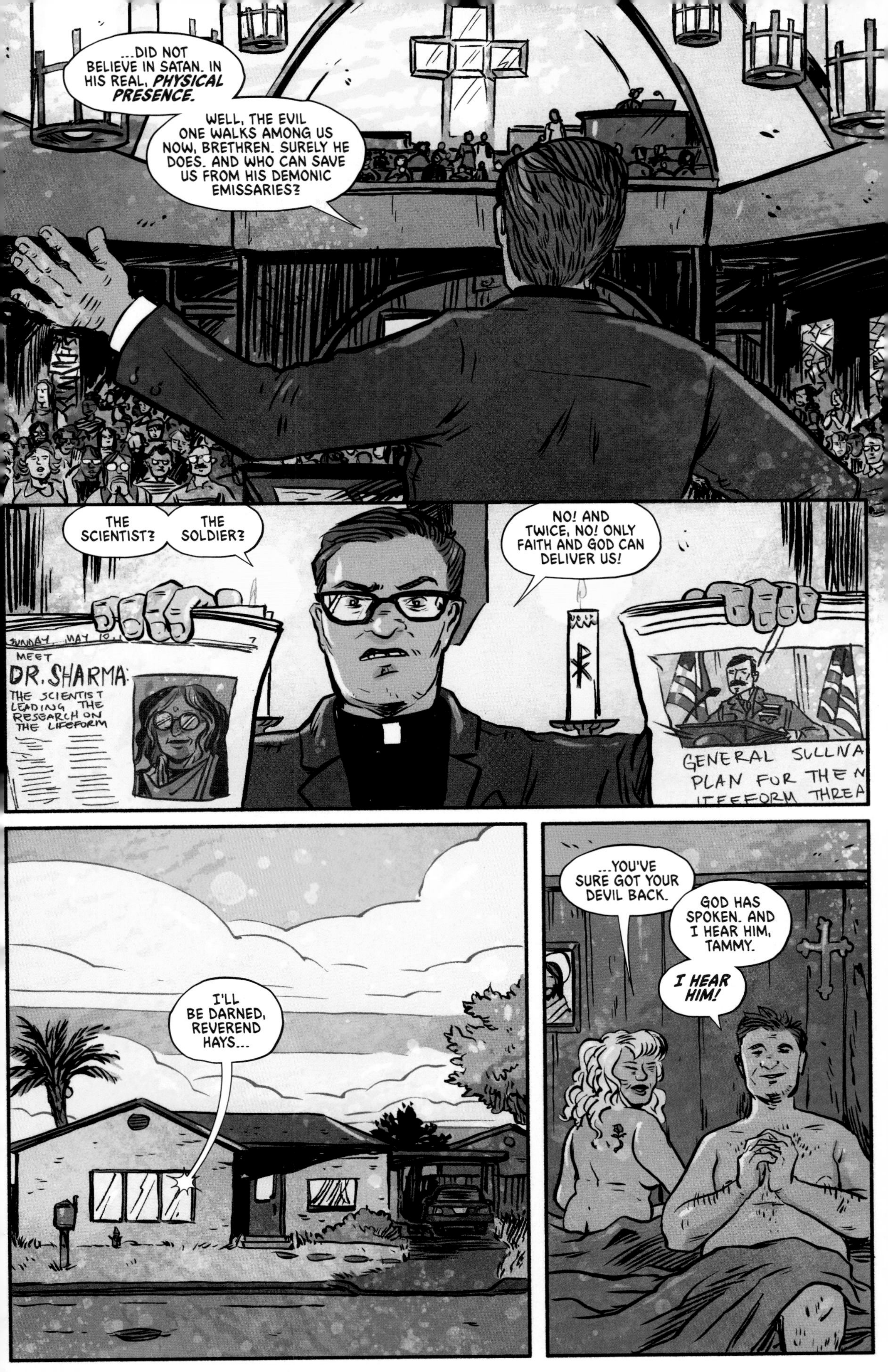
...DID NOT BELIEVE IN SATAN. IN HIS REAL, *PHYSICAL PRESENCE.*
WELL, THE EVIL ONE WALKS AMONG US NOW, BRETHREN. SURELY HE DOES. AND WHO CAN SAVE US FROM HIS DEMONIC EMISSARIES?
THE SCIENTIST?
THE SOLDIER?
NO! AND TWICE, NO! ONLY FAITH AND GOD CAN DELIVER US!
SUNDAY MAY 1
MEET DR. SHARMA: THE SCIENTIST LEADING THE RESEARCH ON THE LIFEFORM
GENERAL SULLIVA
PLAN FOR THE N
I'LL BE DARNED, REVEREND HAYS...
...YOU'VE SURE GOT YOUR DEVIL BACK.
GOD HAS SPOKEN. AND I HEAR HIM, TAMMY.
I HEAR HIM!

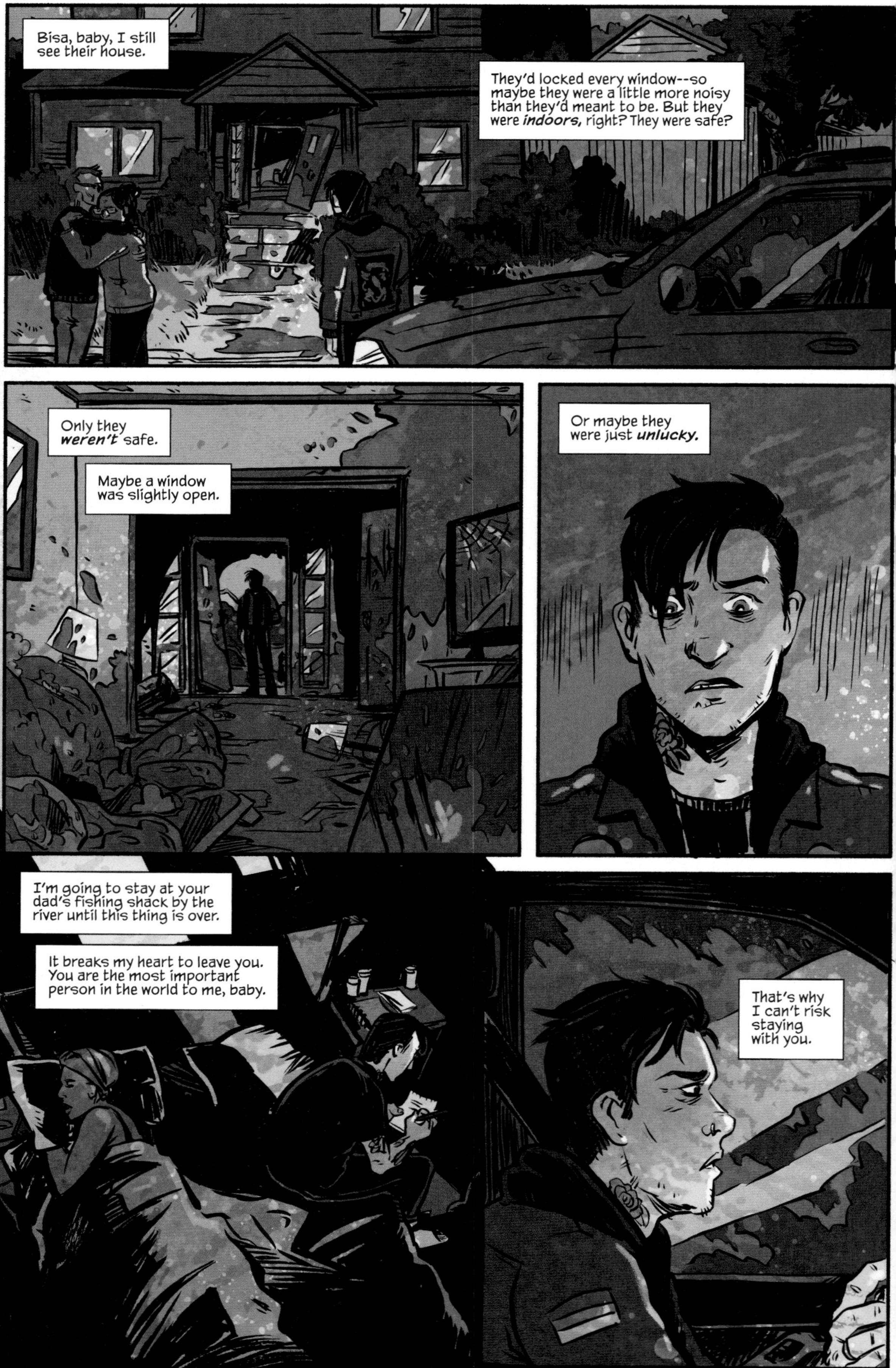
Bisa, baby, I still see their house.
They'd locked every window--so maybe they were a little more noisy than they'd meant to be. But they were *indoors,* right? They were safe?
Only they ***weren't*** safe.
Maybe a window was slightly open.
Or maybe they were just ***unlucky.***
I'm going to stay at your dad's fishing shack by the river until this thing is over.
It breaks my heart to leave you. You are the most important person in the world to me, baby.
That's why I can't risk staying with you.

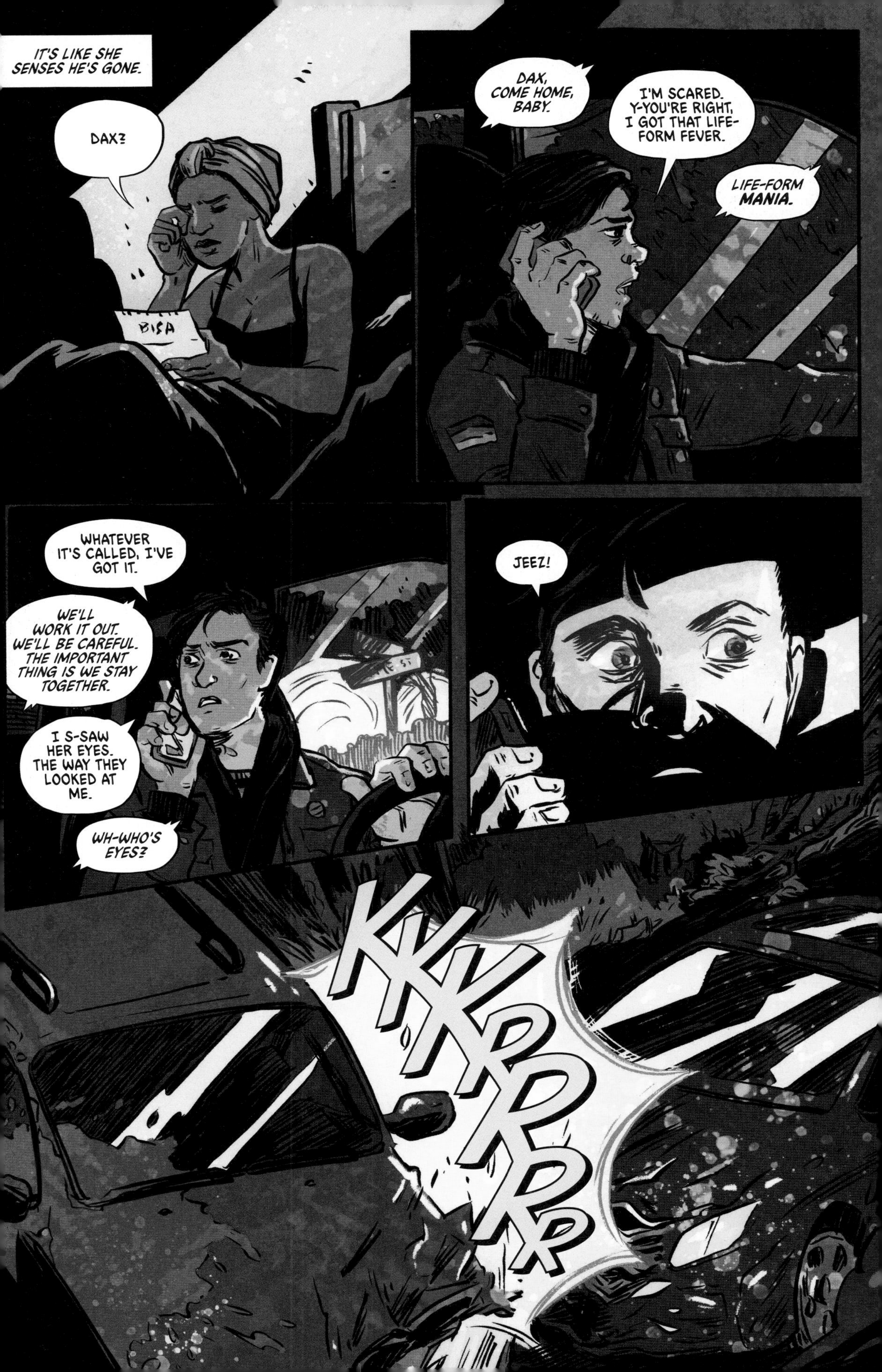
IT'S LIKE SHE SENSES HE'S GONE.
DAX?
BISA
DAX, COME HOME, BABY.
I'M SCARED. Y-YOU'RE RIGHT, I GOT THAT LIFE-FORM FEVER.
LIFE-FORM MANIA.
WHATEVER IT'S CALLED, I'VE GOT IT.
WE'LL WORK IT OUT. WE'LL BE CAREFUL. THE IMPORTANT THING IS WE STAY TOGETHER.
I S-SAW HER EYES. THE WAY THEY LOOKED AT ME.
WH-WHO'S EYES?
JEEZ!
KKKRRRRR

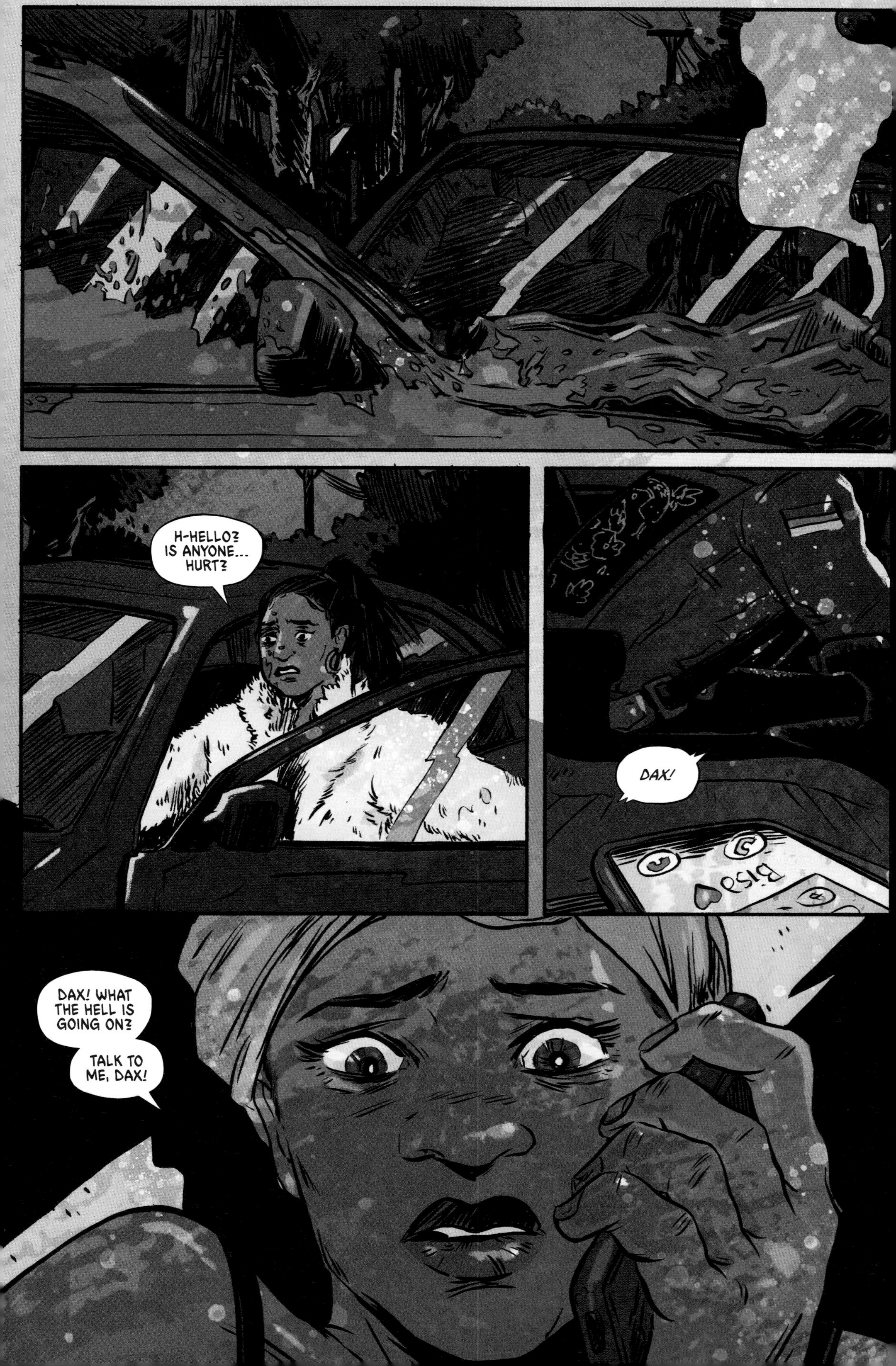
H-HELLO? IS ANYONE... HURT?
DAX!
Bisa
DAX! WHAT THE HELL IS GOING ON?
TALK TO ME, DAX!

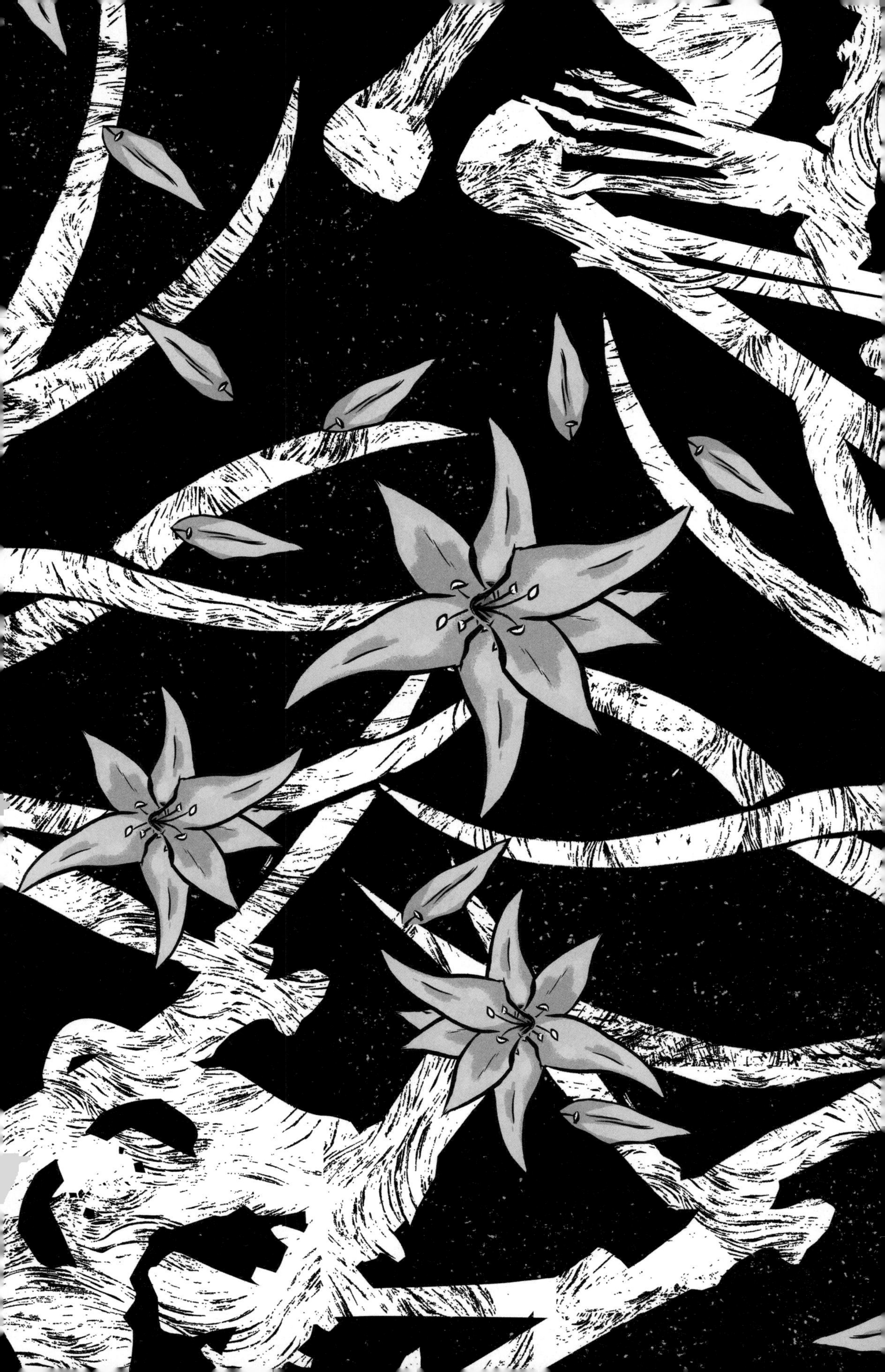

CHAPTER THREE

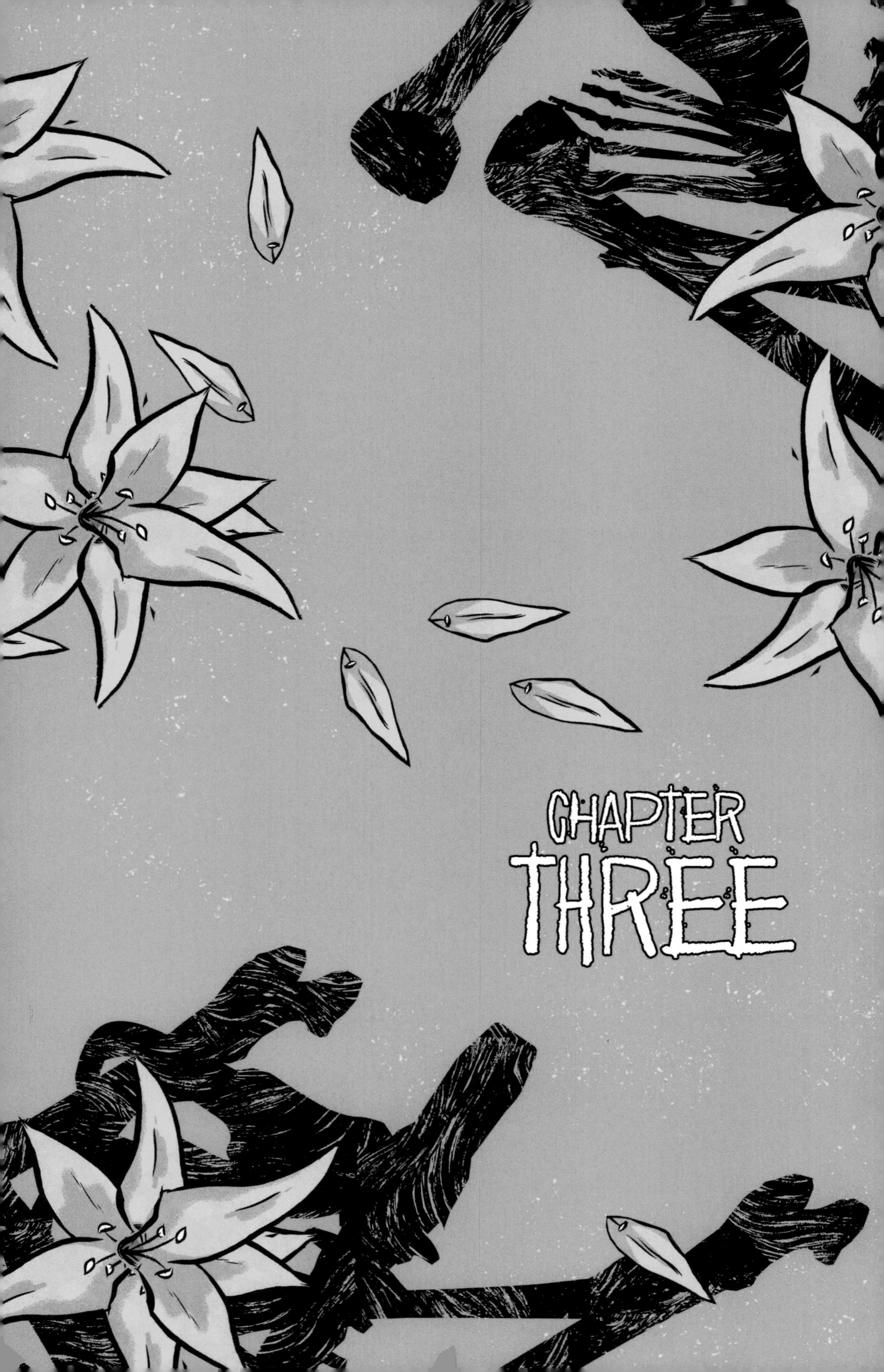

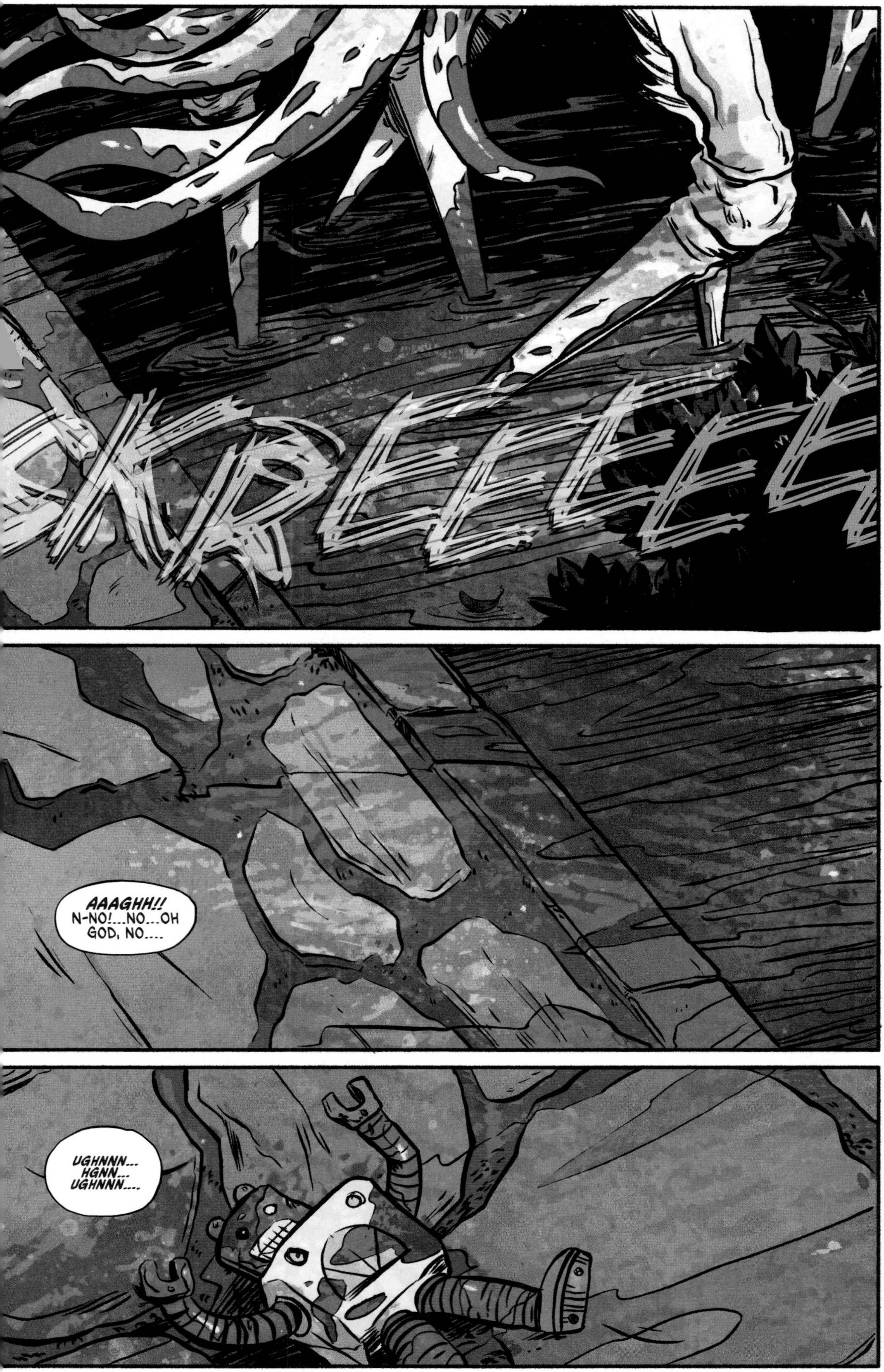
SKREEEEE
AAAGHH!! N-NO!...NO...OH GOD, NO....
UGHNNN... HGNN... UGHNNN....

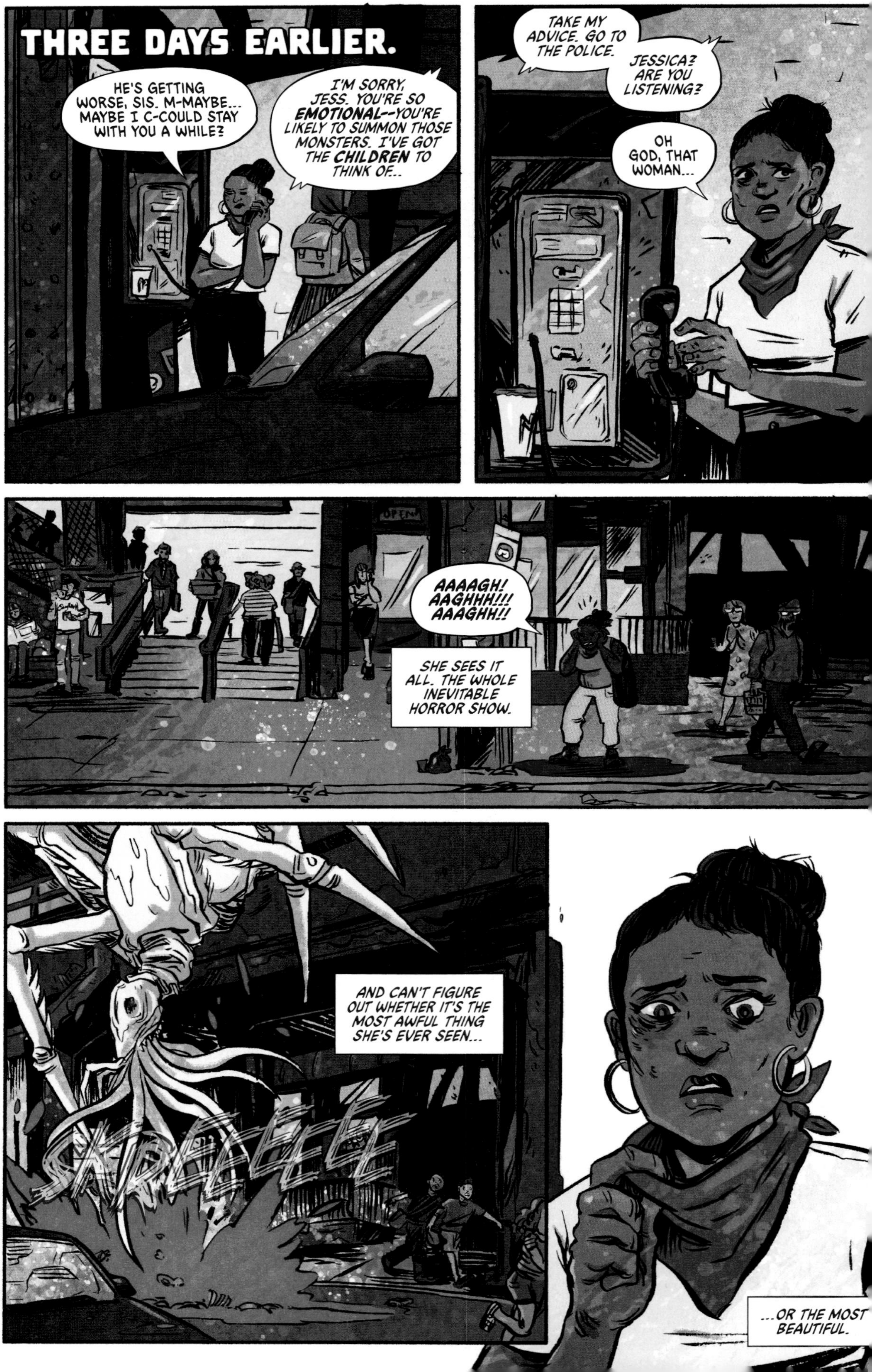
THREE DAYS EARLIER.
HE'S GETTING WORSE, SIS. M-MAYBE... MAYBE I C-COULD STAY WITH YOU A WHILE?
I'M SORRY, JESS. YOU'RE SO EMOTIONAL--YOU'RE LIKELY TO SUMMON THOSE MONSTERS. I'VE GOT THE CHILDREN TO THINK OF...
TAKE MY ADVICE. GO TO THE POLICE.
JESSICA? ARE YOU LISTENING?
OH GOD, THAT WOMAN...
OPEN
AAAAGH! AAGHHH!!! AAAGHH!!
SHE SEES IT ALL. THE WHOLE INEVITABLE HORROR SHOW.
AND CAN'T FIGURE OUT WHETHER IT'S THE MOST AWFUL THING SHE'S EVER SEEN...
...OR THE MOST BEAUTIFUL.

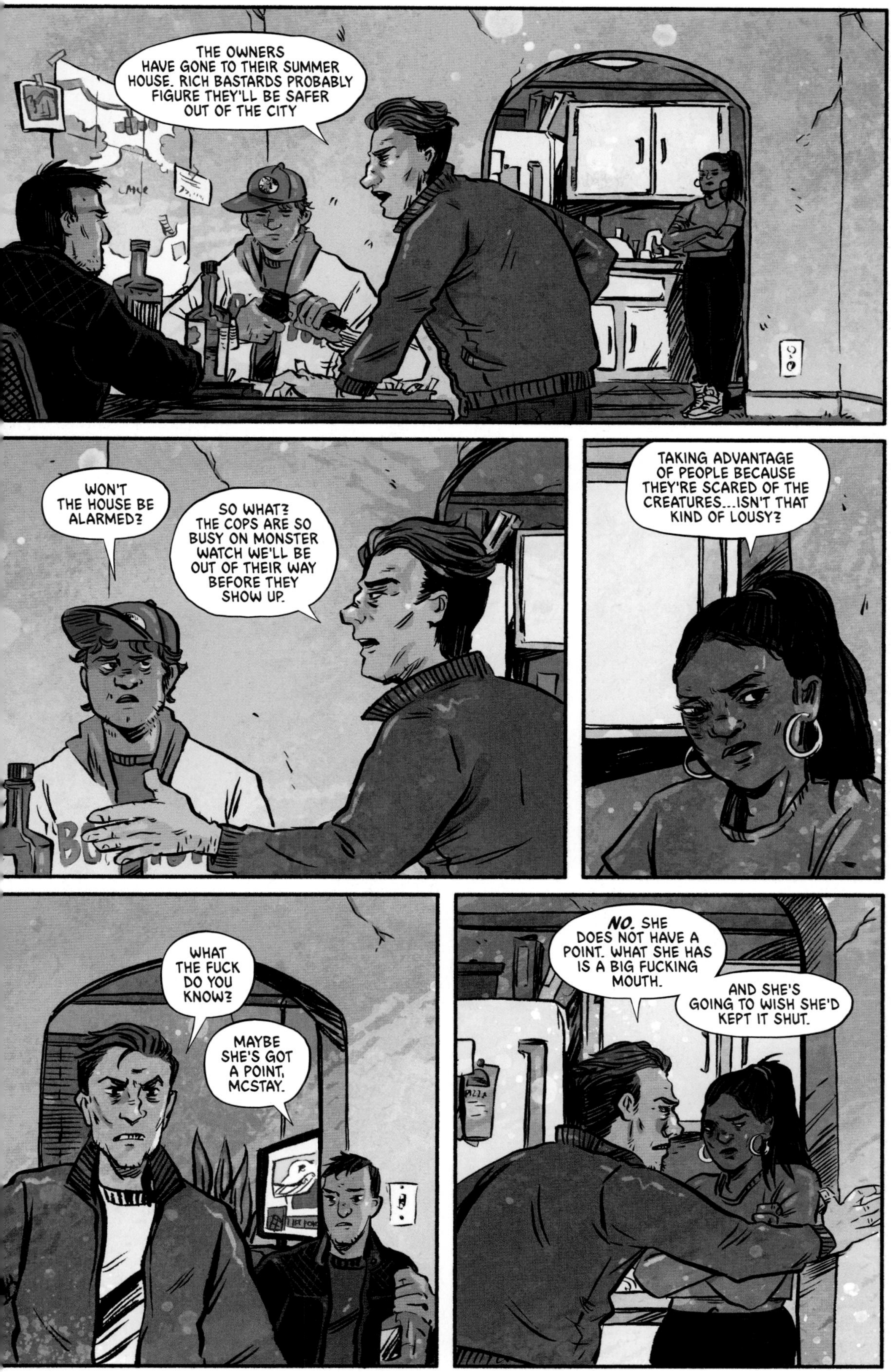
THE OWNERS HAVE GONE TO THEIR SUMMER HOUSE. RICH BASTARDS PROBABLY FIGURE THEY'LL BE SAFER OUT OF THE CITY
WON'T THE HOUSE BE ALARMED?
SO WHAT? THE COPS ARE SO BUSY ON MONSTER WATCH WE'LL BE OUT OF THEIR WAY BEFORE THEY SHOW UP.
TAKING ADVANTAGE OF PEOPLE BECAUSE THEY'RE SCARED OF THE CREATURES...ISN'T THAT KIND OF LOUSY?
WHAT THE FUCK DO YOU KNOW?
MAYBE SHE'S GOT A POINT, MCSTAY.
NO. SHE DOES NOT HAVE A POINT. WHAT SHE HAS IS A BIG FUCKING MOUTH.
AND SHE'S GOING TO WISH SHE'D KEPT IT SHUT.

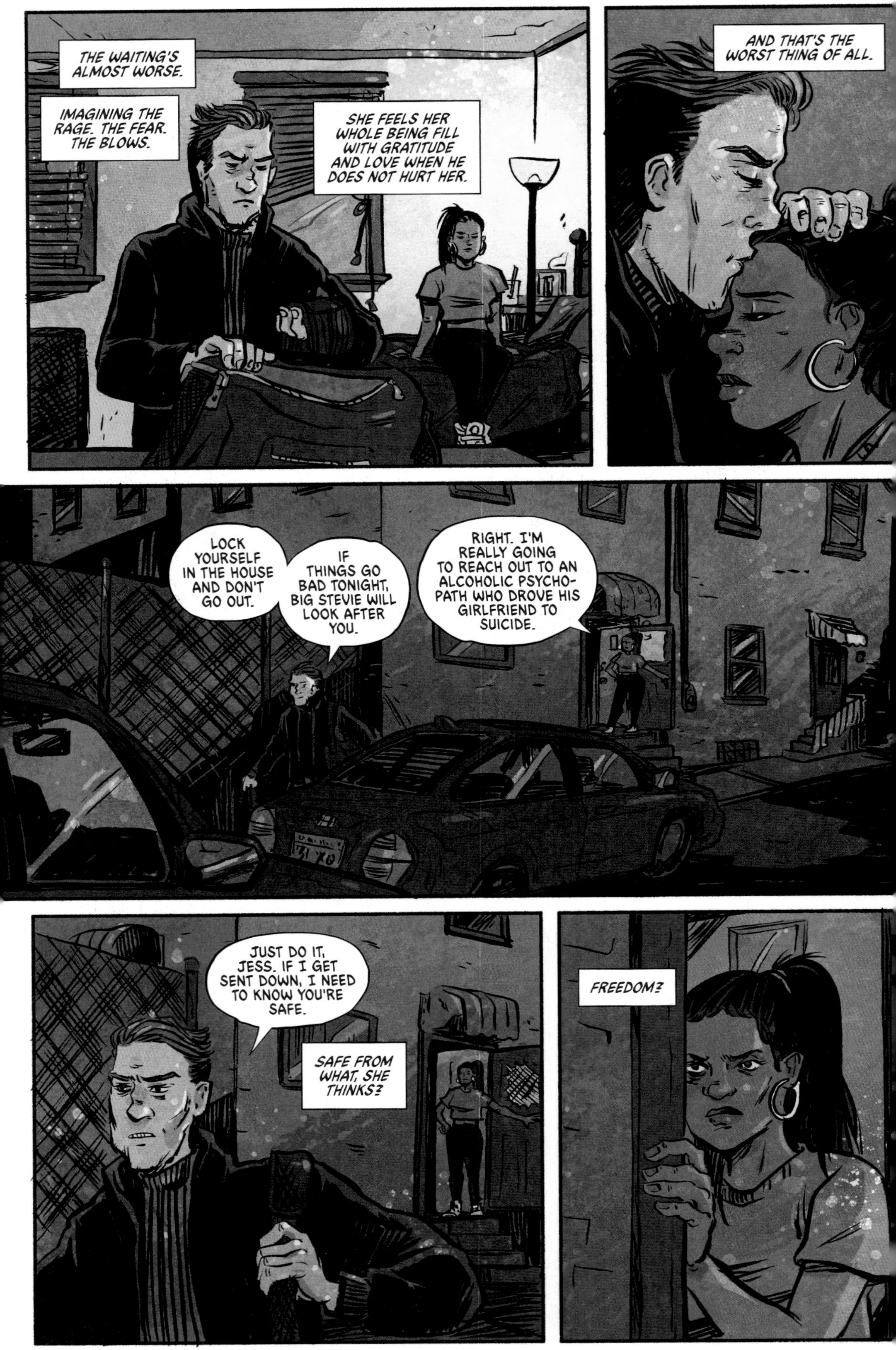
THE WAITING'S ALMOST WORSE.
IMAGINING THE RAGE. THE FEAR. THE BLOWS.
SHE FEELS HER WHOLE BEING FILL WITH GRATITUDE AND LOVE WHEN HE DOES NOT HURT HER.
AND THAT'S THE WORST THING OF ALL.
LOCK YOURSELF IN THE HOUSE AND DON'T GO OUT.
IF THINGS GO BAD TONIGHT, BIG STEVIE WILL LOOK AFTER YOU.
RIGHT. I'M REALLY GOING TO REACH OUT TO AN ALCOHOLIC PSYCHO-PATH WHO DROVE HIS GIRLFRIEND TO SUICIDE.
JUST DO IT, JESS. IF I GET SENT DOWN, I NEED TO KNOW YOU'RE SAFE.
SAFE FROM WHAT, SHE THINKS?
FREEDOM?

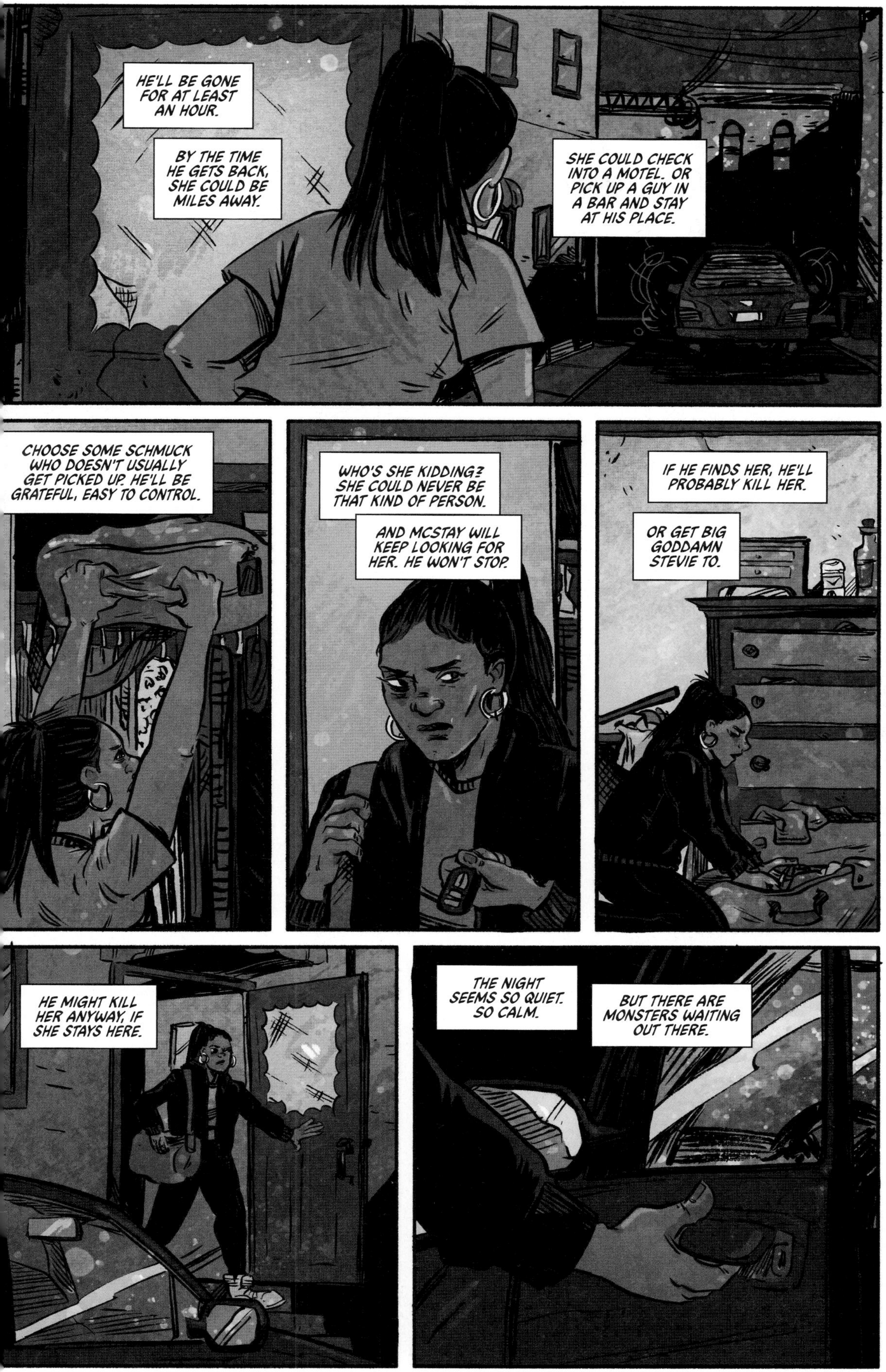
HE'LL BE GONE FOR AT LEAST AN HOUR.
BY THE TIME HE GETS BACK, SHE COULD BE MILES AWAY.
SHE COULD CHECK INTO A MOTEL. OR PICK UP A GUY IN A BAR AND STAY AT HIS PLACE.
CHOOSE SOME SCHMUCK WHO DOESN'T USUALLY GET PICKED UP. HE'LL BE GRATEFUL, EASY TO CONTROL.
WHO'S SHE KIDDING? SHE COULD NEVER BE THAT KIND OF PERSON.
AND MCSTAY WILL KEEP LOOKING FOR HER. HE WON'T STOP.
IF HE FINDS HER, HE'LL PROBABLY KILL HER.
OR GET BIG GODDAMN STEVIE TO.
HE MIGHT KILL HER ANYWAY, IF SHE STAYS HERE.
THE NIGHT SEEMS SO QUIET. SO CALM.
BUT THERE ARE MONSTERS WAITING OUT THERE.

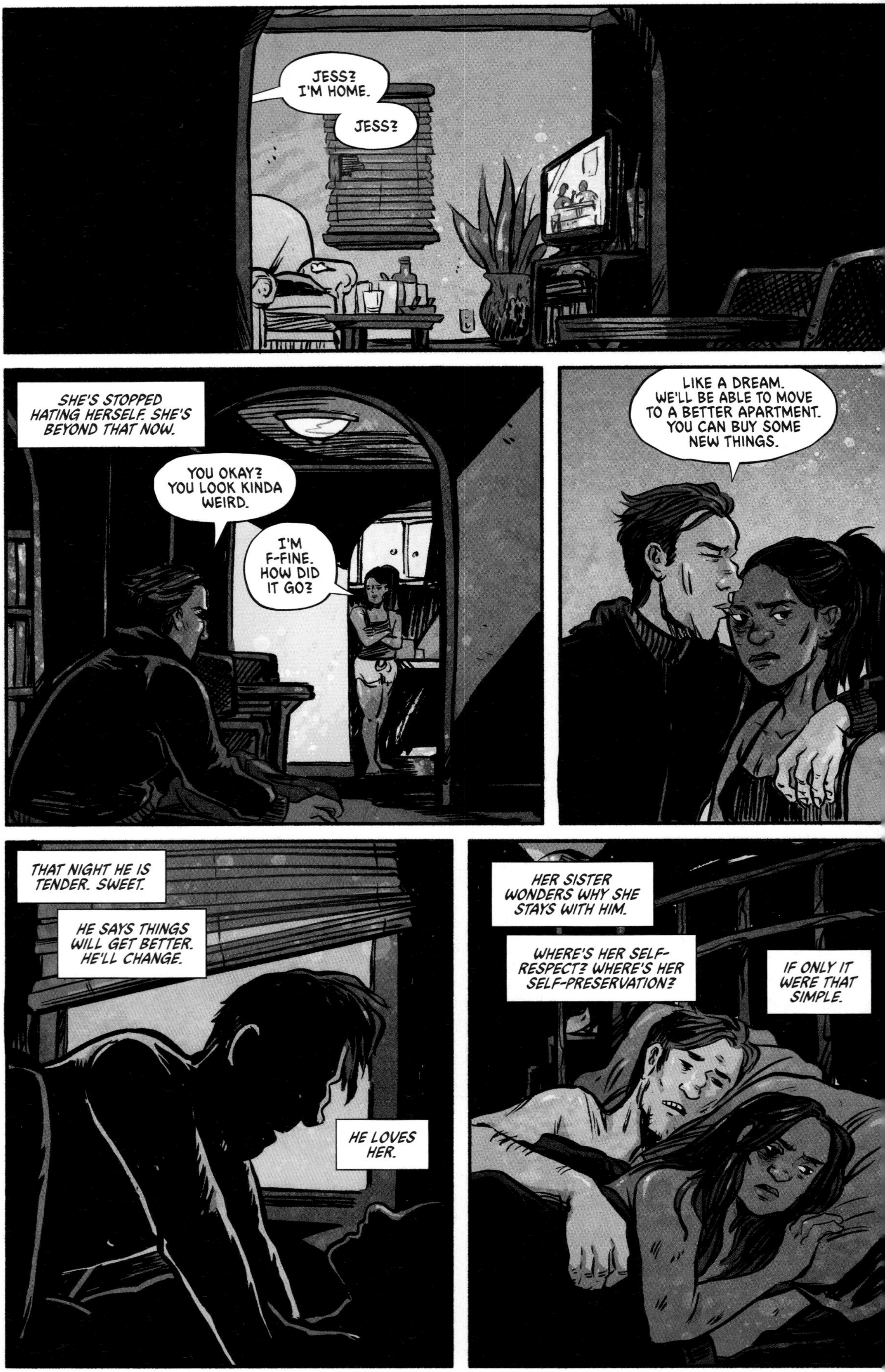
JESS? I'M HOME.
JESS?
SHE'S STOPPED HATING HERSELF. SHE'S BEYOND THAT NOW.
YOU OKAY? YOU LOOK KINDA WEIRD.
I'M F-FINE. HOW DID IT GO?
LIKE A DREAM. WE'LL BE ABLE TO MOVE TO A BETTER APARTMENT. YOU CAN BUY SOME NEW THINGS.
THAT NIGHT HE IS TENDER. SWEET.
HE SAYS THINGS WILL GET BETTER. HE'LL CHANGE.
HE LOVES HER.
HER SISTER WONDERS WHY SHE STAYS WITH HIM.
WHERE'S HER SELF-RESPECT? WHERE'S HER SELF-PRESERVATION?
IF ONLY IT WERE THAT SIMPLE.

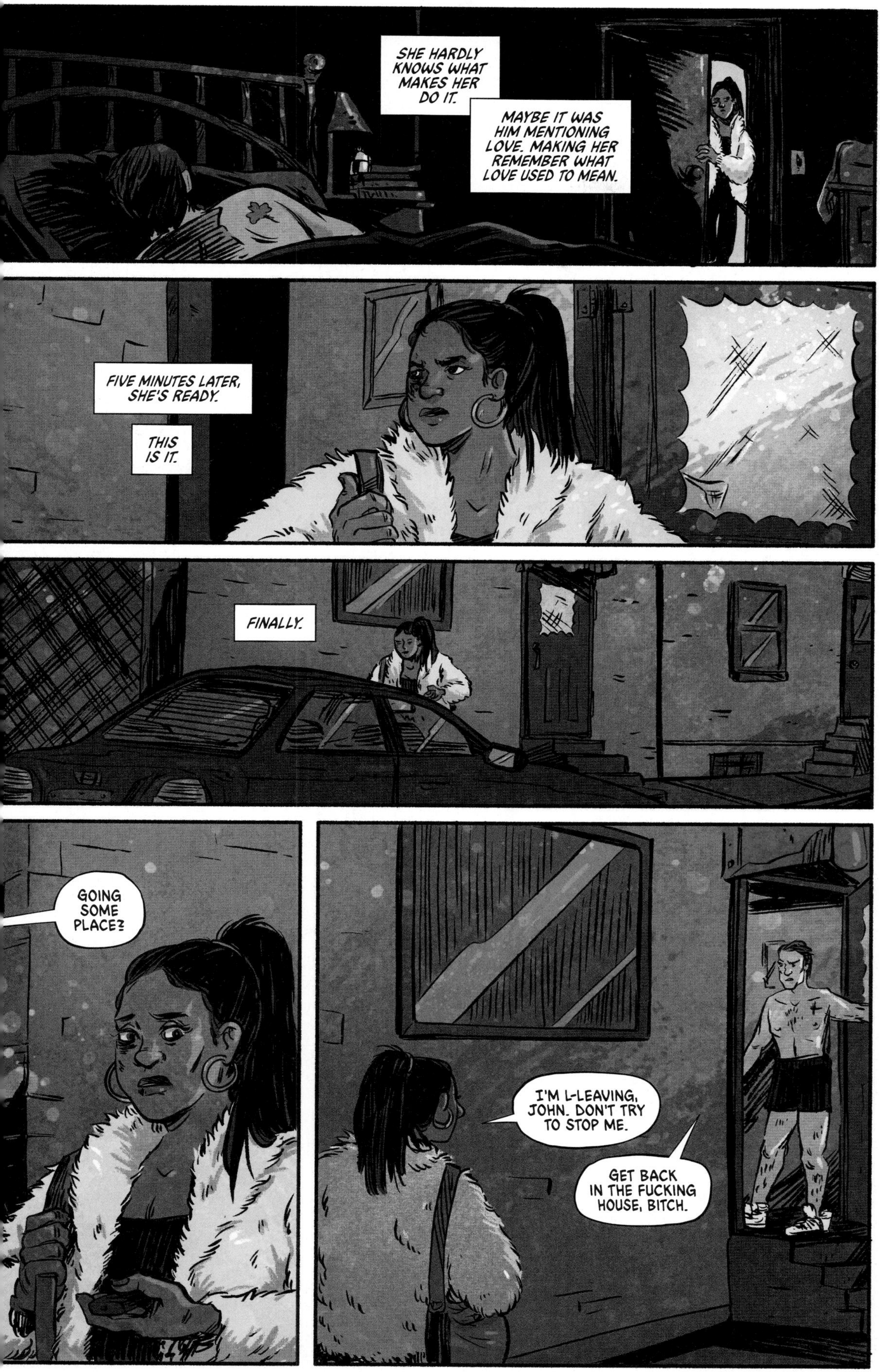
SHE HARDLY KNOWS WHAT MAKES HER DO IT.
MAYBE IT WAS HIM MENTIONING LOVE. MAKING HER REMEMBER WHAT LOVE USED TO MEAN.
FIVE MINUTES LATER, SHE'S READY.
THIS IS IT.
FINALLY.
GOING SOME PLACE?
I'M L-LEAVING, JOHN. DON'T TRY TO STOP ME.
GET BACK IN THE FUCKING HOUSE, BITCH.

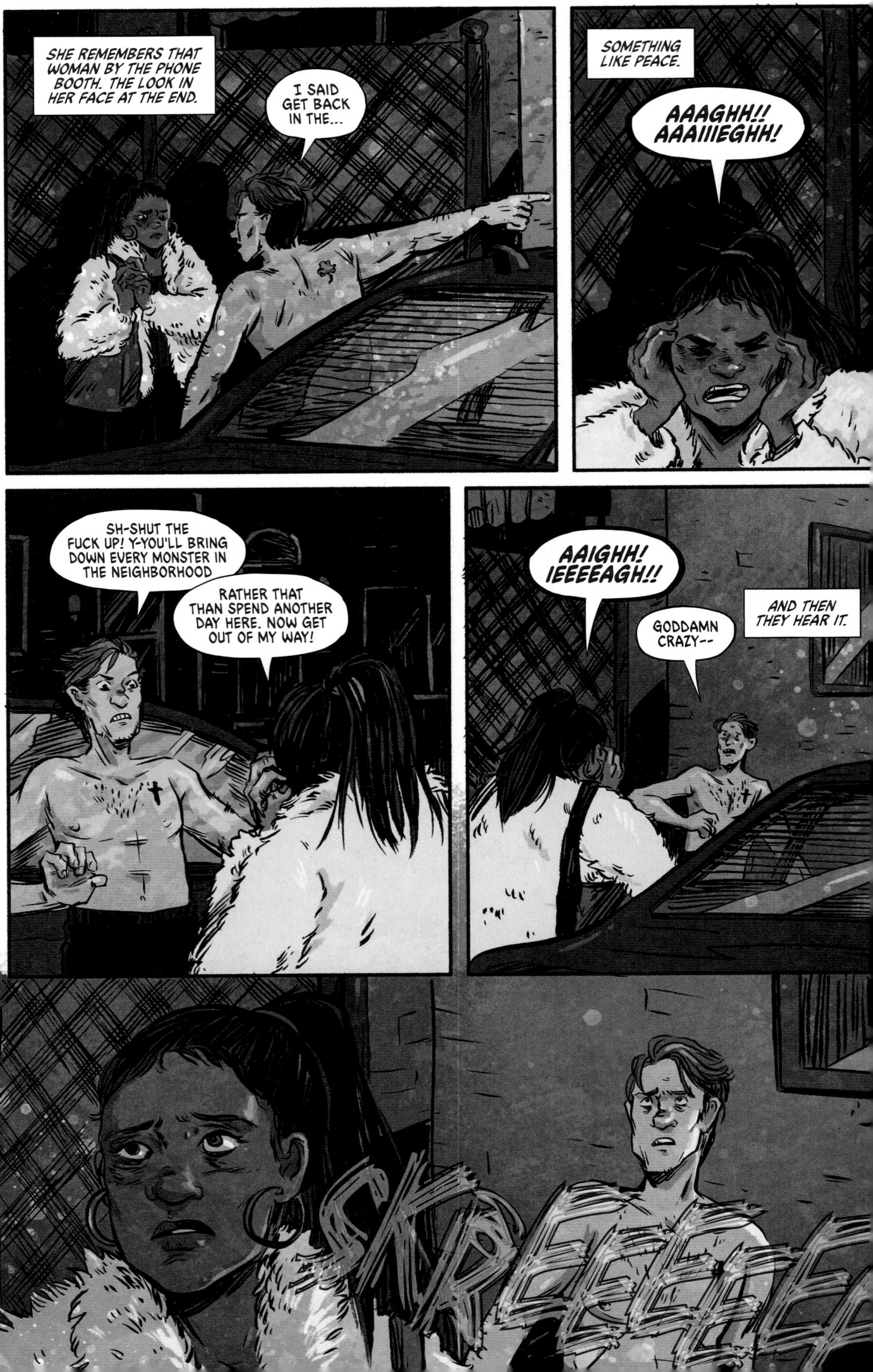
SHE REMEMBERS THAT WOMAN BY THE PHONE BOOTH. THE LOOK IN HER FACE AT THE END.
I SAID GET BACK IN THE...
SOMETHING LIKE PEACE.
AAAGHH!! AAAIIIEGHH!
SH-SHUT THE FUCK UP! Y-YOU'LL BRING DOWN EVERY MONSTER IN THE NEIGHBORHOOD
RATHER THAT THAN SPEND ANOTHER DAY HERE. NOW GET OUT OF MY WAY!
AAIGHH! IEEEEAGH!!
GODDAMN CRAZY--
AND THEN THEY HEAR IT.
SKREEEEEEE

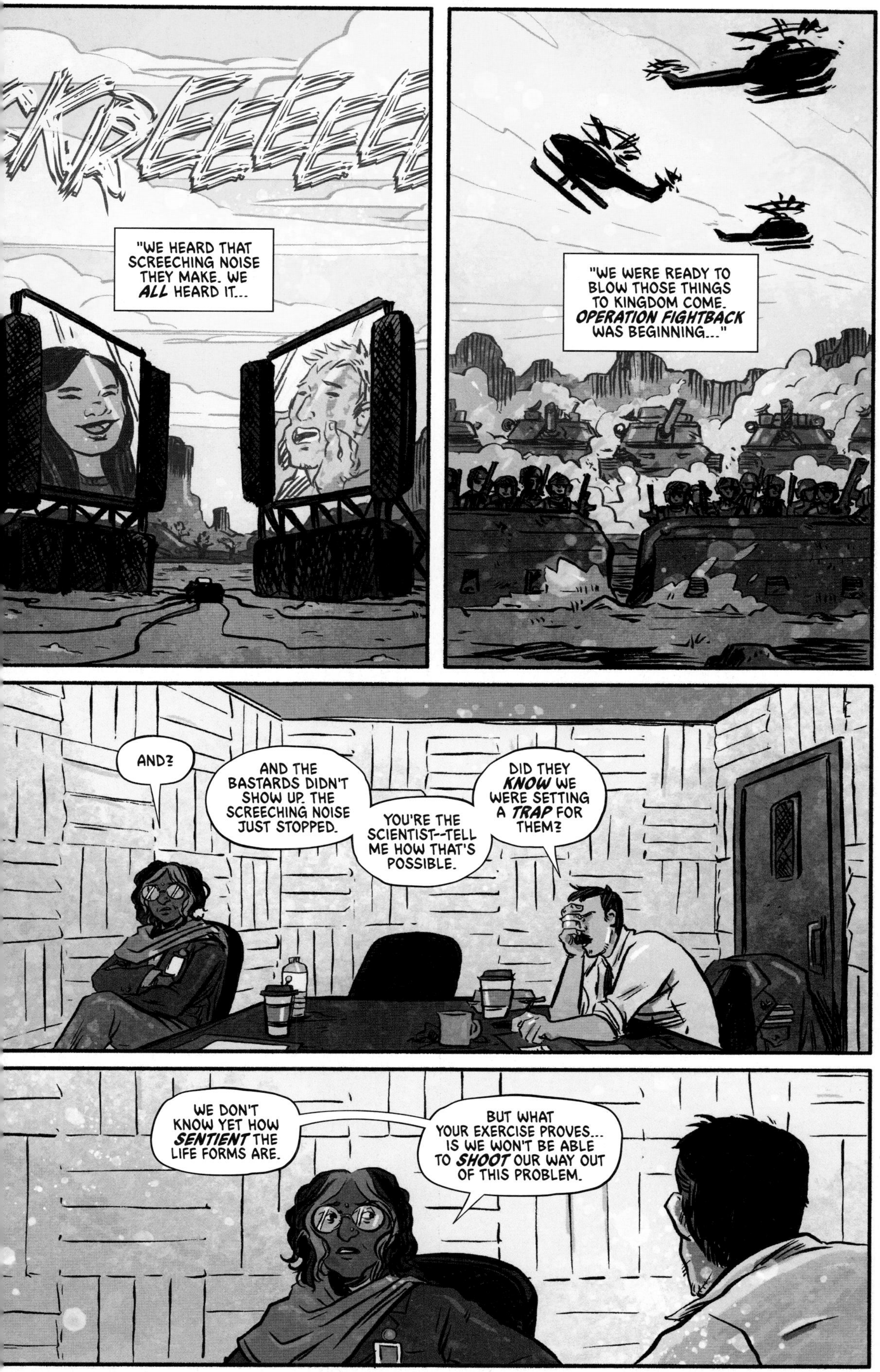
KREEEEEE
"WE HEARD THAT SCREECHING NOISE THEY MAKE. WE ALL HEARD IT...
"WE WERE READY TO BLOW THOSE THINGS TO KINGDOM COME. OPERATION FIGHTBACK WAS BEGINNING..."
AND?
AND THE BASTARDS DIDN'T SHOW UP. THE SCREECHING NOISE JUST STOPPED.
YOU'RE THE SCIENTIST--TELL ME HOW THAT'S POSSIBLE.
DID THEY KNOW WE WERE SETTING A TRAP FOR THEM?
WE DON'T KNOW YET HOW SENTIENT THE LIFE FORMS ARE.
BUT WHAT YOUR EXERCISE PROVES... IS WE WON'T BE ABLE TO SHOOT OUR WAY OUT OF THIS PROBLEM.

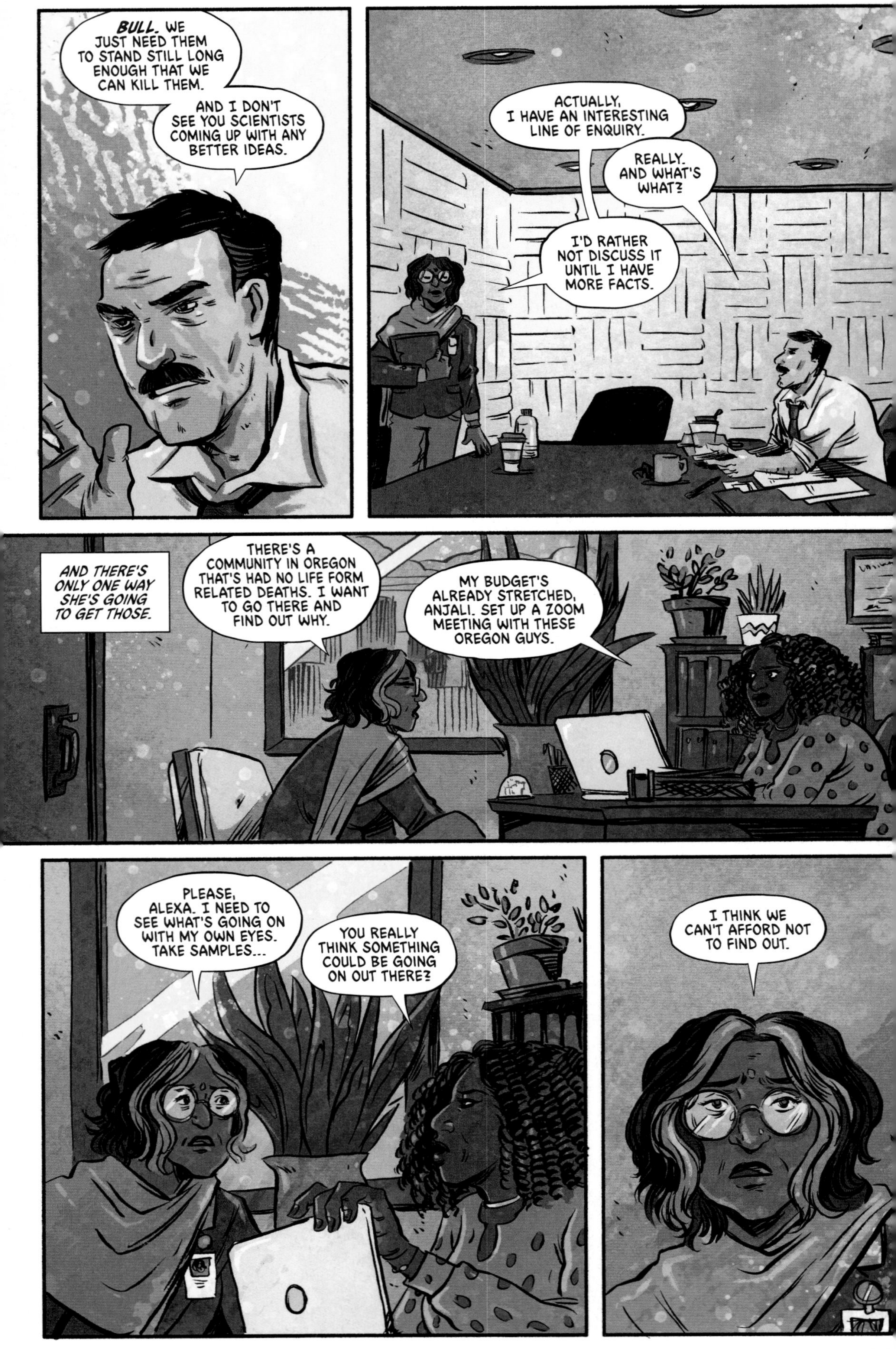
BULL. WE JUST NEED THEM TO STAND STILL LONG ENOUGH THAT WE CAN KILL THEM.
AND I DON'T SEE YOU SCIENTISTS COMING UP WITH ANY BETTER IDEAS.
ACTUALLY, I HAVE AN INTERESTING LINE OF ENQUIRY.
REALLY. AND WHAT'S WHAT?
I'D RATHER NOT DISCUSS IT UNTIL I HAVE MORE FACTS.
AND THERE'S ONLY ONE WAY SHE'S GOING TO GET THOSE.
THERE'S A COMMUNITY IN OREGON THAT'S HAD NO LIFE FORM RELATED DEATHS. I WANT TO GO THERE AND FIND OUT WHY.
MY BUDGET'S ALREADY STRETCHED, ANJALI. SET UP A ZOOM MEETING WITH THESE OREGON GUYS.
PLEASE, ALEXA. I NEED TO SEE WHAT'S GOING ON WITH MY OWN EYES. TAKE SAMPLES...
YOU REALLY THINK SOMETHING COULD BE GOING ON OUT THERE?
I THINK WE CAN'T AFFORD NOT TO FIND OUT.

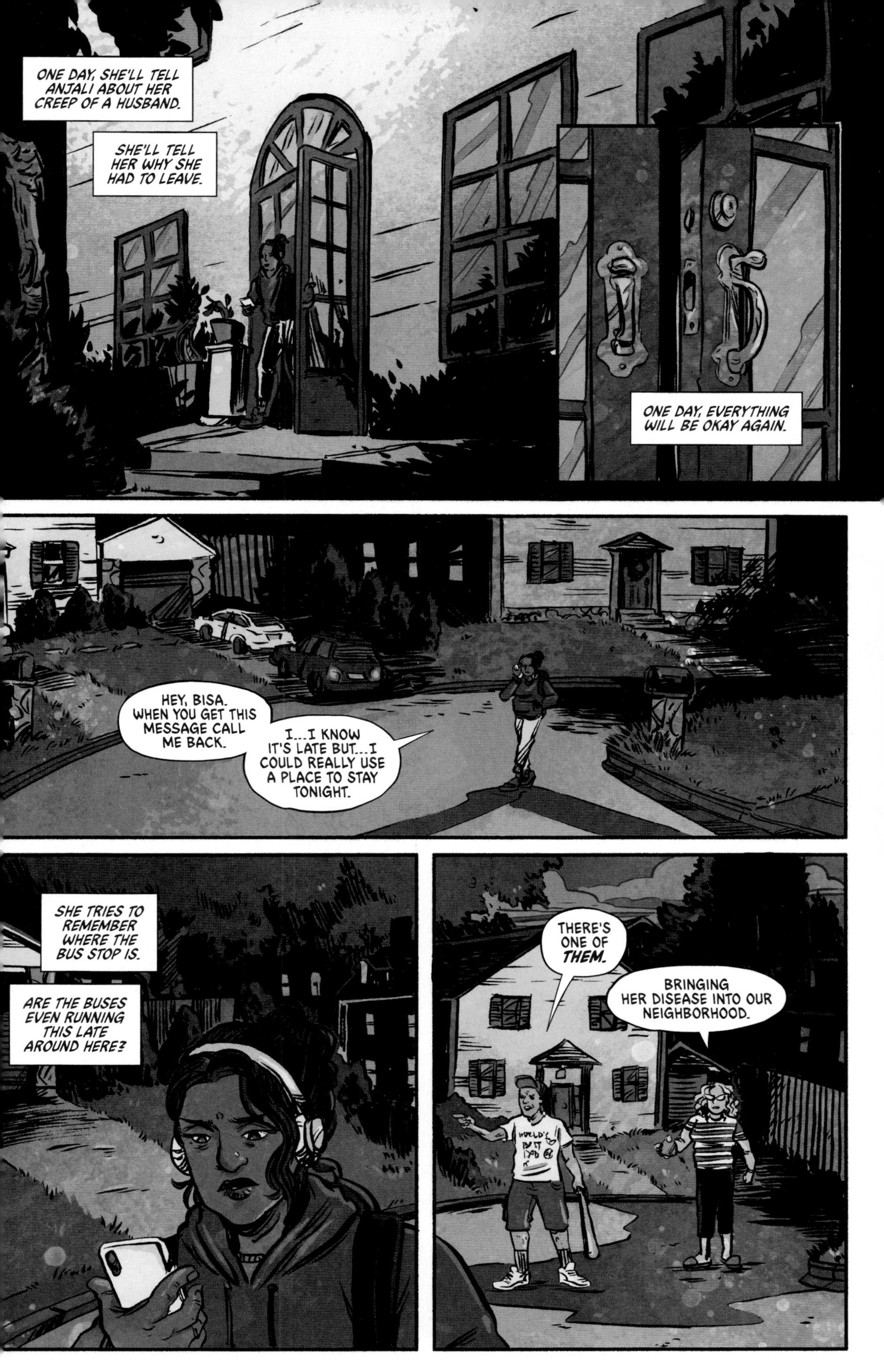
ONE DAY, SHE'LL TELL ANJALI ABOUT HER CREEP OF A HUSBAND.
SHE'LL TELL HER WHY SHE HAD TO LEAVE.
ONE DAY, EVERYTHING WILL BE OKAY AGAIN.
HEY, BISA. WHEN YOU GET THIS MESSAGE CALL ME BACK.
I...I KNOW IT'S LATE BUT...I COULD REALLY USE A PLACE TO STAY TONIGHT.
SHE TRIES TO REMEMBER WHERE THE BUS STOP IS.
ARE THE BUSES EVEN RUNNING THIS LATE AROUND HERE?
THERE'S ONE OF *THEM*.
BRINGING HER DISEASE INTO OUR NEIGHBORHOOD.

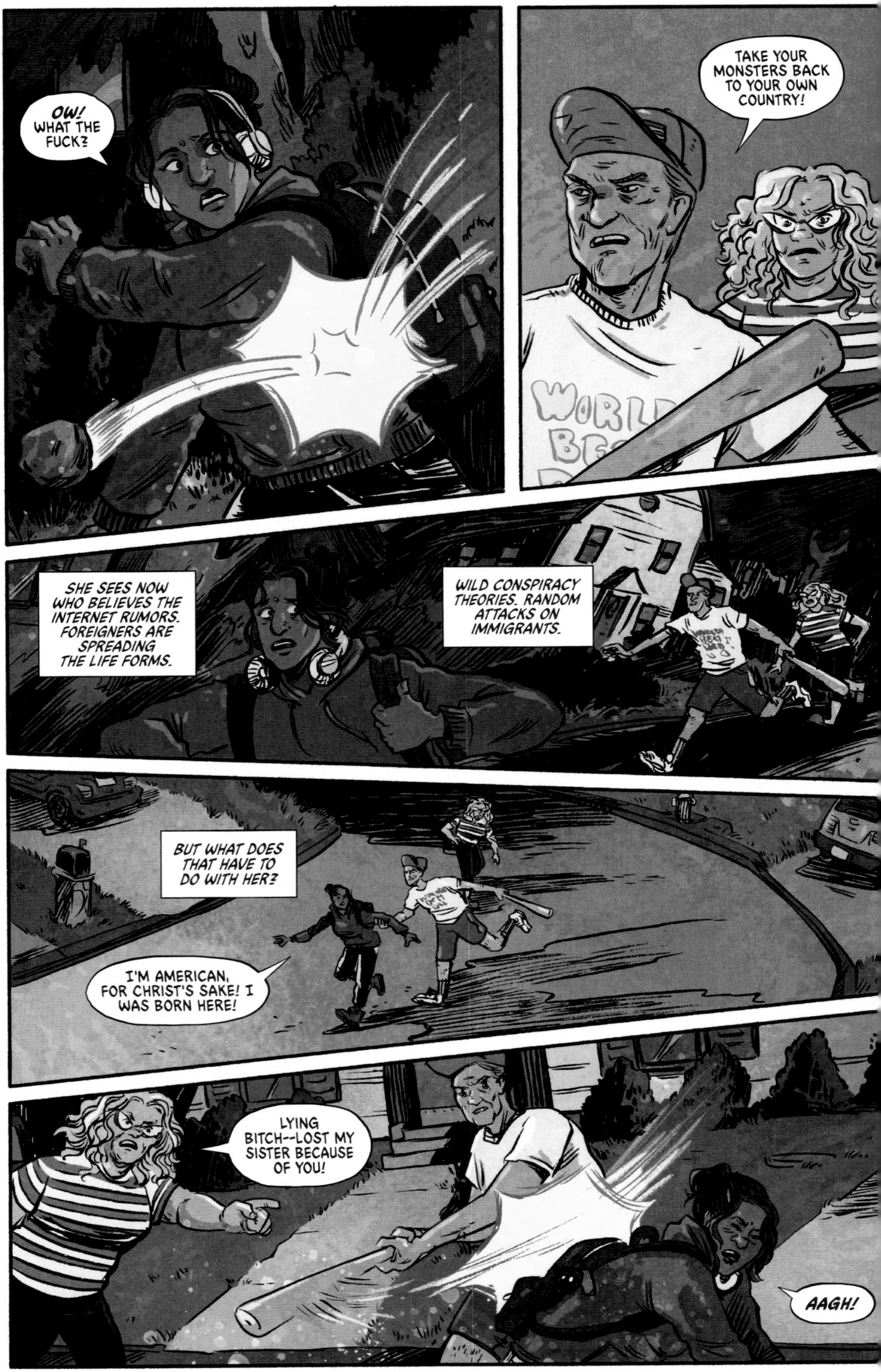
OW! WHAT THE FUCK?
TAKE YOUR MONSTERS BACK TO YOUR OWN COUNTRY!
SHE SEES NOW WHO BELIEVES THE INTERNET RUMORS. FOREIGNERS ARE SPREADING THE LIFE FORMS.
WILD CONSPIRACY THEORIES. RANDOM ATTACKS ON IMMIGRANTS.
BUT WHAT DOES THAT HAVE TO DO WITH HER?
I'M AMERICAN, FOR CHRIST'S SAKE! I WAS BORN HERE!
LYING BITCH--LOST MY SISTER BECAUSE OF YOU!
AAGH!

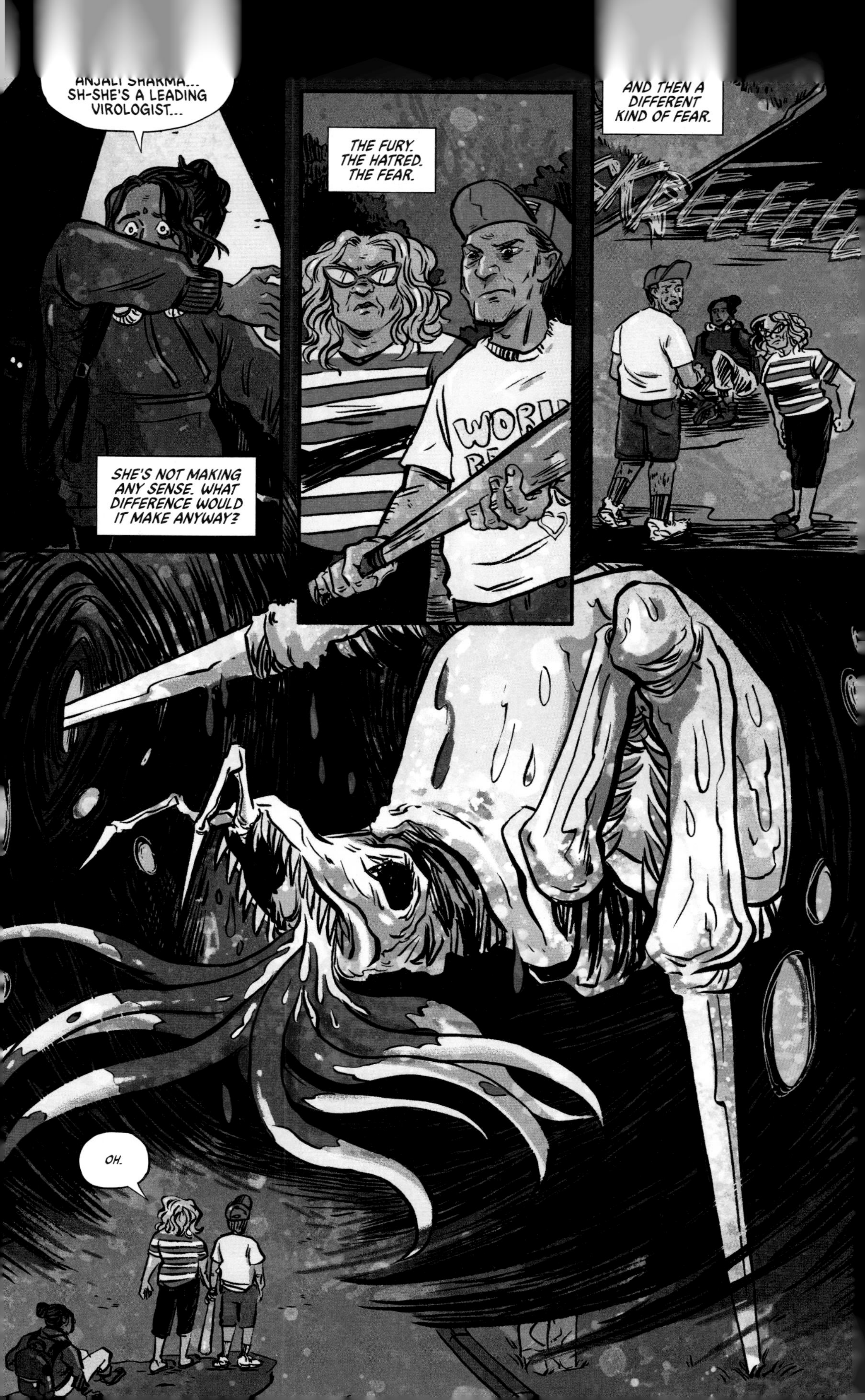
ANJALI SHARMA... SH-SHE'S A LEADING VIROLOGIST...
SHE'S NOT MAKING ANY SENSE. WHAT DIFFERENCE WOULD IT MAKE ANYWAY?
THE FURY. THE HATRED. THE FEAR.
AND THEN A DIFFERENT KIND OF FEAR.
KREEEEEE
OH.

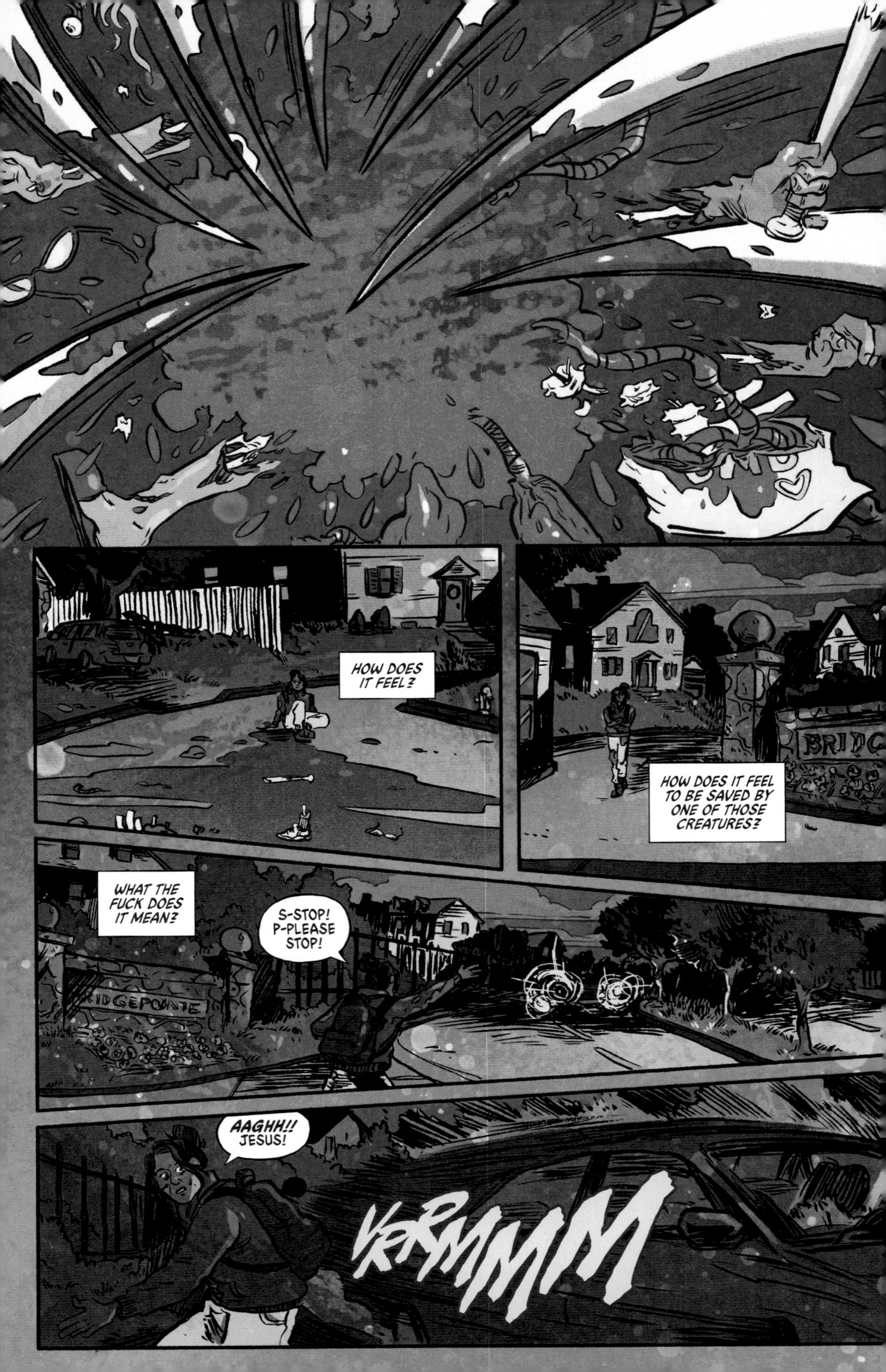
HOW DOES
IT FEEL?
HOW DOES IT FEEL
TO BE SAVED BY
ONE OF THOSE
CREATURES?
BRIDG
WHAT THE
FUCK DOES
IT MEAN?
S-STOP!
P-PLEASE
STOP!
RIDGEPOINTE
AAGHH!!
JESUS!
VRRMMMM

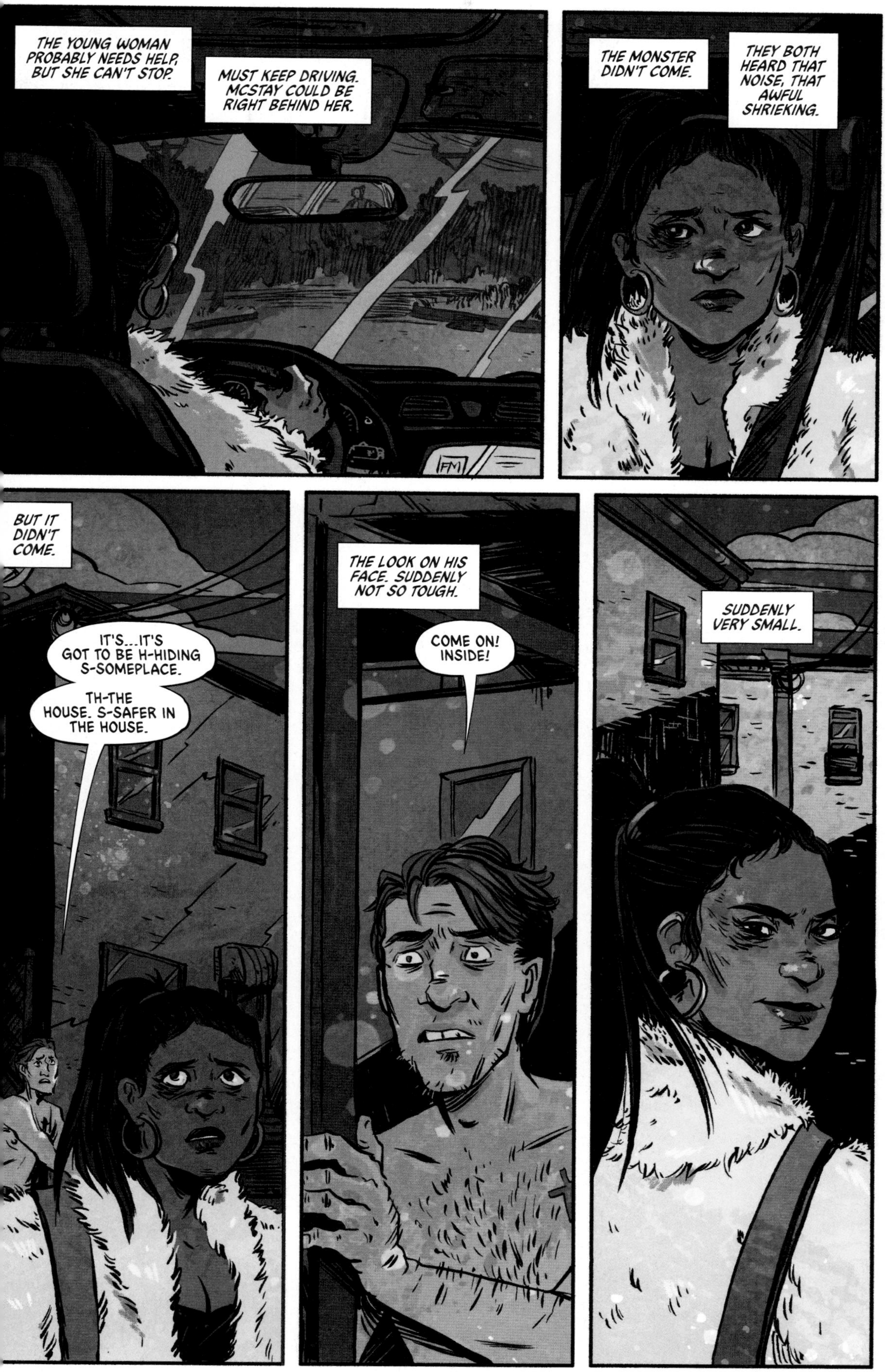
THE YOUNG WOMAN PROBABLY NEEDS HELP, BUT SHE CAN'T STOP.
MUST KEEP DRIVING. MCSTAY COULD BE RIGHT BEHIND HER.
THE MONSTER DIDN'T COME.
THEY BOTH HEARD THAT NOISE, THAT AWFUL SHRIEKING.
BUT IT DIDN'T COME.
IT'S...IT'S GOT TO BE H-HIDING S-SOMEPLACE.
TH-THE HOUSE. S-SAFER IN THE HOUSE.
THE LOOK ON HIS FACE. SUDDENLY NOT SO TOUGH.
COME ON! INSIDE!
SUDDENLY VERY SMALL.

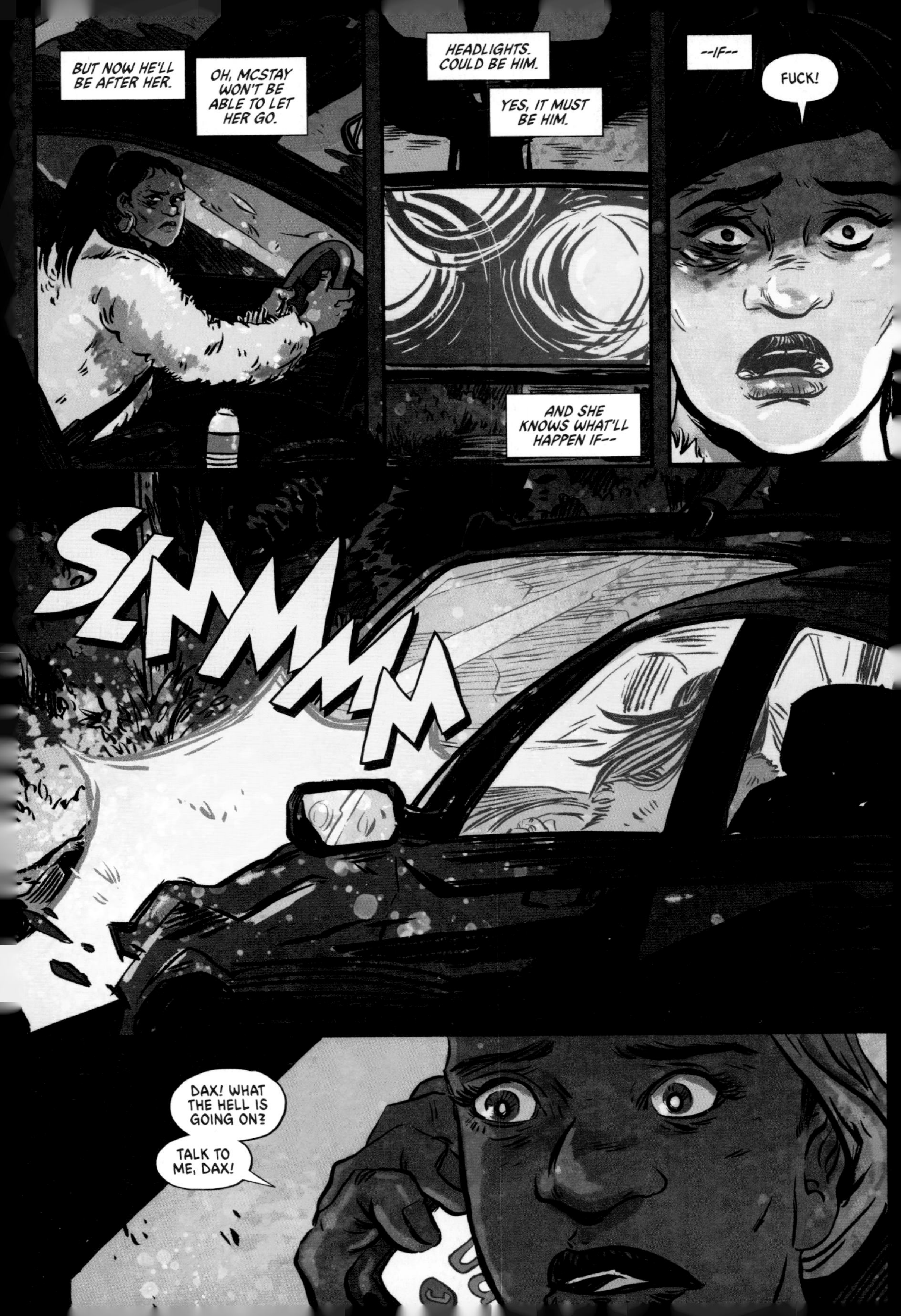
BUT NOW HE'LL BE AFTER HER.
OH, MCSTAY WON'T BE ABLE TO LET HER GO.
HEADLIGHTS. COULD BE HIM.
YES, IT MUST BE HIM.
AND SHE KNOWS WHAT'LL HAPPEN IF--
--IF--
FUCK!
SLMMMM
DAX! WHAT THE HELL IS GOING ON?
TALK TO ME, DAX!

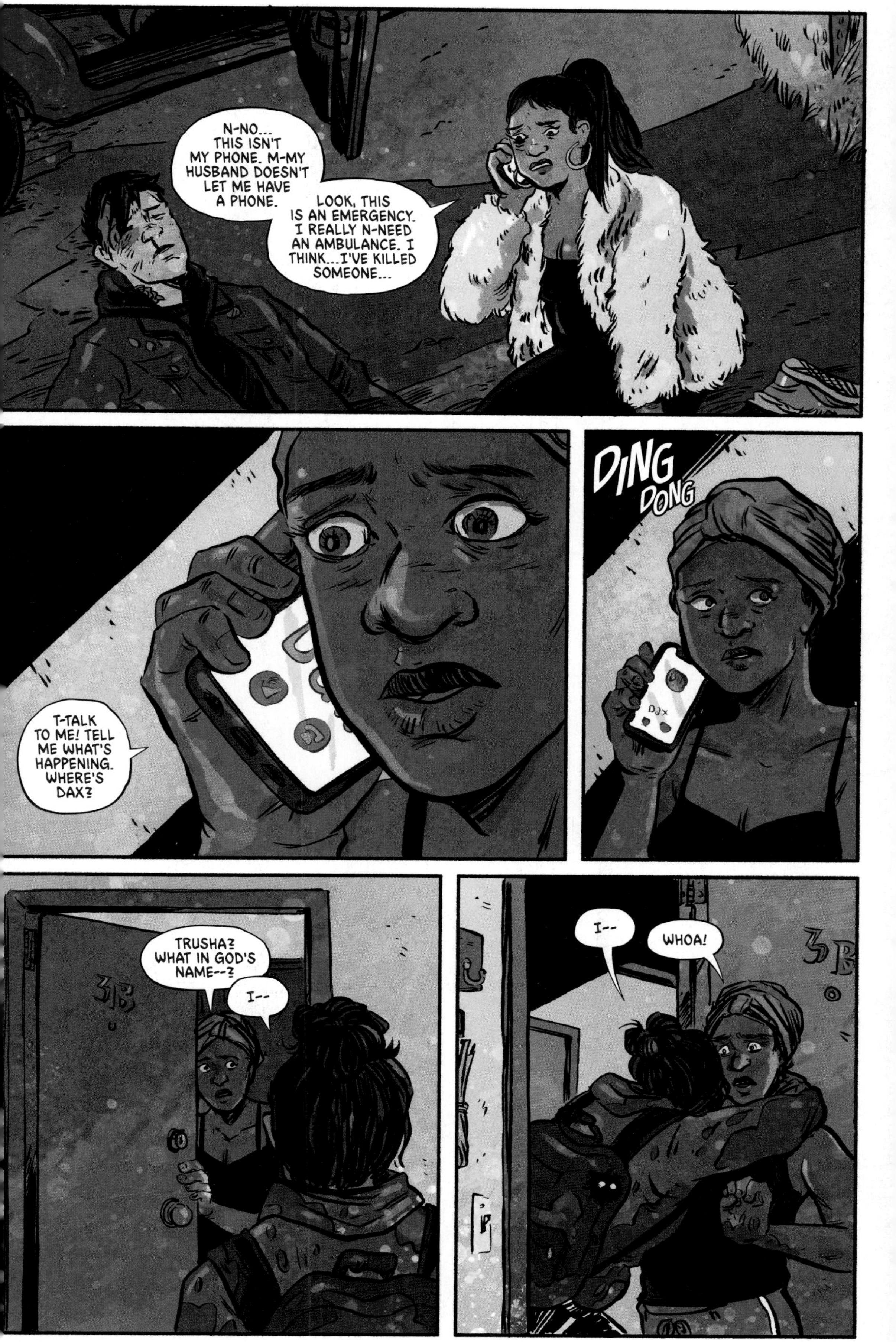
N-NO... THIS ISN'T MY PHONE. M-MY HUSBAND DOESN'T LET ME HAVE A PHONE.
LOOK, THIS IS AN EMERGENCY. I REALLY N-NEED AN AMBULANCE. I THINK...I'VE KILLED SOMEONE...
T-TALK TO ME! TELL ME WHAT'S HAPPENING. WHERE'S DAX?
DING DONG
TRUSHA? WHAT IN GOD'S NAME--?
I--
3B
I--
WHOA!
3B

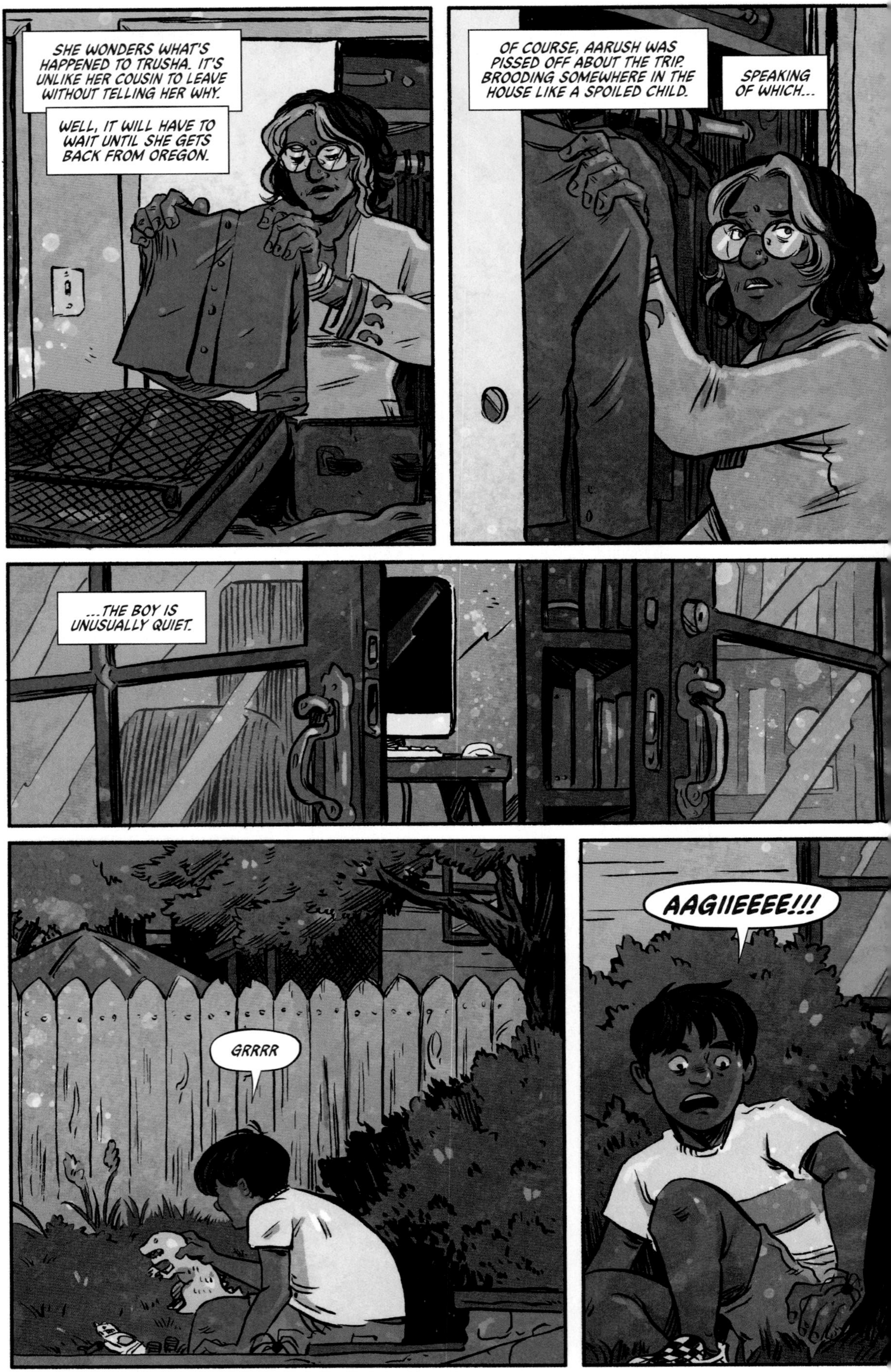
SHE WONDERS WHAT'S HAPPENED TO TRUSHA. IT'S UNLIKE HER COUSIN TO LEAVE WITHOUT TELLING HER WHY.
WELL, IT WILL HAVE TO WAIT UNTIL SHE GETS BACK FROM OREGON.
OF COURSE, AARUSH WAS PISSED OFF ABOUT THE TRIP. BROODING SOMEWHERE IN THE HOUSE LIKE A SPOILED CHILD.
SPEAKING OF WHICH...
...THE BOY IS UNUSUALLY QUIET.
GRRRR
AAGIIEEEE!!!

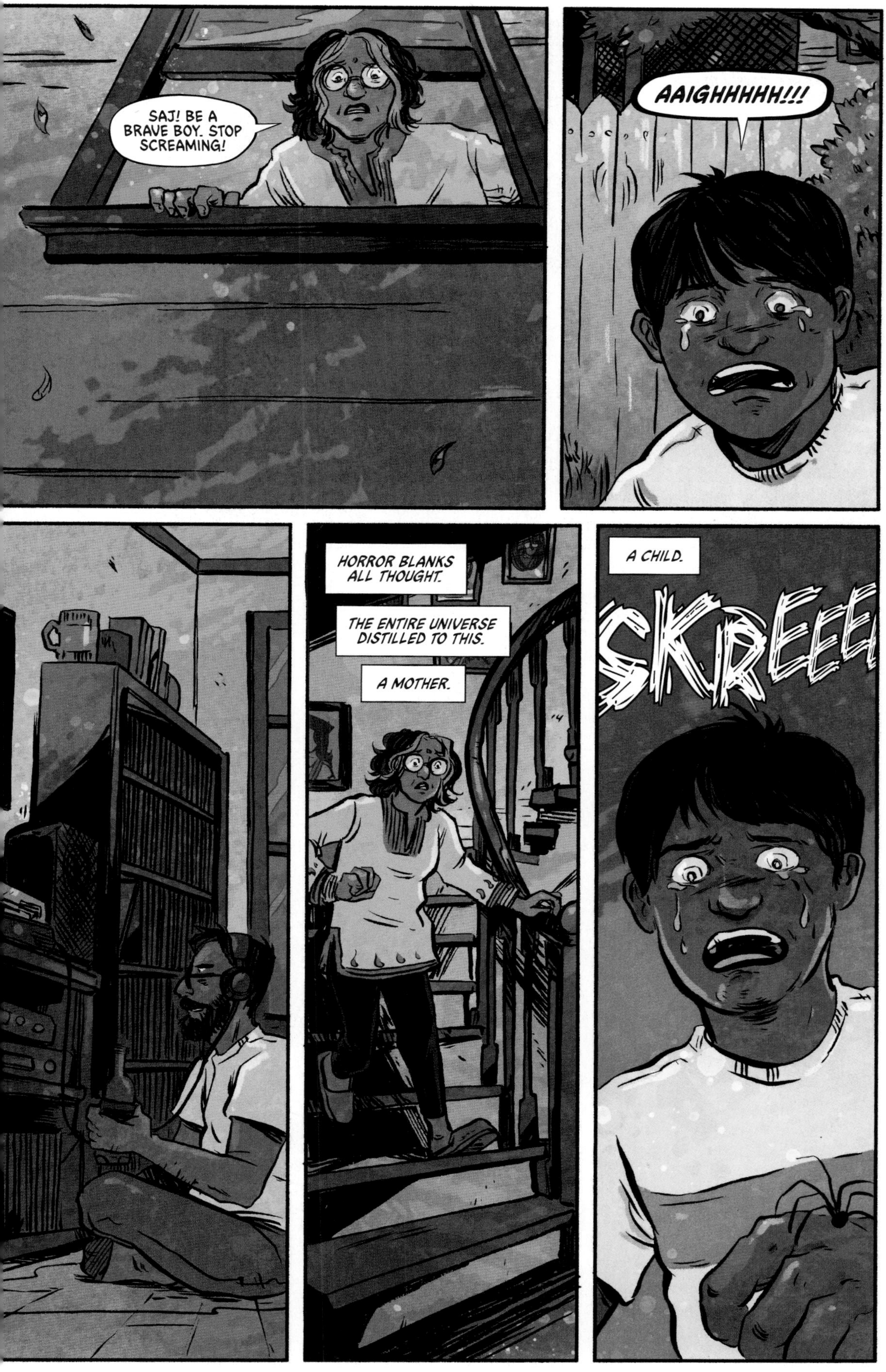
SAJ! BE A BRAVE BOY. STOP SCREAMING!
AAIGHHHHH!!!
HORROR BLANKS ALL THOUGHT.
THE ENTIRE UNIVERSE DISTILLED TO THIS.
A MOTHER.
A CHILD.
SKREEE

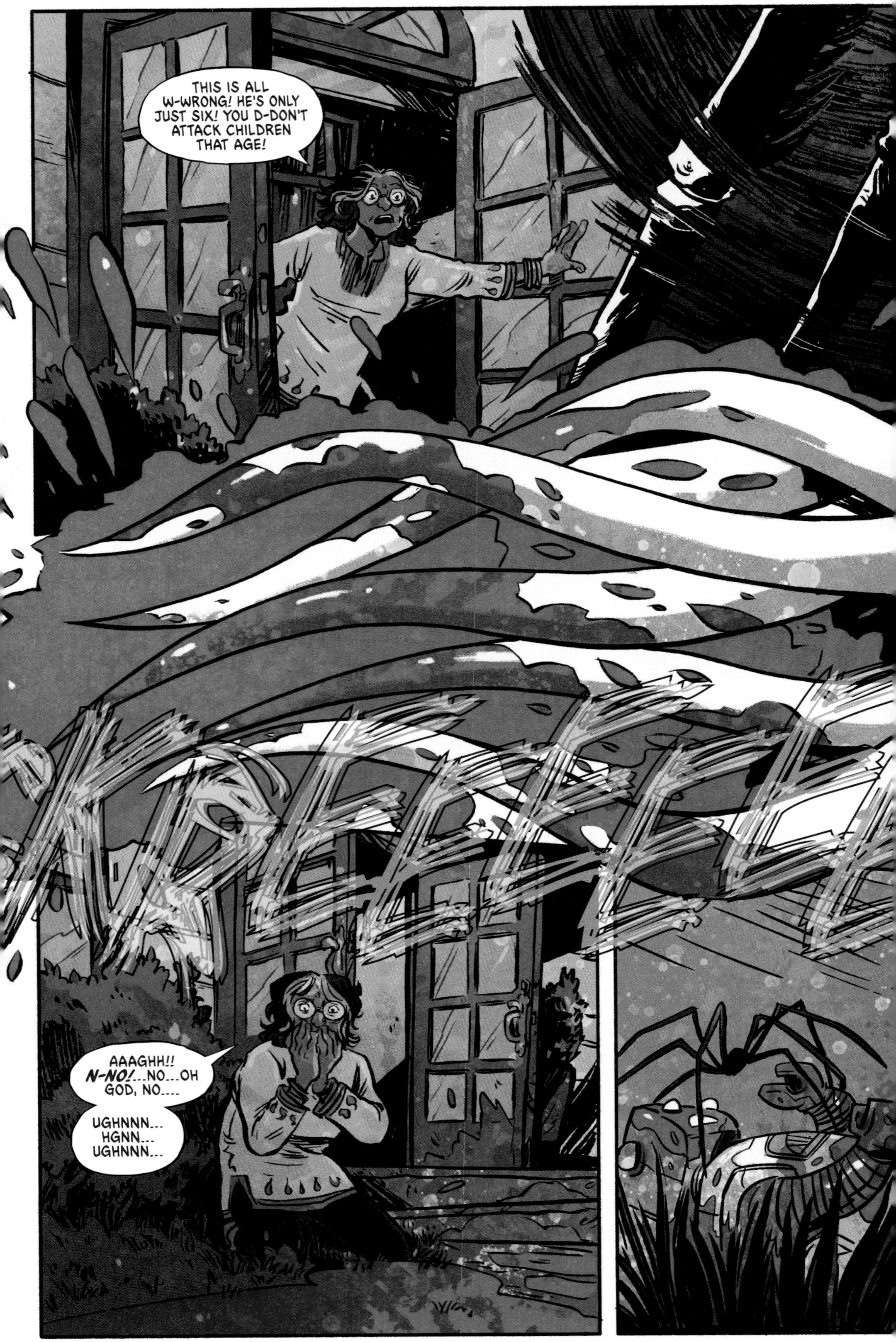
THIS IS ALL W-WRONG! HE'S ONLY JUST SIX! YOU D-DON'T ATTACK CHILDREN THAT AGE!
AAAGHH!! *N-NO!*...NO...OH GOD, NO....
UGHNNN... HGNN... UGHNNN...

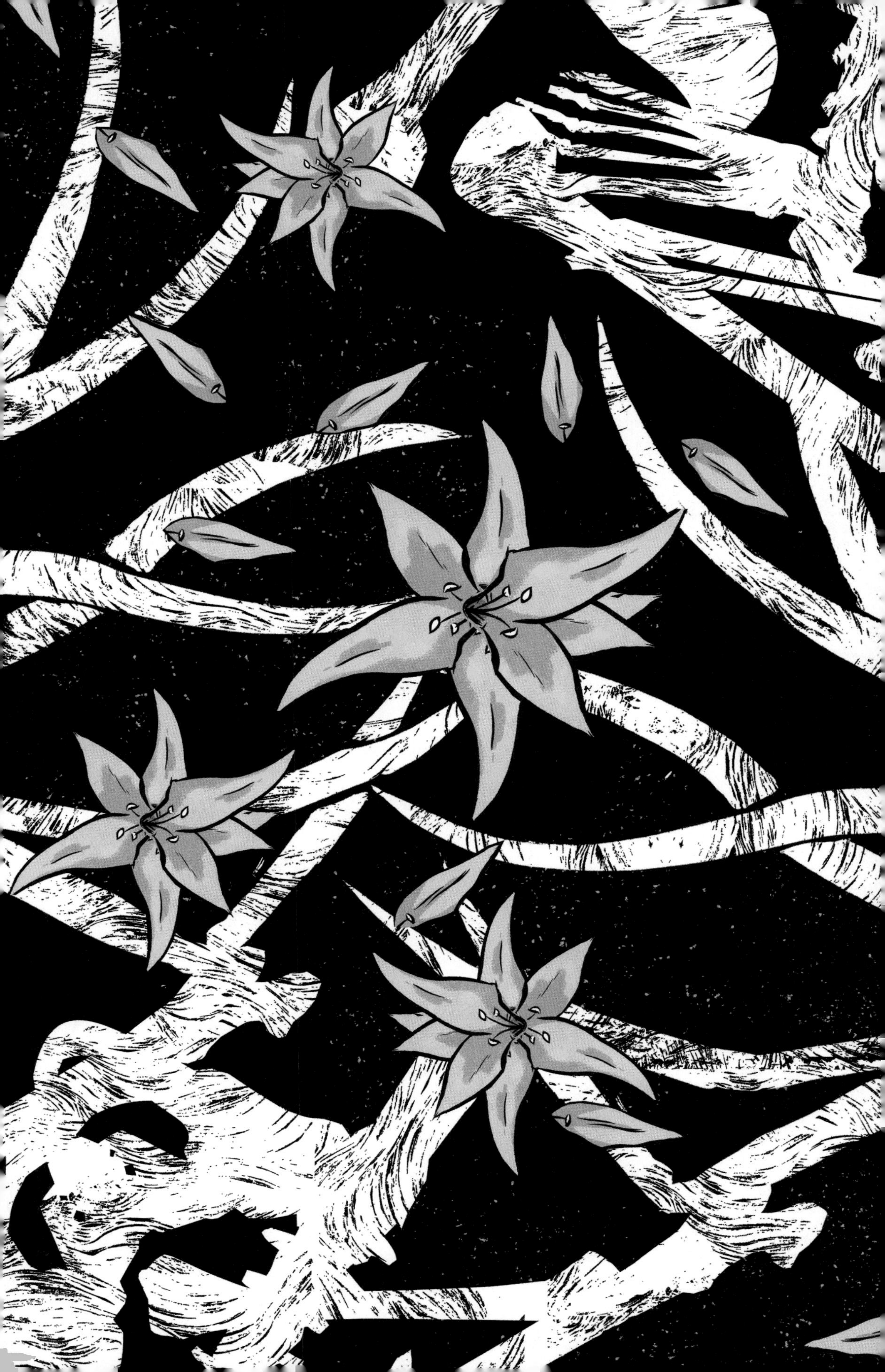

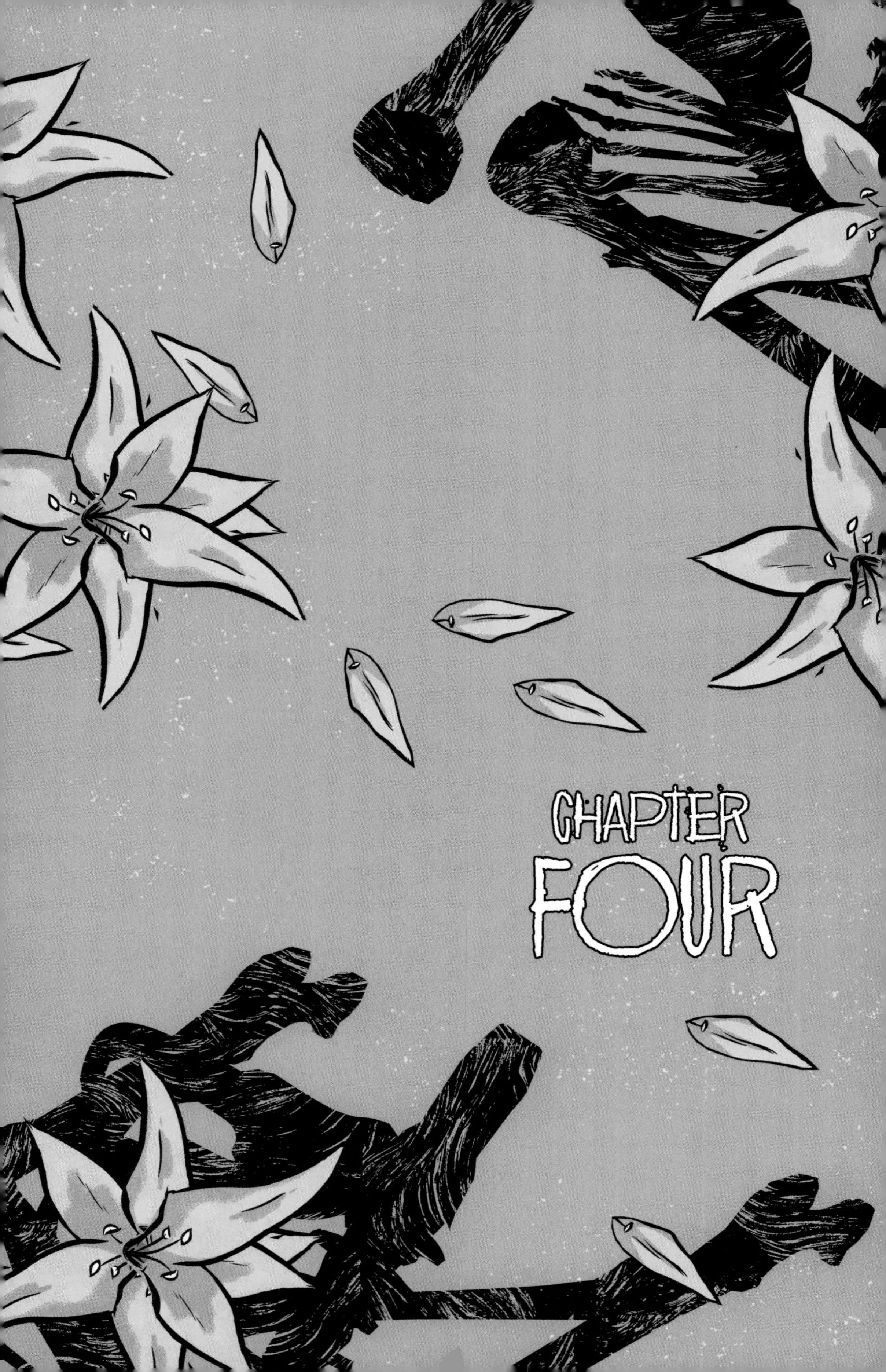
CHAPTER
FOUR

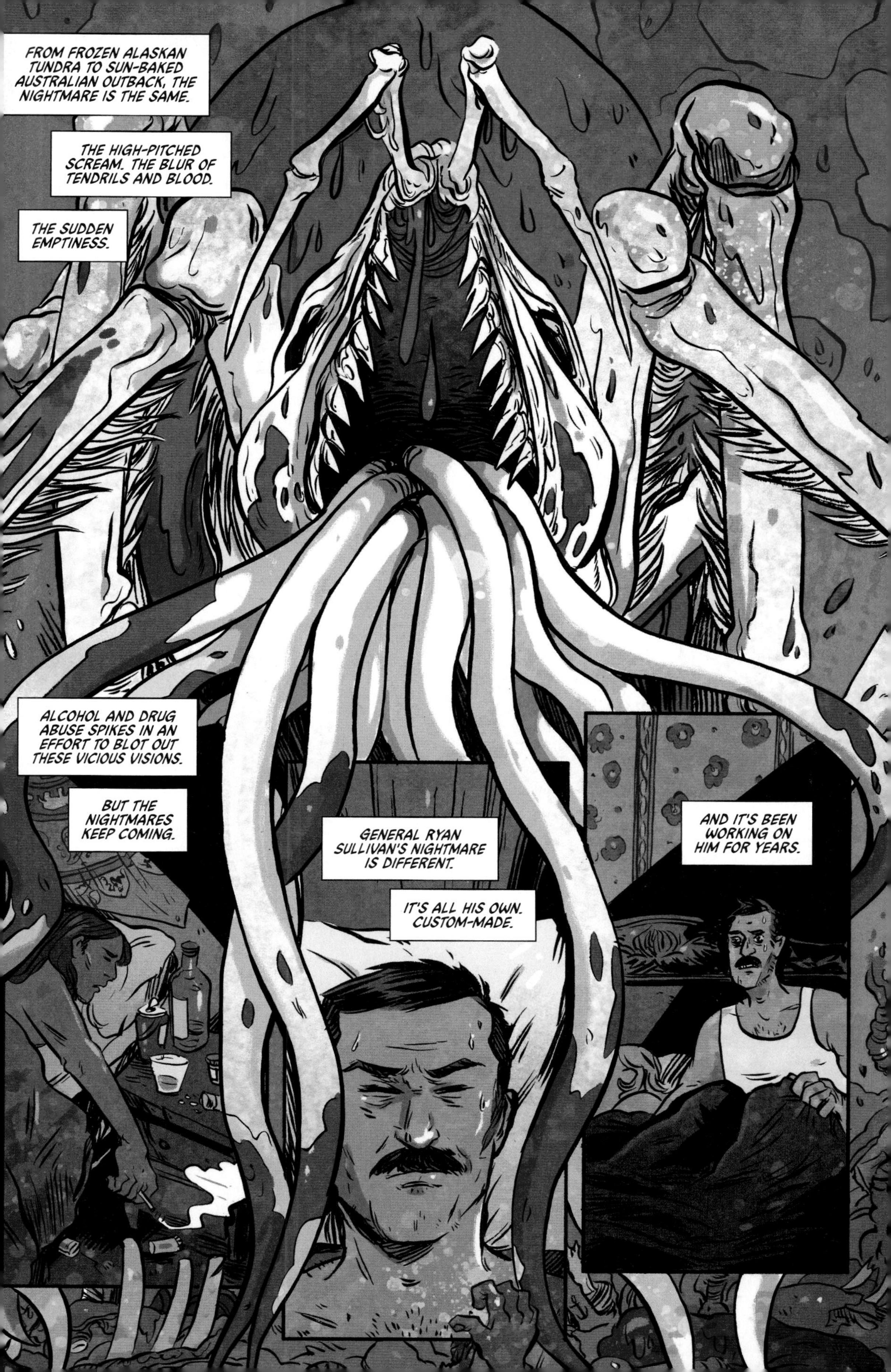
FROM FROZEN ALASKAN TUNDRA TO SUN-BAKED AUSTRALIAN OUTBACK, THE NIGHTMARE IS THE SAME.
THE HIGH-PITCHED SCREAM. THE BLUR OF TENDRILS AND BLOOD.
THE SUDDEN EMPTINESS.
ALCOHOL AND DRUG ABUSE SPIKES IN AN EFFORT TO BLOT OUT THESE VICIOUS VISIONS.
BUT THE NIGHTMARES KEEP COMING.
GENERAL RYAN SULLIVAN'S NIGHTMARE IS DIFFERENT.
IT'S ALL HIS OWN. CUSTOM-MADE.
AND IT'S BEEN WORKING ON HIM FOR YEARS.

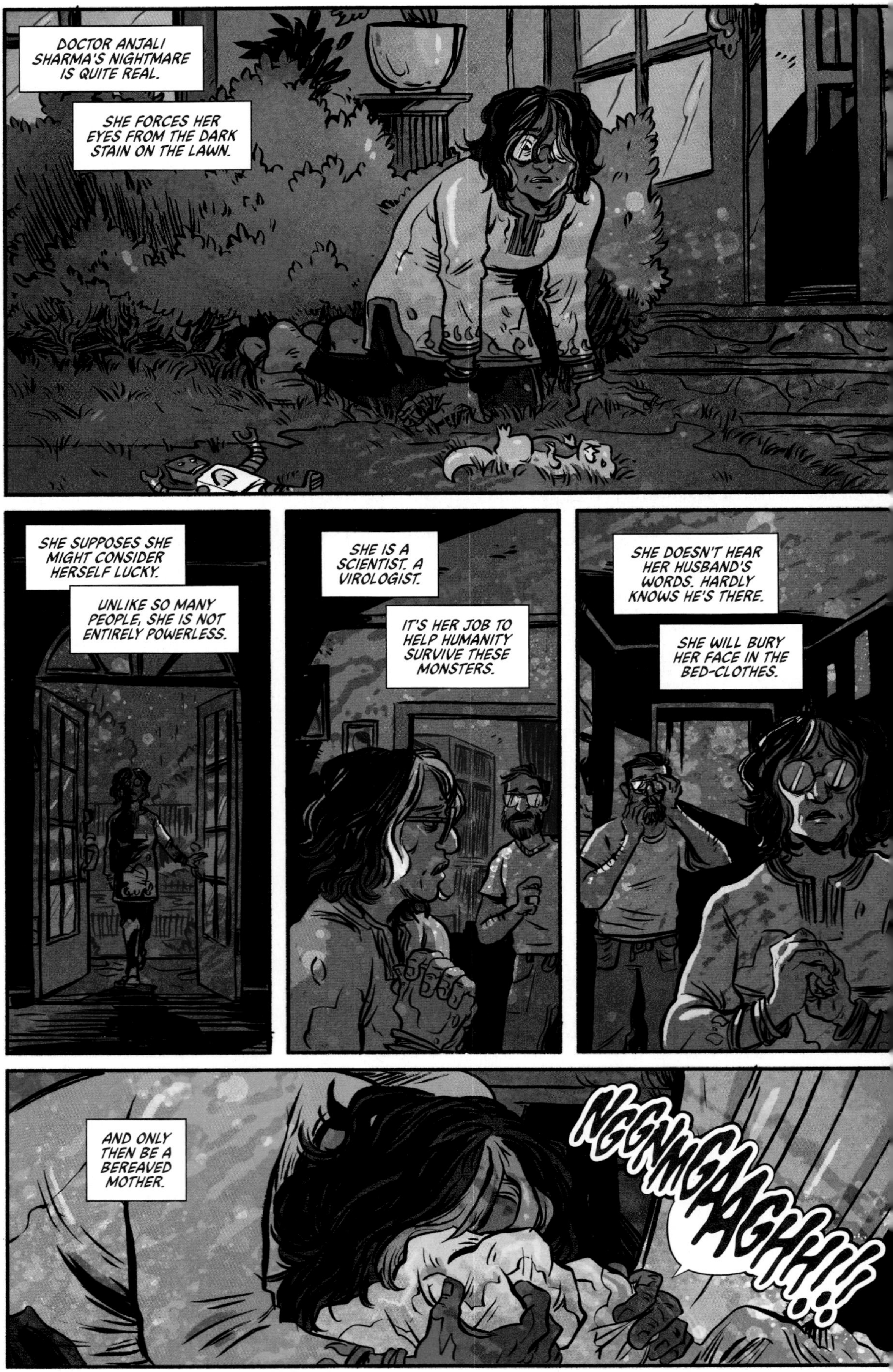
DOCTOR ANJALI SHARMA'S NIGHTMARE IS QUITE REAL.
SHE FORCES HER EYES FROM THE DARK STAIN ON THE LAWN.
SHE SUPPOSES SHE MIGHT CONSIDER HERSELF LUCKY.
UNLIKE SO MANY PEOPLE, SHE IS NOT ENTIRELY POWERLESS.
SHE IS A SCIENTIST. A VIROLOGIST.
IT'S HER JOB TO HELP HUMANITY SURVIVE THESE MONSTERS.
SHE DOESN'T HEAR HER HUSBAND'S WORDS. HARDLY KNOWS HE'S THERE.
SHE WILL BURY HER FACE IN THE BED-CLOTHES.
AND ONLY THEN BE A BEREAVED MOTHER.
NGGNNGAAGHH!!!

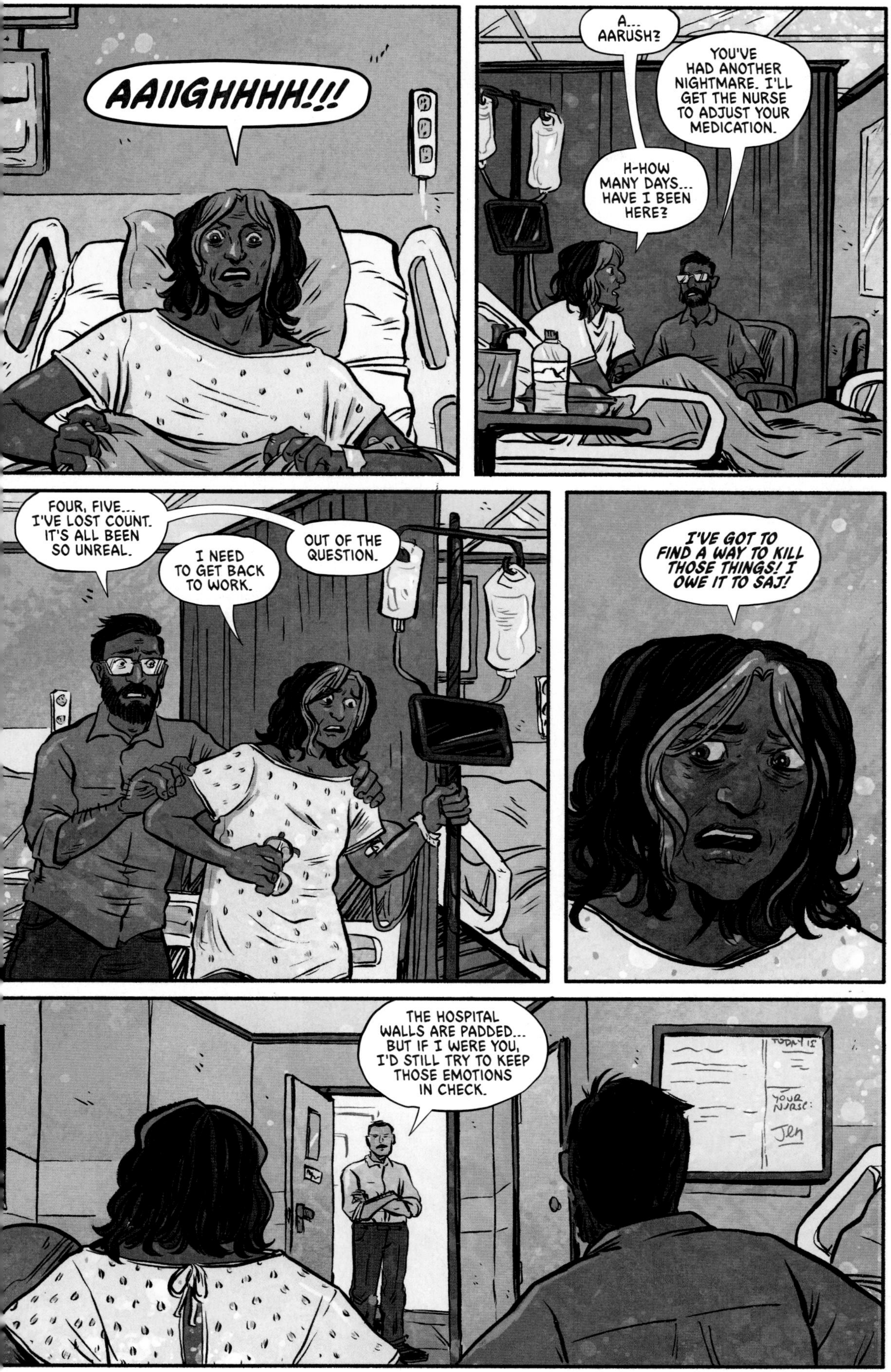
AAIIGHHHH!!!
A... AARUSH?
YOU'VE HAD ANOTHER NIGHTMARE. I'LL GET THE NURSE TO ADJUST YOUR MEDICATION.
H-HOW MANY DAYS... HAVE I BEEN HERE?
FOUR, FIVE... I'VE LOST COUNT. IT'S ALL BEEN SO UNREAL.
I NEED TO GET BACK TO WORK.
OUT OF THE QUESTION.
I'VE GOT TO FIND A WAY TO KILL THOSE THINGS! I OWE IT TO SAJ!
THE HOSPITAL WALLS ARE PADDED... BUT IF I WERE YOU, I'D STILL TRY TO KEEP THOSE EMOTIONS IN CHECK.
TODAY IS
YOUR NURSE:
Jen

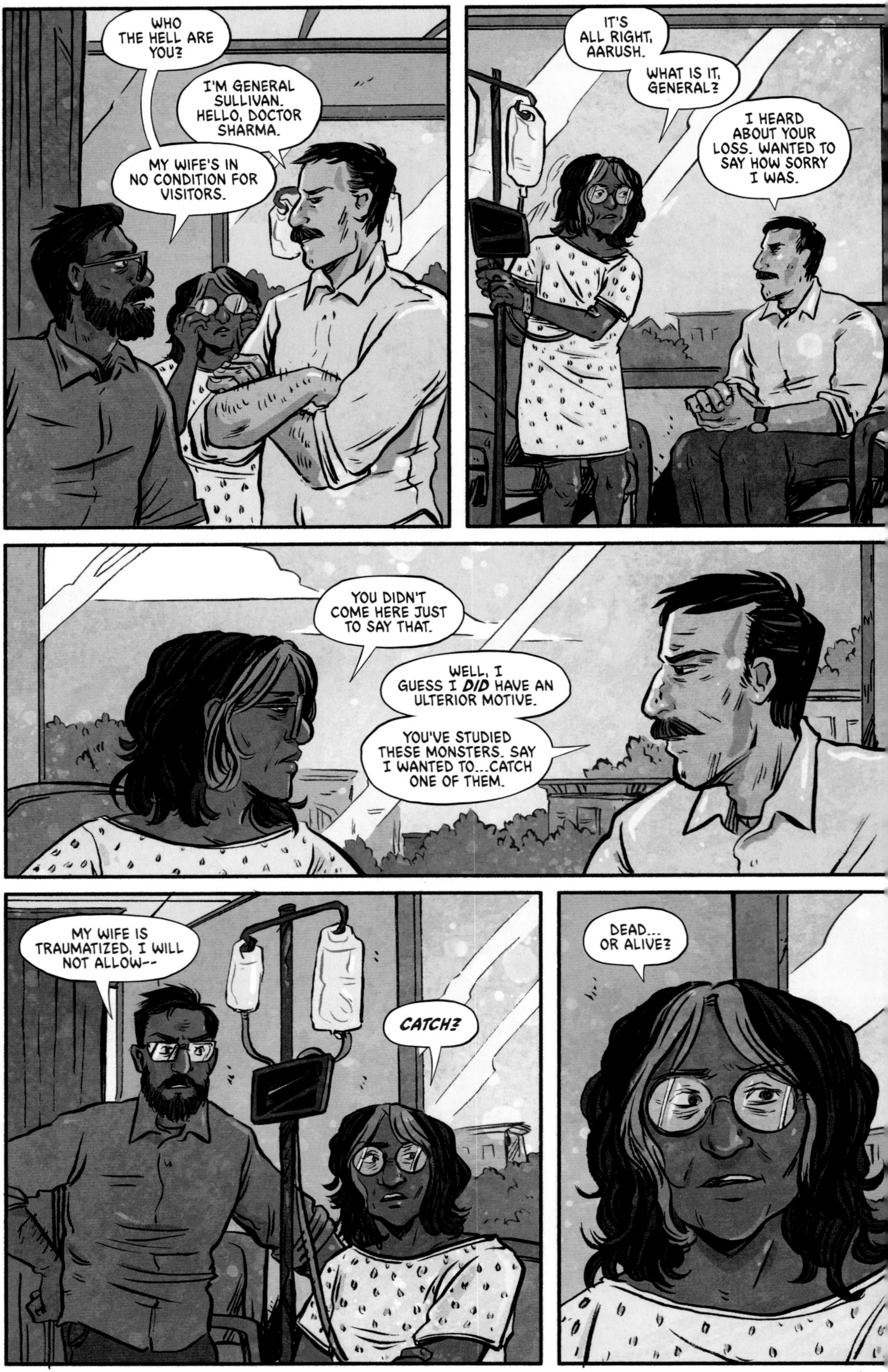
WHO THE HELL ARE YOU?
I'M GENERAL SULLIVAN. HELLO, DOCTOR SHARMA.
MY WIFE'S IN NO CONDITION FOR VISITORS.
IT'S ALL RIGHT, AARUSH.
WHAT IS IT, GENERAL?
I HEARD ABOUT YOUR LOSS. WANTED TO SAY HOW SORRY I WAS.
YOU DIDN'T COME HERE JUST TO SAY THAT.
WELL, I GUESS I DID HAVE AN ULTERIOR MOTIVE.
YOU'VE STUDIED THESE MONSTERS. SAY I WANTED TO...CATCH ONE OF THEM.
MY WIFE IS TRAUMATIZED, I WILL NOT ALLOW--
CATCH?
DEAD... OR ALIVE?

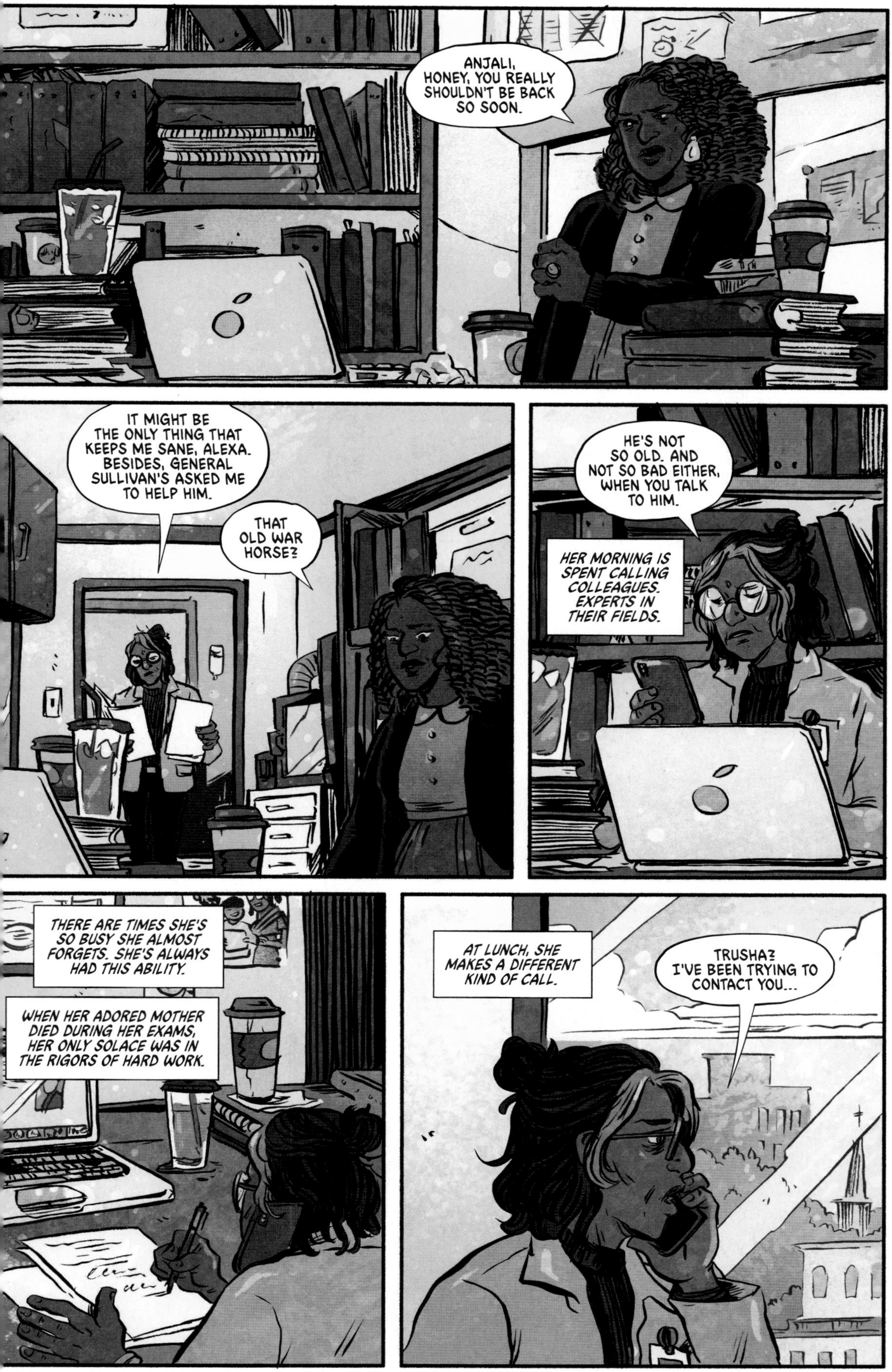
ANJALI, HONEY, YOU REALLY SHOULDN'T BE BACK SO SOON.
IT MIGHT BE THE ONLY THING THAT KEEPS ME SANE, ALEXA. BESIDES, GENERAL SULLIVAN'S ASKED ME TO HELP HIM.
THAT OLD WAR HORSE?
HE'S NOT SO OLD. AND NOT SO BAD EITHER, WHEN YOU TALK TO HIM.
HER MORNING IS SPENT CALLING COLLEAGUES. EXPERTS IN THEIR FIELDS.
THERE ARE TIMES SHE'S SO BUSY SHE ALMOST FORGETS. SHE'S ALWAYS HAD THIS ABILITY.
WHEN HER ADORED MOTHER DIED DURING HER EXAMS, HER ONLY SOLACE WAS IN THE RIGORS OF HARD WORK.
AT LUNCH, SHE MAKES A DIFFERENT KIND OF CALL.
TRUSHA? I'VE BEEN TRYING TO CONTACT YOU...

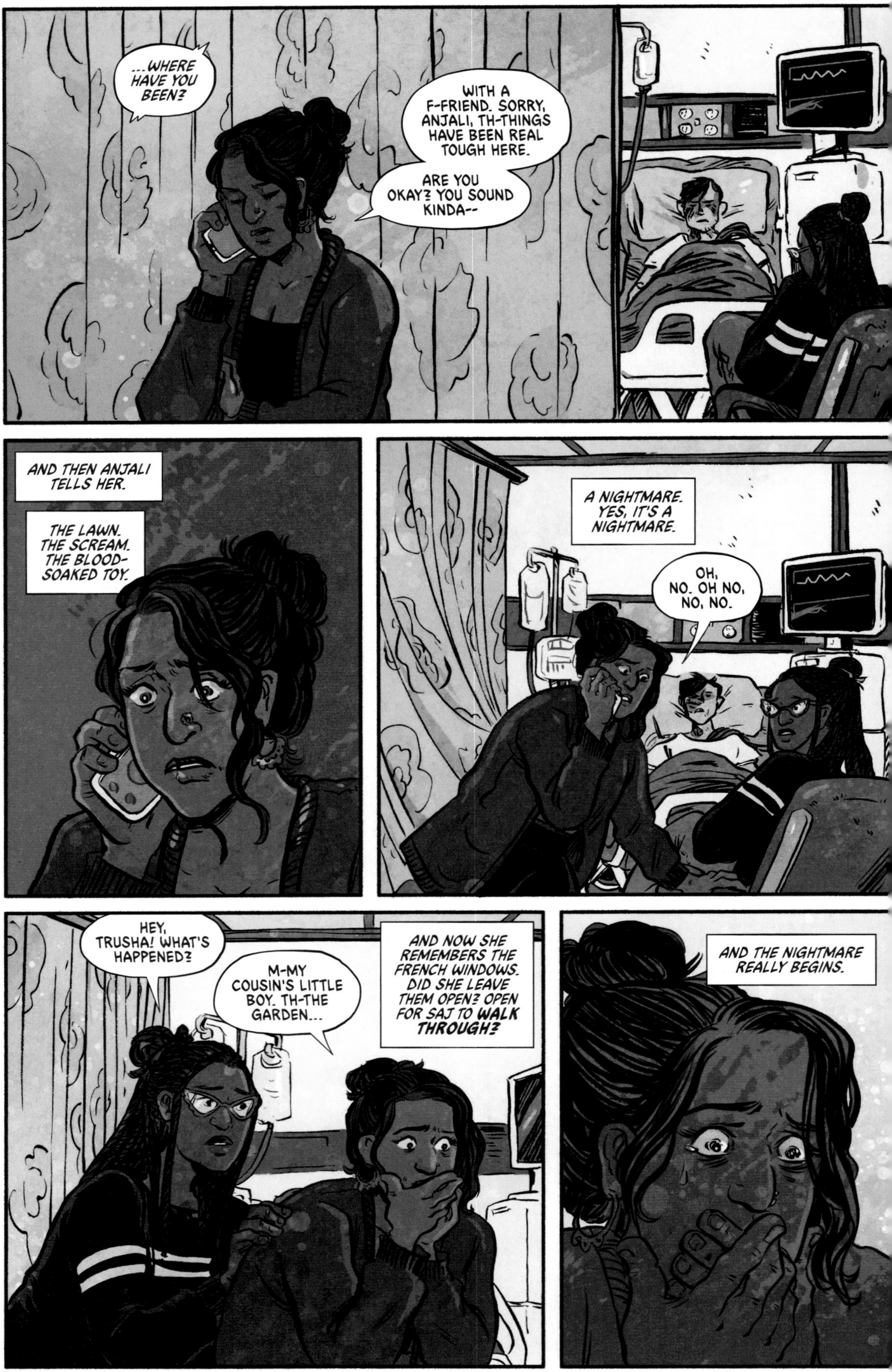
...WHERE HAVE YOU BEEN?
WITH A F-FRIEND. SORRY, ANJALI, TH-THINGS HAVE BEEN REAL TOUGH HERE.
ARE YOU OKAY? YOU SOUND KINDA--
AND THEN ANJALI TELLS HER.
THE LAWN. THE SCREAM. THE BLOOD-SOAKED TOY.
A NIGHTMARE. YES, IT'S A NIGHTMARE.
OH, NO. OH NO, NO, NO.
HEY, TRUSHA! WHAT'S HAPPENED?
M-MY COUSIN'S LITTLE BOY. TH-THE GARDEN...
AND NOW SHE REMEMBERS THE FRENCH WINDOWS. DID SHE LEAVE THEM OPEN? OPEN FOR SAJ TO WALK THROUGH?
AND THE NIGHTMARE REALLY BEGINS.

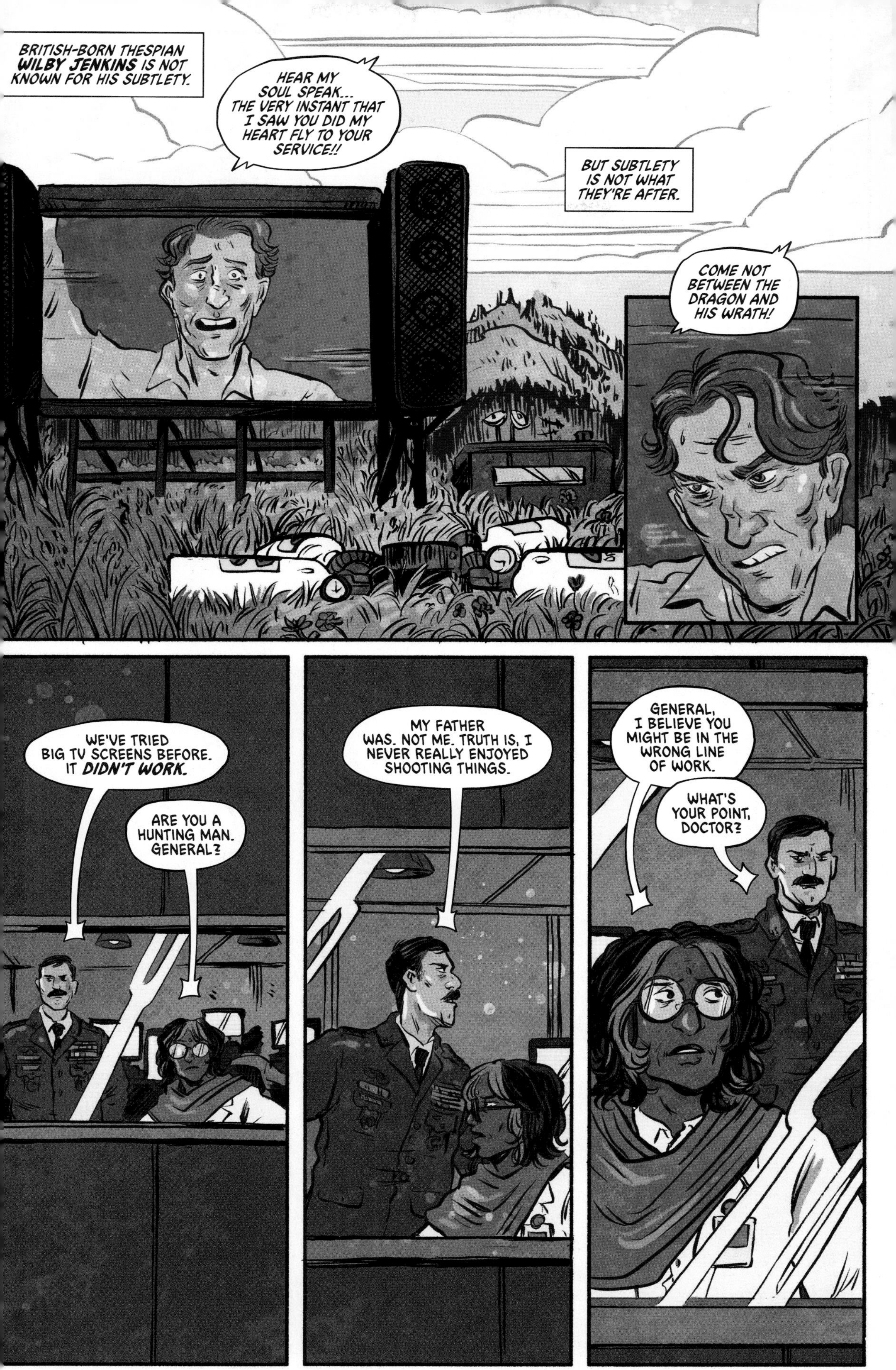

BRITISH-BORN THESPIAN **WILBY JENKINS** IS NOT KNOWN FOR HIS SUBTLETY.
HEAR MY SOUL SPEAK... THE VERY INSTANT THAT I SAW YOU DID MY HEART FLY TO YOUR SERVICE!!
BUT SUBTLETY IS NOT WHAT THEY'RE AFTER.
COME NOT BETWEEN THE DRAGON AND HIS WRATH!
WE'VE TRIED BIG TV SCREENS BEFORE. IT ***DIDN'T WORK.***
ARE YOU A HUNTING MAN, GENERAL?
MY FATHER WAS. NOT ME. TRUTH IS, I NEVER REALLY ENJOYED SHOOTING THINGS.
GENERAL, I BELIEVE YOU MIGHT BE IN THE WRONG LINE OF WORK.
WHAT'S YOUR POINT, DOCTOR?

LIAM HERE IS A DOCTOR OF AUDIOLOGY.

TELL GENERAL SULLIVAN ABOUT THE *HUMAN VOICE*, LIAM.

YEAH, *AH*... BASICALLY TH-THE FREQUENCY RESPONSE OF THE HUMAN VOICE AS RELAYED ON A REGULAR TV OR RADIO IS DIFFERENT FROM A *NATURAL* VOICE.

WH-WHICH MEANS, TO REPLICATE A NORMAL HUMAN FREQUENCY RANGE, CERTAIN *MODIFICATIONS* MUST BE MADE...

IN SHORT, YOUR TV SCREENS DIDN'T SOUND *REAL ENOUGH* TO FOOL WHATEVER PASSES FOR THE LIFE-FORMS' AUDITORY SYSTEM.

I THINK I'M PICKING SOMETHING UP! YES...OH, JESUS...

"...SOMETHING'S *COMING!*"

SKREEEEEE

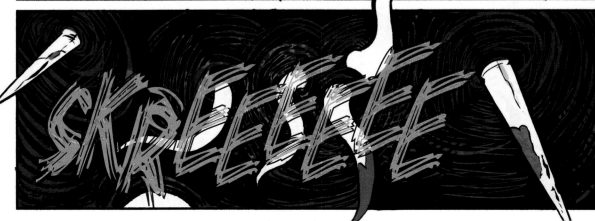

SKREEEEEE

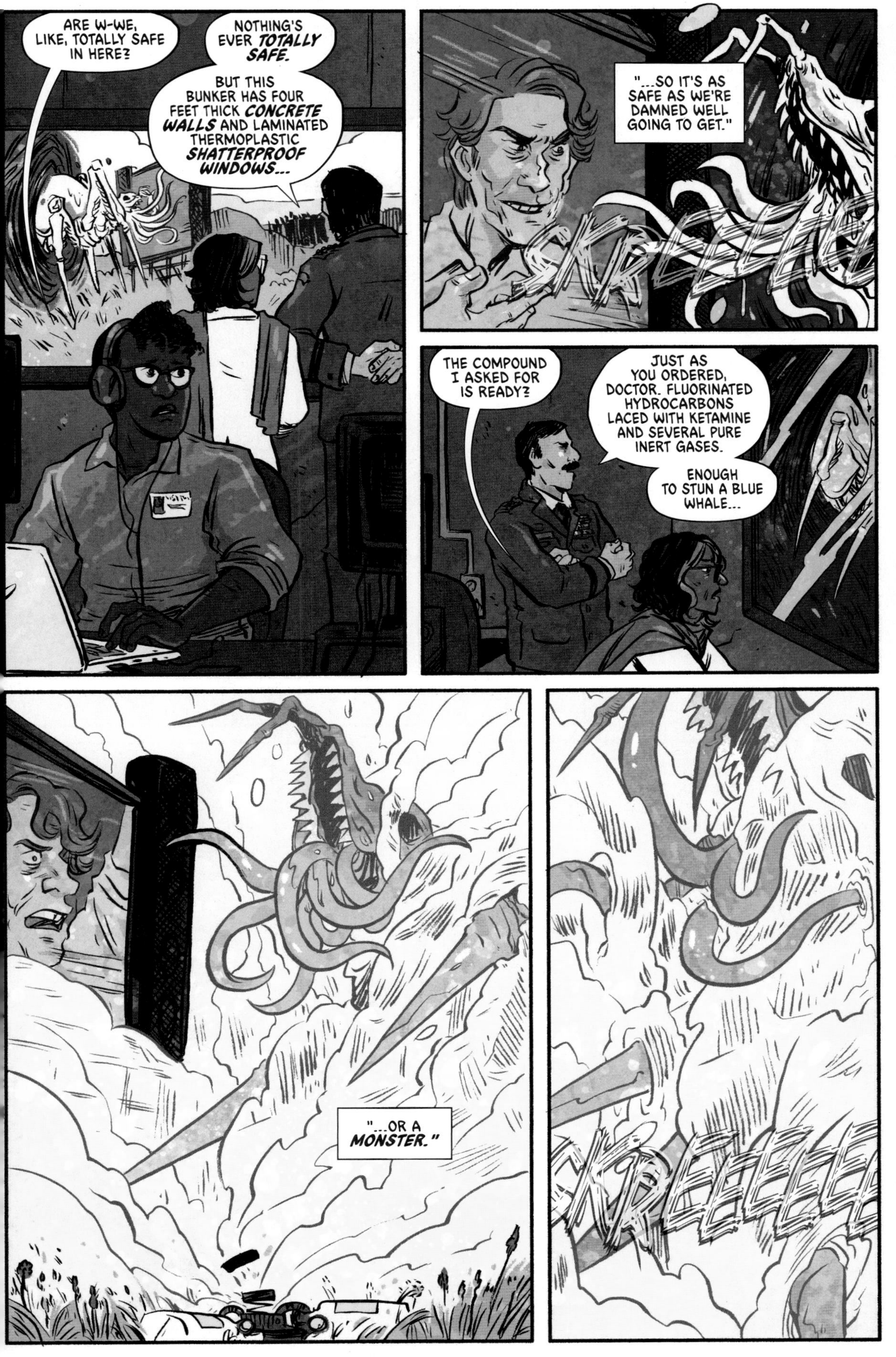
ARE W-WE, LIKE, TOTALLY SAFE IN HERE?
NOTHING'S EVER *TOTALLY SAFE.*
BUT THIS BUNKER HAS FOUR FEET THICK *CONCRETE WALLS* AND LAMINATED THERMOPLASTIC *SHATTERPROOF WINDOWS...*
"...SO IT'S AS SAFE AS WE'RE DAMNED WELL GOING TO GET."
SKREEEEE
THE COMPOUND I ASKED FOR IS READY?
JUST AS YOU ORDERED, DOCTOR. FLUORINATED HYDROCARBONS LACED WITH KETAMINE AND SEVERAL PURE INERT GASES.
ENOUGH TO STUN A BLUE WHALE...
"...OR A *MONSTER.*"
SKREEEEEE

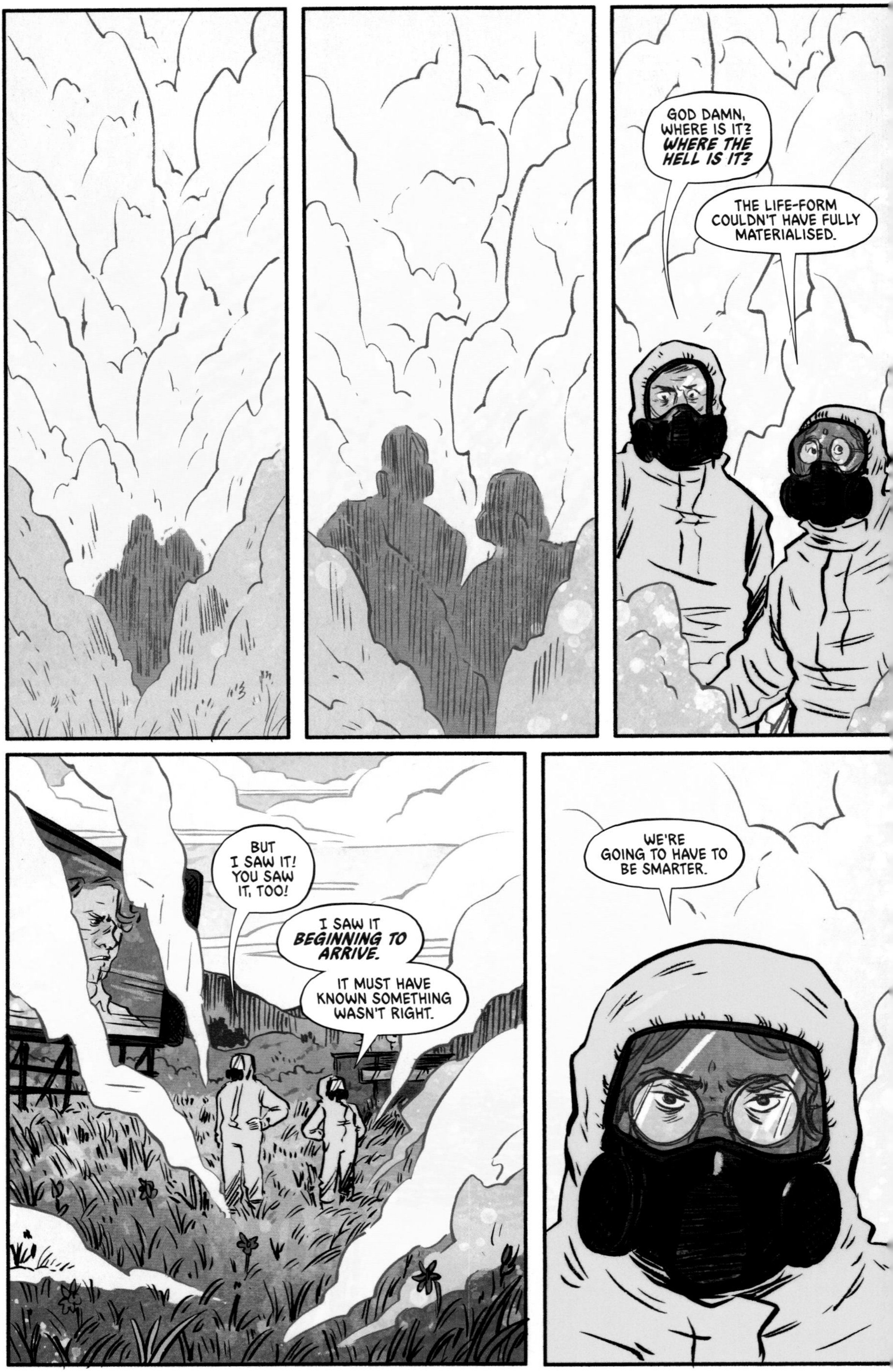
GOD DAMN, WHERE IS IT? WHERE THE HELL IS IT?
THE LIFE-FORM COULDN'T HAVE FULLY MATERIALISED.
BUT I SAW IT! YOU SAW IT, TOO!
I SAW IT BEGINNING TO ARRIVE.
IT MUST HAVE KNOWN SOMETHING WASN'T RIGHT.
WE'RE GOING TO HAVE TO BE SMARTER.

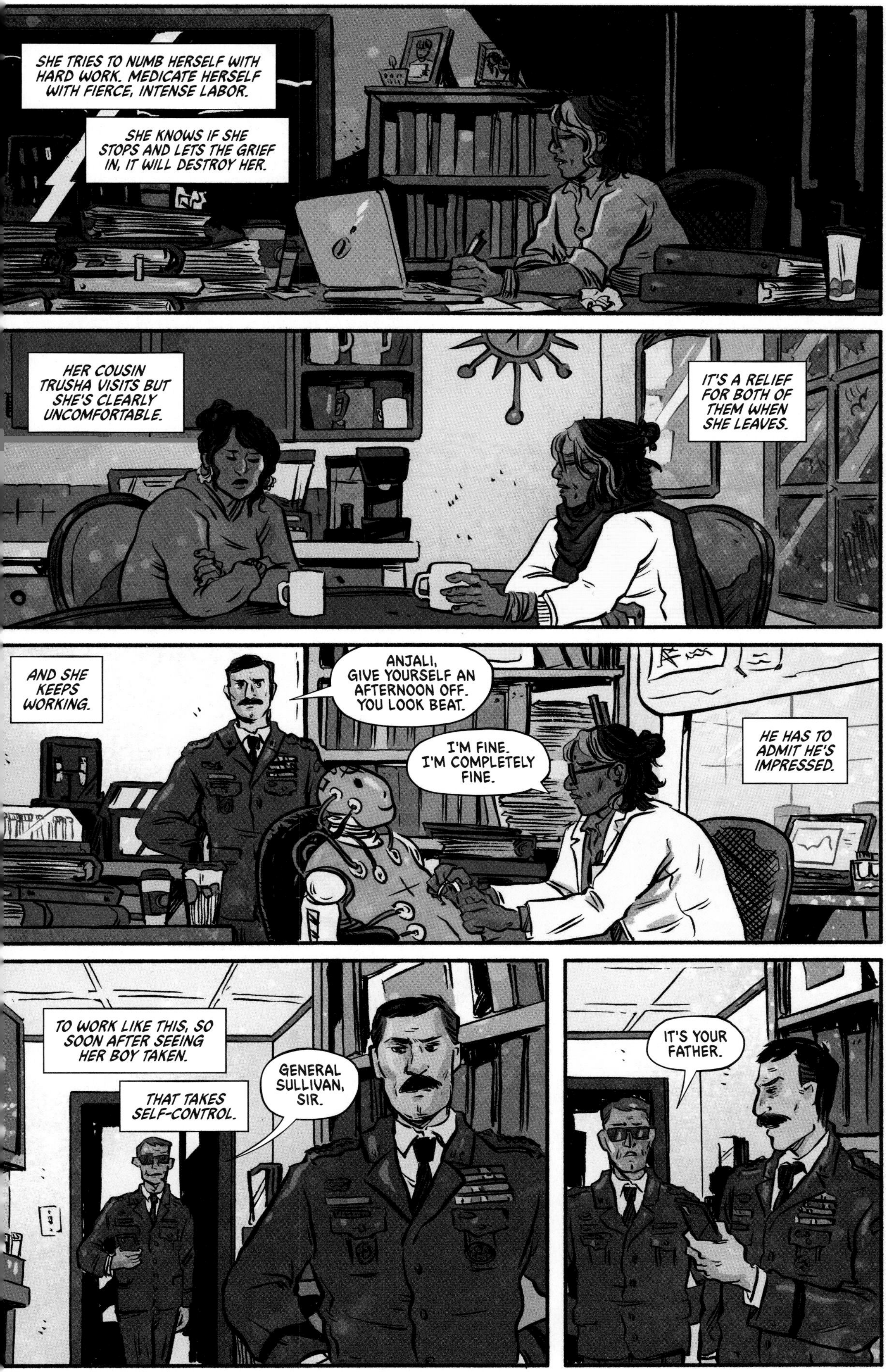

SHE TRIES TO NUMB HERSELF WITH HARD WORK. MEDICATE HERSELF WITH FIERCE, INTENSE LABOR.
SHE KNOWS IF SHE STOPS AND LETS THE GRIEF IN, IT WILL DESTROY HER.
HER COUSIN TRUSHA VISITS BUT SHE'S CLEARLY UNCOMFORTABLE.
IT'S A RELIEF FOR BOTH OF THEM WHEN SHE LEAVES.
AND SHE KEEPS WORKING.
ANJALI, GIVE YOURSELF AN AFTERNOON OFF. YOU LOOK BEAT.
I'M FINE. I'M COMPLETELY FINE.
HE HAS TO ADMIT HE'S IMPRESSED.
TO WORK LIKE THIS, SO SOON AFTER SEEING HER BOY TAKEN.
THAT TAKES SELF-CONTROL.
GENERAL SULLIVAN, SIR.
IT'S YOUR FATHER.

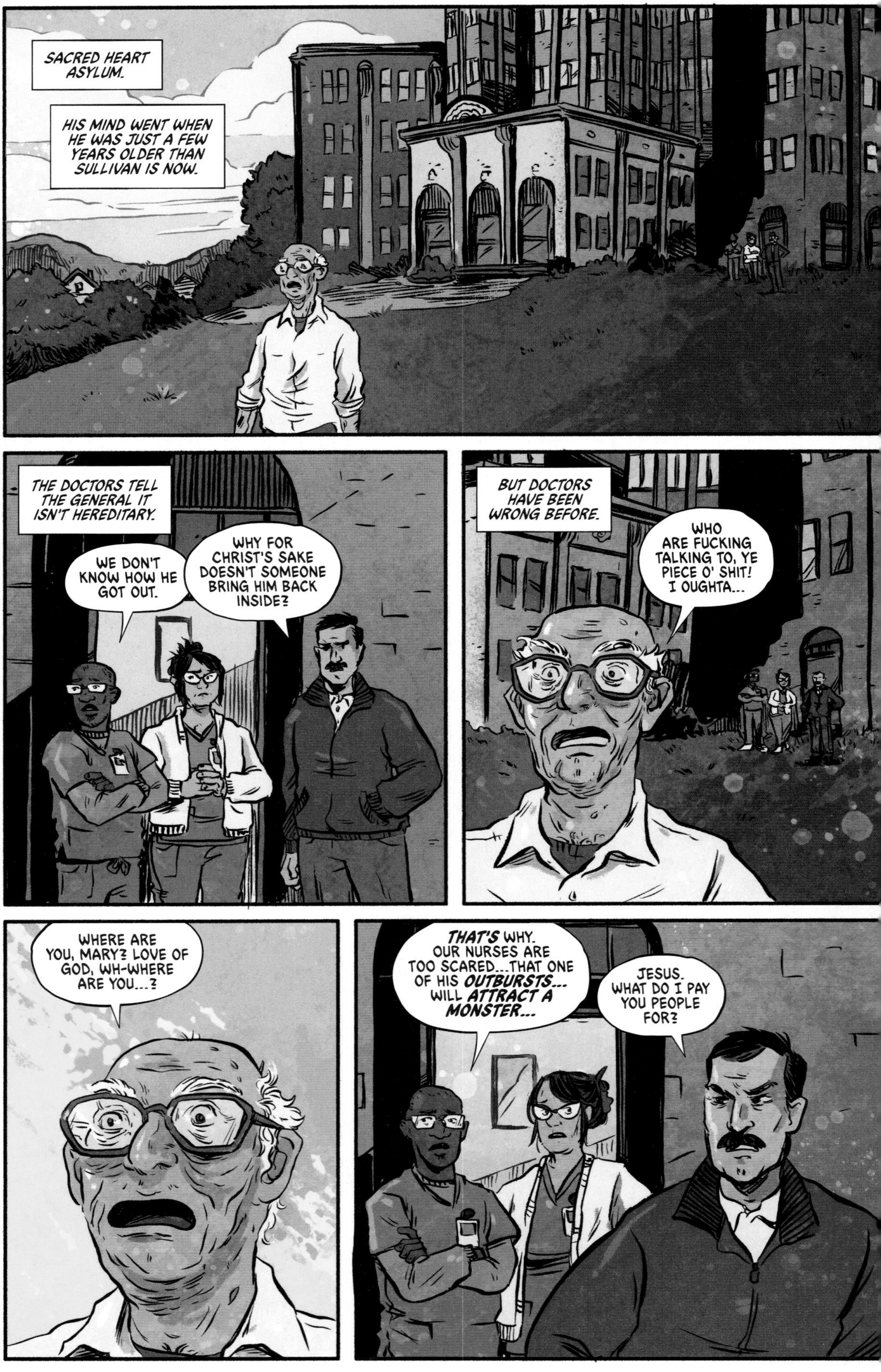
SACRED HEART ASYLUM.
HIS MIND WENT WHEN HE WAS JUST A FEW YEARS OLDER THAN SULLIVAN IS NOW.
THE DOCTORS TELL THE GENERAL IT ISN'T HEREDITARY.
WE DON'T KNOW HOW HE GOT OUT.
WHY FOR CHRIST'S SAKE DOESN'T SOMEONE BRING HIM BACK INSIDE?
BUT DOCTORS HAVE BEEN WRONG BEFORE.
WHO ARE FUCKING TALKING TO, YE PIECE O' SHIT! I OUGHTA...
WHERE ARE YOU, MARY? LOVE OF GOD, WH-WHERE ARE YOU...?
THAT'S WHY. OUR NURSES ARE TOO SCARED...THAT ONE OF HIS OUTBURSTS... WILL ATTRACT A MONSTER...
JESUS. WHAT DO I PAY YOU PEOPLE FOR?

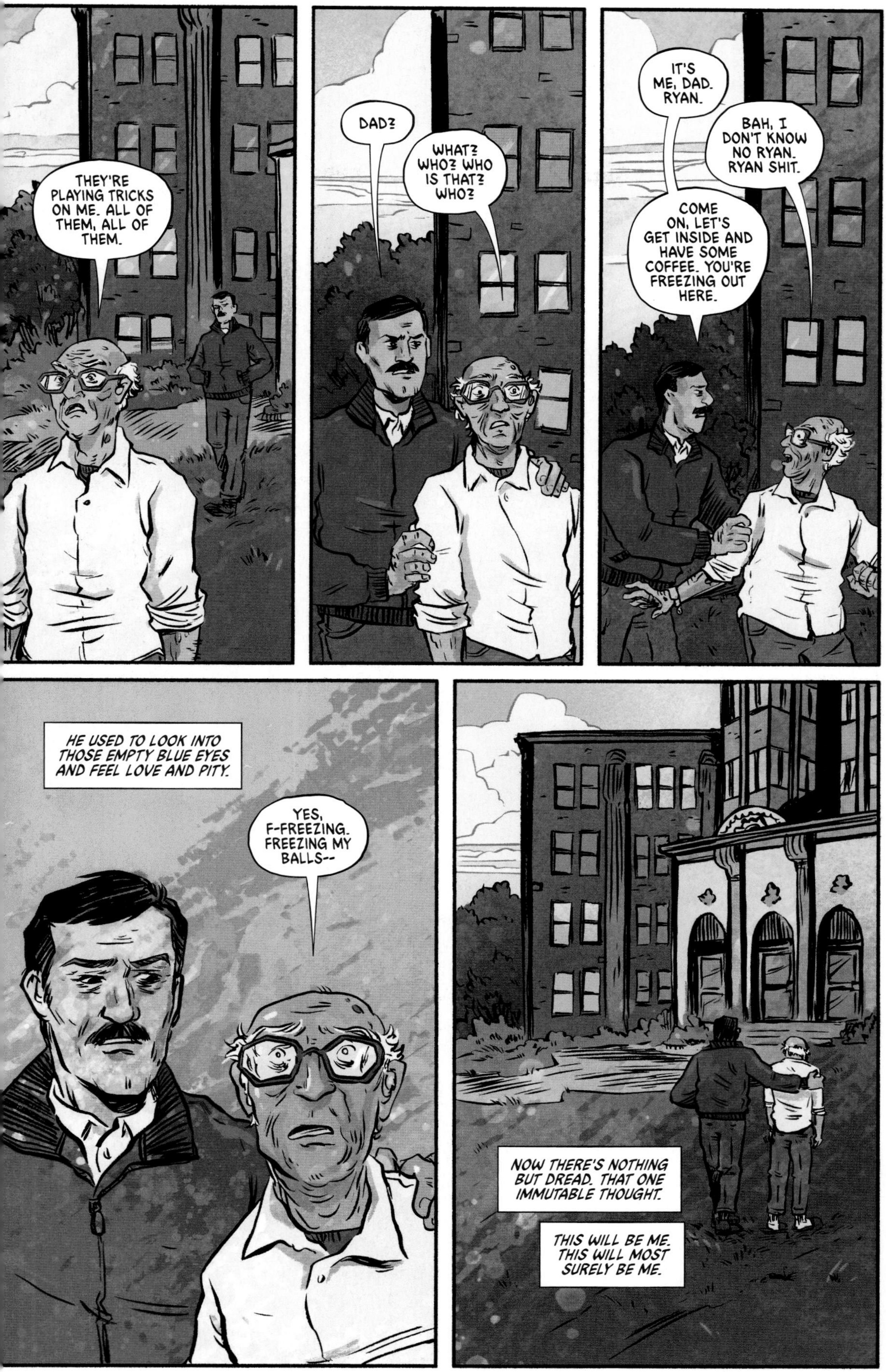
THEY'RE PLAYING TRICKS ON ME. ALL OF THEM, ALL OF THEM.
DAD?
WHAT? WHO? WHO IS THAT? WHO?
IT'S ME, DAD. RYAN.
BAH, I DON'T KNOW NO RYAN. RYAN SHIT.
COME ON, LET'S GET INSIDE AND HAVE SOME COFFEE. YOU'RE FREEZING OUT HERE.
HE USED TO LOOK INTO THOSE EMPTY BLUE EYES AND FEEL LOVE AND PITY.
YES, F-FREEZING. FREEZING MY BALLS--
NOW THERE'S NOTHING BUT DREAD. THAT ONE IMMUTABLE THOUGHT.
THIS WILL BE ME. THIS WILL MOST SURELY BE ME.

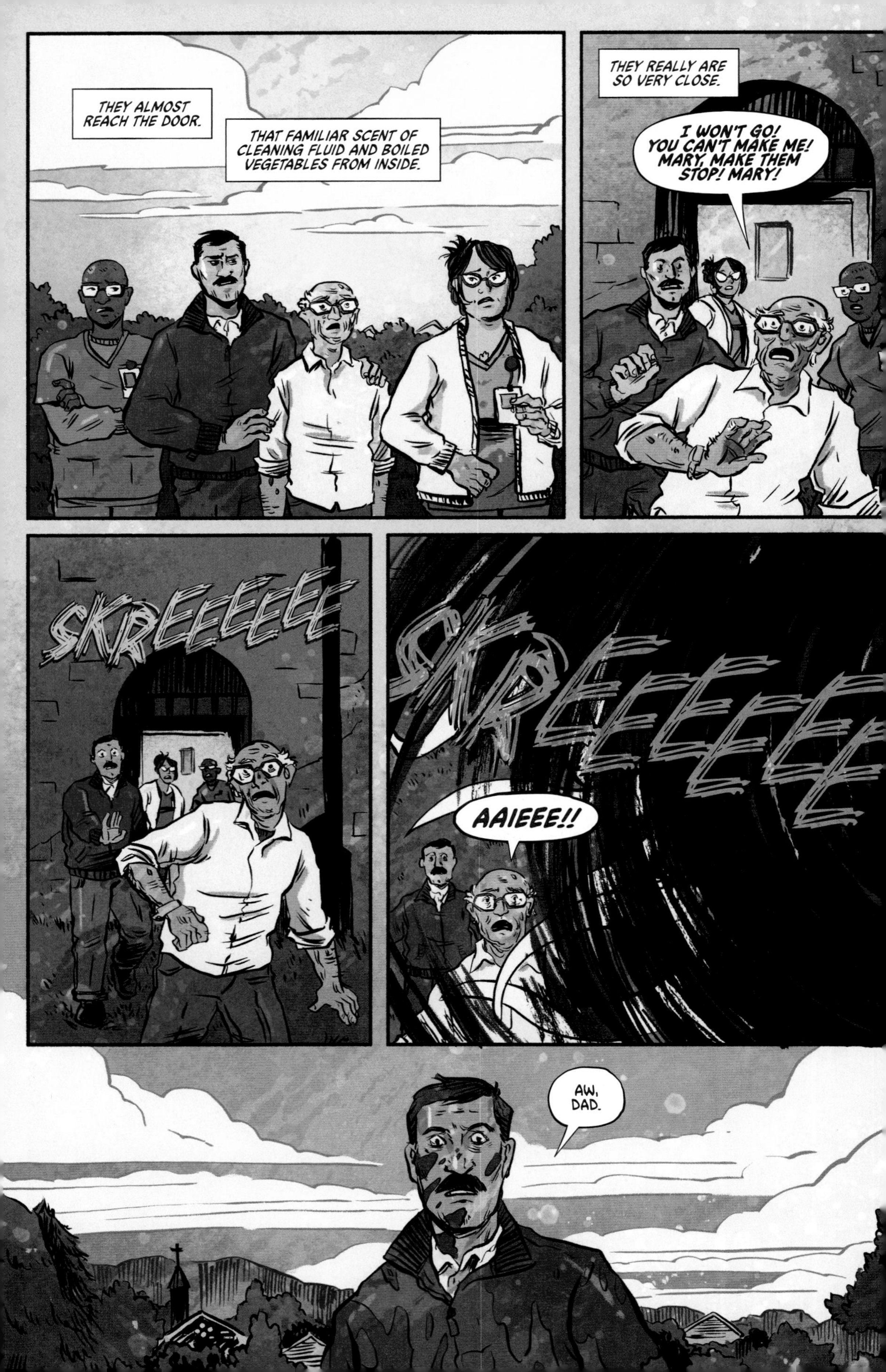
THEY ALMOST REACH THE DOOR.
THAT FAMILIAR SCENT OF CLEANING FLUID AND BOILED VEGETABLES FROM INSIDE.
THEY REALLY ARE SO VERY CLOSE.
I WON'T GO! YOU CAN'T MAKE ME! MARY, MAKE THEM STOP! MARY!
SKREEEEEEE
SKREEEEEE
AAIEEE!!
AW, DAD.

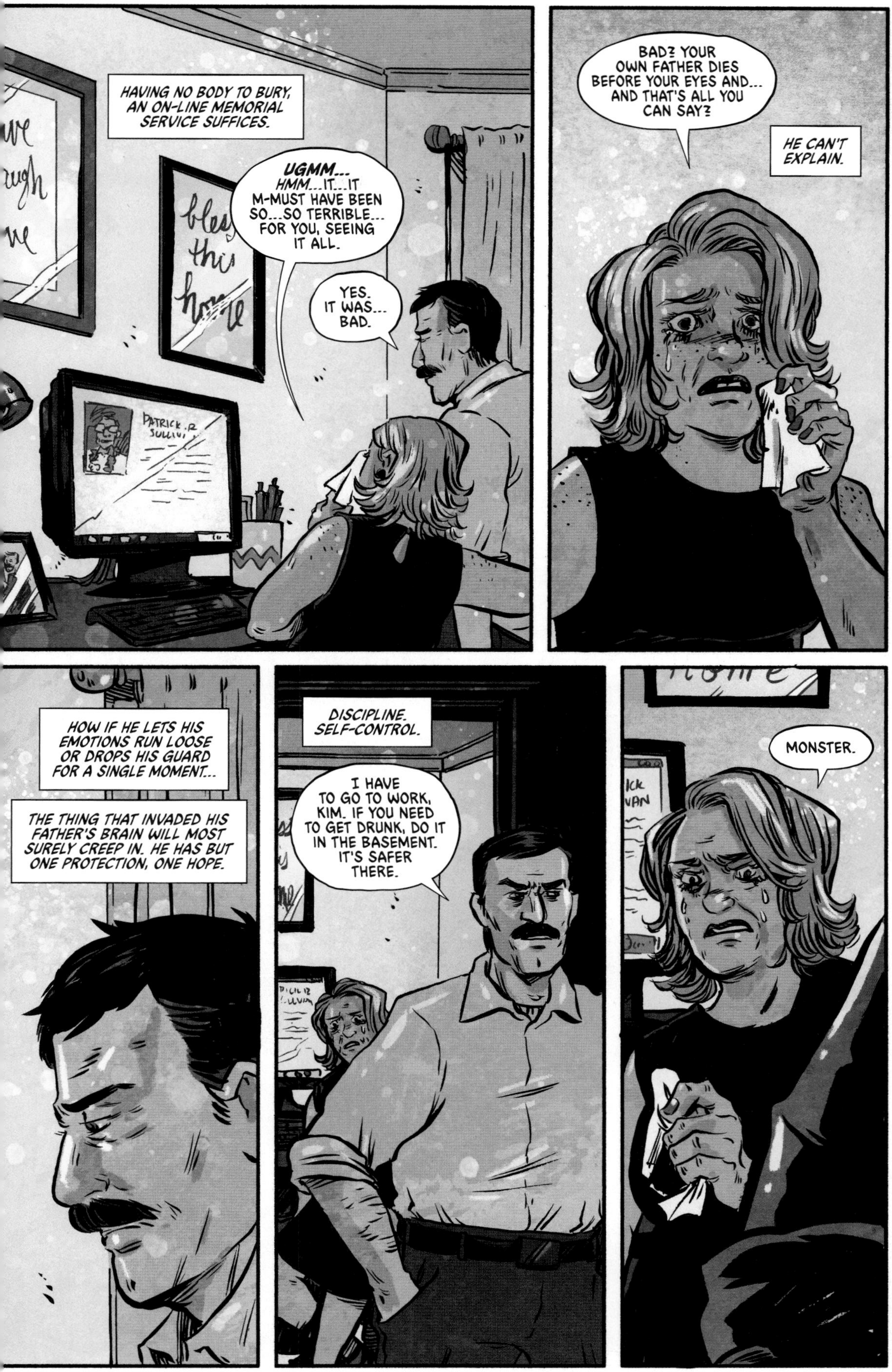
HAVING NO BODY TO BURY, AN ON-LINE MEMORIAL SERVICE SUFFICES.
UGMM... HMM...IT...IT M-MUST HAVE BEEN SO...SO TERRIBLE... FOR YOU, SEEING IT ALL.
YES. IT WAS... BAD.
PATRICK .R SULLIVI
BAD? YOUR OWN FATHER DIES BEFORE YOUR EYES AND... AND THAT'S ALL YOU CAN SAY?
HE CAN'T EXPLAIN.
HOW IF HE LETS HIS EMOTIONS RUN LOOSE OR DROPS HIS GUARD FOR A SINGLE MOMENT...
THE THING THAT INVADED HIS FATHER'S BRAIN WILL MOST SURELY CREEP IN. HE HAS BUT ONE PROTECTION, ONE HOPE.
DISCIPLINE. SELF-CONTROL.
I HAVE TO GO TO WORK, KIM. IF YOU NEED TO GET DRUNK, DO IT IN THE BASEMENT. IT'S SAFER THERE.
MONSTER.

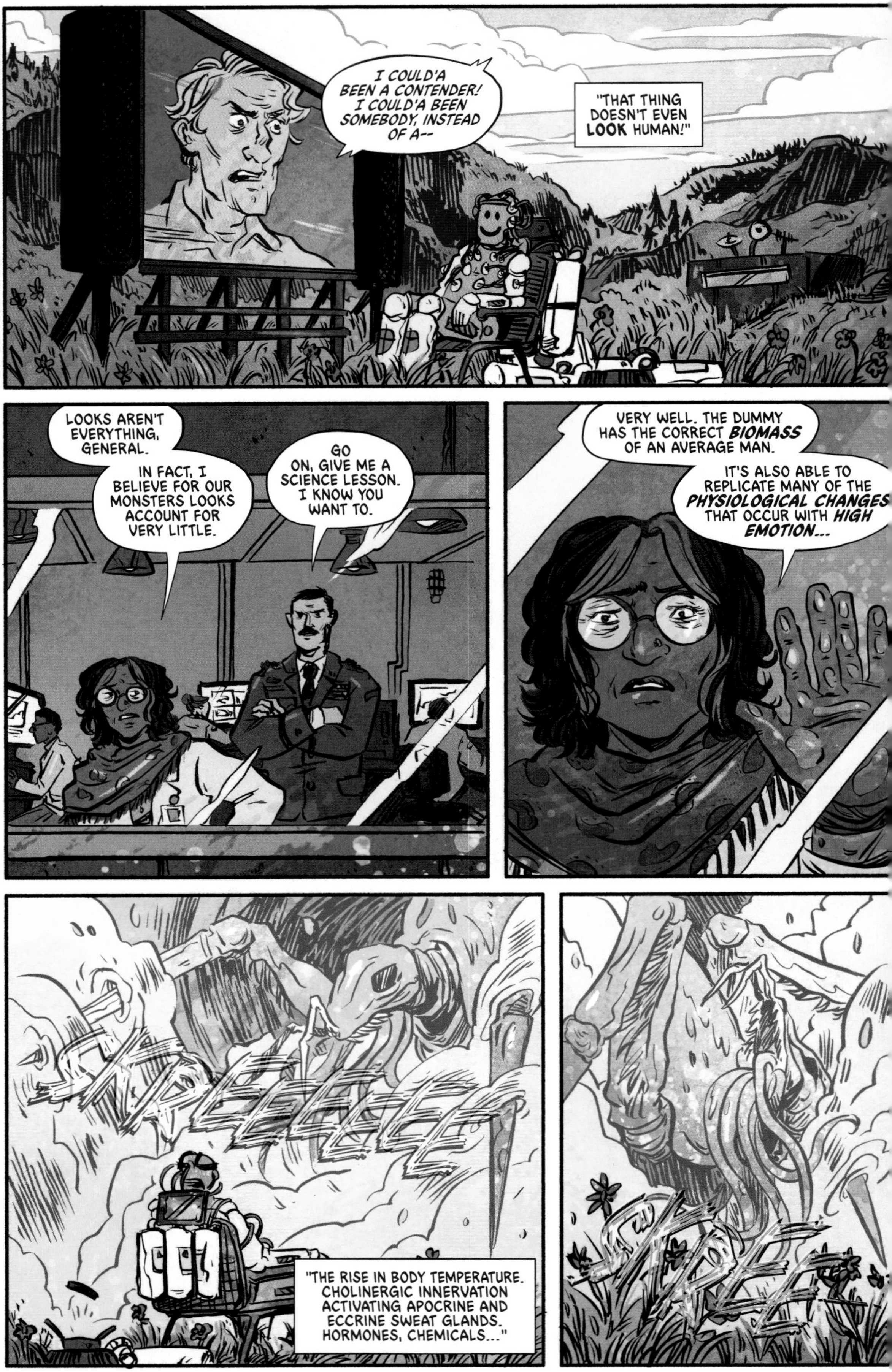
I COULD'A BEEN A CONTENDER! I COULD'A BEEN SOMEBODY, INSTEAD OF A--
"THAT THING DOESN'T EVEN LOOK HUMAN!"
LOOKS AREN'T EVERYTHING, GENERAL.
IN FACT, I BELIEVE FOR OUR MONSTERS LOOKS ACCOUNT FOR VERY LITTLE.
GO ON, GIVE ME A SCIENCE LESSON. I KNOW YOU WANT TO.
VERY WELL. THE DUMMY HAS THE CORRECT BIOMASS OF AN AVERAGE MAN.
IT'S ALSO ABLE TO REPLICATE MANY OF THE PHYSIOLOGICAL CHANGES THAT OCCUR WITH HIGH EMOTION...
"THE RISE IN BODY TEMPERATURE. CHOLINERGIC INNERVATION ACTIVATING APOCRINE AND ECCRINE SWEAT GLANDS. HORMONES, CHEMICALS..."

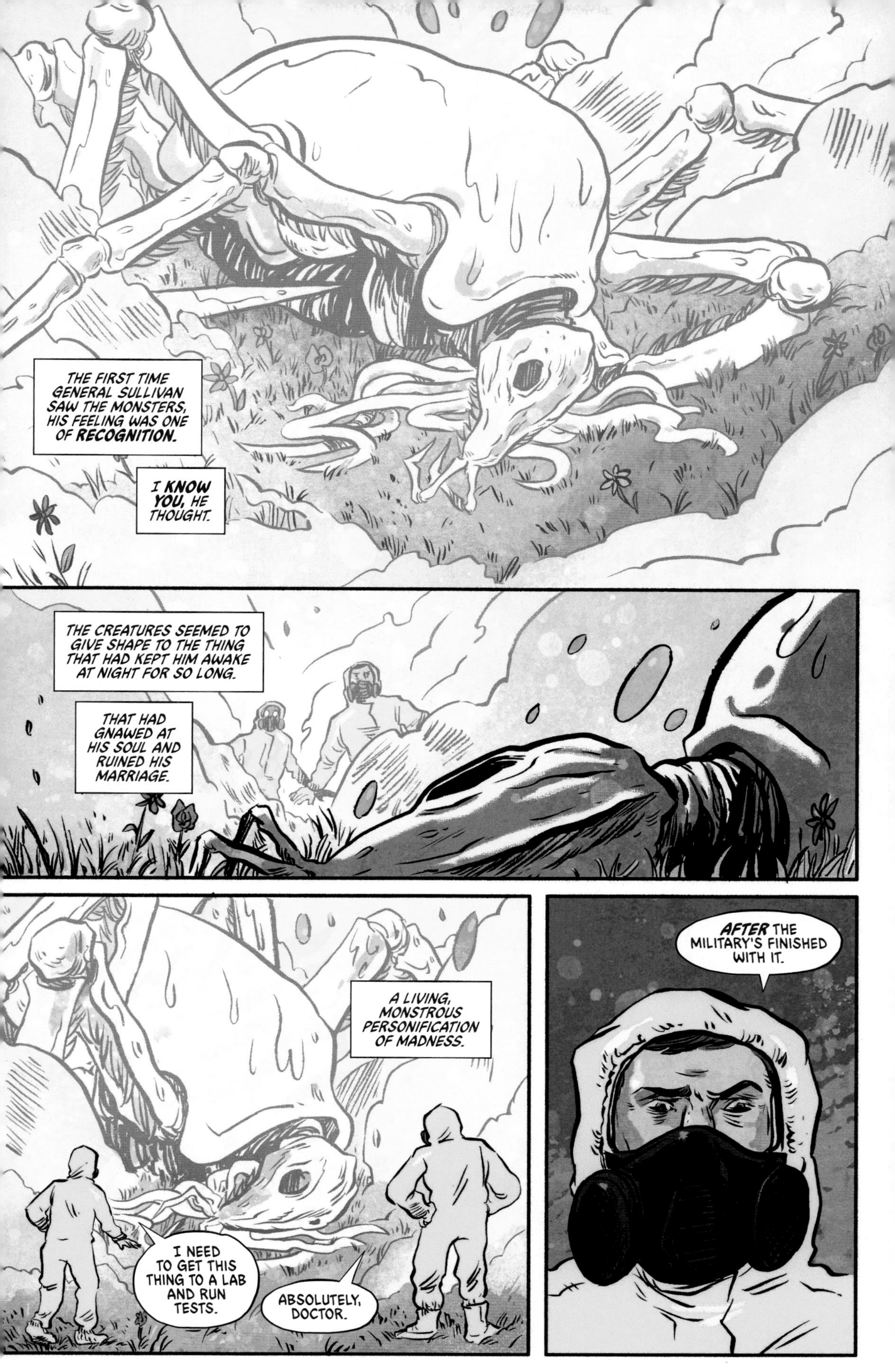
THE FIRST TIME GENERAL SULLIVAN SAW THE MONSTERS, HIS FEELING WAS ONE OF **RECOGNITION.**
I **KNOW YOU,** HE THOUGHT.
THE CREATURES SEEMED TO GIVE SHAPE TO THE THING THAT HAD KEPT HIM AWAKE AT NIGHT FOR SO LONG.
THAT HAD GNAWED AT HIS SOUL AND RUINED HIS MARRIAGE.
A LIVING, MONSTROUS PERSONIFICATION OF MADNESS.
I NEED TO GET THIS THING TO A LAB AND RUN TESTS.
ABSOLUTELY, DOCTOR.
AFTER THE MILITARY'S FINISHED WITH IT.

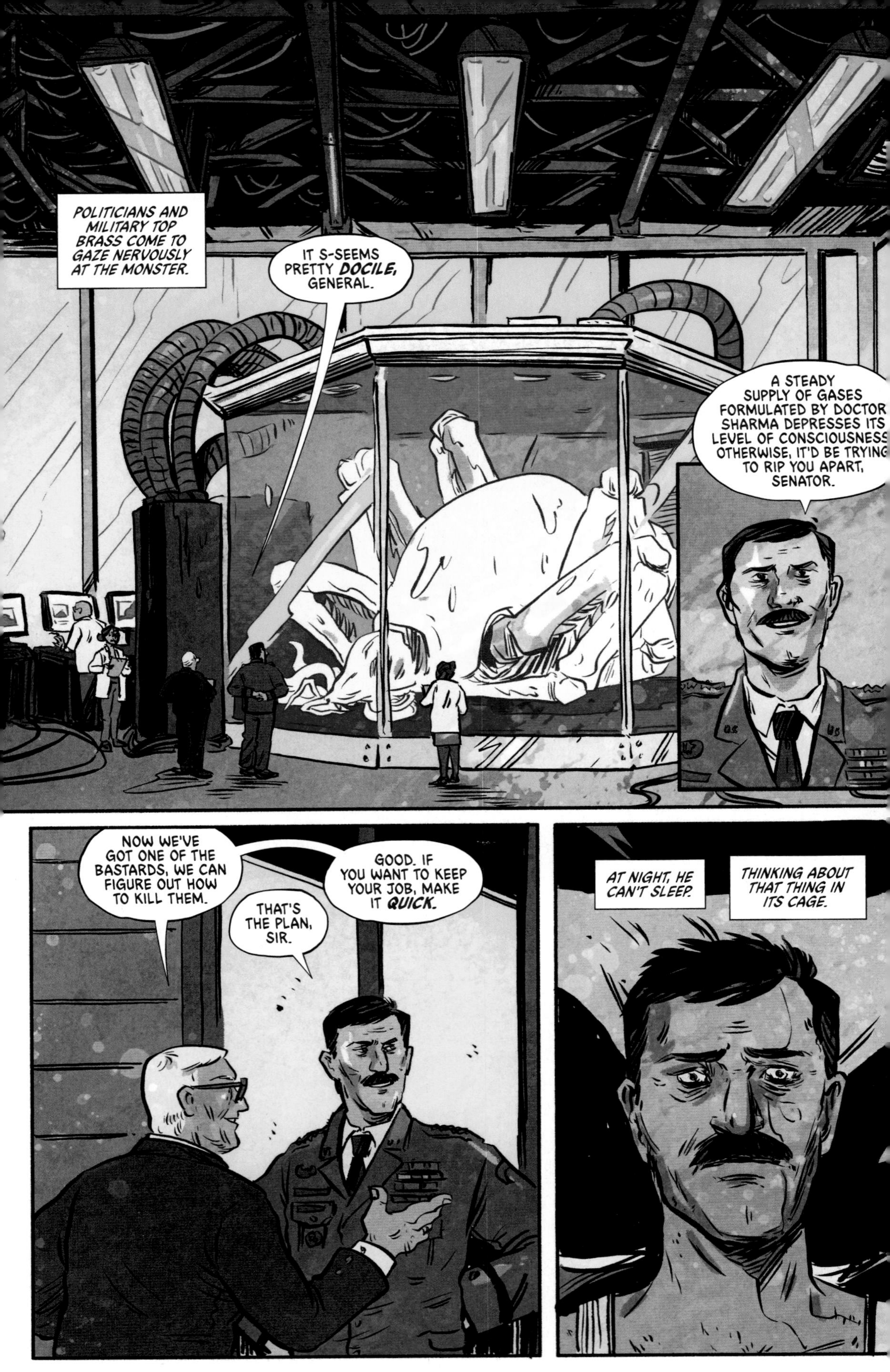
POLITICIANS AND MILITARY TOP BRASS COME TO GAZE NERVOUSLY AT THE MONSTER.
IT S-SEEMS PRETTY **DOCILE,** GENERAL.
A STEADY SUPPLY OF GASES FORMULATED BY DOCTOR SHARMA DEPRESSES ITS LEVEL OF CONSCIOUSNESS OTHERWISE, IT'D BE TRYING TO RIP YOU APART, SENATOR.
NOW WE'VE GOT ONE OF THE BASTARDS, WE CAN FIGURE OUT HOW TO KILL THEM.
THAT'S THE PLAN, SIR.
GOOD. IF YOU WANT TO KEEP YOUR JOB, MAKE IT **QUICK.**
AT NIGHT, HE CAN'T SLEEP.
THINKING ABOUT THAT THING IN ITS CAGE.

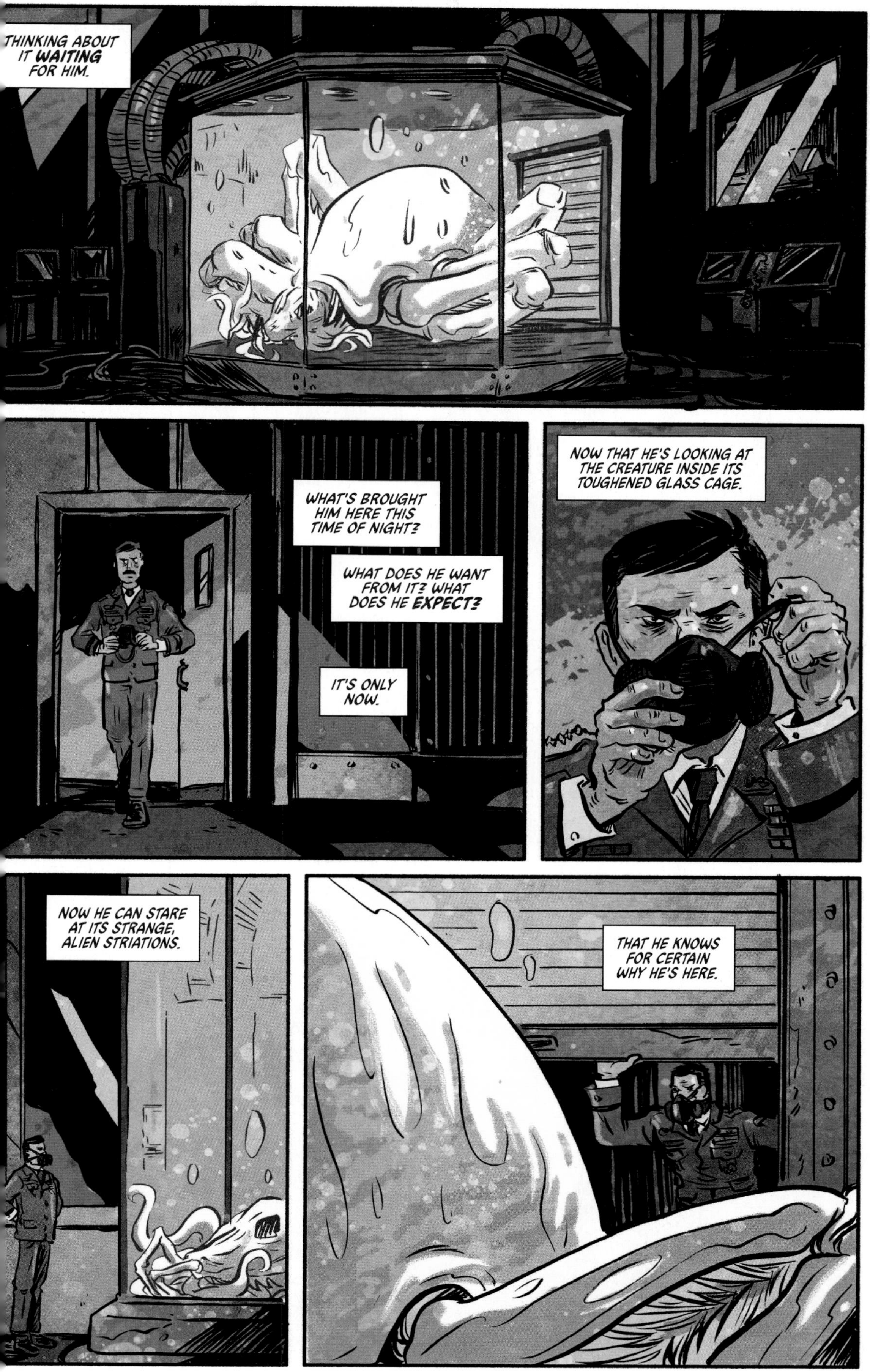
THINKING ABOUT IT WAITING FOR HIM.
WHAT'S BROUGHT HIM HERE THIS TIME OF NIGHT?
WHAT DOES HE WANT FROM IT? WHAT DOES HE EXPECT?
IT'S ONLY NOW.
NOW THAT HE'S LOOKING AT THE CREATURE INSIDE ITS TOUGHENED GLASS CAGE.
NOW HE CAN STARE AT ITS STRANGE, ALIEN STRIATIONS.
THAT HE KNOWS FOR CERTAIN WHY HE'S HERE.

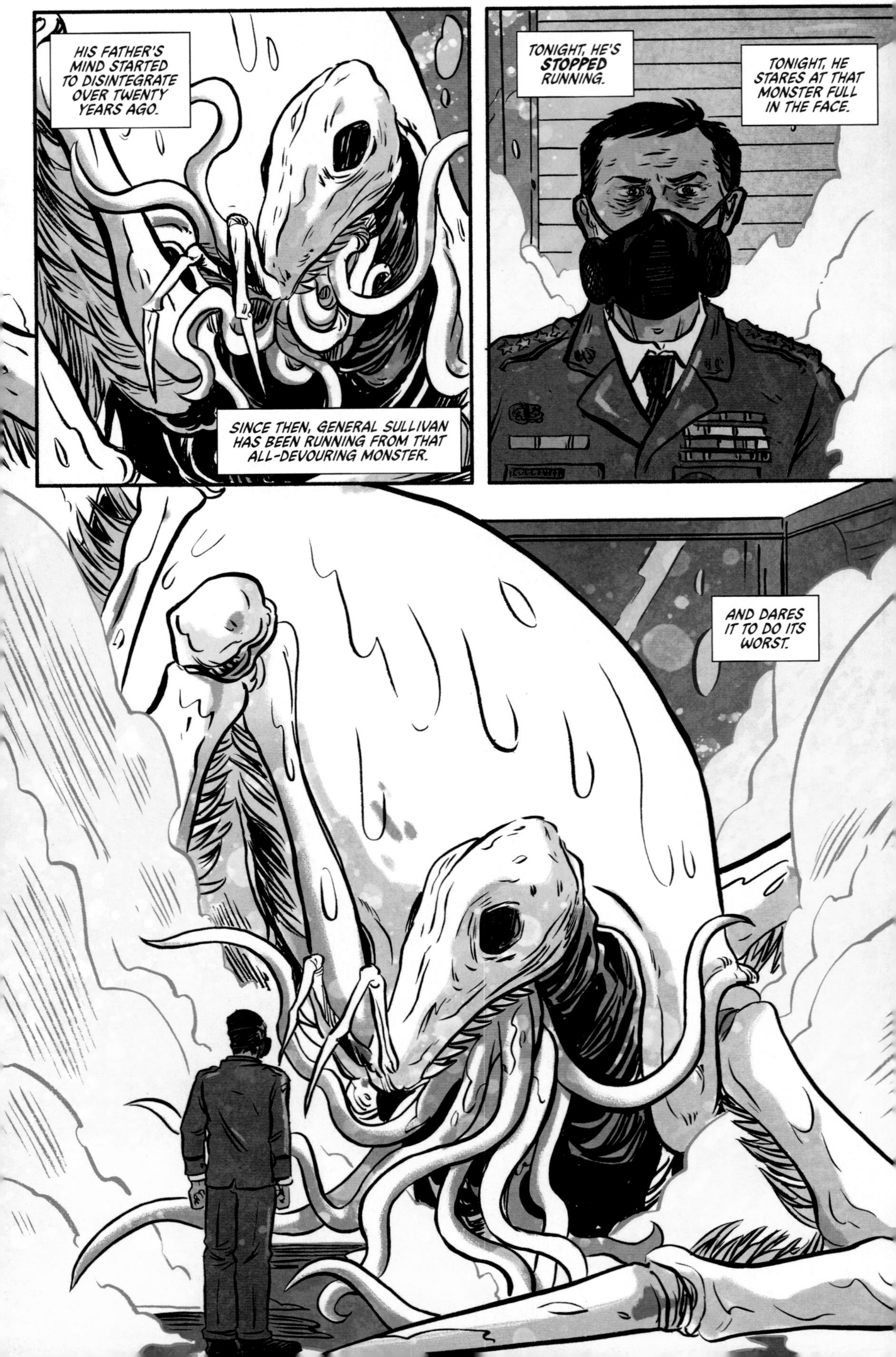
HIS FATHER'S MIND STARTED TO DISINTEGRATE OVER TWENTY YEARS AGO.
SINCE THEN, GENERAL SULLIVAN HAS BEEN RUNNING FROM THAT ALL-DEVOURING MONSTER.
TONIGHT, HE'S **STOPPED** RUNNING.
TONIGHT, HE STARES AT THAT MONSTER FULL IN THE FACE.
AND DARES IT TO DO ITS WORST.

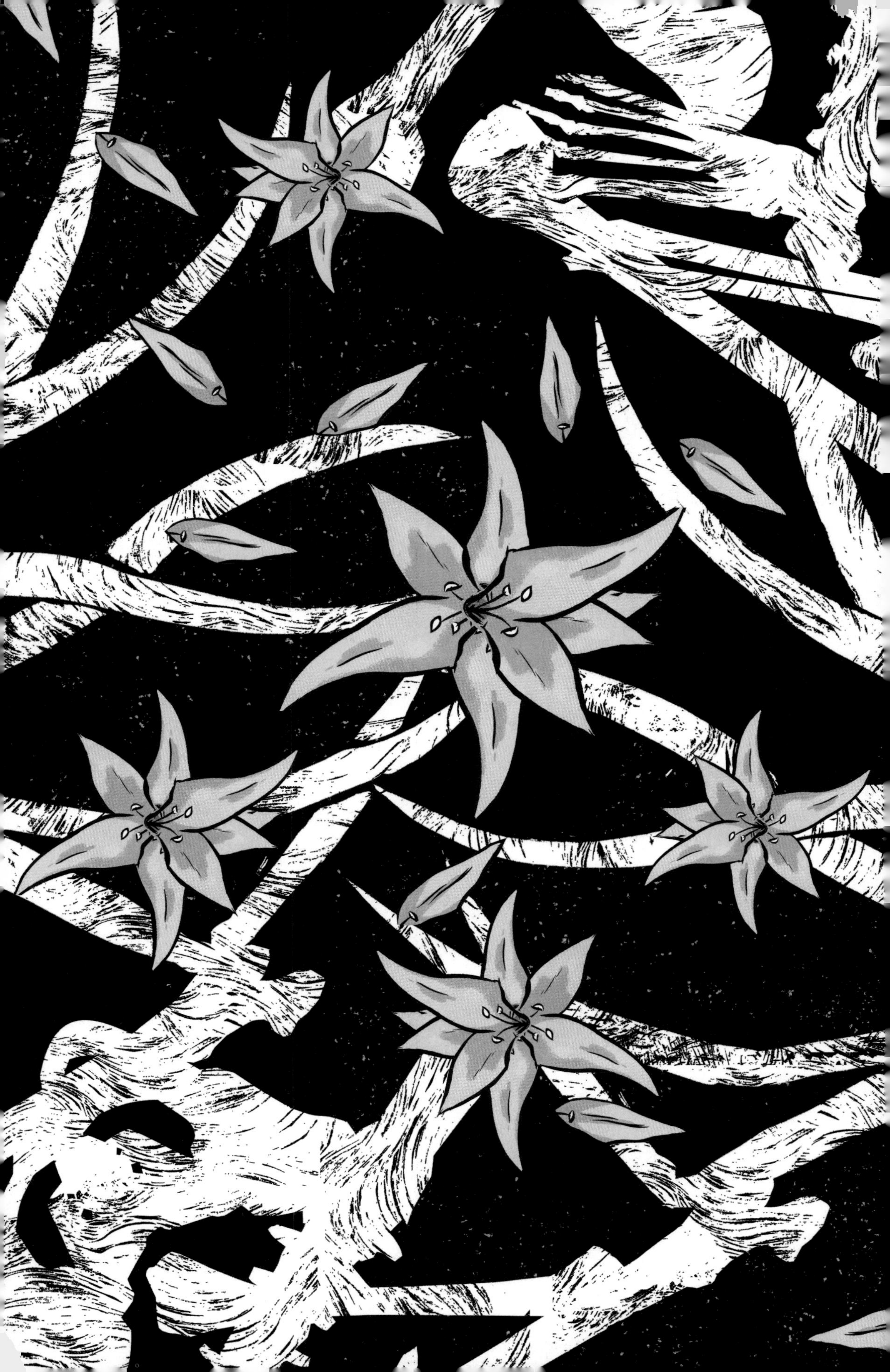

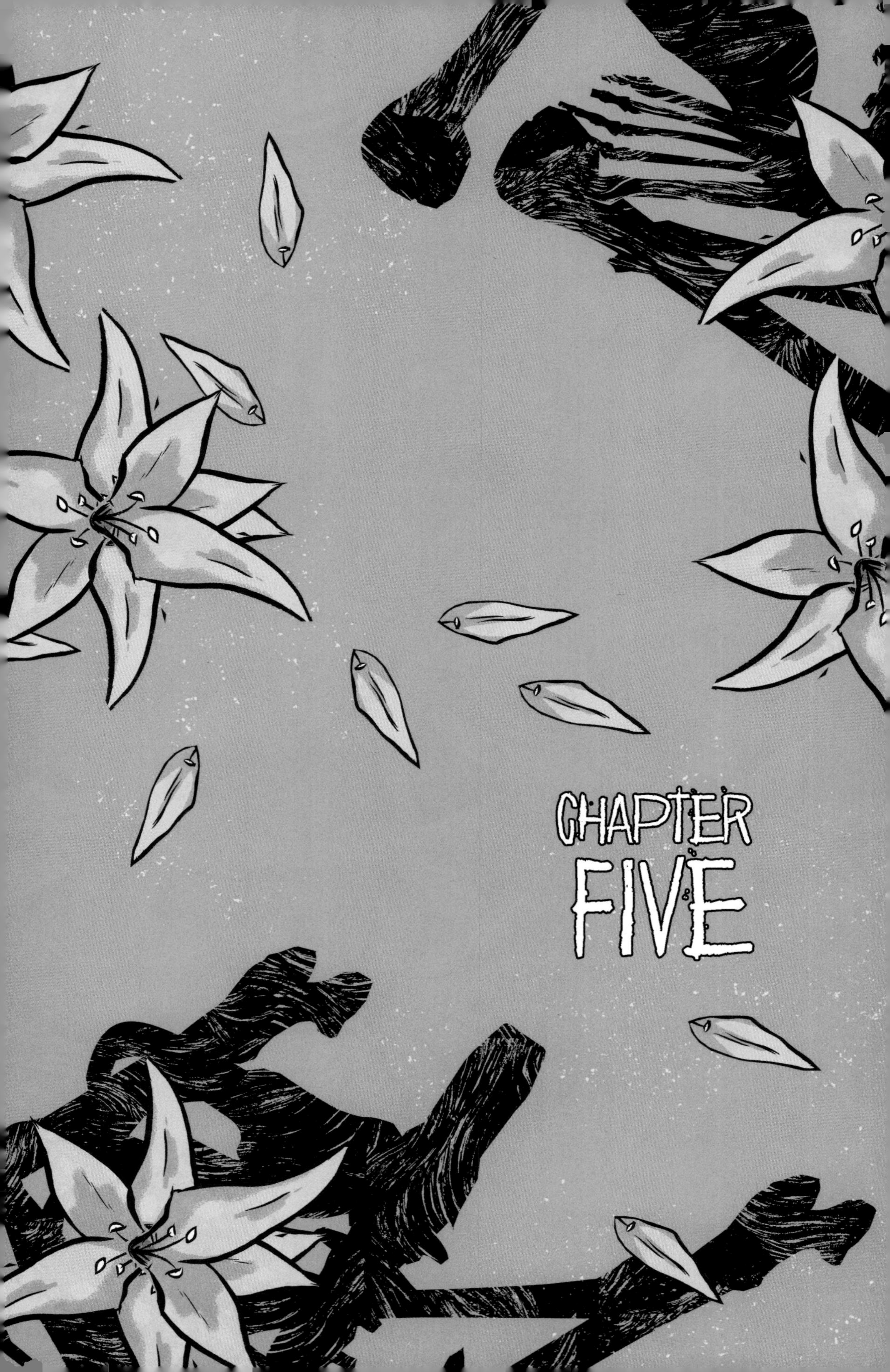
CHAPTER
FIVE

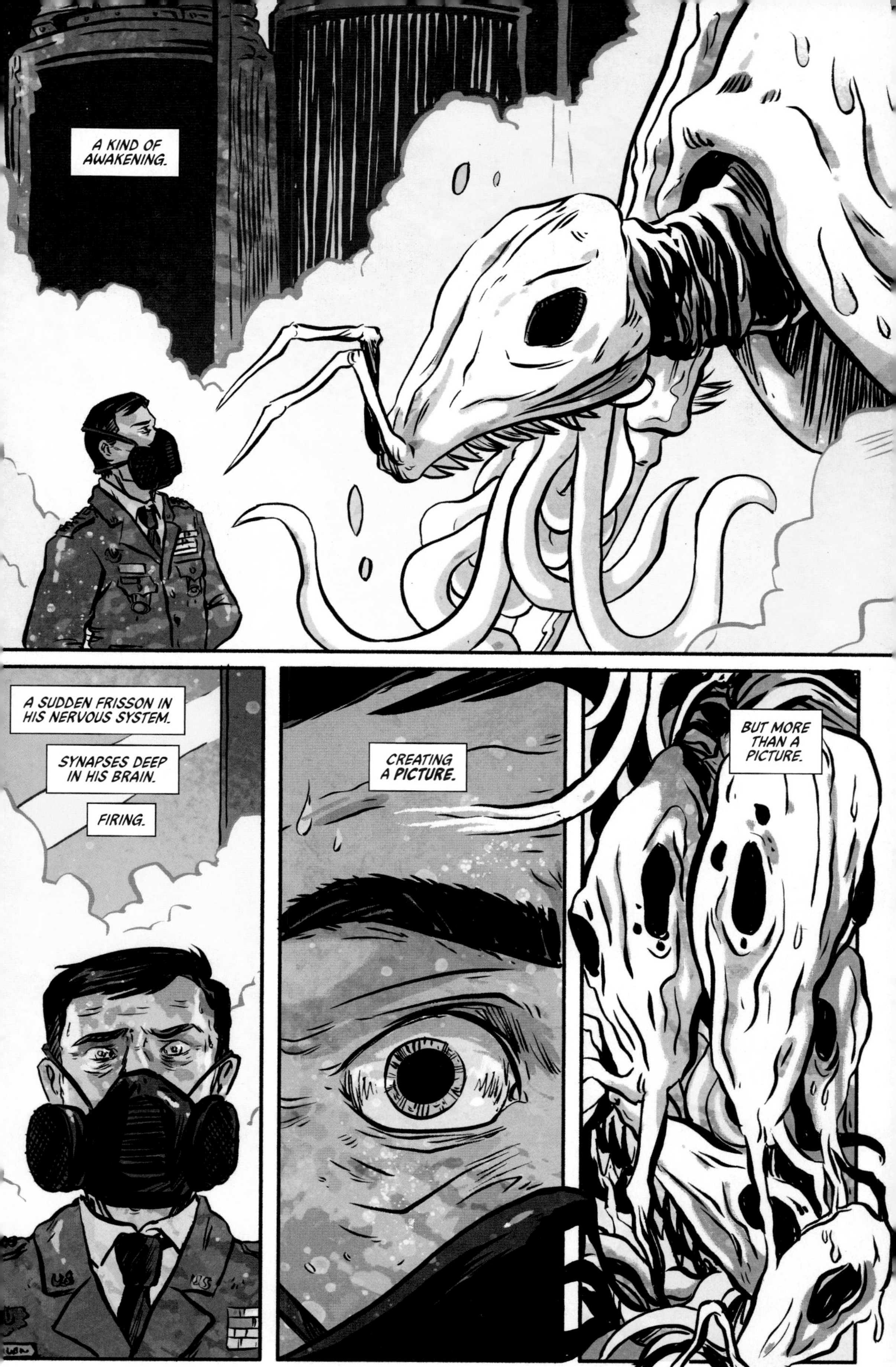
A KIND OF AWAKENING.
A SUDDEN FRISSON IN HIS NERVOUS SYSTEM.
SYNAPSES DEEP IN HIS BRAIN.
FIRING.
CREATING A PICTURE.
BUT MORE THAN A PICTURE.

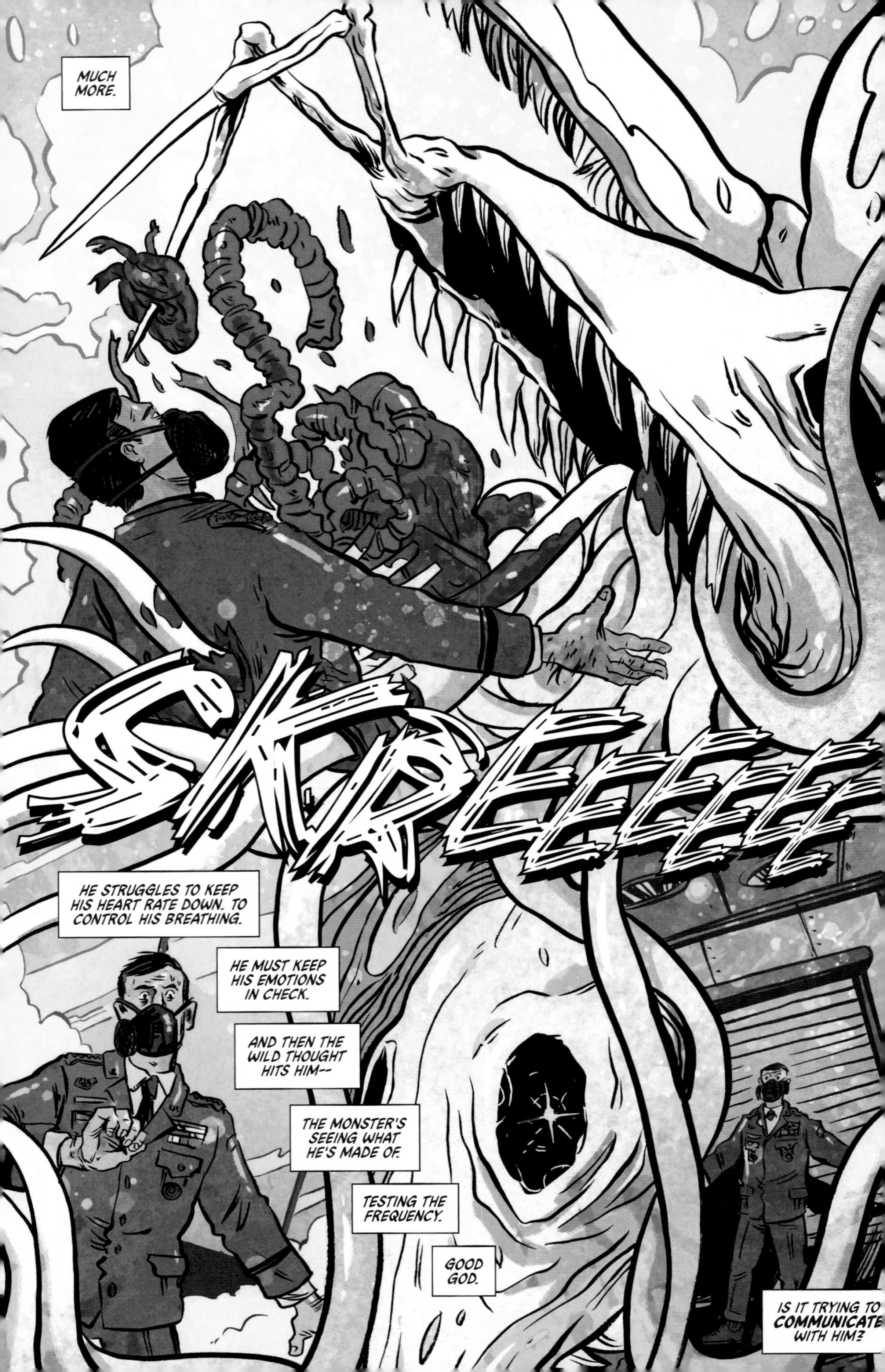
MUCH MORE.
SKREEEEEE
HE STRUGGLES TO KEEP HIS HEART RATE DOWN. TO CONTROL HIS BREATHING.
HE MUST KEEP HIS EMOTIONS IN CHECK.
AND THEN THE WILD THOUGHT HITS HIM--
THE MONSTER'S SEEING WHAT HE'S MADE OF.
TESTING THE FREQUENCY.
GOOD GOD.
IS IT TRYING TO COMMUNICATE WITH HIM?

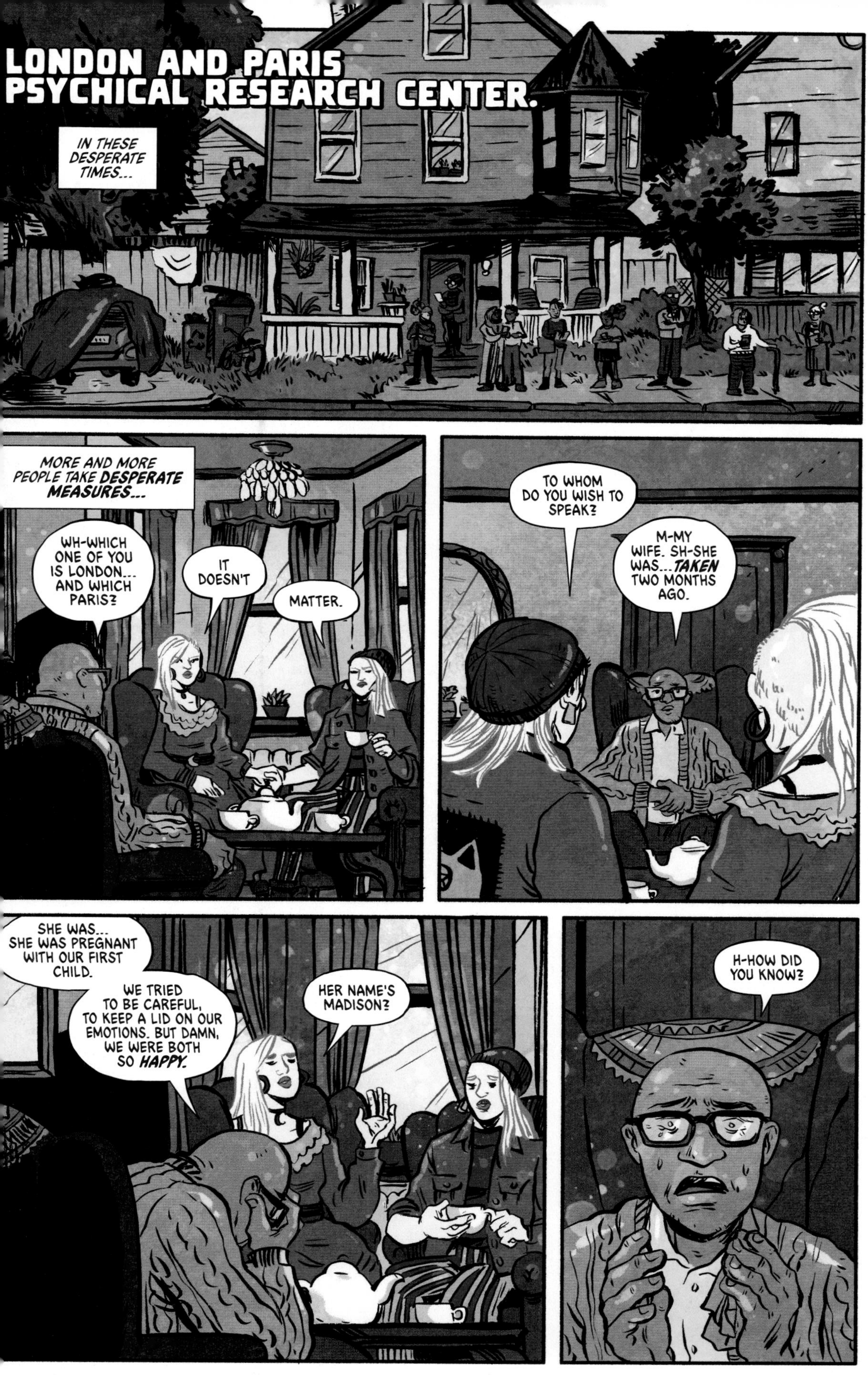
LONDON AND PARIS PSYCHICAL RESEARCH CENTER.
IN THESE DESPERATE TIMES...
MORE AND MORE PEOPLE TAKE DESPERATE MEASURES...
WH-WHICH ONE OF YOU IS LONDON... AND WHICH PARIS?
IT DOESN'T
MATTER.
TO WHOM DO YOU WISH TO SPEAK?
M-MY WIFE. SH-SHE WAS... TAKEN TWO MONTHS AGO.
SHE WAS... SHE WAS PREGNANT WITH OUR FIRST CHILD.
WE TRIED TO BE CAREFUL, TO KEEP A LID ON OUR EMOTIONS. BUT DAMN, WE WERE BOTH SO HAPPY.
HER NAME'S MADISON?
H-HOW DID YOU KNOW?

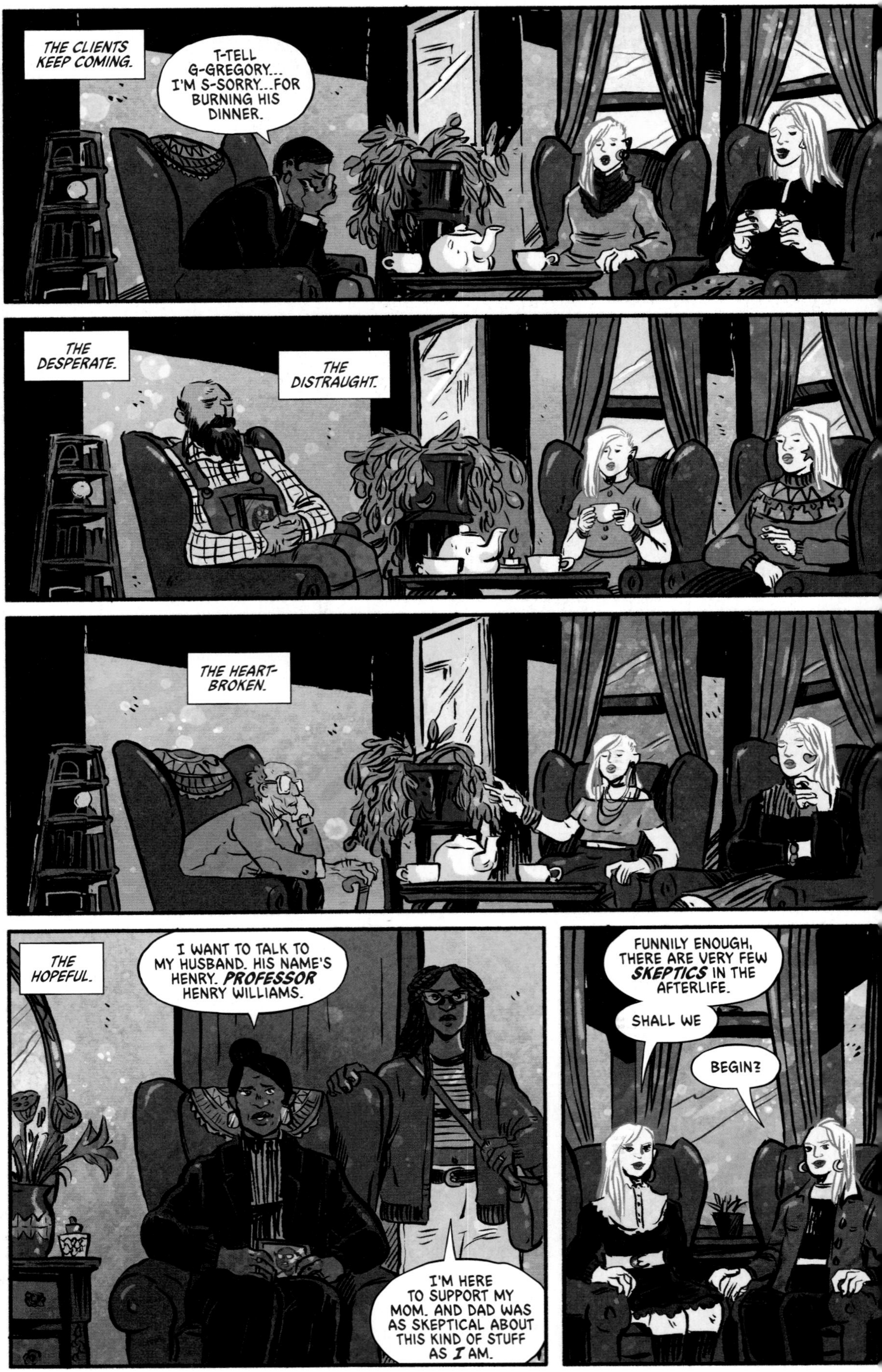
THE CLIENTS KEEP COMING.
T-TELL G-GREGORY... I'M S-SORRY...FOR BURNING HIS DINNER.
THE DESPERATE.
THE DISTRAUGHT.
THE HEART-BROKEN.
THE HOPEFUL.
I WANT TO TALK TO MY HUSBAND. HIS NAME'S HENRY. PROFESSOR HENRY WILLIAMS.
I'M HERE TO SUPPORT MY MOM. AND DAD WAS AS SKEPTICAL ABOUT THIS KIND OF STUFF AS I AM.
FUNNILY ENOUGH, THERE ARE VERY FEW SKEPTICS IN THE AFTERLIFE.
SHALL WE
BEGIN?

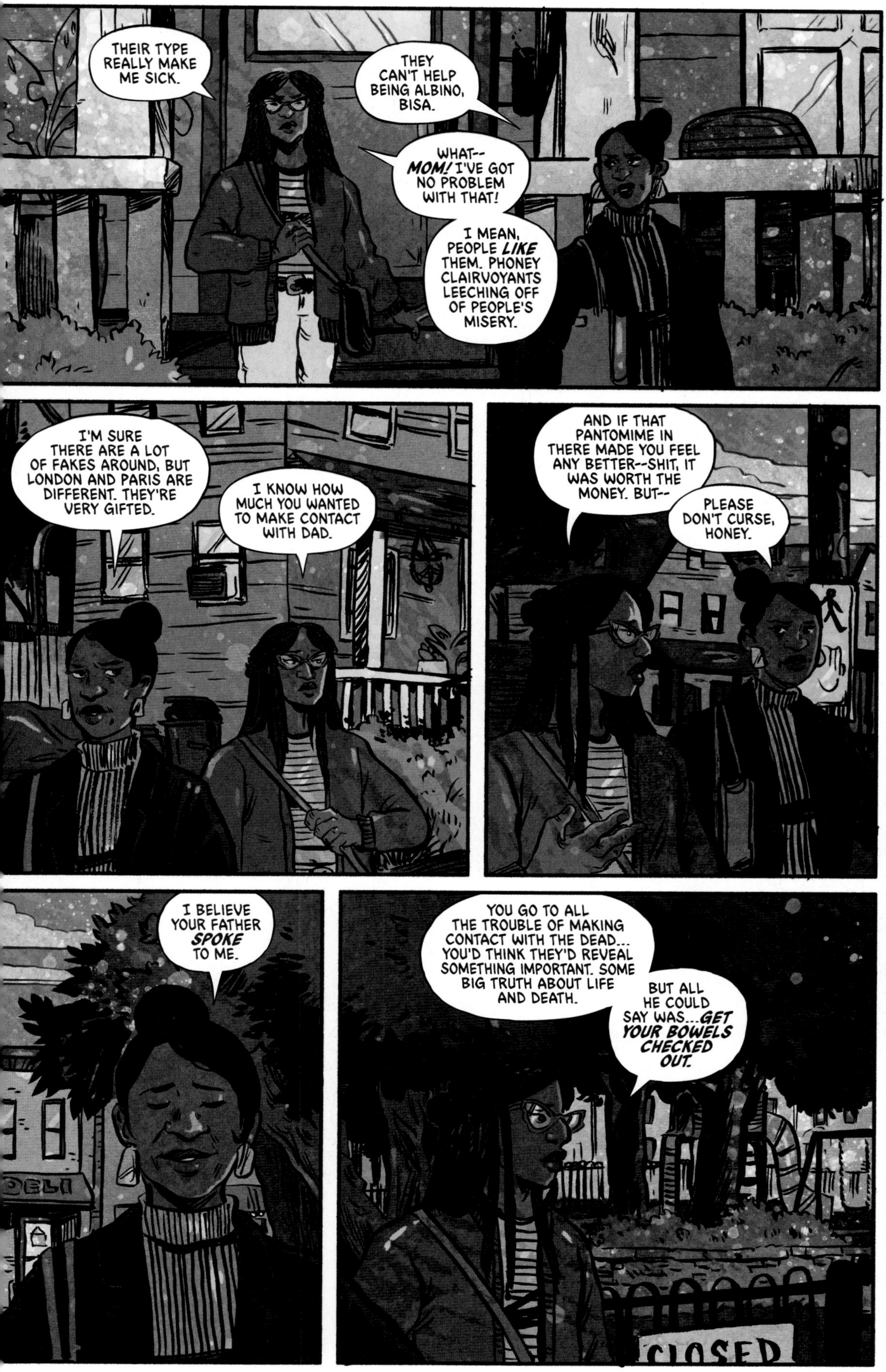
THEIR TYPE REALLY MAKE ME SICK.
THEY CAN'T HELP BEING ALBINO, BISA.
WHAT-- MOM! I'VE GOT NO PROBLEM WITH THAT!
I MEAN, PEOPLE LIKE THEM. PHONEY CLAIRVOYANTS LEECHING OFF OF PEOPLE'S MISERY.
I'M SURE THERE ARE A LOT OF FAKES AROUND, BUT LONDON AND PARIS ARE DIFFERENT. THEY'RE VERY GIFTED.
I KNOW HOW MUCH YOU WANTED TO MAKE CONTACT WITH DAD.
AND IF THAT PANTOMIME IN THERE MADE YOU FEEL ANY BETTER--SHIT, IT WAS WORTH THE MONEY. BUT--
PLEASE DON'T CURSE, HONEY.
I BELIEVE YOUR FATHER SPOKE TO ME.
DELI
YOU GO TO ALL THE TROUBLE OF MAKING CONTACT WITH THE DEAD... YOU'D THINK THEY'D REVEAL SOMETHING IMPORTANT. SOME BIG TRUTH ABOUT LIFE AND DEATH.
BUT ALL HE COULD SAY WAS... GET YOUR BOWELS CHECKED OUT.
CLOSED

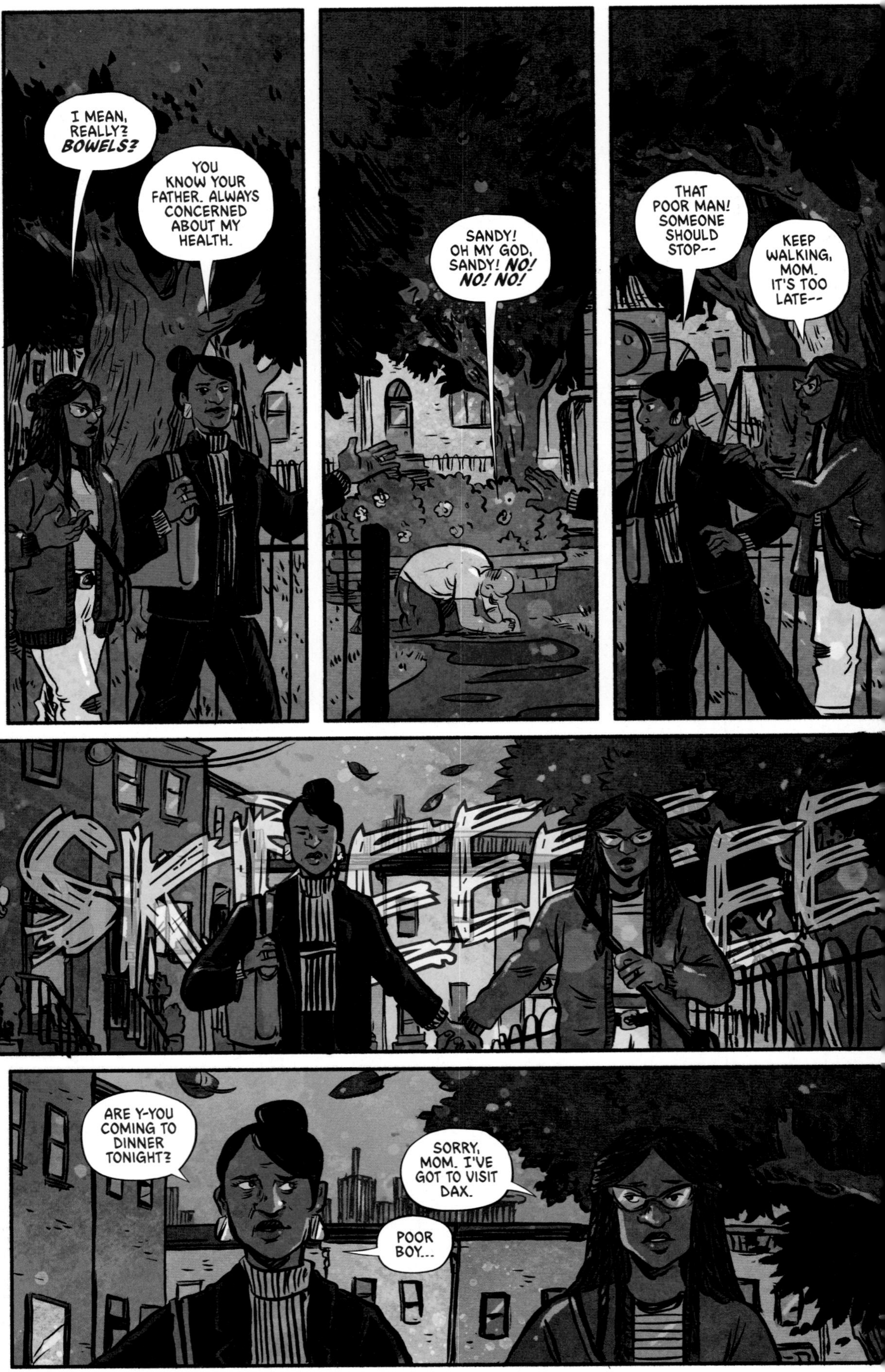
I MEAN, REALLY? ***BOWELS?***
YOU KNOW YOUR FATHER. ALWAYS CONCERNED ABOUT MY HEALTH.
SANDY! OH MY GOD, SANDY! ***NO! NO! NO!***
THAT POOR MAN! SOMEONE SHOULD STOP--
KEEP WALKING, MOM. IT'S TOO LATE--
ARE Y-YOU COMING TO DINNER TONIGHT?
SORRY, MOM. I'VE GOT TO VISIT DAX.
POOR BOY...

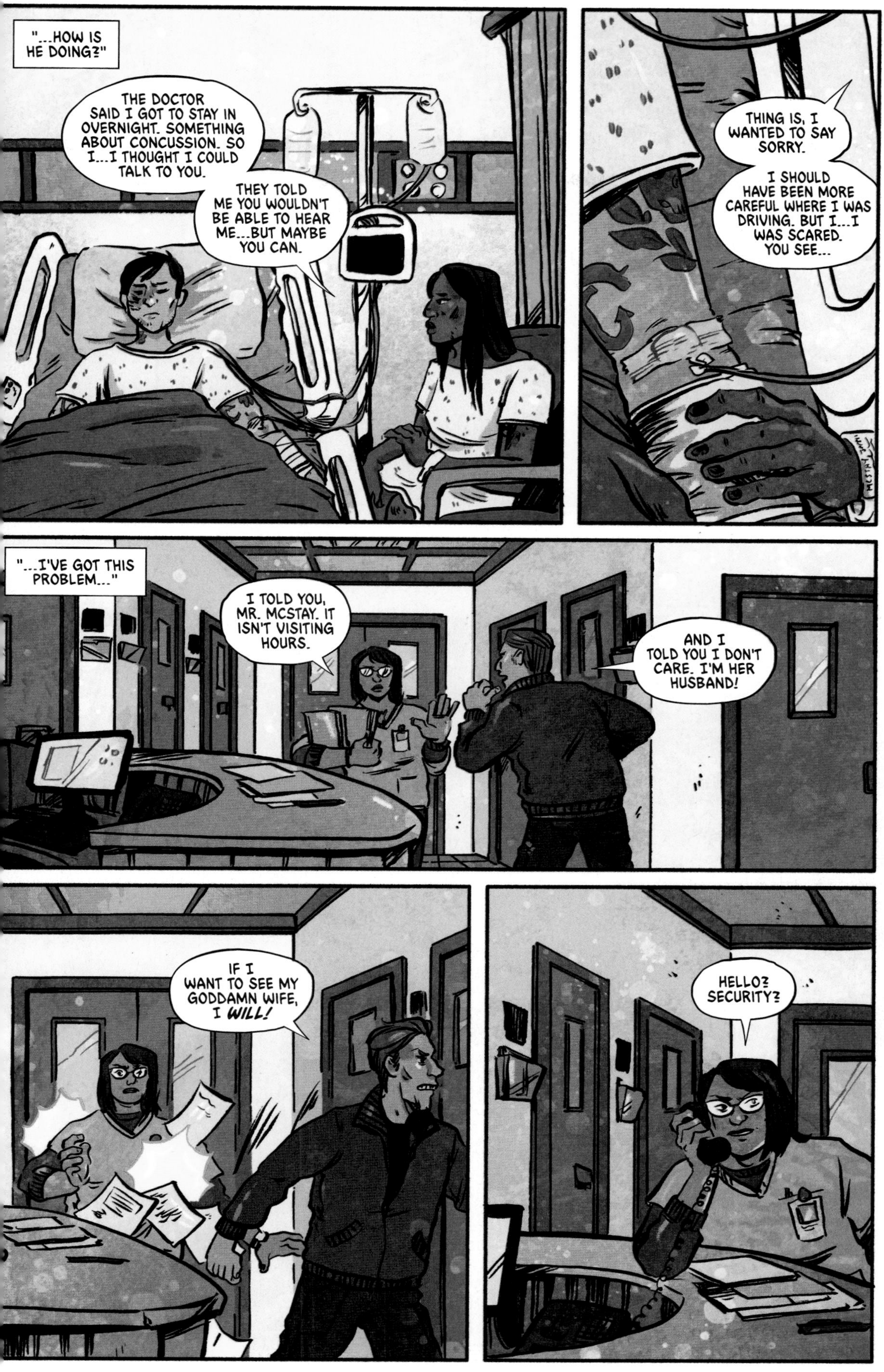
"...HOW IS HE DOING?"
THE DOCTOR SAID I GOT TO STAY IN OVERNIGHT. SOMETHING ABOUT CONCUSSION. SO I...I THOUGHT I COULD TALK TO YOU.
THEY TOLD ME YOU WOULDN'T BE ABLE TO HEAR ME...BUT MAYBE YOU CAN.
THING IS, I WANTED TO SAY SORRY.
I SHOULD HAVE BEEN MORE CAREFUL WHERE I WAS DRIVING. BUT I...I WAS SCARED. YOU SEE...
"...I'VE GOT THIS PROBLEM..."
I TOLD YOU, MR. MCSTAY. IT ISN'T VISITING HOURS.
AND I TOLD YOU I DON'T CARE. I'M HER HUSBAND!
IF I WANT TO SEE MY GODDAMN WIFE, I *WILL!*
HELLO? SECURITY?

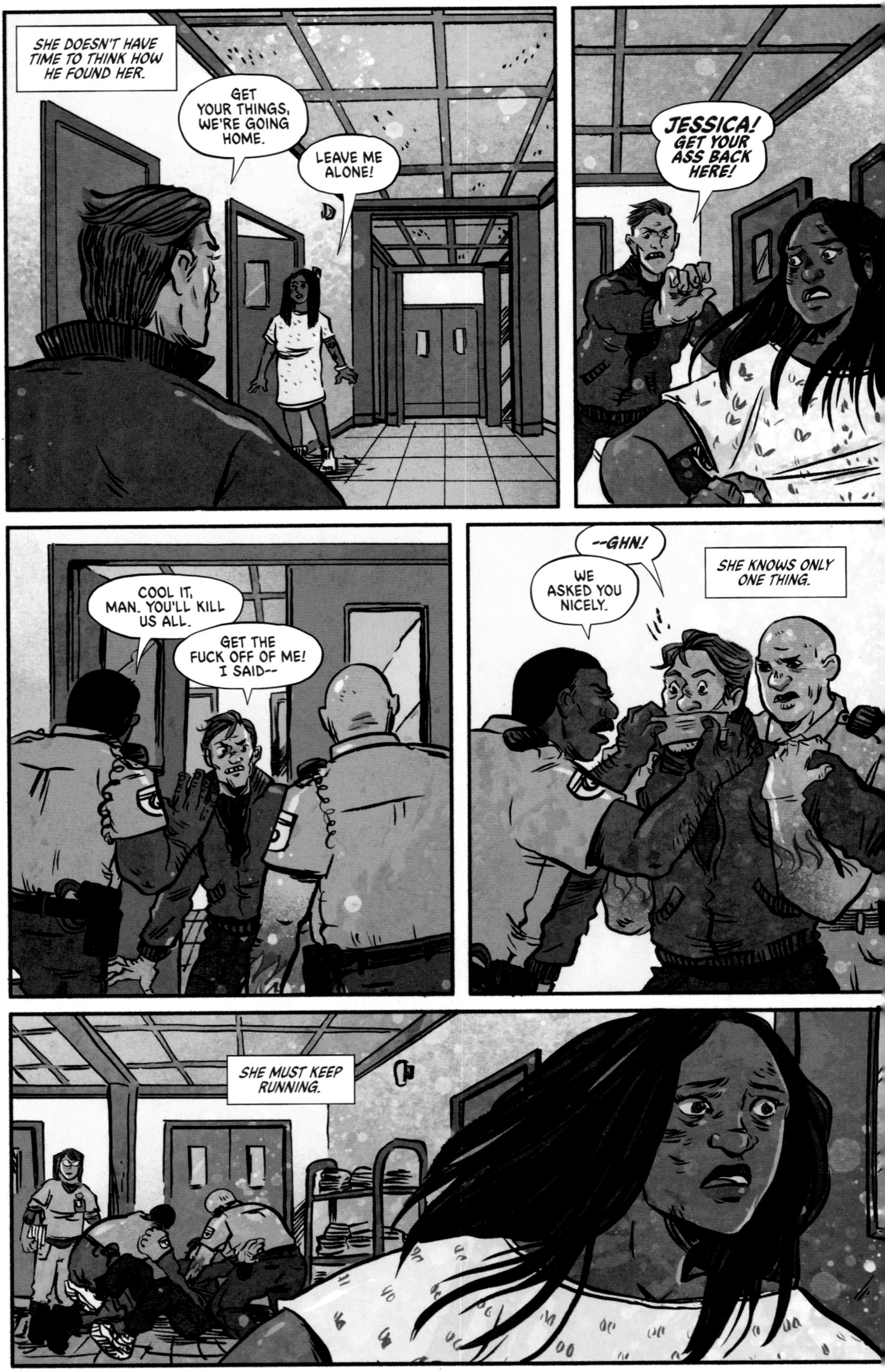
SHE DOESN'T HAVE TIME TO THINK HOW HE FOUND HER.
GET YOUR THINGS, WE'RE GOING HOME.
LEAVE ME ALONE!
JESSICA! GET YOUR ASS BACK HERE!
COOL IT, MAN. YOU'LL KILL US ALL.
GET THE FUCK OFF OF ME! I SAID--
--GHN!
WE ASKED YOU NICELY.
SHE KNOWS ONLY ONE THING.
SHE MUST KEEP RUNNING.

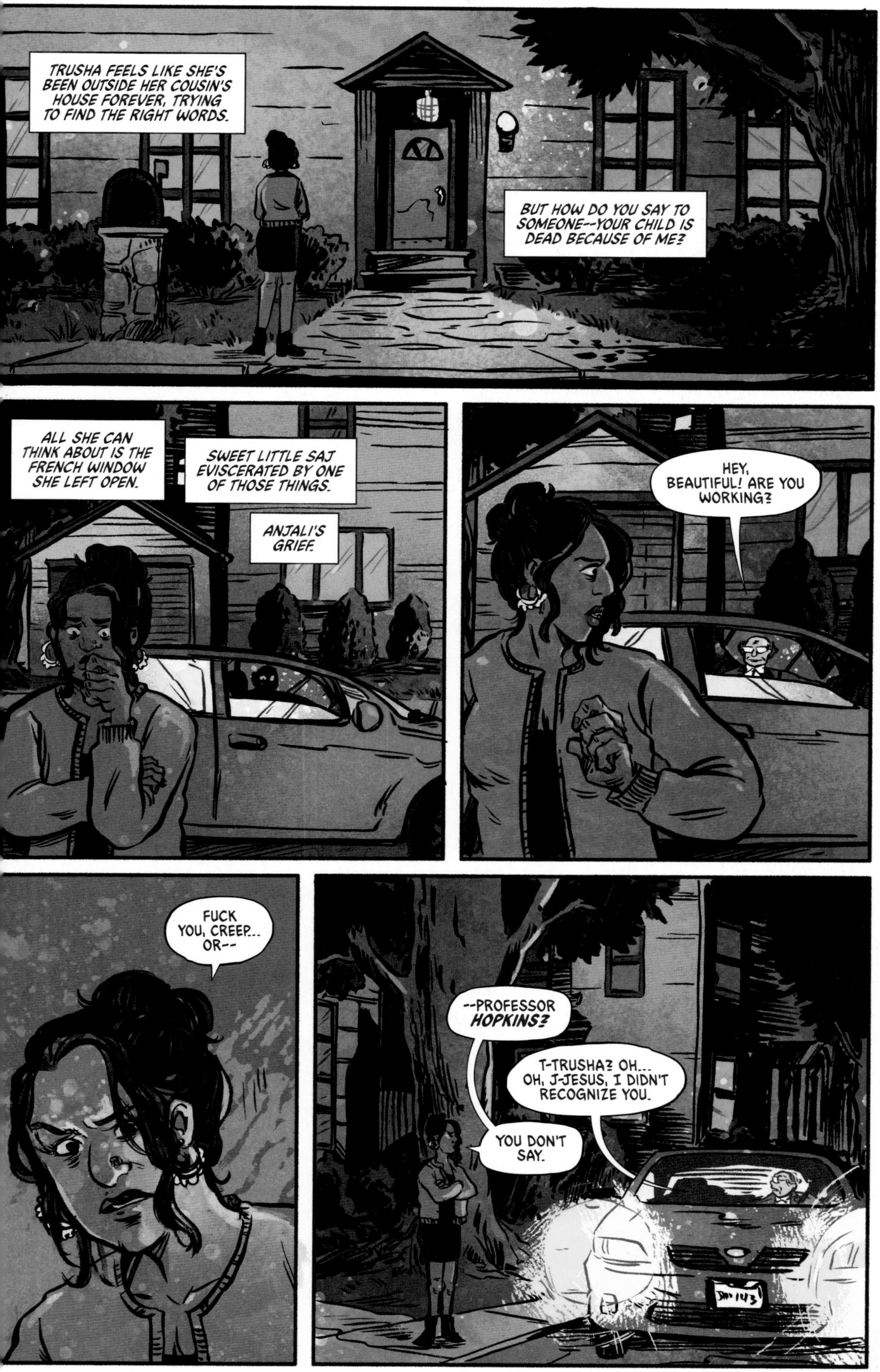
TRUSHA FEELS LIKE SHE'S BEEN OUTSIDE HER COUSIN'S HOUSE FOREVER, TRYING TO FIND THE RIGHT WORDS.
BUT HOW DO YOU SAY TO SOMEONE--YOUR CHILD IS DEAD BECAUSE OF ME?
ALL SHE CAN THINK ABOUT IS THE FRENCH WINDOW SHE LEFT OPEN.
SWEET LITTLE SAJ EVISCERATED BY ONE OF THOSE THINGS.
ANJALI'S GRIEF.
HEY, BEAUTIFUL! ARE YOU WORKING?
FUCK YOU, CREEP... OR--
--PROFESSOR HOPKINS?
T-TRUSHA? OH... OH, J-JESUS, I DIDN'T RECOGNIZE YOU.
YOU DON'T SAY.

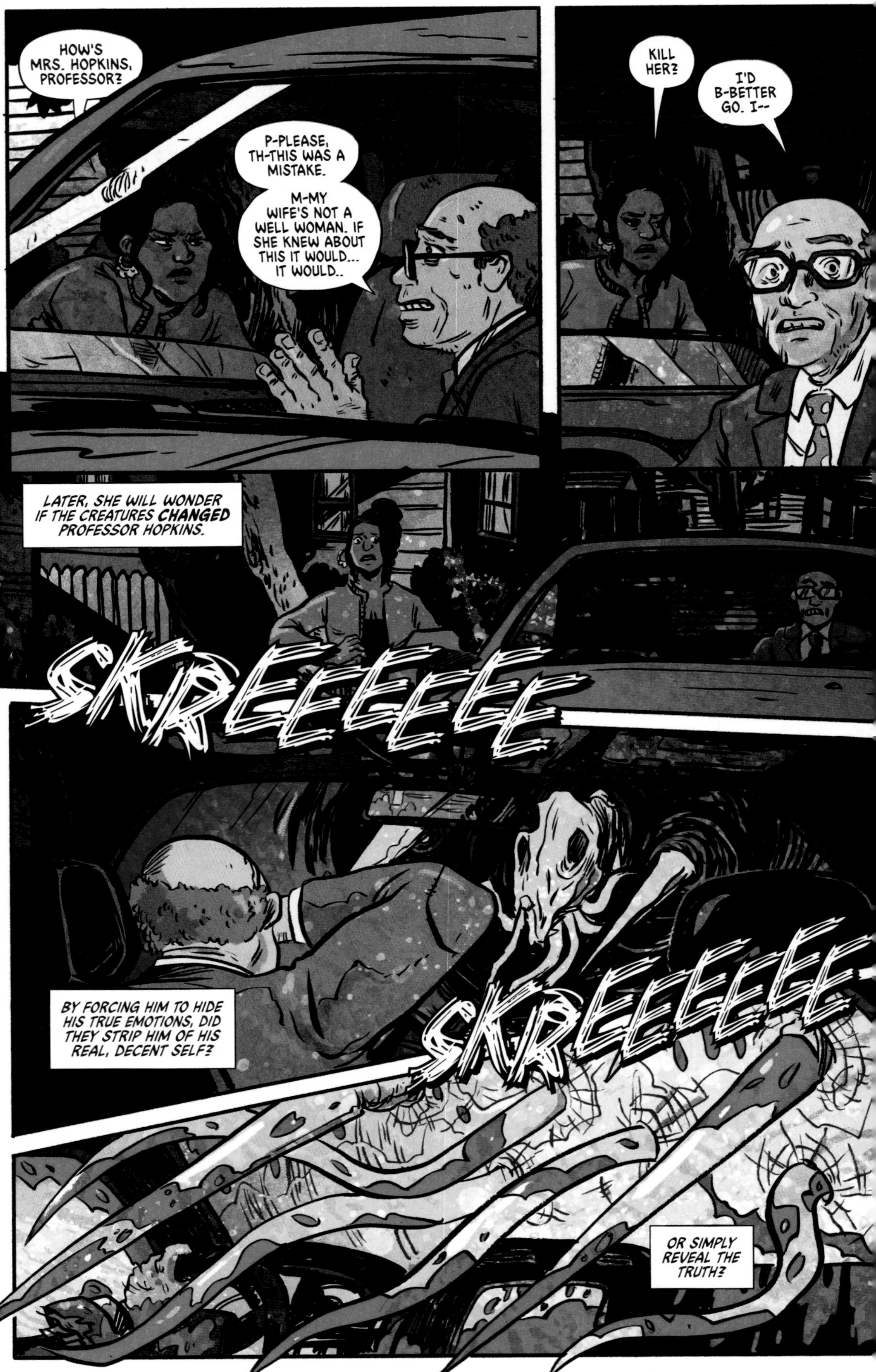
HOW'S MRS. HOPKINS, PROFESSOR?
P-PLEASE, TH-THIS WAS A MISTAKE.
M-MY WIFE'S NOT A WELL WOMAN. IF SHE KNEW ABOUT THIS IT WOULD... IT WOULD..
KILL HER?
I'D B-BETTER GO. I--
LATER, SHE WILL WONDER IF THE CREATURES CHANGED PROFESSOR HOPKINS.
SKREEEEEE
BY FORCING HIM TO HIDE HIS TRUE EMOTIONS, DID THEY STRIP HIM OF HIS REAL, DECENT SELF?
SKREEEEEE
OR SIMPLY REVEAL THE TRUTH?

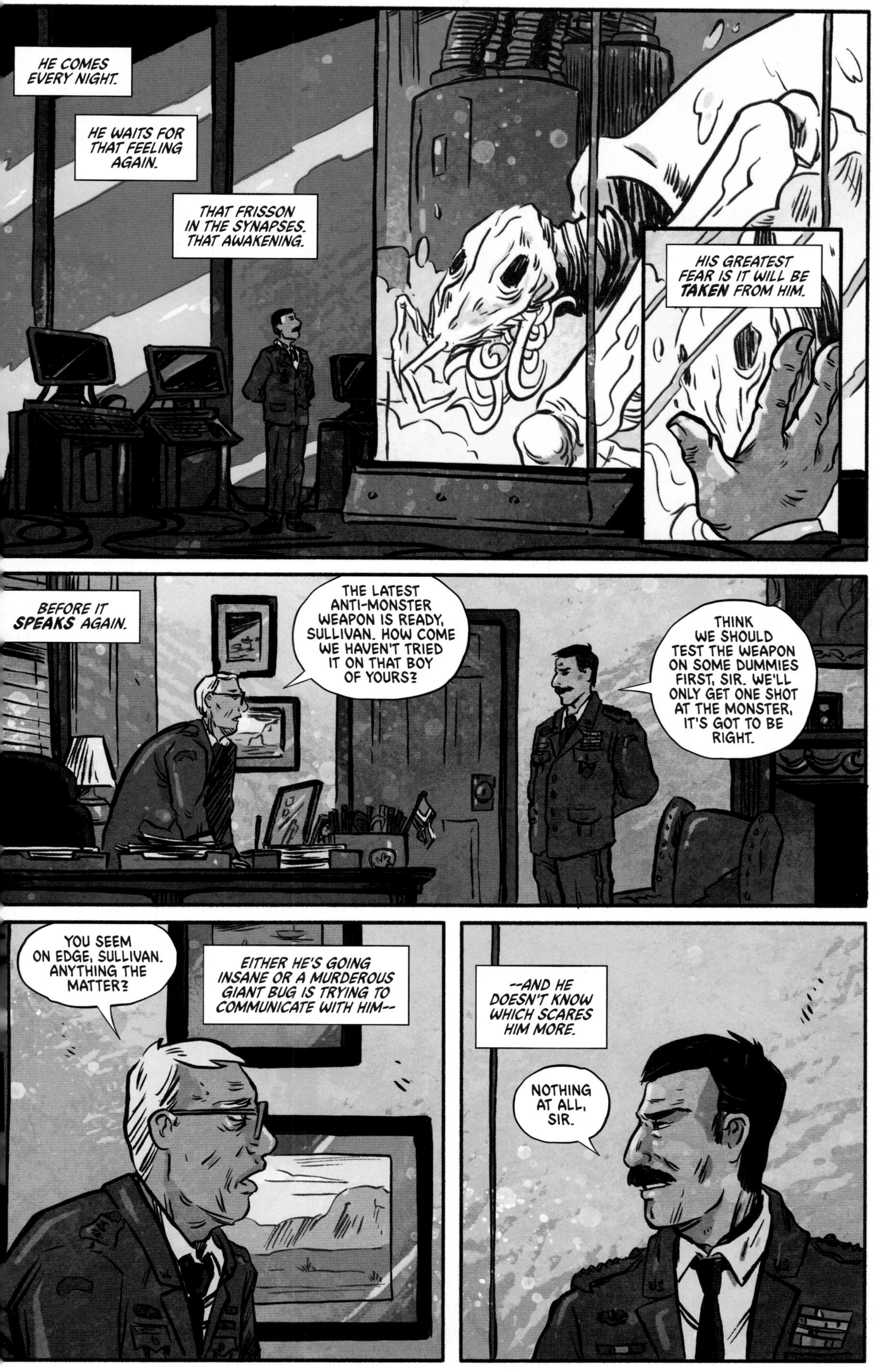
HE COMES EVERY NIGHT.
HE WAITS FOR THAT FEELING AGAIN.
THAT FRISSON IN THE SYNAPSES. THAT AWAKENING.
HIS GREATEST FEAR IS IT WILL BE TAKEN FROM HIM.
BEFORE IT SPEAKS AGAIN.
THE LATEST ANTI-MONSTER WEAPON IS READY, SULLIVAN. HOW COME WE HAVEN'T TRIED IT ON THAT BOY OF YOURS?
THINK WE SHOULD TEST THE WEAPON ON SOME DUMMIES FIRST, SIR. WE'LL ONLY GET ONE SHOT AT THE MONSTER, IT'S GOT TO BE RIGHT.
YOU SEEM ON EDGE, SULLIVAN. ANYTHING THE MATTER?
EITHER HE'S GOING INSANE OR A MURDEROUS GIANT BUG IS TRYING TO COMMUNICATE WITH HIM--
--AND HE DOESN'T KNOW WHICH SCARES HIM MORE.
NOTHING AT ALL, SIR.

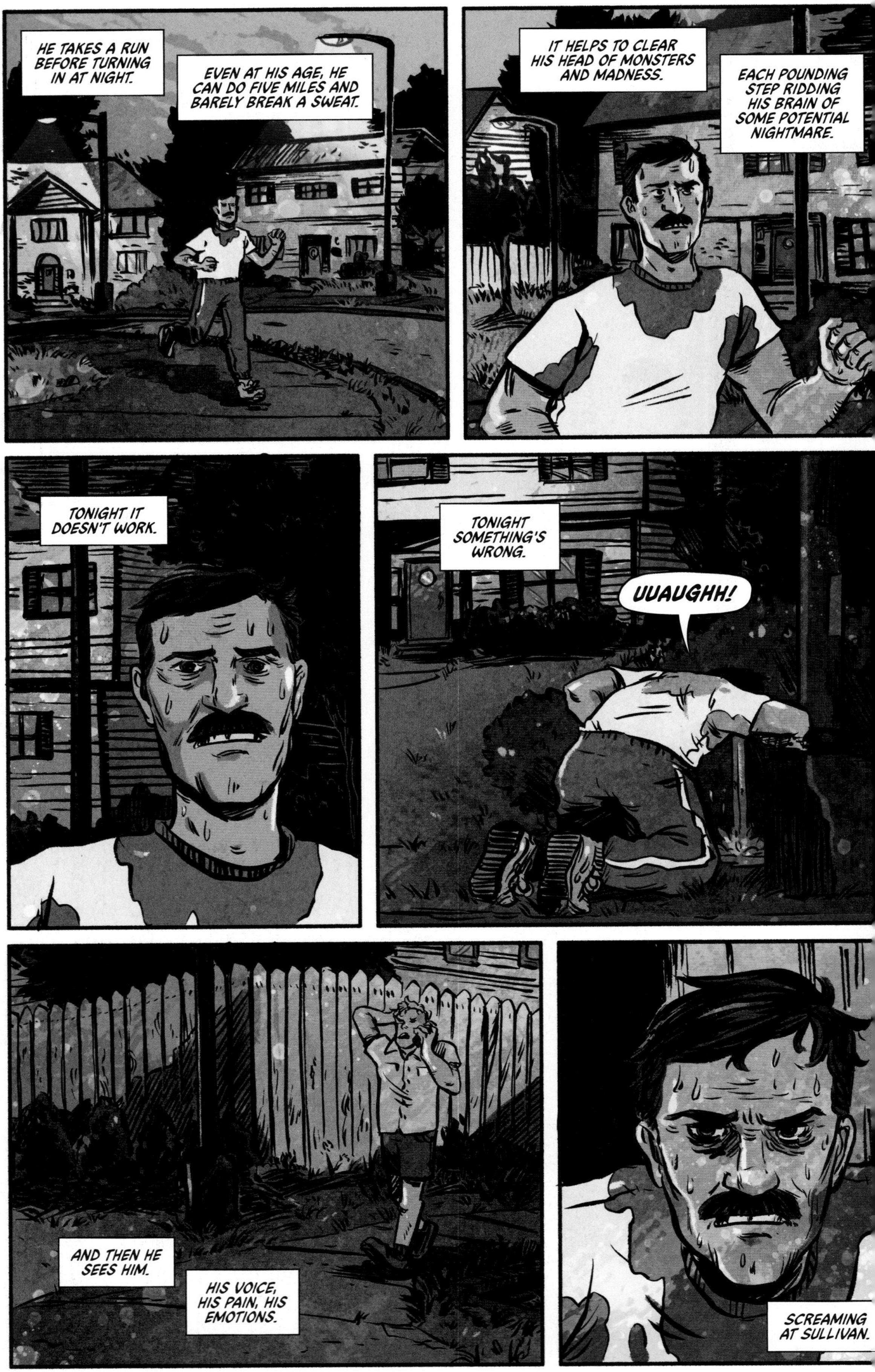
HE TAKES A RUN BEFORE TURNING IN AT NIGHT.
EVEN AT HIS AGE, HE CAN DO FIVE MILES AND BARELY BREAK A SWEAT.
IT HELPS TO CLEAR HIS HEAD OF MONSTERS AND MADNESS.
EACH POUNDING STEP RIDDING HIS BRAIN OF SOME POTENTIAL NIGHTMARE.
TONIGHT IT DOESN'T WORK.
TONIGHT SOMETHING'S WRONG.
UUAUGHH!
AND THEN HE SEES HIM.
HIS VOICE, HIS PAIN, HIS EMOTIONS.
SCREAMING AT SULLIVAN.

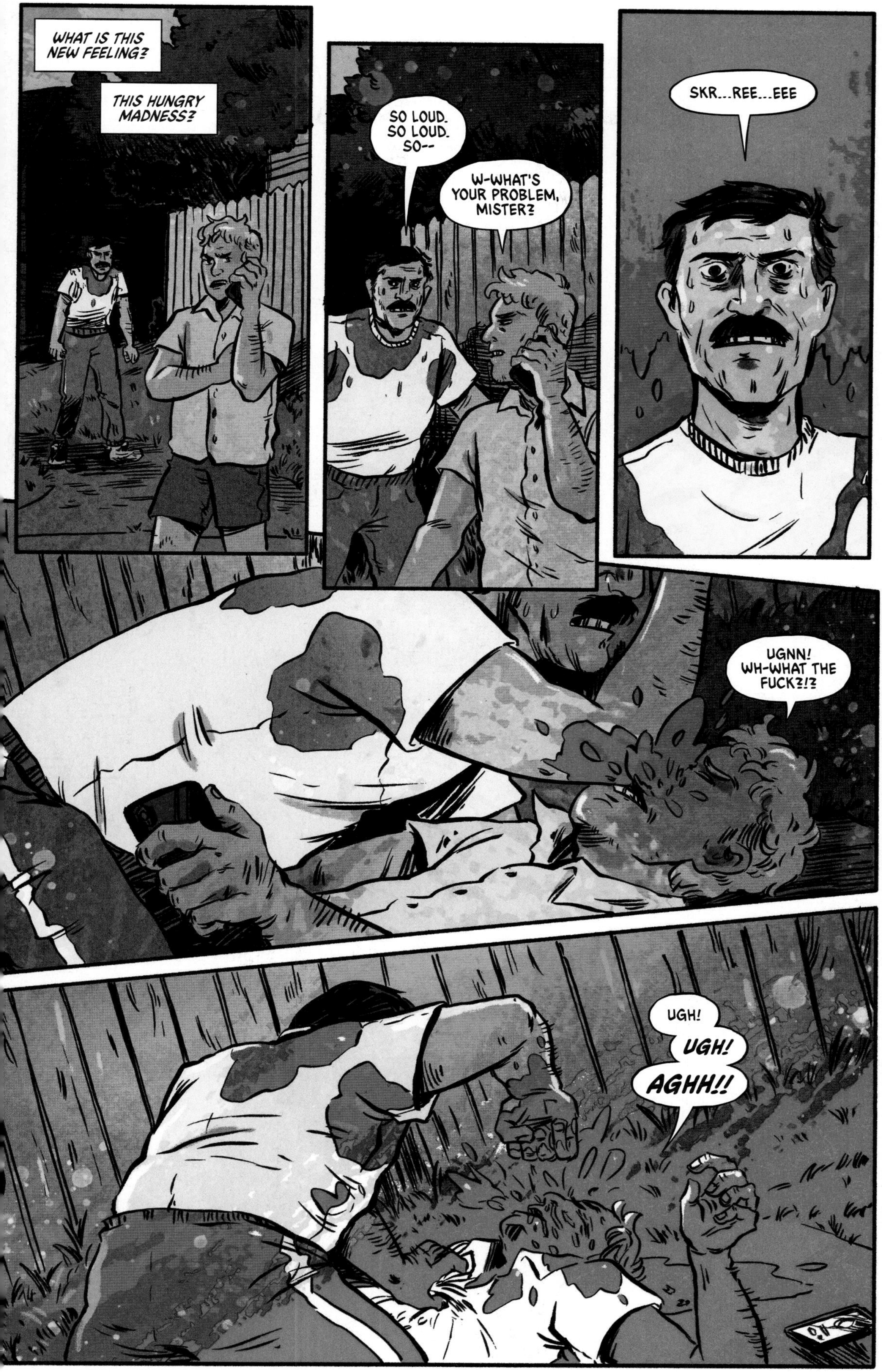
WHAT IS THIS NEW FEELING?
THIS HUNGRY MADNESS?
SO LOUD. SO LOUD. SO--
W-WHAT'S YOUR PROBLEM, MISTER?
SKR...REE...EEE
UGNN! WH-WHAT THE FUCK?!?
UGH!
UGH!
AGHH!!

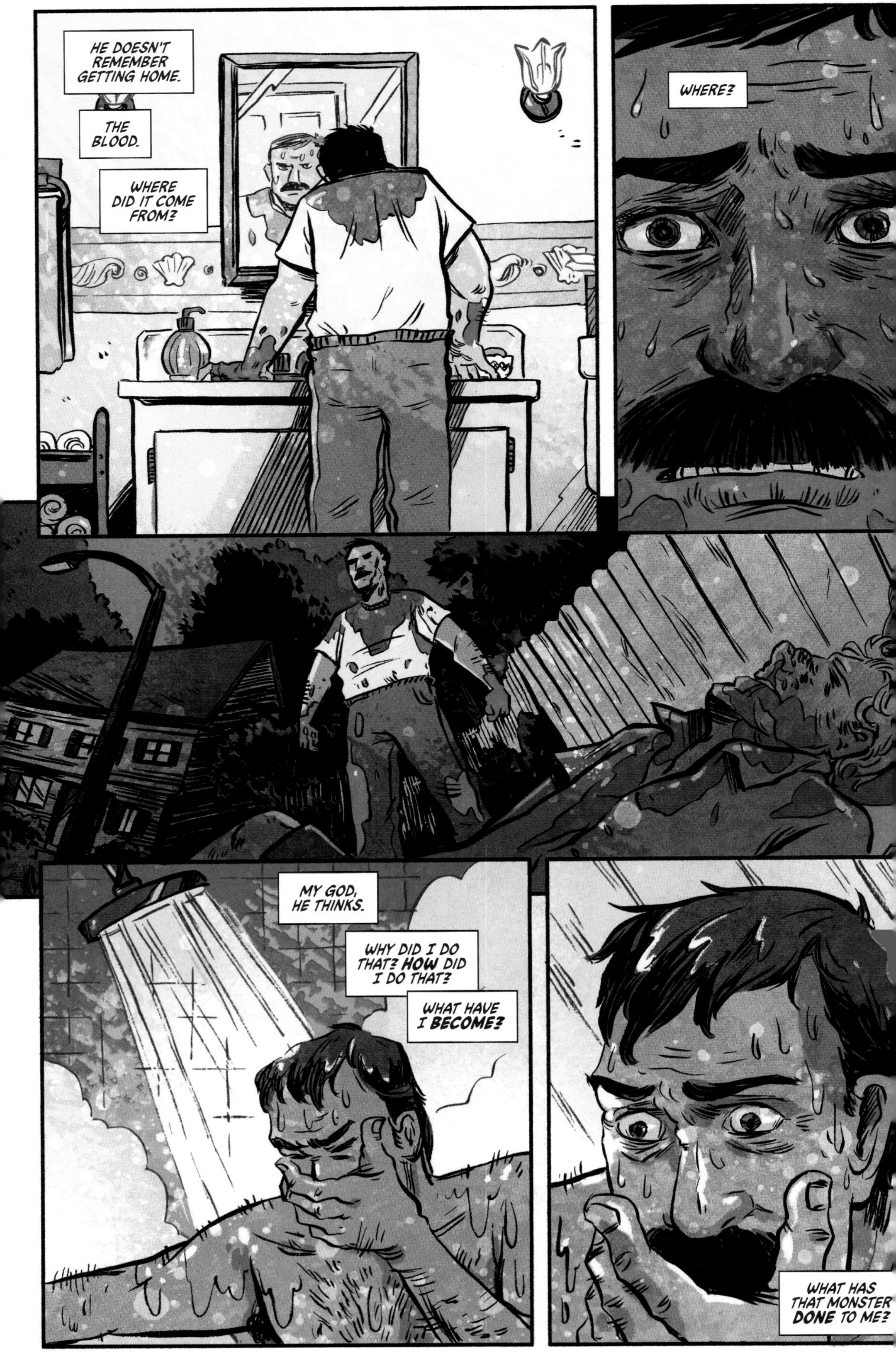
HE DOESN'T REMEMBER GETTING HOME.
THE BLOOD.
WHERE DID IT COME FROM?
WHERE?
MY GOD, HE THINKS.
WHY DID I DO THAT? **HOW** DID I DO THAT?
WHAT HAVE I **BECOME?**
WHAT HAS THAT MONSTER **DONE** TO ME?

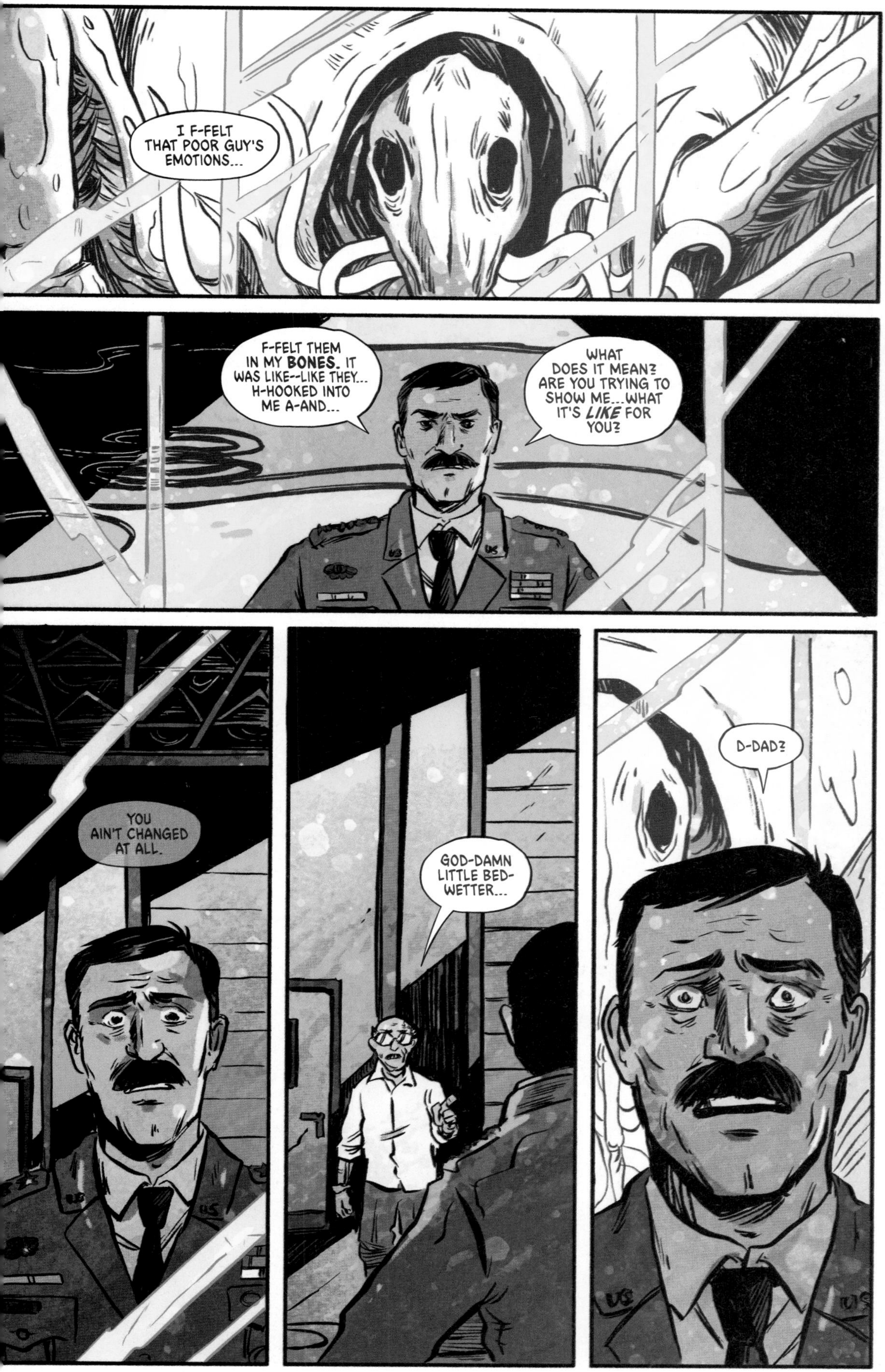
I F-FELT THAT POOR GUY'S EMOTIONS...
F-FELT THEM IN MY **BONES.** IT WAS LIKE--LIKE THEY... H-HOOKED INTO ME A-AND...
WHAT DOES IT MEAN? ARE YOU TRYING TO SHOW ME...WHAT IT'S *LIKE* FOR YOU?
YOU AIN'T CHANGED AT ALL.
GOD-DAMN LITTLE BED-WETTER...
D-DAD?

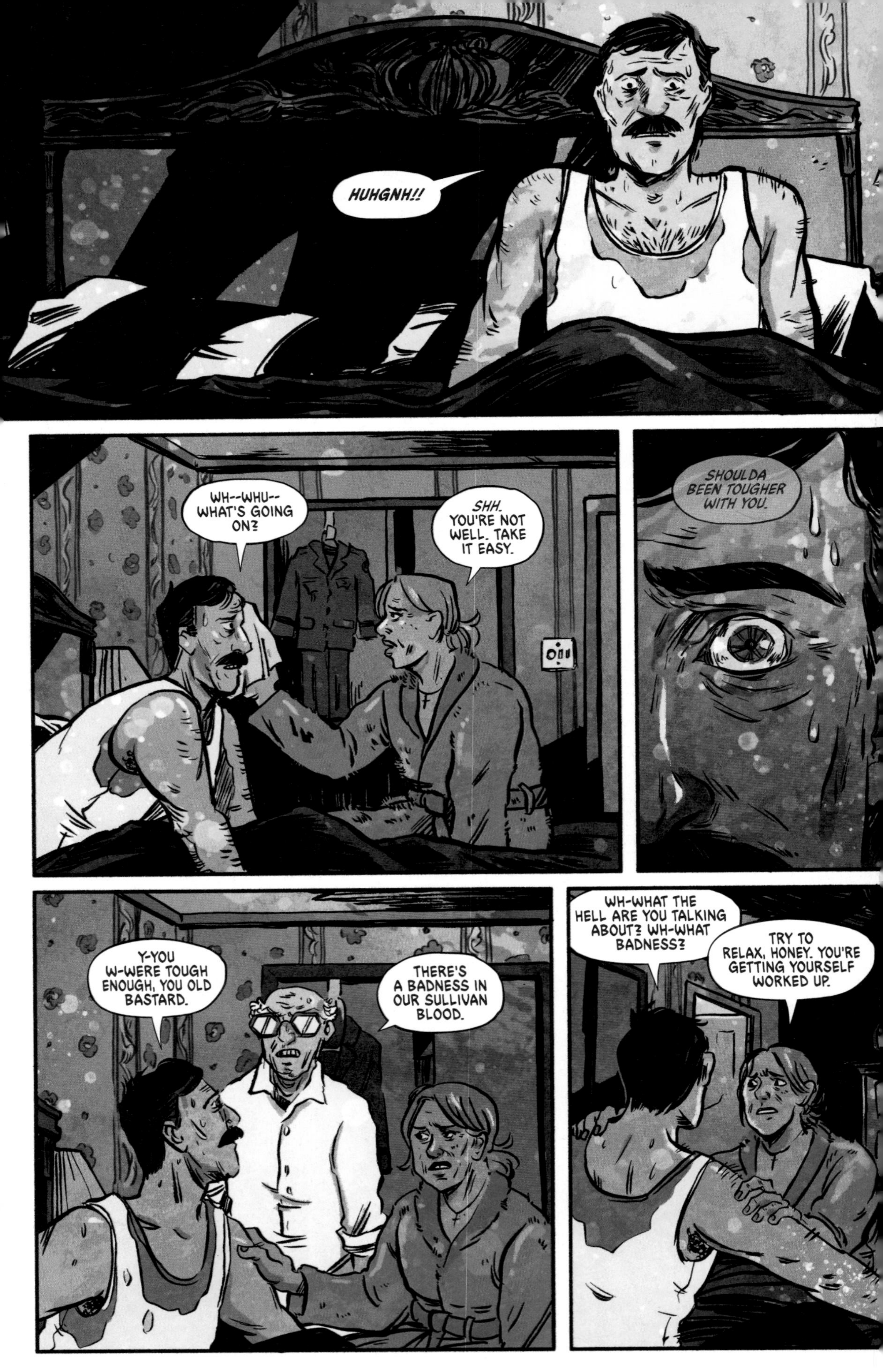
HUHGNH!!
WH--WHU-- WHAT'S GOING ON?
SHH. YOU'RE NOT WELL. TAKE IT EASY.
SHOULDA BEEN TOUGHER WITH YOU.
Y-YOU W-WERE TOUGH ENOUGH, YOU OLD BASTARD.
THERE'S A BADNESS IN OUR SULLIVAN BLOOD.
WH-WHAT THE HELL ARE YOU TALKING ABOUT? WH-WHAT BADNESS?
TRY TO RELAX, HONEY. YOU'RE GETTING YOURSELF WORKED UP.

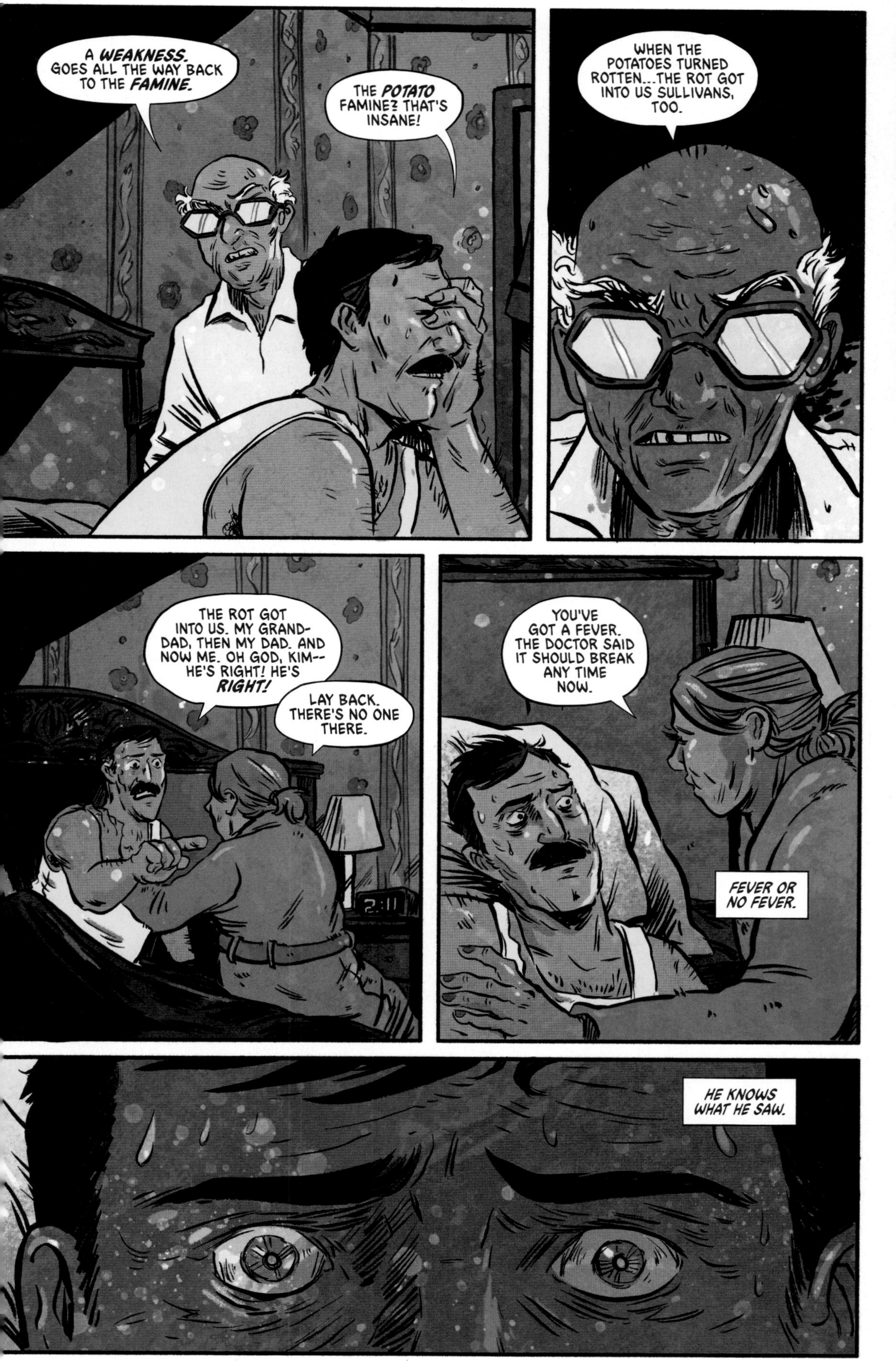
A WEAKNESS. GOES ALL THE WAY BACK TO THE FAMINE.
THE POTATO FAMINE? THAT'S INSANE!
WHEN THE POTATOES TURNED ROTTEN...THE ROT GOT INTO US SULLIVANS, TOO.
THE ROT GOT INTO US. MY GRAND-DAD, THEN MY DAD. AND NOW ME. OH GOD, KIM-- HE'S RIGHT! HE'S RIGHT!
LAY BACK. THERE'S NO ONE THERE.
2:11
YOU'VE GOT A FEVER. THE DOCTOR SAID IT SHOULD BREAK ANY TIME NOW.
FEVER OR NO FEVER.
HE KNOWS WHAT HE SAW.

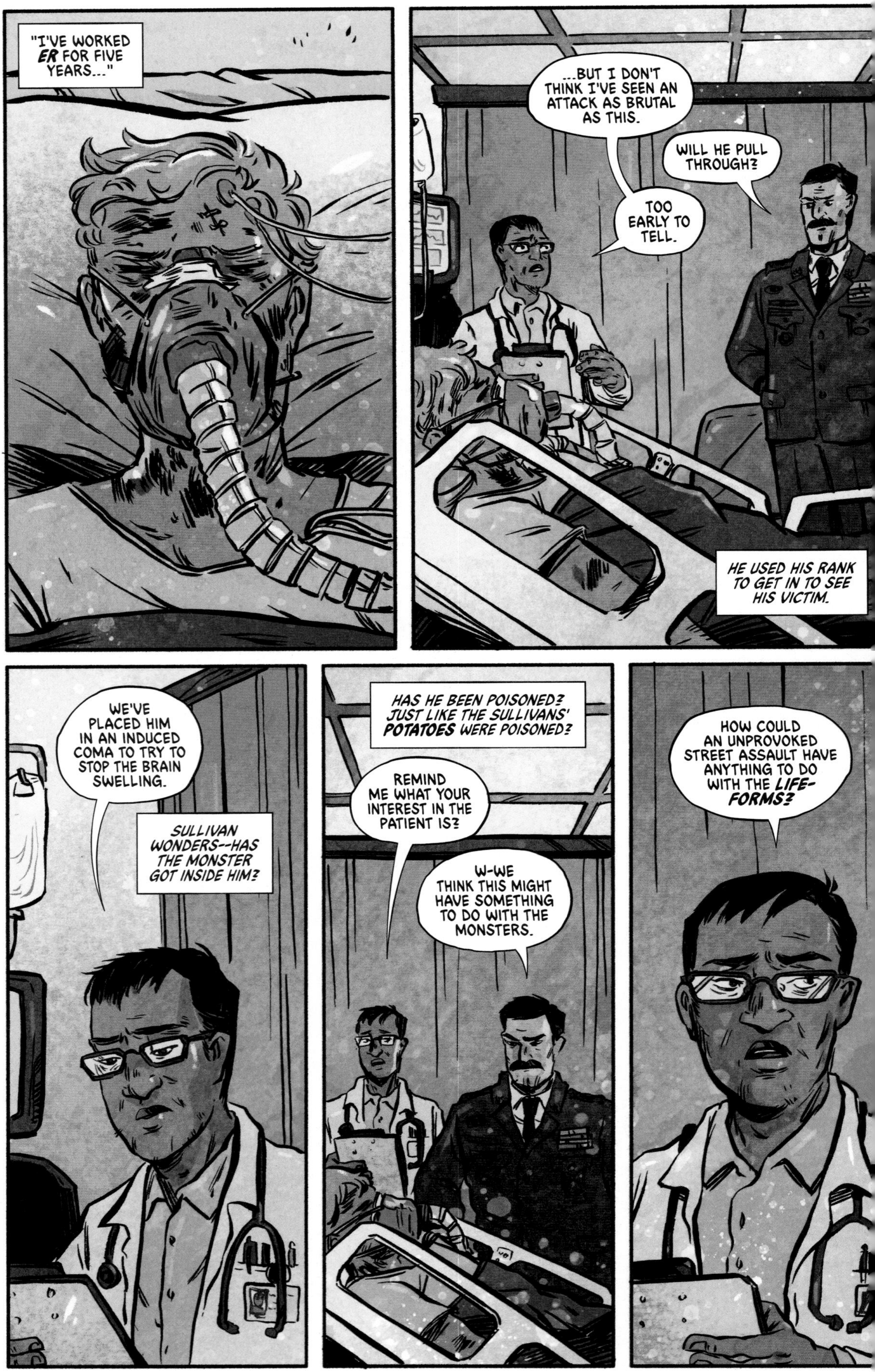
"I'VE WORKED ER FOR FIVE YEARS..."
...BUT I DON'T THINK I'VE SEEN AN ATTACK AS BRUTAL AS THIS.
WILL HE PULL THROUGH?
TOO EARLY TO TELL.
HE USED HIS RANK TO GET IN TO SEE HIS VICTIM.
WE'VE PLACED HIM IN AN INDUCED COMA TO TRY TO STOP THE BRAIN SWELLING.
SULLIVAN WONDERS--HAS THE MONSTER GOT INSIDE HIM?
HAS HE BEEN POISONED? JUST LIKE THE SULLIVANS' POTATOES WERE POISONED?
REMIND ME WHAT YOUR INTEREST IN THE PATIENT IS?
W-WE THINK THIS MIGHT HAVE SOMETHING TO DO WITH THE MONSTERS.
HOW COULD AN UNPROVOKED STREET ASSAULT HAVE ANYTHING TO DO WITH THE LIFE-FORMS?

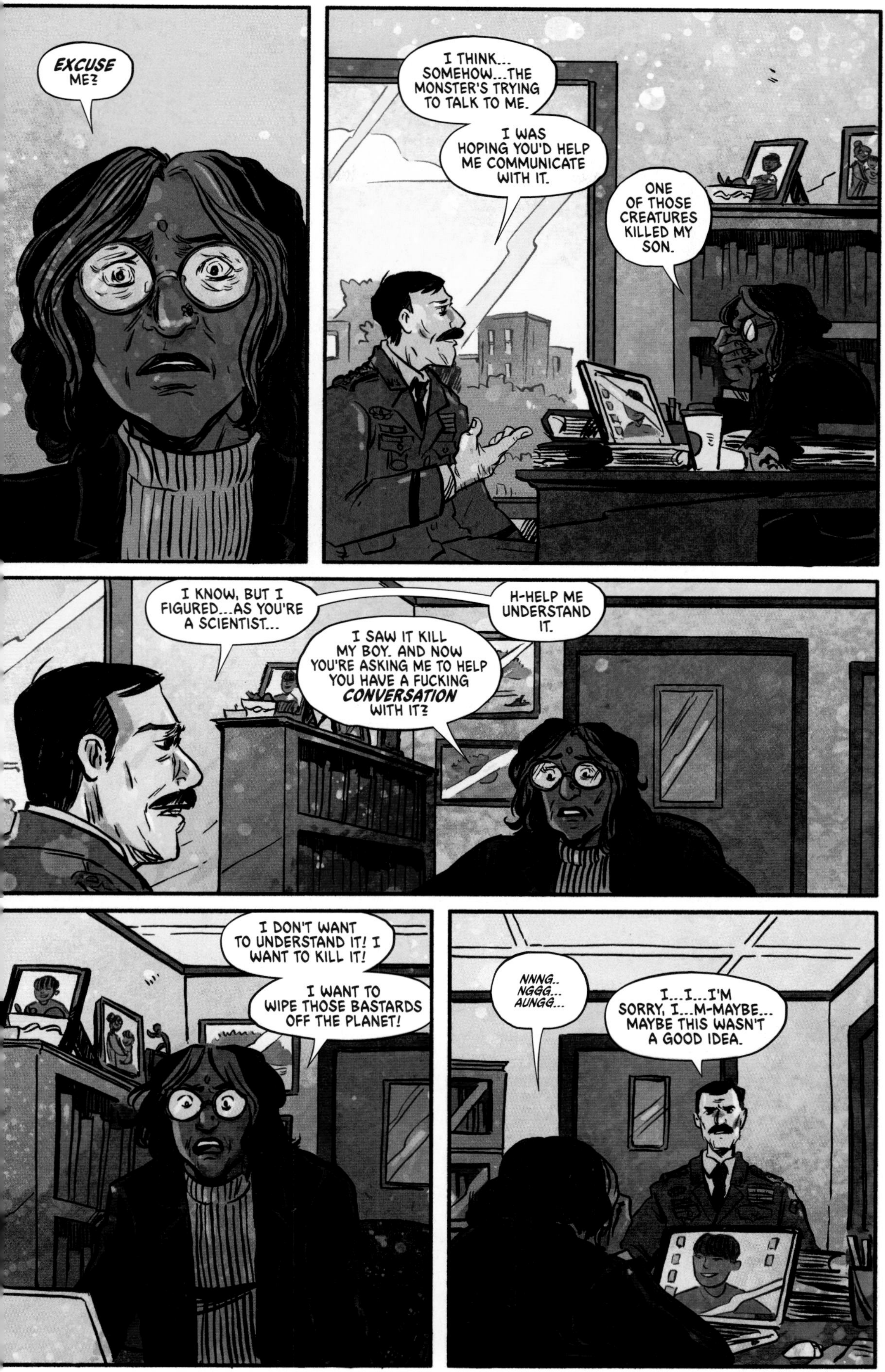
EXCUSE ME?
I THINK... SOMEHOW...THE MONSTER'S TRYING TO TALK TO ME.
I WAS HOPING YOU'D HELP ME COMMUNICATE WITH IT.
ONE OF THOSE CREATURES KILLED MY SON.
I KNOW, BUT I FIGURED...AS YOU'RE A SCIENTIST...
H-HELP ME UNDERSTAND IT.
I SAW IT KILL MY BOY. AND NOW YOU'RE ASKING ME TO HELP YOU HAVE A FUCKING CONVERSATION WITH IT?
I DON'T WANT TO UNDERSTAND IT! I WANT TO KILL IT!
I WANT TO WIPE THOSE BASTARDS OFF THE PLANET!
NNNG.. NGGG... AUNGG...
I...I...I'M SORRY, I...M-MAYBE... MAYBE THIS WASN'T A GOOD IDEA.

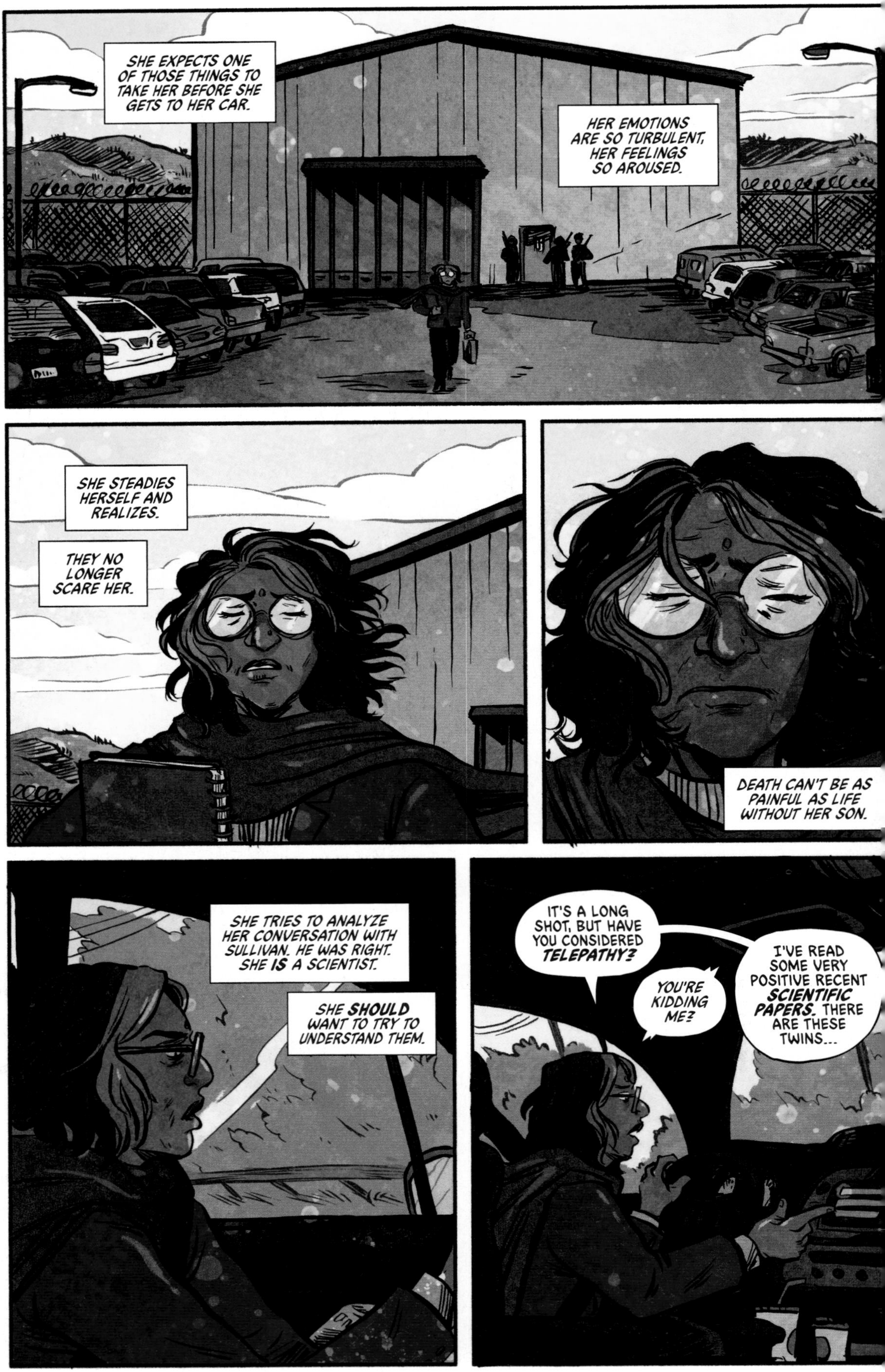
SHE EXPECTS ONE OF THOSE THINGS TO TAKE HER BEFORE SHE GETS TO HER CAR.
HER EMOTIONS ARE SO TURBULENT, HER FEELINGS SO AROUSED.
SHE STEADIES HERSELF AND REALIZES.
THEY NO LONGER SCARE HER.
DEATH CAN'T BE AS PAINFUL AS LIFE WITHOUT HER SON.
SHE TRIES TO ANALYZE HER CONVERSATION WITH SULLIVAN. HE WAS RIGHT. SHE IS A SCIENTIST.
SHE SHOULD WANT TO TRY TO UNDERSTAND THEM.
IT'S A LONG SHOT, BUT HAVE YOU CONSIDERED TELEPATHY?
YOU'RE KIDDING ME?
I'VE READ SOME VERY POSITIVE RECENT SCIENTIFIC PAPERS. THERE ARE THESE TWINS...

SHE WORKS SO LATE IT NUMBS HER BRAIN.

THE MILITARY GAVE THEM A SHAVING FROM THE CAPTURED MONSTER AND DNA RESULTS HAVE JUST COME BACK.

ONLY IT'S NOT DNA. MAYBE CLOSER TO RNA, HINTING THAT THE LIFE-FORMS PRE-DATE PRESENT LIFE ON EARTH-- OR DID NOT ORIGINATE ON EARTH.

ACTGG
ATTA c
XCA_A
G__A
XTXG
CCCA
TBAT
CC_T
_ATA
X_TT
X_TA
TAGA
CCA
XX_-

SPAM

start   9:27

IT'S LIKE A LONG-DEAD LANGUAGE, A CODEX IN NEED OF A *ROSETTA STONE*.

AS SHE RETURNS HOME, SHE SEES THE SHADOW.

SOME SCIENTISTS HAVE BEEN ATTACKED RECENTLY.

BUT SHE'S TOO WEARY TO CALL 911.

WHO IS THAT?

TRUSHA?

A-ANJALI, I...

I'VE GOT SOMETHING TO TELL YOU...

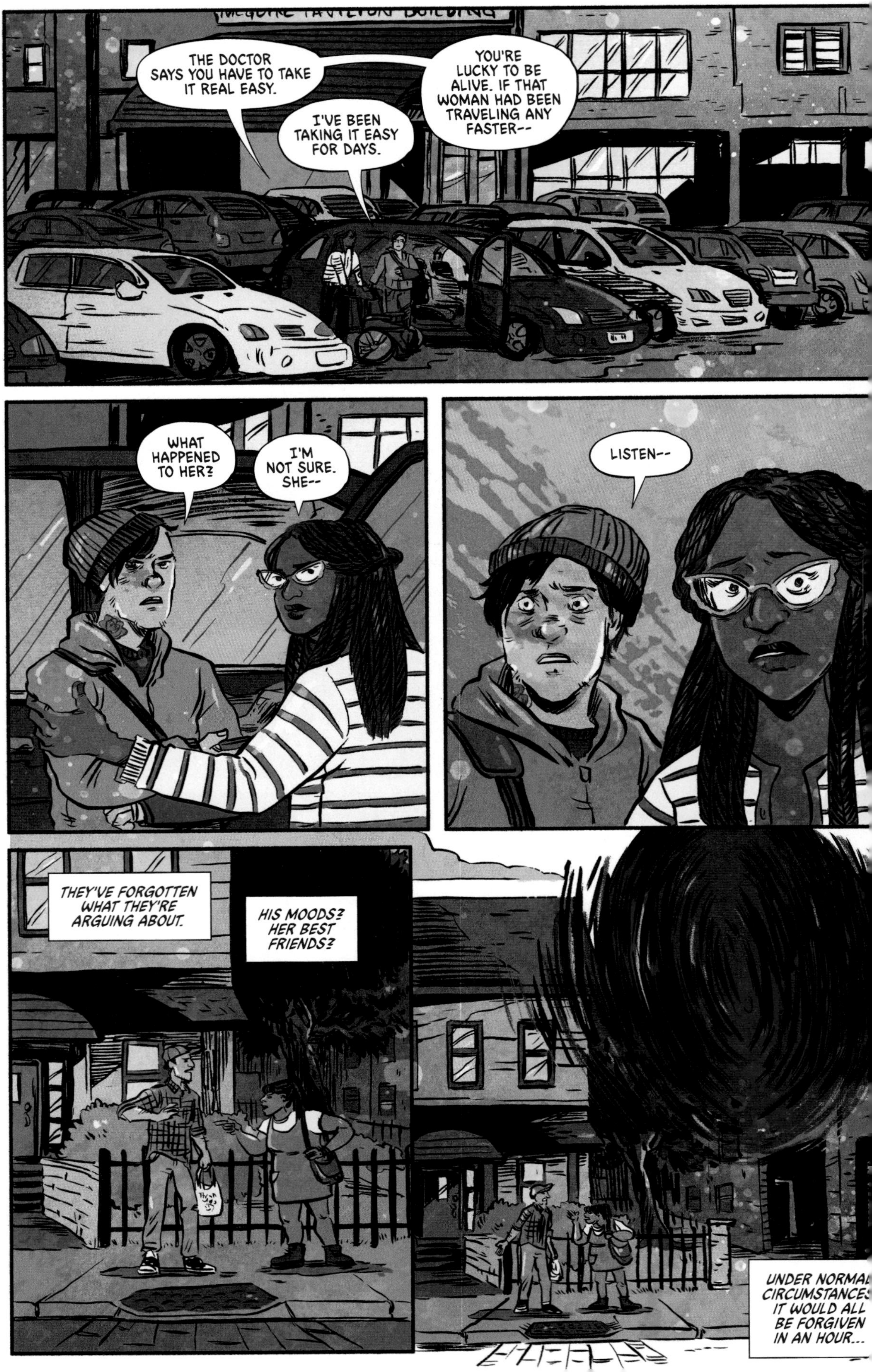
THE DOCTOR SAYS YOU HAVE TO TAKE IT REAL EASY.
I'VE BEEN TAKING IT EASY FOR DAYS.
YOU'RE LUCKY TO BE ALIVE. IF THAT WOMAN HAD BEEN TRAVELING ANY FASTER--
WHAT HAPPENED TO HER?
I'M NOT SURE. SHE--
LISTEN--
THEY'VE FORGOTTEN WHAT THEY'RE ARGUING ABOUT.
HIS MOODS? HER BEST FRIENDS?
UNDER NORMAL CIRCUMSTANCES IT WOULD ALL BE FORGIVEN IN AN HOUR...

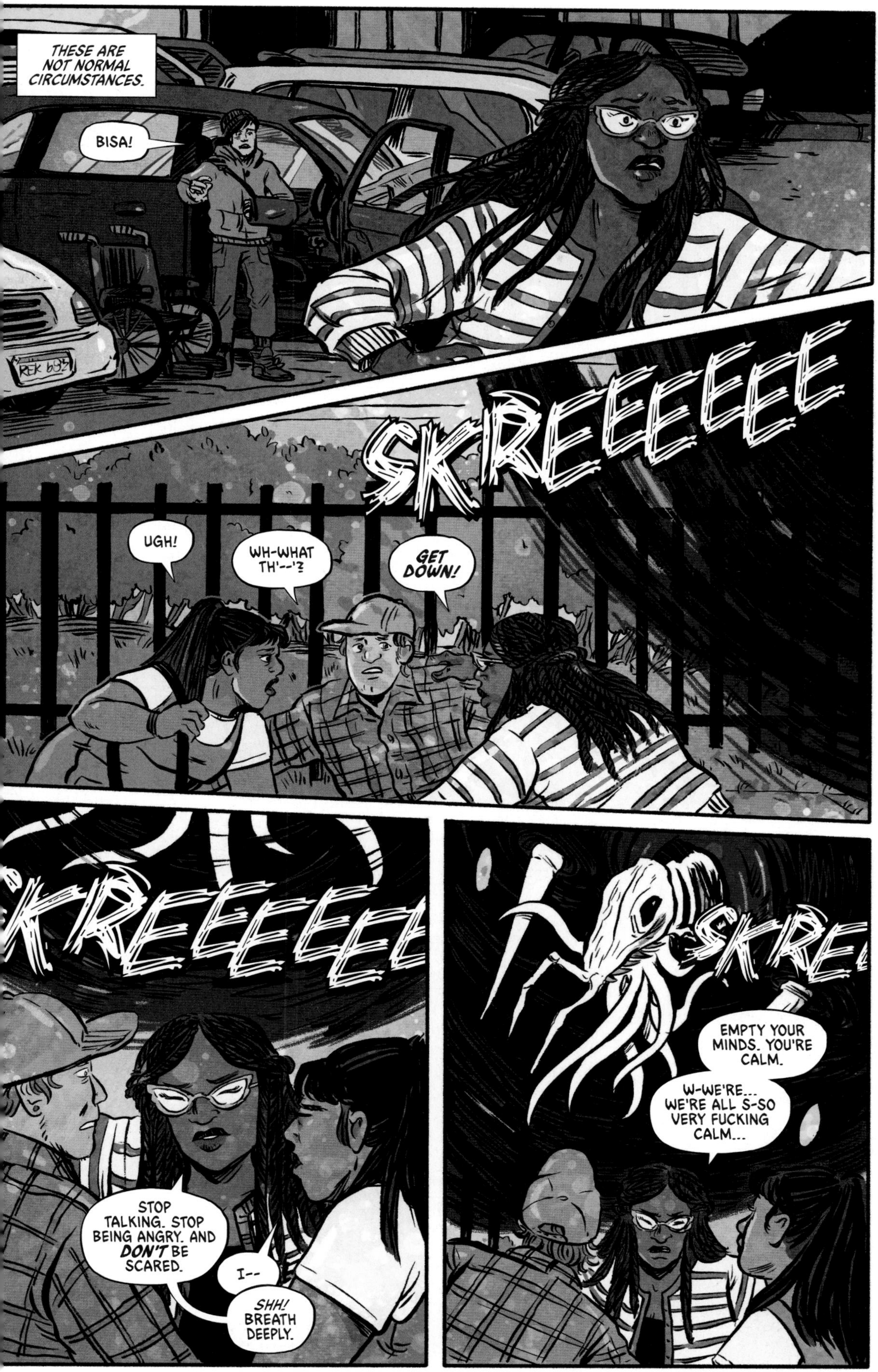

THESE ARE NOT NORMAL CIRCUMSTANCES.
BISA!
REK 685
SKREEEEEEE
UGH!
WH-WHAT TH'--'?
GET DOWN!
SKREEEEEEE
STOP TALKING. STOP BEING ANGRY. AND DON'T BE SCARED.
I--
SHH! BREATH DEEPLY.
SKRE
EMPTY YOUR MINDS. YOU'RE CALM.
W-WE'RE... WE'RE ALL S-SO VERY FUCKING CALM...

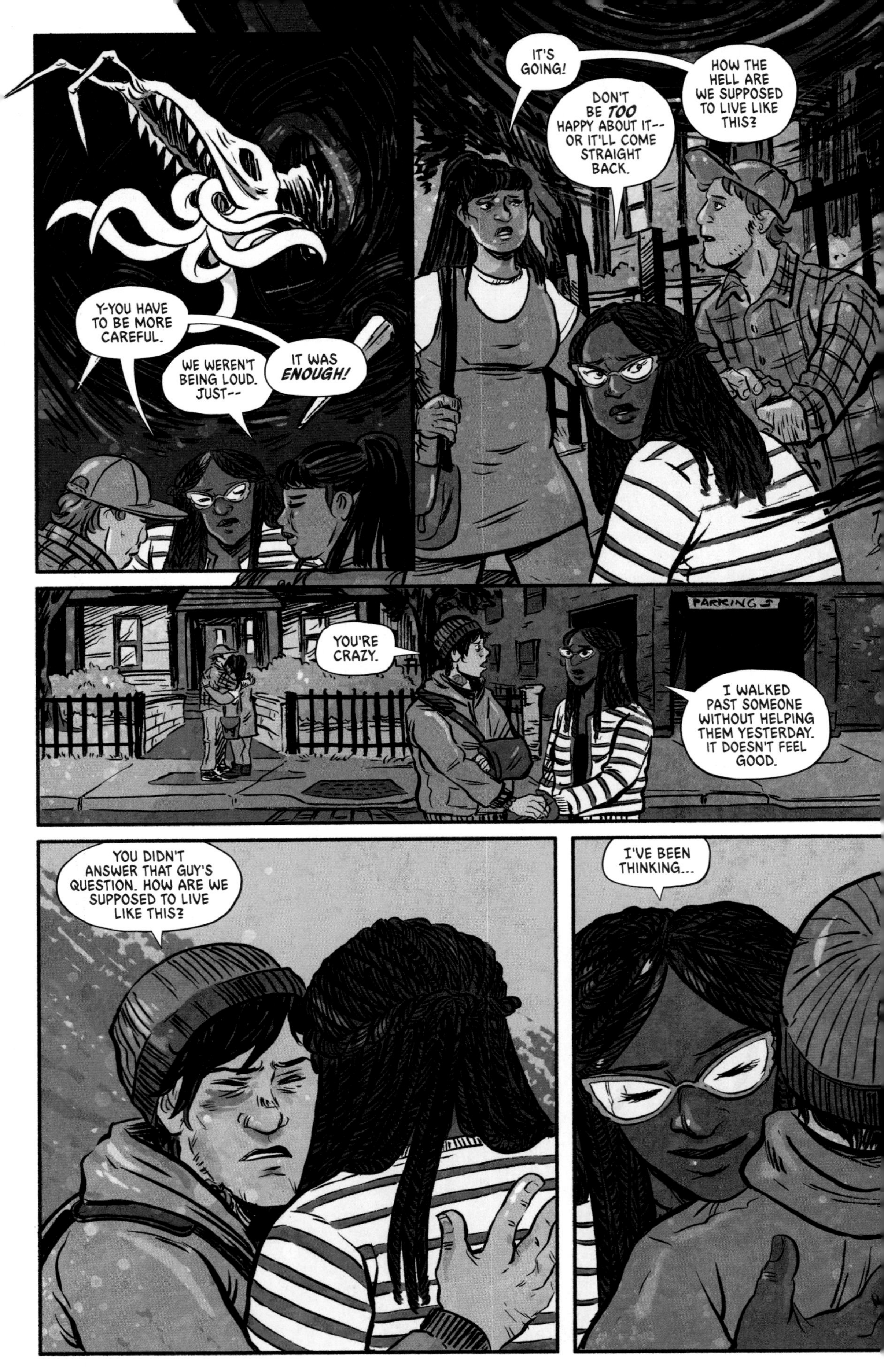
Y-YOU HAVE TO BE MORE CAREFUL.
WE WEREN'T BEING LOUD. JUST--
IT WAS *ENOUGH!*
IT'S GOING!
DON'T BE *TOO* HAPPY ABOUT IT-- OR IT'LL COME STRAIGHT BACK.
HOW THE HELL ARE WE SUPPOSED TO LIVE LIKE THIS?
PARKING
YOU'RE CRAZY.
I WALKED PAST SOMEONE WITHOUT HELPING THEM YESTERDAY. IT DOESN'T FEEL GOOD.
YOU DIDN'T ANSWER THAT GUY'S QUESTION. HOW ARE WE SUPPOSED TO LIVE LIKE THIS?
I'VE BEEN THINKING...

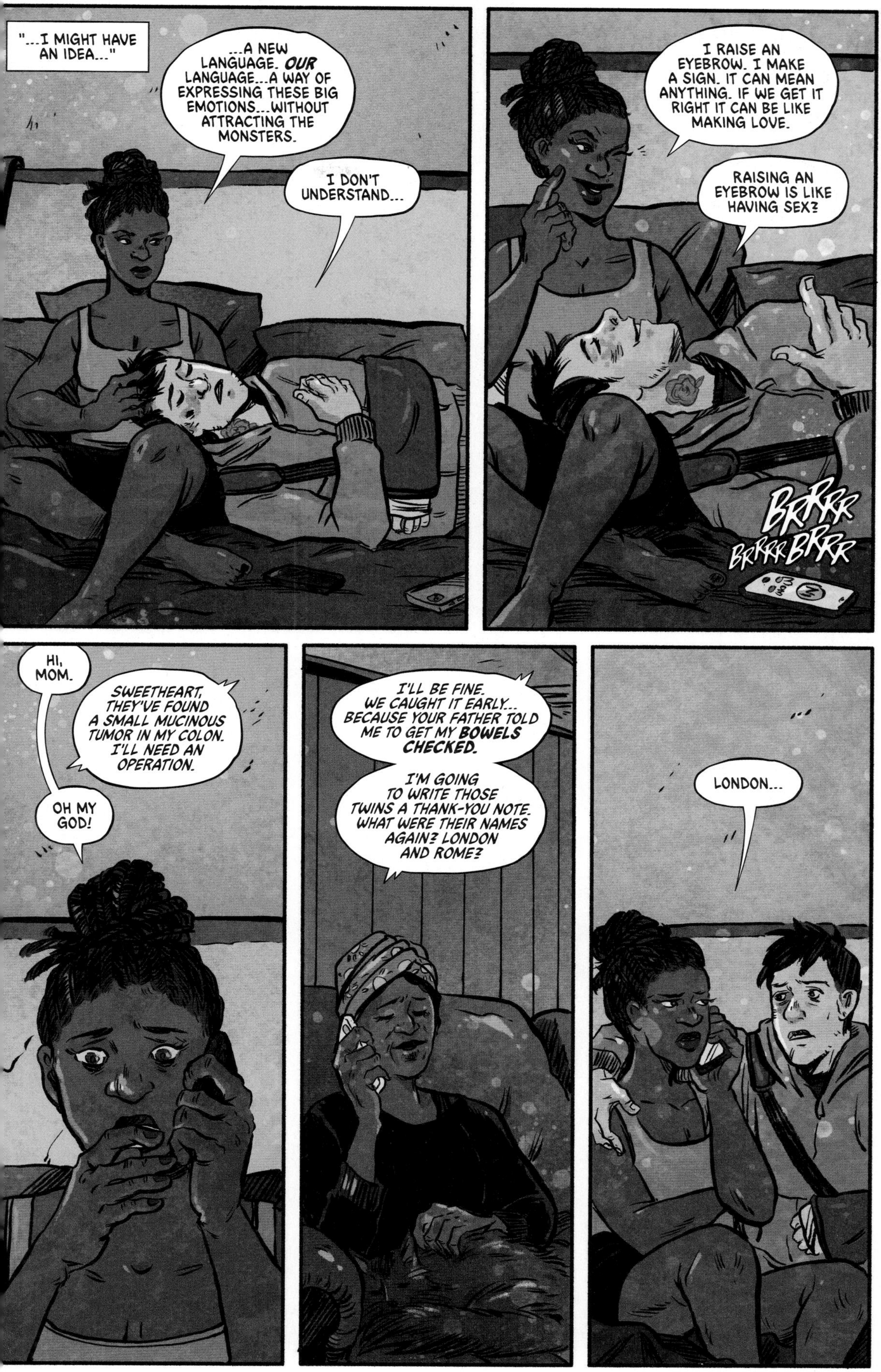
"...I MIGHT HAVE AN IDEA..."
...A NEW LANGUAGE. OUR LANGUAGE...A WAY OF EXPRESSING THESE BIG EMOTIONS...WITHOUT ATTRACTING THE MONSTERS.
I DON'T UNDERSTAND...
I RAISE AN EYEBROW. I MAKE A SIGN. IT CAN MEAN ANYTHING. IF WE GET IT RIGHT IT CAN BE LIKE MAKING LOVE.
RAISING AN EYEBROW IS LIKE HAVING SEX?
BRRRR BRRRR BRRRR
HI, MOM.
SWEETHEART, THEY'VE FOUND A SMALL MUCINOUS TUMOR IN MY COLON. I'LL NEED AN OPERATION.
OH MY GOD!
I'LL BE FINE. WE CAUGHT IT EARLY... BECAUSE YOUR FATHER TOLD ME TO GET MY BOWELS CHECKED.
I'M GOING TO WRITE THOSE TWINS A THANK-YOU NOTE. WHAT WERE THEIR NAMES AGAIN? LONDON AND ROME?
LONDON...

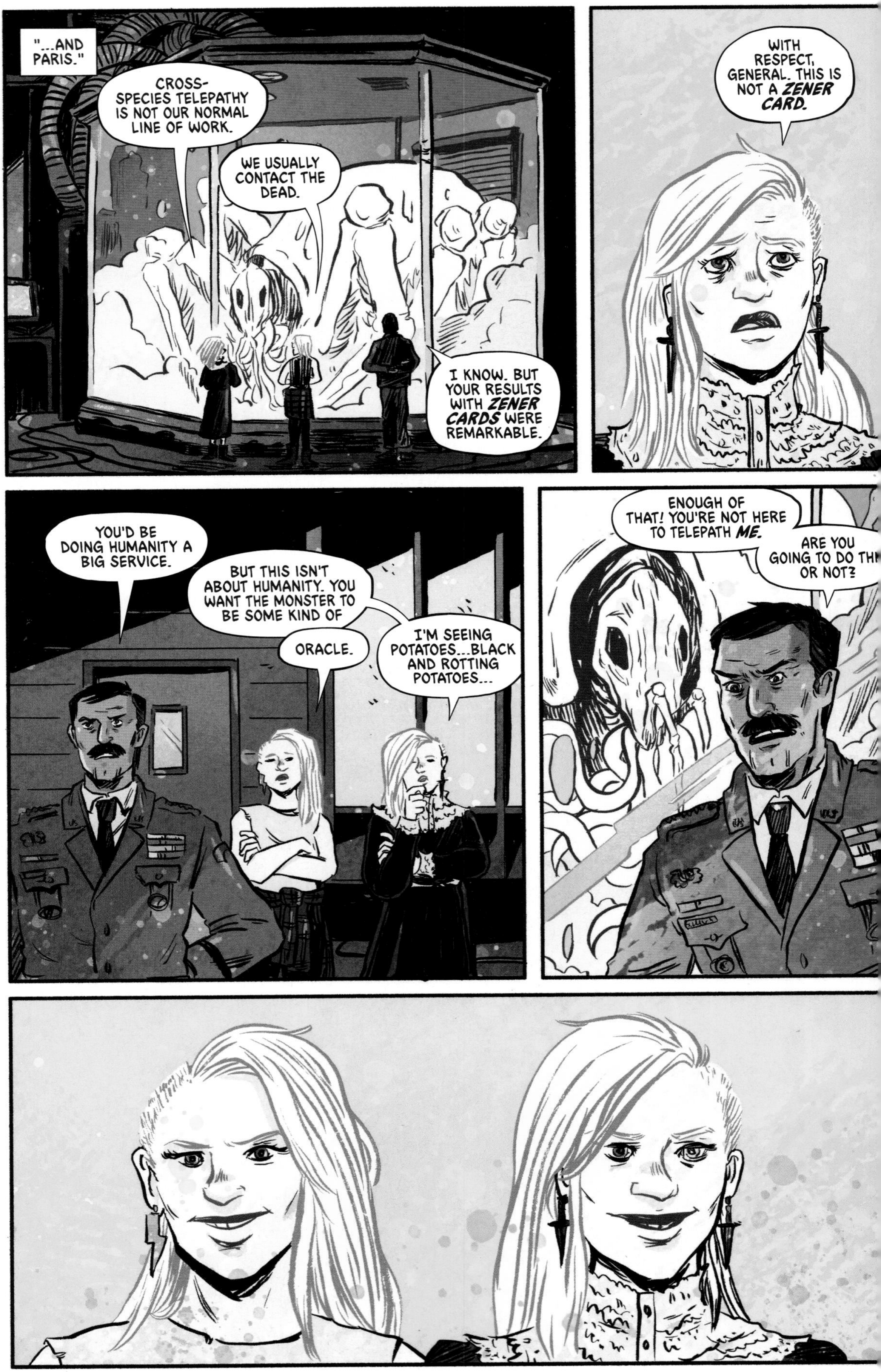
"...AND PARIS."
CROSS-SPECIES TELEPATHY IS NOT OUR NORMAL LINE OF WORK.
WE USUALLY CONTACT THE DEAD.
I KNOW. BUT YOUR RESULTS WITH ZENER CARDS WERE REMARKABLE.
WITH RESPECT, GENERAL. THIS IS NOT A ZENER CARD.
YOU'D BE DOING HUMANITY A BIG SERVICE.
BUT THIS ISN'T ABOUT HUMANITY. YOU WANT THE MONSTER TO BE SOME KIND OF
ORACLE.
I'M SEEING POTATOES...BLACK AND ROTTING POTATOES...
ENOUGH OF THAT! YOU'RE NOT HERE TO TELEPATH ME.
ARE YOU GOING TO DO TH OR NOT?

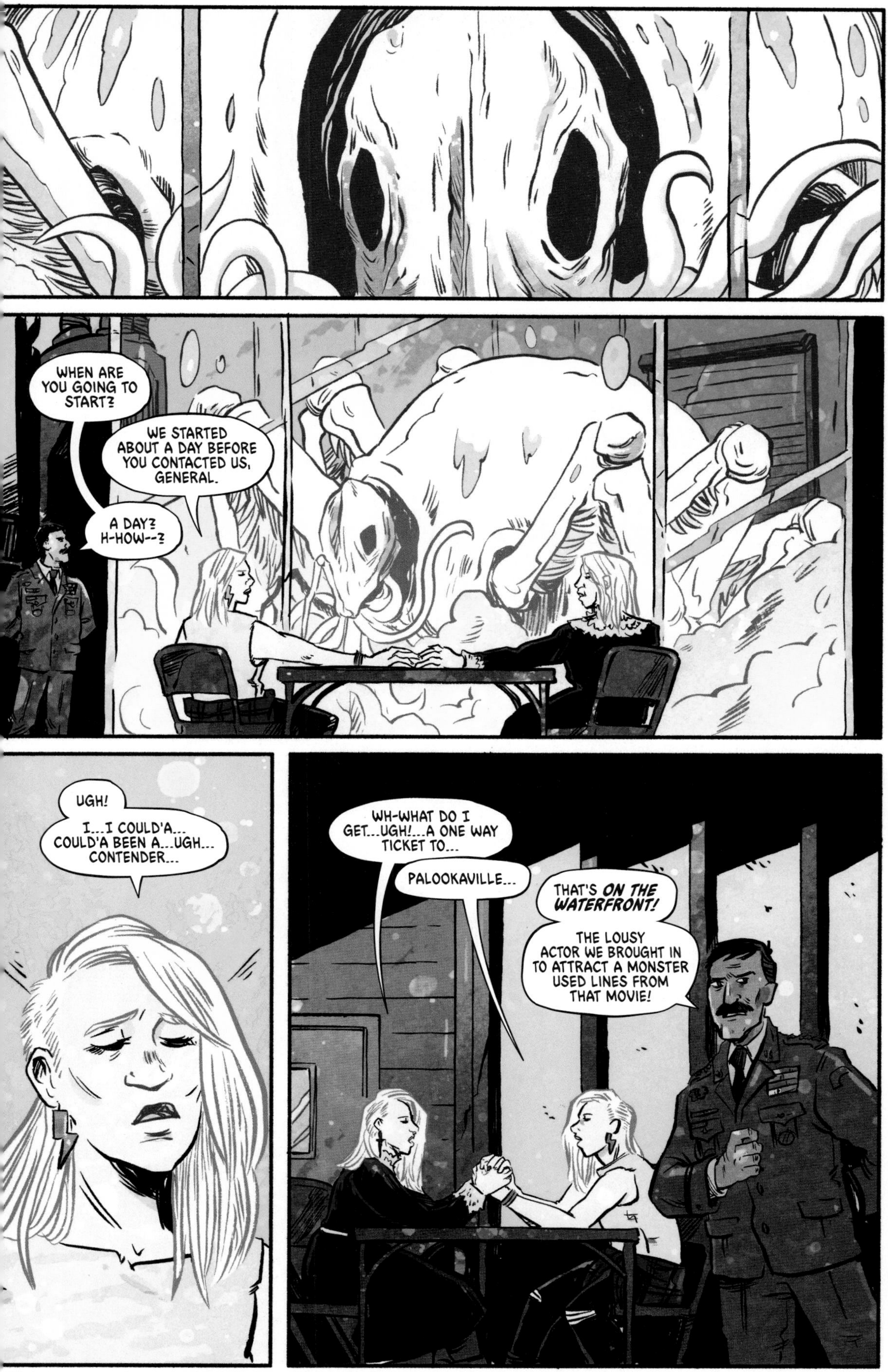
WHEN ARE YOU GOING TO START?
WE STARTED ABOUT A DAY BEFORE YOU CONTACTED US, GENERAL.
A DAY? H-HOW--?
UGH!
I...I COULD'A... COULD'A BEEN A...UGH... CONTENDER...
WH-WHAT DO I GET...UGH!...A ONE WAY TICKET TO...
PALOOKAVILLE...
THAT'S *ON THE WATERFRONT!*
THE LOUSY ACTOR WE BROUGHT IN TO ATTRACT A MONSTER USED LINES FROM THAT MOVIE!

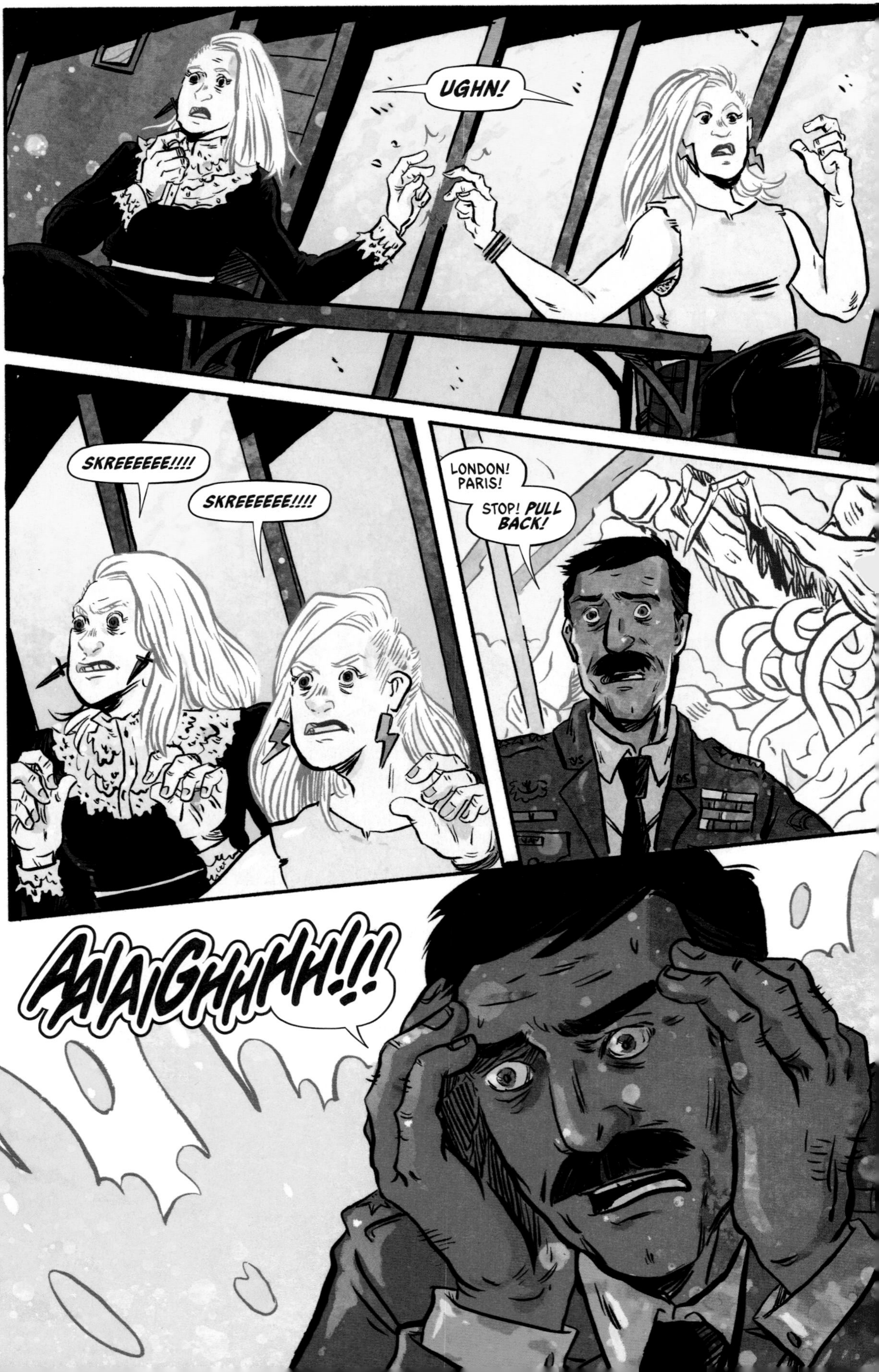
UGHN!
SKREEEEEE!!!!
SKREEEEEE!!!!
LONDON! PARIS!
STOP! PULL BACK!
AAAAGHHHH!!!

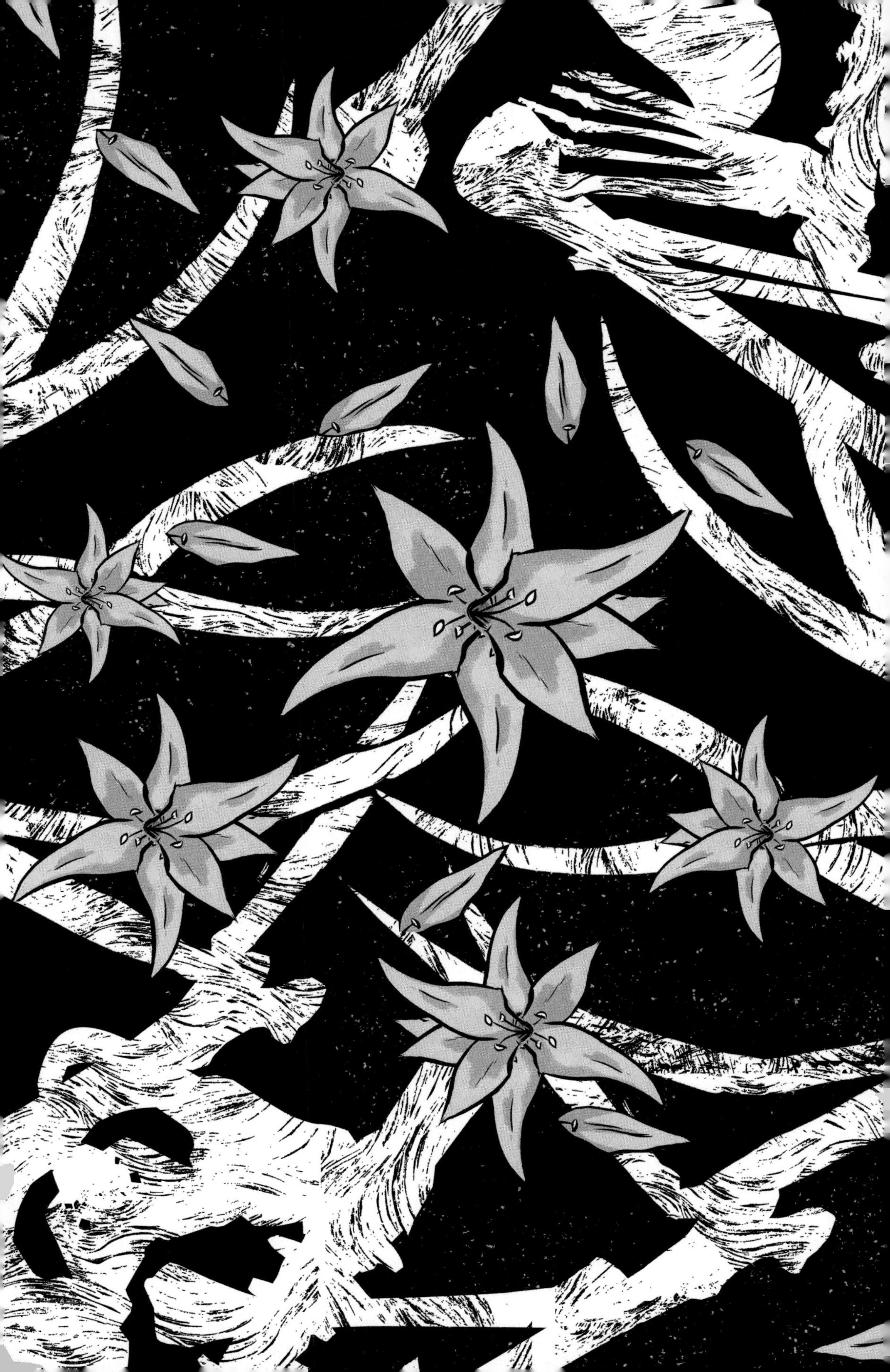

CHAPTER SIX

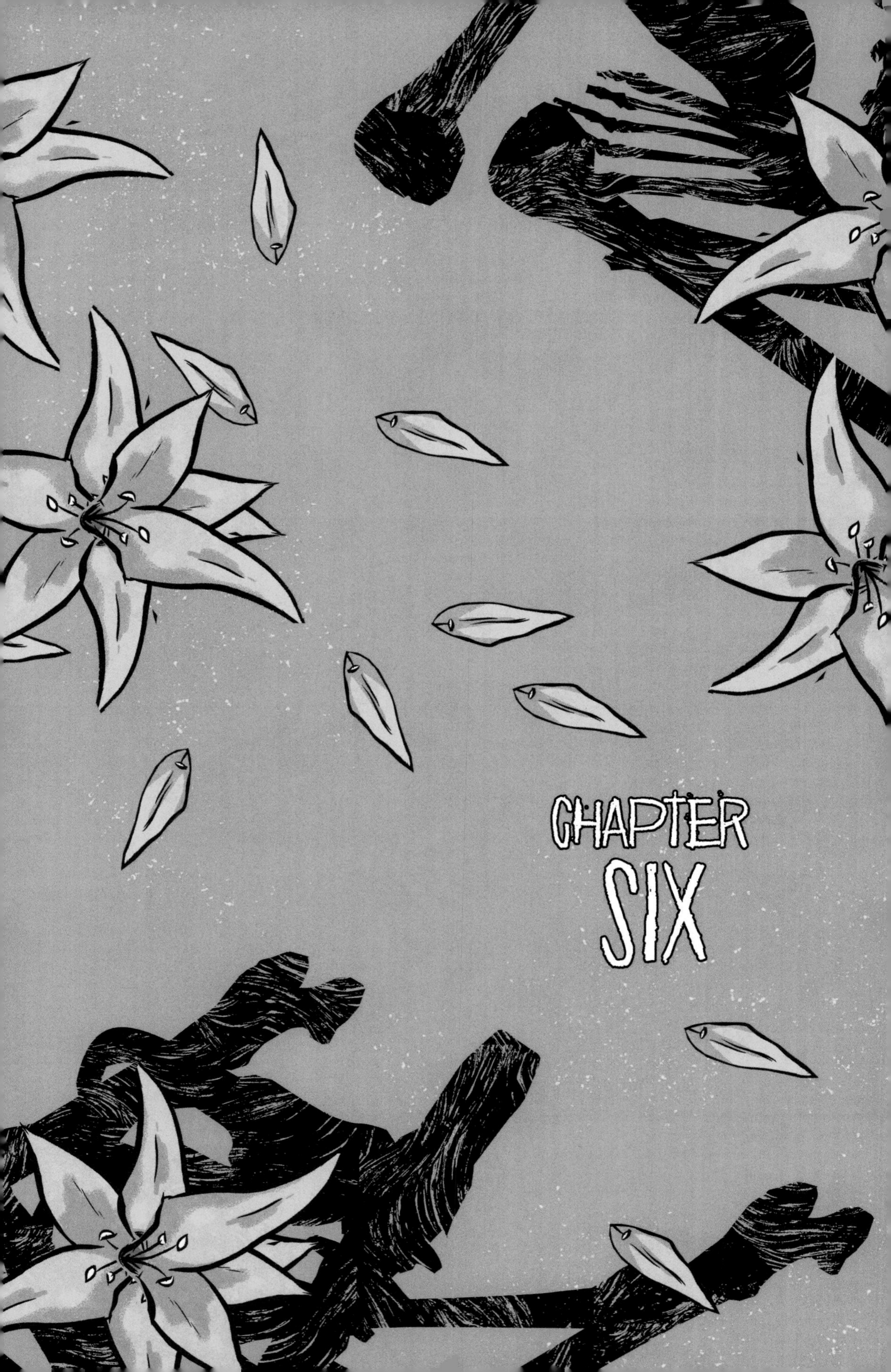

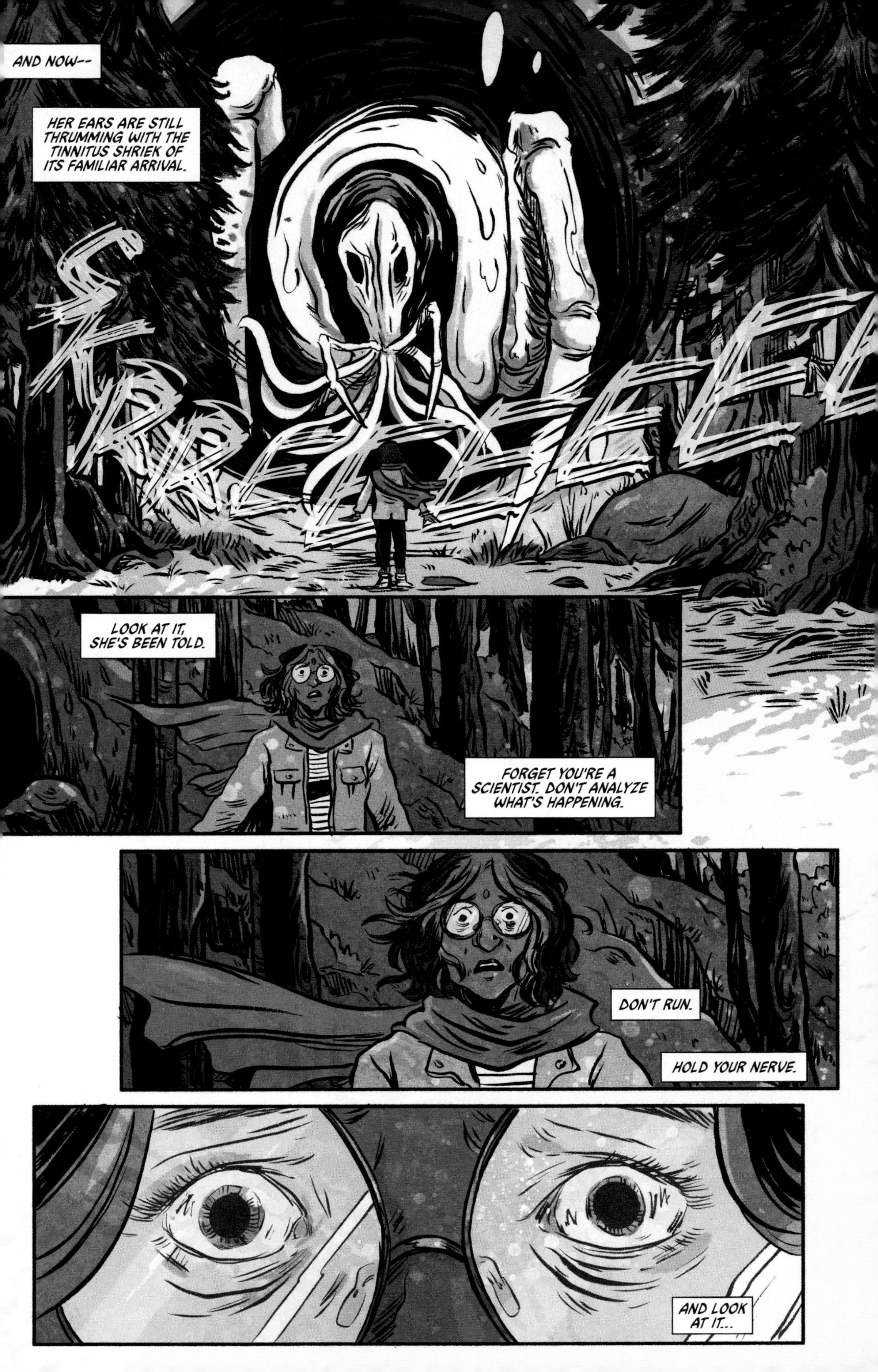
AND NOW--
HER EARS ARE STILL THRUMMING WITH THE TINNITUS SHRIEK OF ITS FAMILIAR ARRIVAL.
SKREEEEEEE
LOOK AT IT, SHE'S BEEN TOLD.
FORGET YOU'RE A SCIENTIST. DON'T ANALYZE WHAT'S HAPPENING.
DON'T RUN.
HOLD YOUR NERVE.
AND LOOK AT IT...

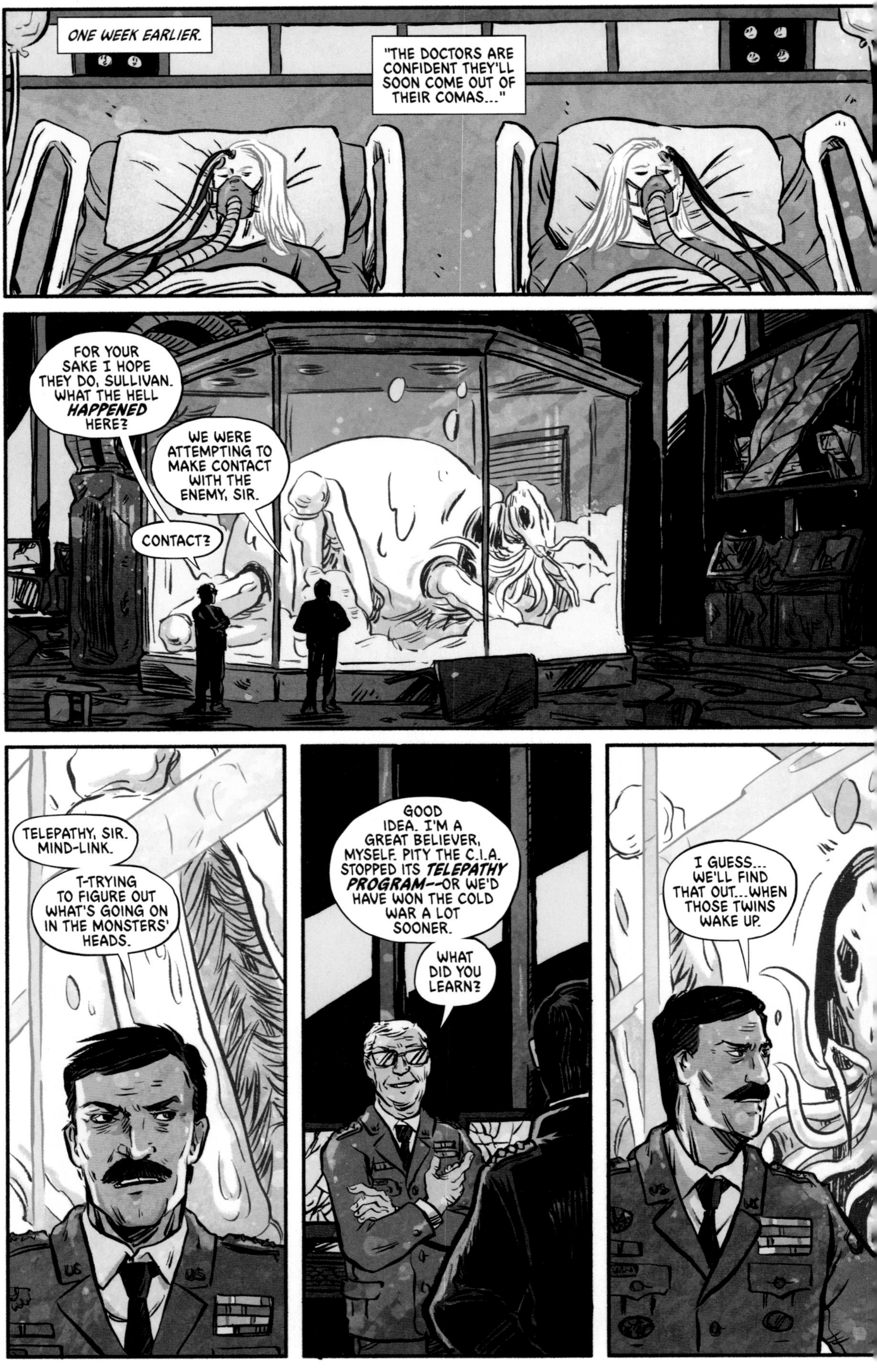
ONE WEEK EARLIER.
"THE DOCTORS ARE CONFIDENT THEY'LL SOON COME OUT OF THEIR COMAS..."
FOR YOUR SAKE I HOPE THEY DO, SULLIVAN. WHAT THE HELL HAPPENED HERE?
WE WERE ATTEMPTING TO MAKE CONTACT WITH THE ENEMY, SIR.
CONTACT?
TELEPATHY, SIR. MIND-LINK.
T-TRYING TO FIGURE OUT WHAT'S GOING ON IN THE MONSTERS' HEADS.
GOOD IDEA. I'M A GREAT BELIEVER, MYSELF. PITY THE C.I.A. STOPPED ITS TELEPATHY PROGRAM--OR WE'D HAVE WON THE COLD WAR A LOT SOONER.
WHAT DID YOU LEARN?
I GUESS... WE'LL FIND THAT OUT...WHEN THOSE TWINS WAKE UP.

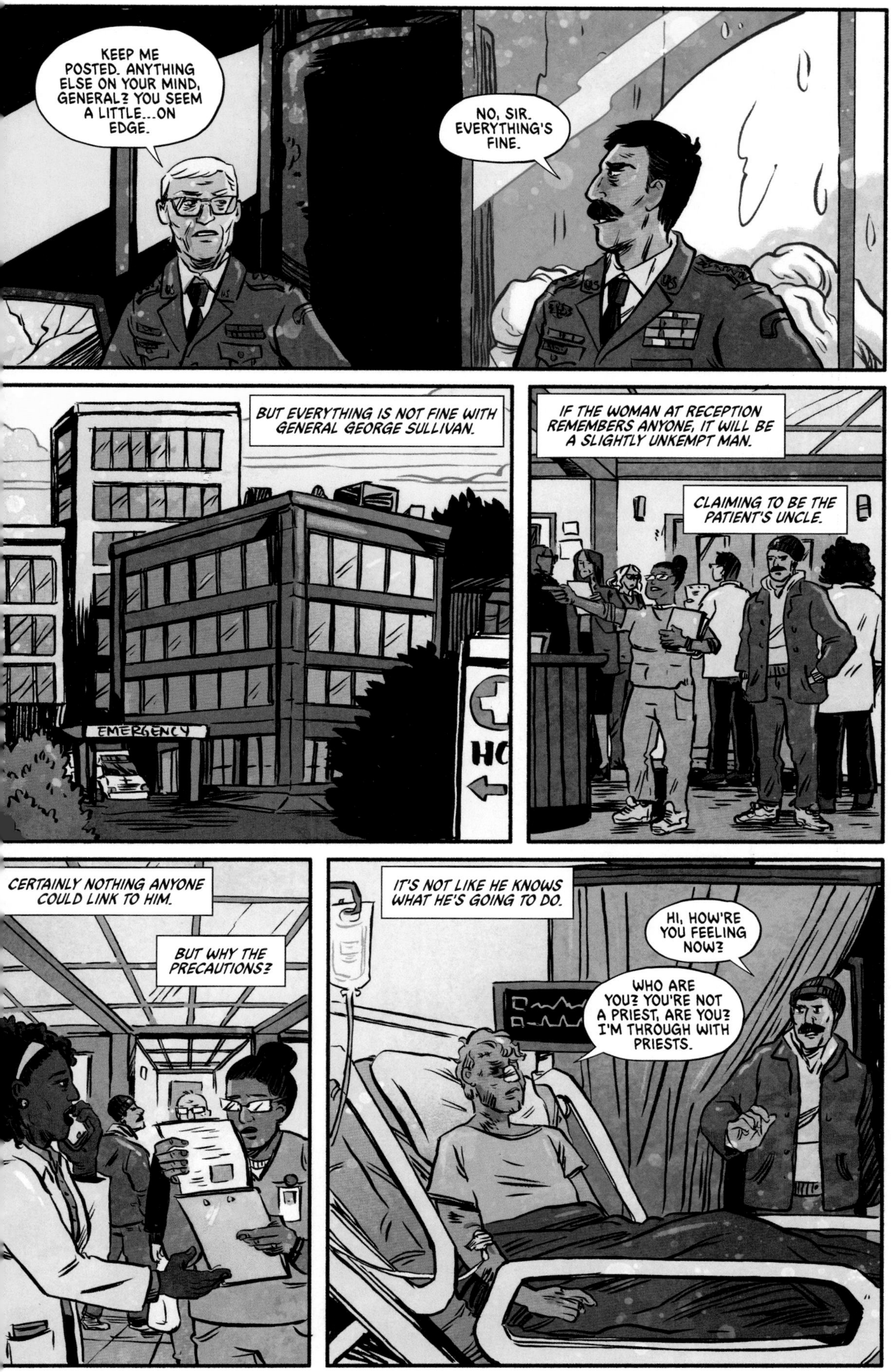
KEEP ME POSTED. ANYTHING ELSE ON YOUR MIND, GENERAL? YOU SEEM A LITTLE...ON EDGE.
NO, SIR. EVERYTHING'S FINE.
BUT EVERYTHING IS NOT FINE WITH GENERAL GEORGE SULLIVAN.
EMERGENCY
HO
IF THE WOMAN AT RECEPTION REMEMBERS ANYONE, IT WILL BE A SLIGHTLY UNKEMPT MAN.
CLAIMING TO BE THE PATIENT'S UNCLE.
CERTAINLY NOTHING ANYONE COULD LINK TO HIM.
BUT WHY THE PRECAUTIONS?
IT'S NOT LIKE HE KNOWS WHAT HE'S GOING TO DO.
HI, HOW'RE YOU FEELING NOW?
WHO ARE YOU? YOU'RE NOT A PRIEST, ARE YOU? I'M THROUGH WITH PRIESTS.

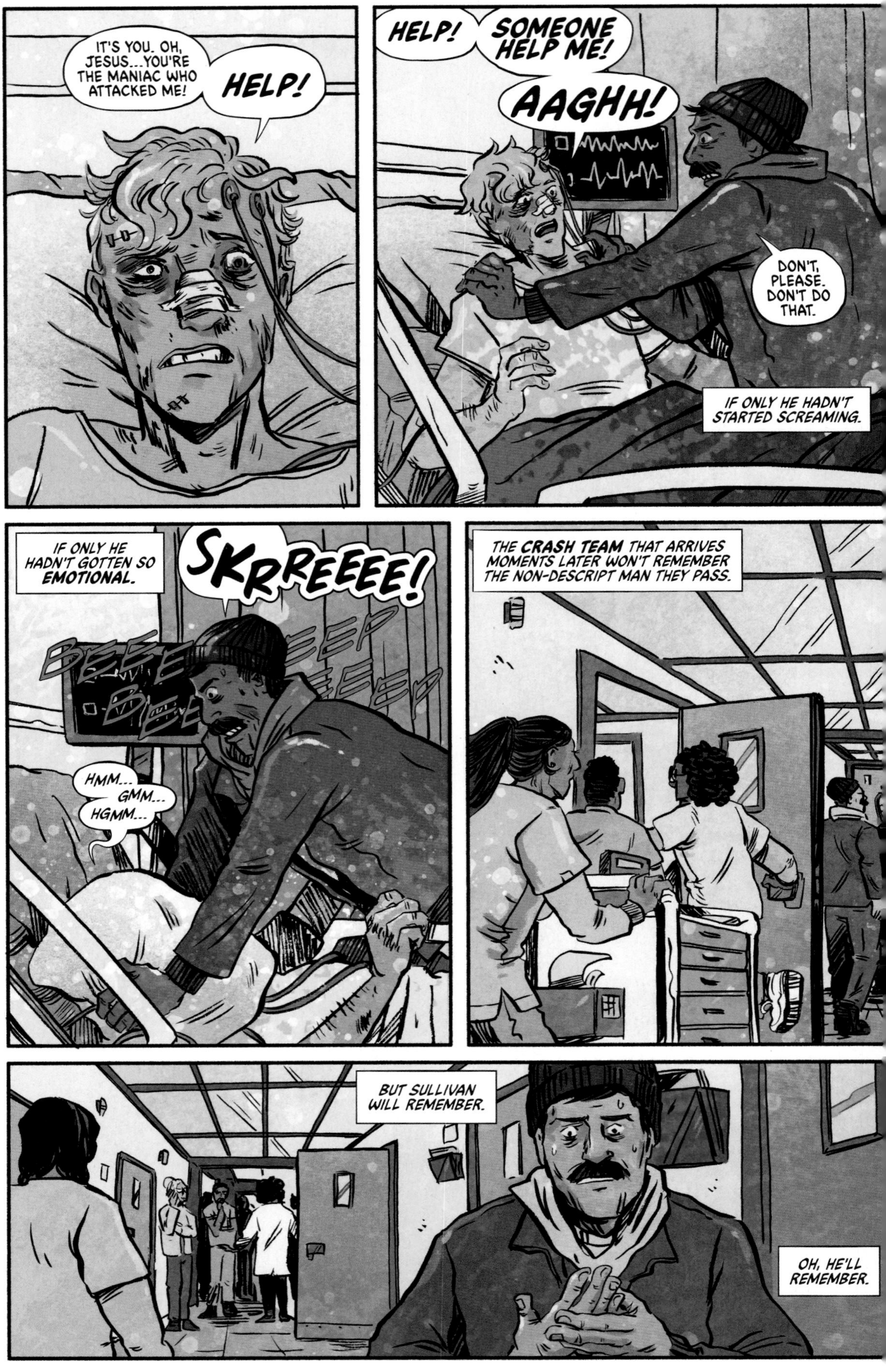
IT'S YOU. OH, JESUS...YOU'RE THE MANIAC WHO ATTACKED ME!
HELP!
HELP!
SOMEONE HELP ME!
AAGHH!
DON'T, PLEASE. DON'T DO THAT.
IF ONLY HE HADN'T STARTED SCREAMING.
IF ONLY HE HADN'T GOTTEN SO EMOTIONAL.
SKRREEEEE!
BEEEEEEEP
BEEEEEEEP
HMM...
GMM...
HGMM...
THE CRASH TEAM THAT ARRIVES MOMENTS LATER WON'T REMEMBER THE NON-DESCRIPT MAN THEY PASS.
BUT SULLIVAN WILL REMEMBER.
OH, HE'LL REMEMBER.

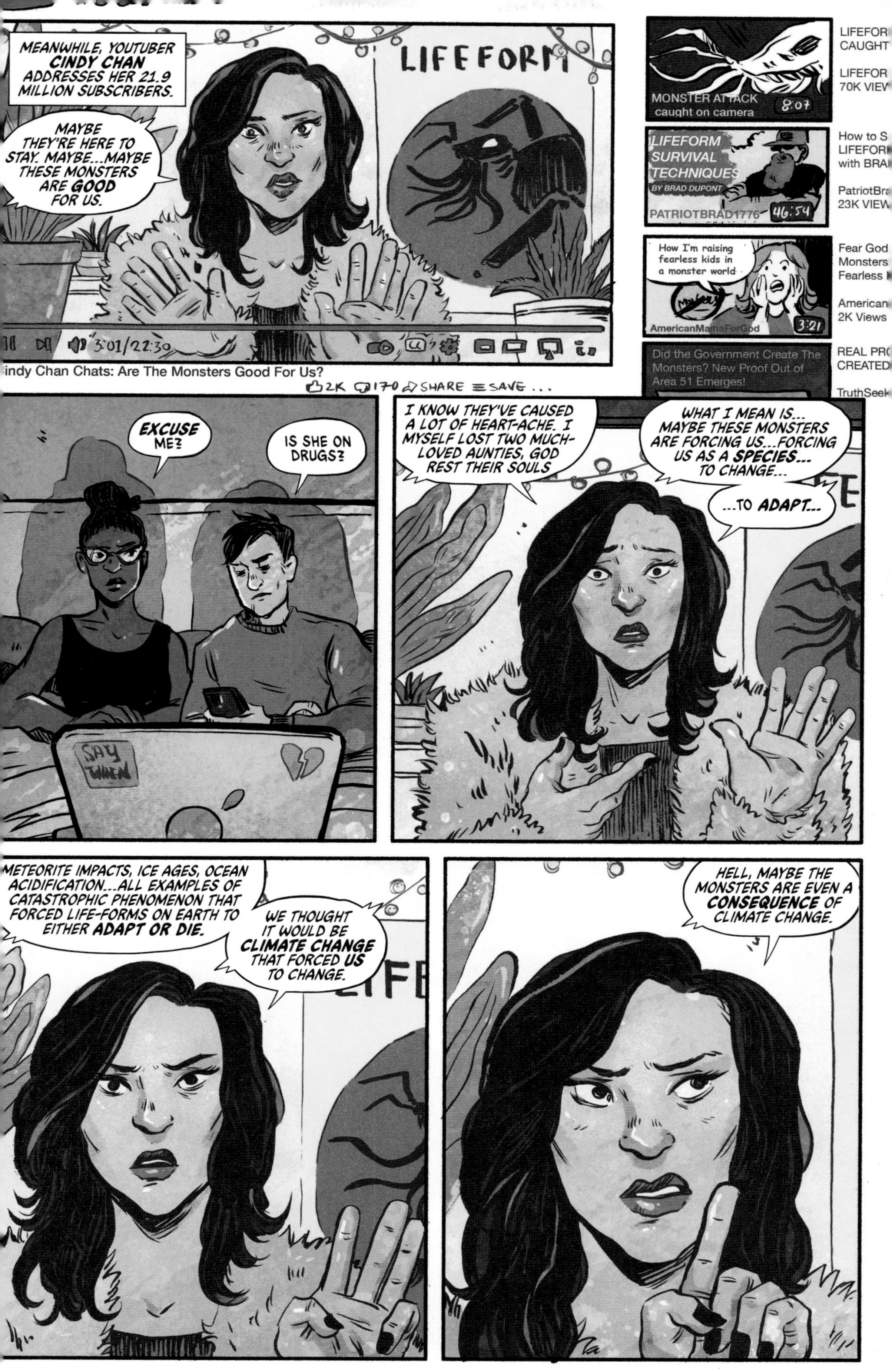

MEANWHILE, YOUTUBER CINDY CHAN ADDRESSES HER 21.9 MILLION SUBSCRIBERS.
MAYBE THEY'RE HERE TO STAY. MAYBE...MAYBE THESE MONSTERS ARE GOOD FOR US.
LIFEFORM
3:01/22:30
Cindy Chan Chats: Are The Monsters Good For Us?
2K 170 SHARE SAVE ...
MONSTER ATTACK caught on camera 8:07
LIFEFOR
CAUGHT
LIFEFOR
70K VIEW
LIFEFORM SURVIVAL TECHNIQUES
BY BRAD DUPONT
PATRIOTBRAD1776 46:54
How to S
LIFEFOR
with BRA
PatriotBra
23K VIEW
How I'm raising fearless kids in a monster world
AmericanMamaForGod 3:21
Fear God
Monsters
Fearless
American
2K Views
Did the Government Create The Monsters? New Proof Out of Area 51 Emerges!
REAL PRO
CREATED
TruthSeek
EXCUSE ME?
IS SHE ON DRUGS?
SAY WHEN
I KNOW THEY'VE CAUSED A LOT OF HEART-ACHE. I MYSELF LOST TWO MUCH-LOVED AUNTIES, GOD REST THEIR SOULS
WHAT I MEAN IS... MAYBE THESE MONSTERS ARE FORCING US...FORCING US AS A SPECIES... TO CHANGE...
...TO ADAPT...
METEORITE IMPACTS, ICE AGES, OCEAN ACIDIFICATION...ALL EXAMPLES OF CATASTROPHIC PHENOMENON THAT FORCED LIFE-FORMS ON EARTH TO EITHER ADAPT OR DIE.
WE THOUGHT IT WOULD BE CLIMATE CHANGE THAT FORCED US TO CHANGE.
HELL, MAYBE THE MONSTERS ARE EVEN A CONSEQUENCE OF CLIMATE CHANGE.

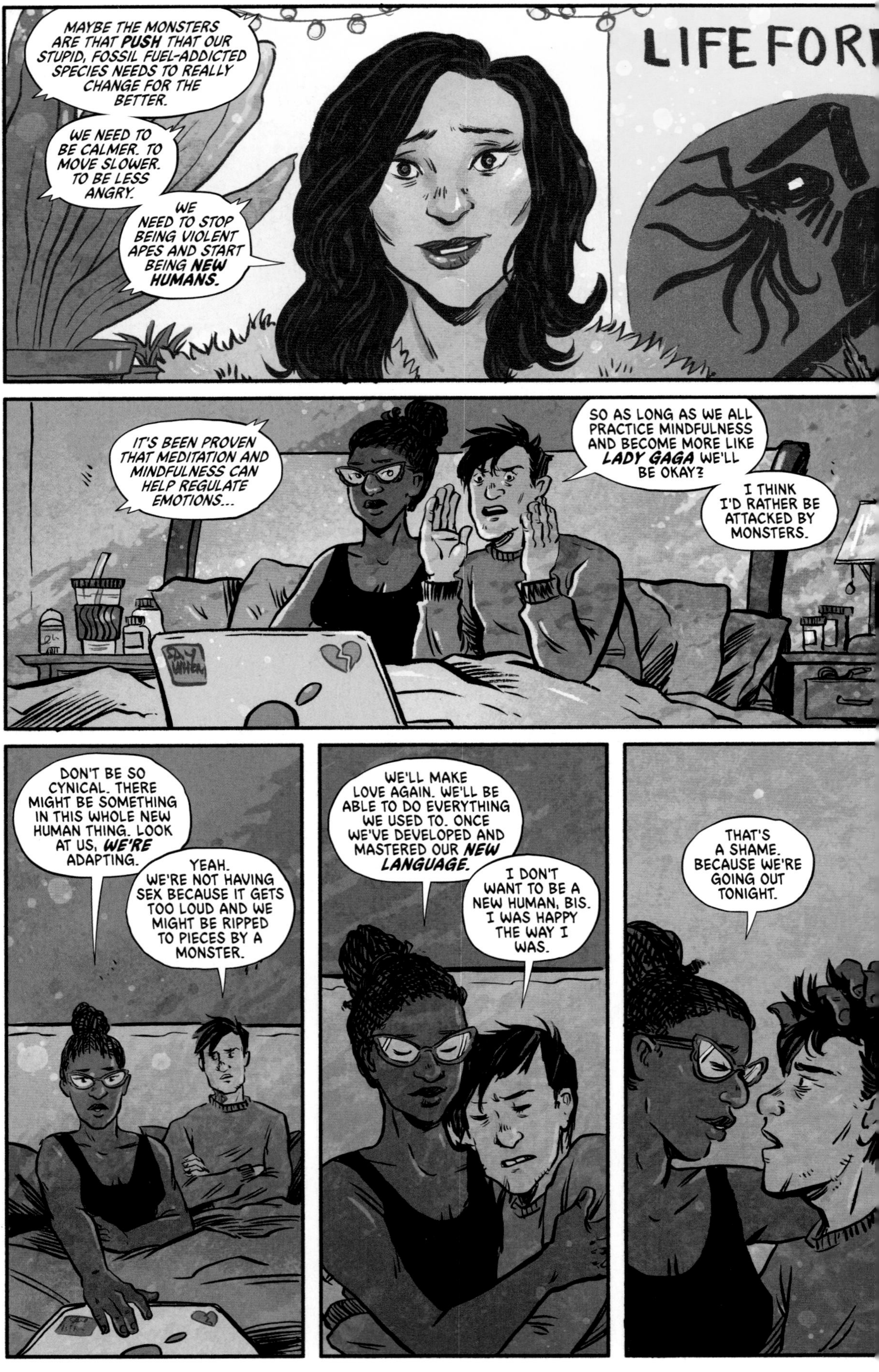
MAYBE THE MONSTERS ARE THAT PUSH THAT OUR STUPID, FOSSIL FUEL-ADDICTED SPECIES NEEDS TO REALLY CHANGE FOR THE BETTER.
WE NEED TO BE CALMER. TO MOVE SLOWER. TO BE LESS ANGRY.
WE NEED TO STOP BEING VIOLENT APES AND START BEING NEW HUMANS.
LIFEFOR
IT'S BEEN PROVEN THAT MEDITATION AND MINDFULNESS CAN HELP REGULATE EMOTIONS...
SO AS LONG AS WE ALL PRACTICE MINDFULNESS AND BECOME MORE LIKE LADY GAGA WE'LL BE OKAY?
I THINK I'D RATHER BE ATTACKED BY MONSTERS.
DON'T BE SO CYNICAL. THERE MIGHT BE SOMETHING IN THIS WHOLE NEW HUMAN THING. LOOK AT US, WE'RE ADAPTING.
YEAH. WE'RE NOT HAVING SEX BECAUSE IT GETS TOO LOUD AND WE MIGHT BE RIPPED TO PIECES BY A MONSTER.
WE'LL MAKE LOVE AGAIN. WE'LL BE ABLE TO DO EVERYTHING WE USED TO. ONCE WE'VE DEVELOPED AND MASTERED OUR NEW LANGUAGE.
I DON'T WANT TO BE A NEW HUMAN, BIS. I WAS HAPPY THE WAY I WAS.
THAT'S A SHAME. BECAUSE WE'RE GOING OUT TONIGHT.

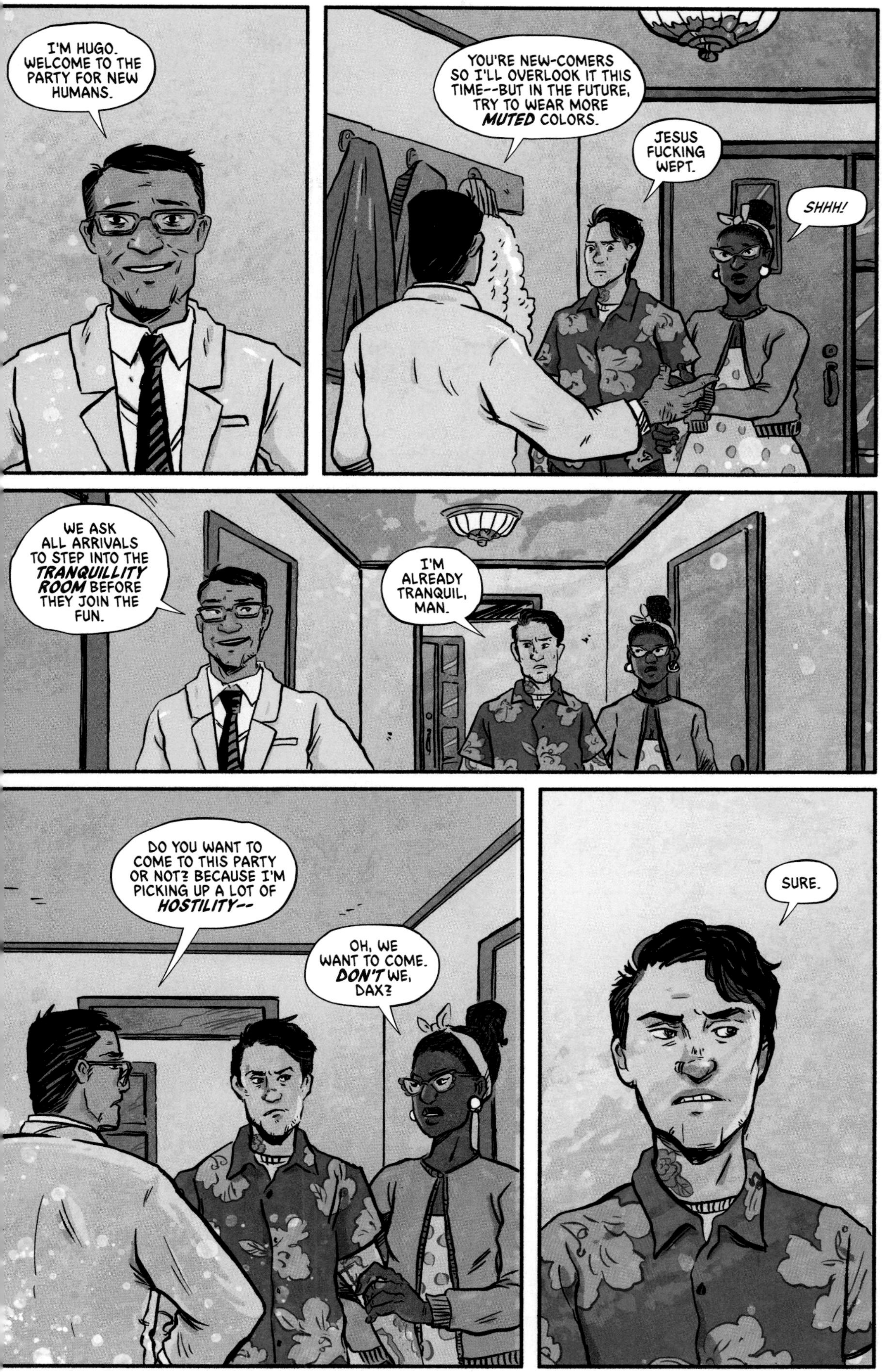
I'M HUGO. WELCOME TO THE PARTY FOR NEW HUMANS.
YOU'RE NEW-COMERS SO I'LL OVERLOOK IT THIS TIME--BUT IN THE FUTURE, TRY TO WEAR MORE MUTED COLORS.
JESUS FUCKING WEPT.
SHHH!
WE ASK ALL ARRIVALS TO STEP INTO THE TRANQUILLITY ROOM BEFORE THEY JOIN THE FUN.
I'M ALREADY TRANQUIL, MAN.
DO YOU WANT TO COME TO THIS PARTY OR NOT? BECAUSE I'M PICKING UP A LOT OF HOSTILITY--
OH, WE WANT TO COME. DON'T WE, DAX?
SURE.

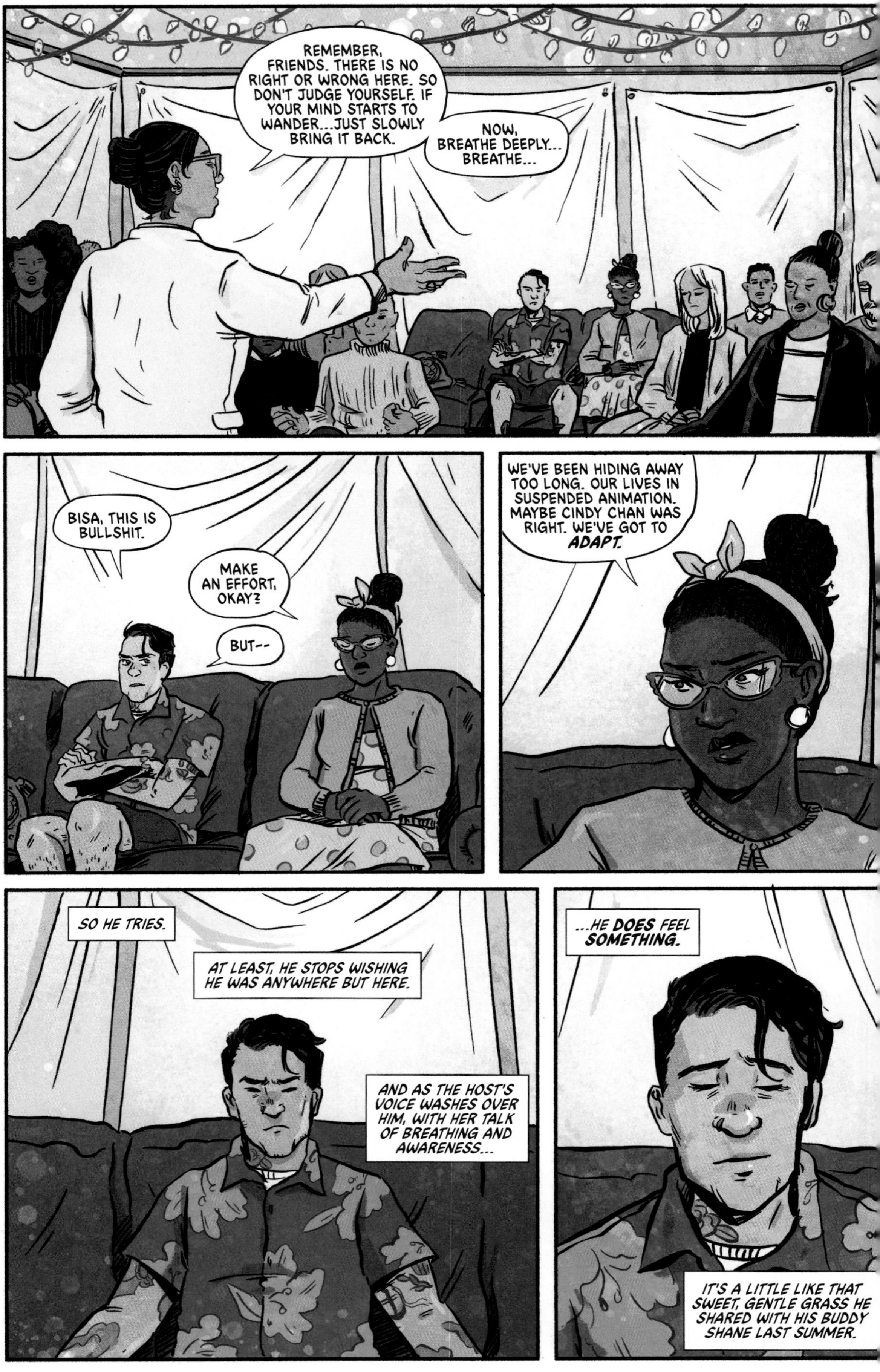
REMEMBER, FRIENDS. THERE IS NO RIGHT OR WRONG HERE. SO DON'T JUDGE YOURSELF. IF YOUR MIND STARTS TO WANDER...JUST SLOWLY BRING IT BACK.
NOW, BREATHE DEEPLY... BREATHE...
BISA, THIS IS BULLSHIT.
MAKE AN EFFORT, OKAY?
BUT--
WE'VE BEEN HIDING AWAY TOO LONG. OUR LIVES IN SUSPENDED ANIMATION. MAYBE CINDY CHAN WAS RIGHT. WE'VE GOT TO ***ADAPT***.
SO HE TRIES.
AT LEAST, HE STOPS WISHING HE WAS ANYWHERE BUT HERE.
AND AS THE HOST'S VOICE WASHES OVER HIM, WITH HER TALK OF BREATHING AND AWARENESS...
...HE ***DOES*** *FEEL* ***SOMETHING.***
IT'S A LITTLE LIKE THAT SWEET, GENTLE GRASS HE SHARED WITH HIS BUDDY SHANE LAST SUMMER.

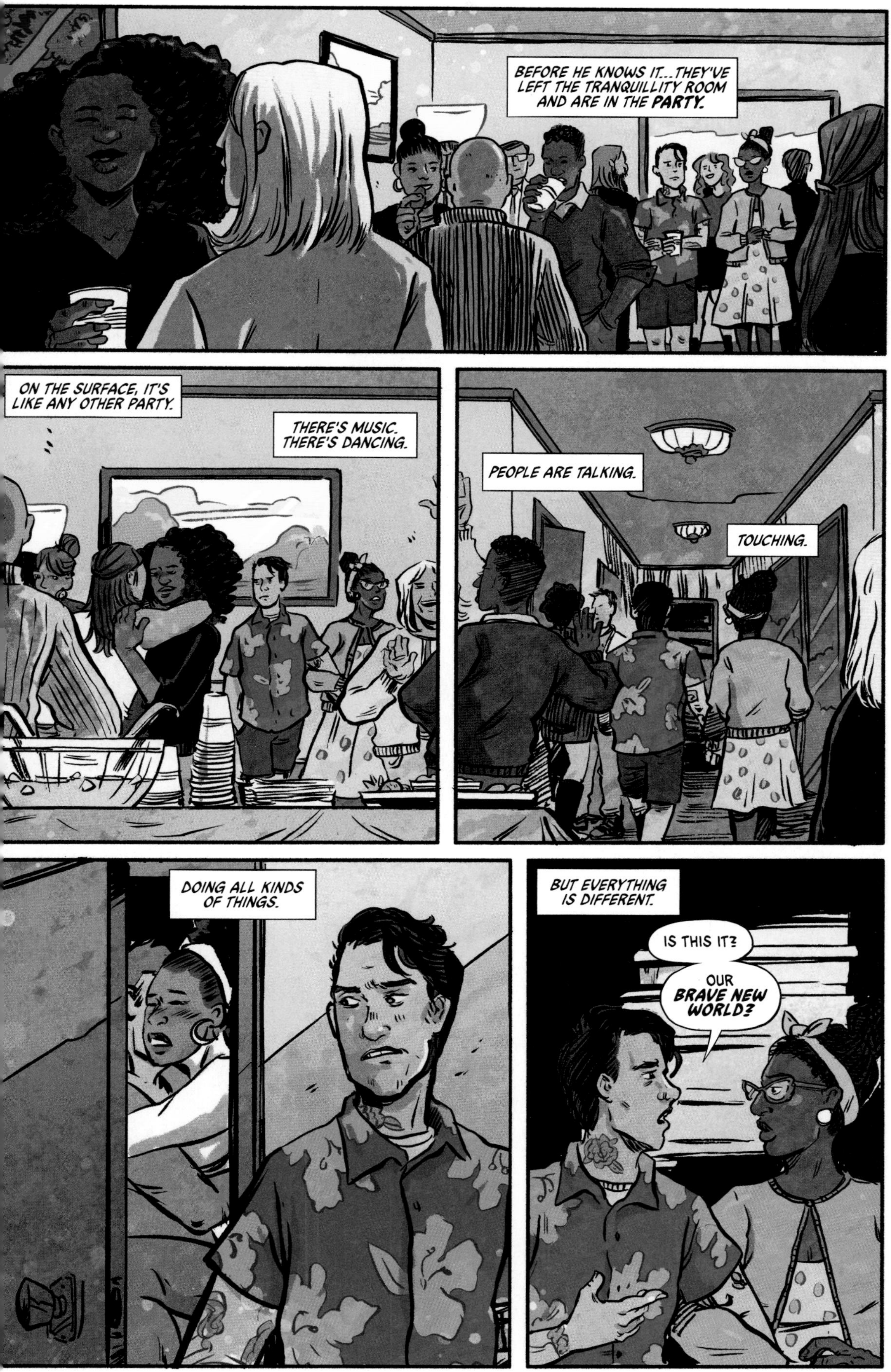
BEFORE HE KNOWS IT... THEY'VE LEFT THE TRANQUILLITY ROOM AND ARE IN THE PARTY.
ON THE SURFACE, IT'S LIKE ANY OTHER PARTY.
THERE'S MUSIC. THERE'S DANCING.
PEOPLE ARE TALKING.
TOUCHING.
DOING ALL KINDS OF THINGS.
BUT EVERYTHING IS DIFFERENT.
IS THIS IT?
OUR BRAVE NEW WORLD?

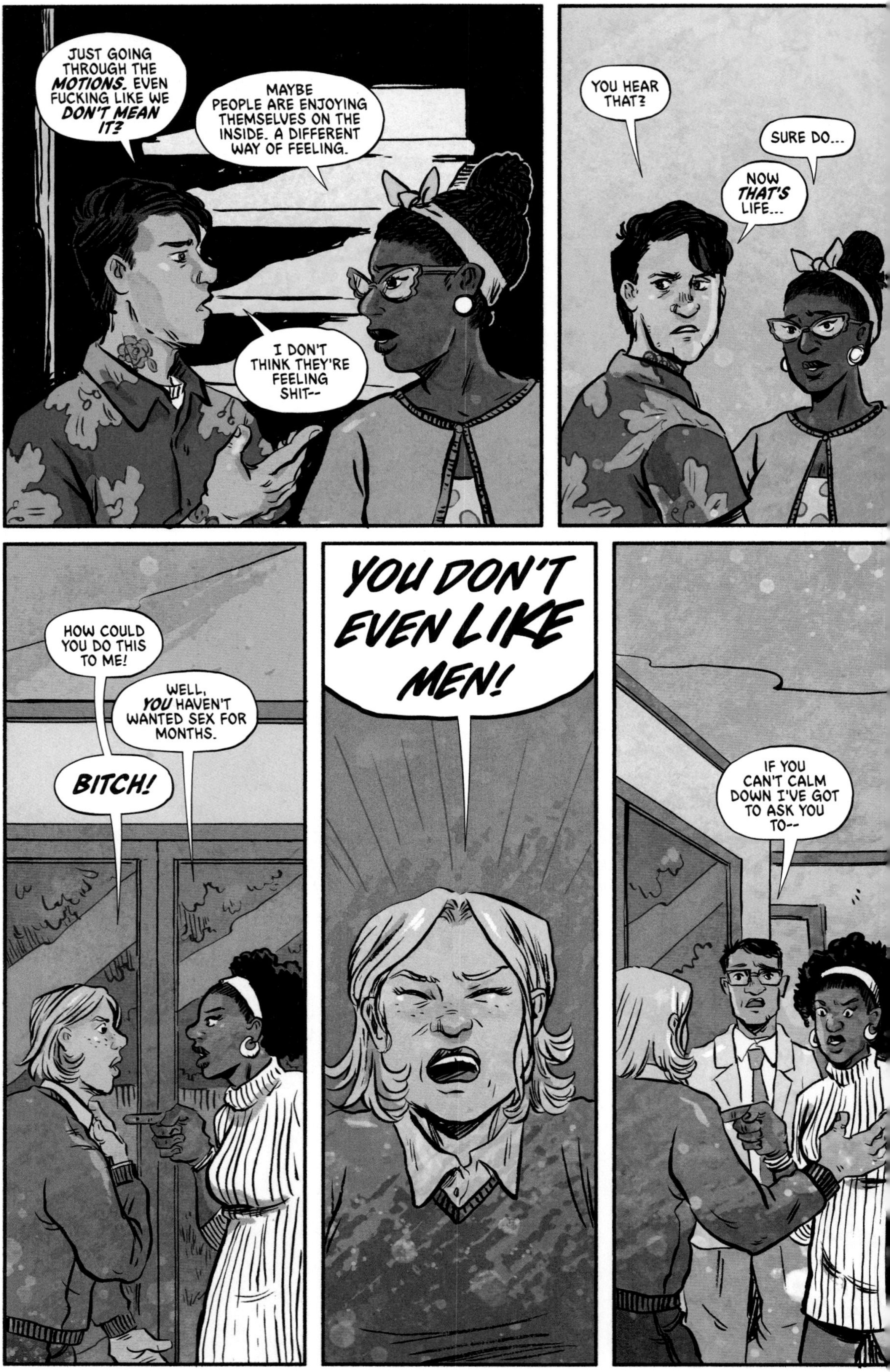
JUST GOING THROUGH THE MOTIONS. EVEN FUCKING LIKE WE DON'T MEAN IT?
MAYBE PEOPLE ARE ENJOYING THEMSELVES ON THE INSIDE. A DIFFERENT WAY OF FEELING.
I DON'T THINK THEY'RE FEELING SHIT--
YOU HEAR THAT?
SURE DO...
NOW THAT'S LIFE...
HOW COULD YOU DO THIS TO ME!
WELL, YOU HAVEN'T WANTED SEX FOR MONTHS.
BITCH!
YOU DON'T EVEN LIKE MEN!
IF YOU CAN'T CALM DOWN I'VE GOT TO ASK YOU TO--

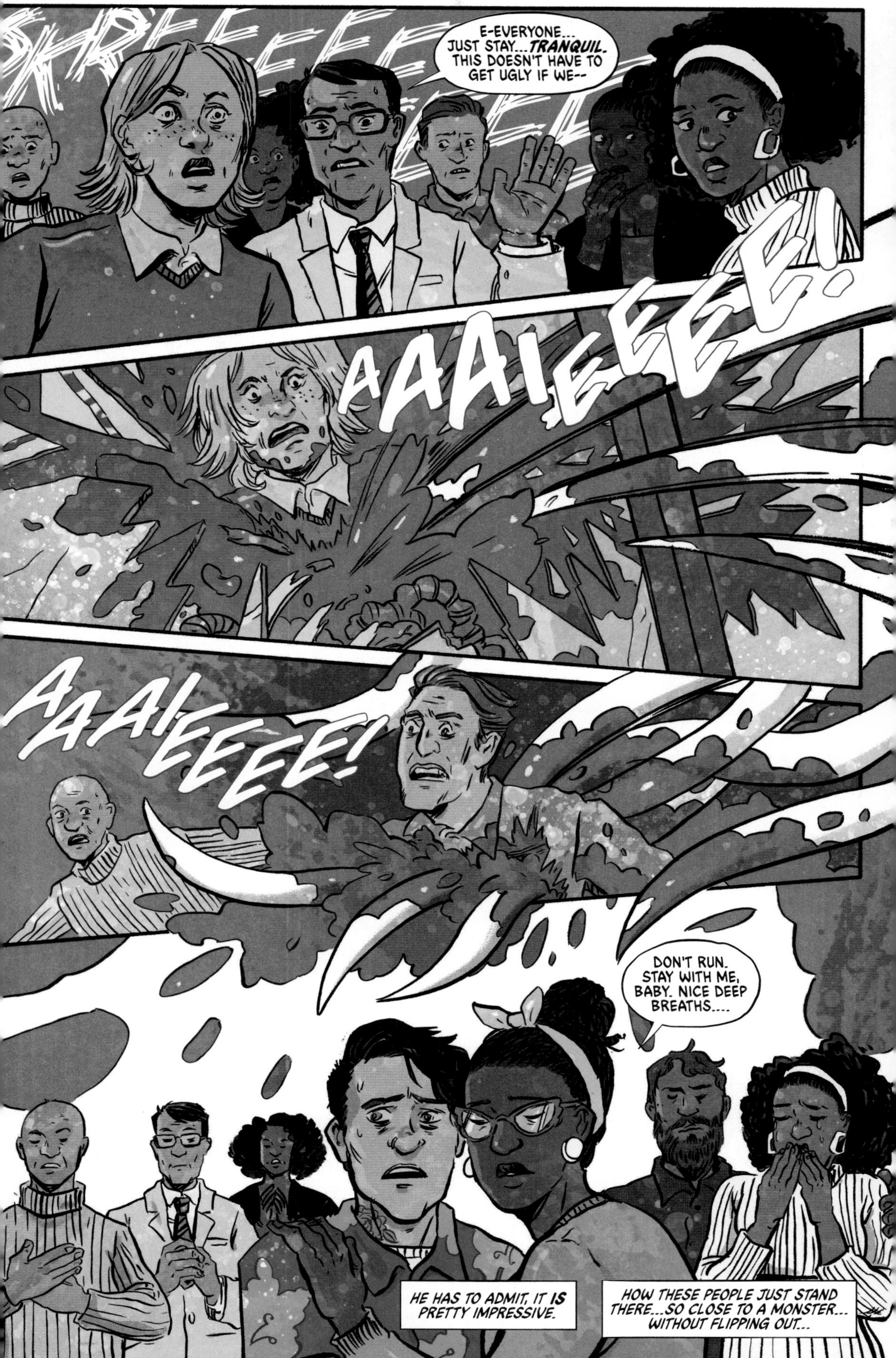
SKREEEEEEEEEE
E-EVERYONE... JUST STAY...TRANQUIL. THIS DOESN'T HAVE TO GET UGLY IF WE--
AAAIEEEEE!
AAAIEEEEE!
DON'T RUN. STAY WITH ME, BABY. NICE DEEP BREATHS....
HE HAS TO ADMIT, IT IS PRETTY IMPRESSIVE.
HOW THESE PEOPLE JUST STAND THERE...SO CLOSE TO A MONSTER... WITHOUT FLIPPING OUT...

NOW.

THE MONSTER GROWS.
SEEMS TO COME AT HER.

SHE EXPECTS
ANY MOMENT TO
BE HER LAST.

BUT SHE STILL DOES
NOT RUN. STILL KEEPS
LOOKING AT IT.

SHE FEELS THE FUNGUS THAT
RICHARD GAVE HER BLUNTING
HER EDGES. MAYBE BLUNTING
HER FEAR, TOO.

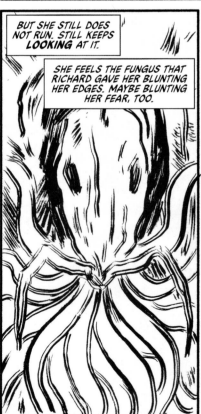

HE SAID THIS FEELING WOULD PASS,
BUT SHE'S NOT SURE SHE *WANTS* IT
TO PASS. IT MAKES THE MEMORIES
JUST A *LITTLE* EASIER TO BEAR.

HER HELPLESS EFFORTS
TO SAVE SAJ.

WHAT THAT MONSTER
DID TO HER BEAUTIFUL,
HAPPY LITTLE BOY.

HER COUSIN
TRUSHA STANDING
IN FRONT OF HER...

ANJALI KNEW WHAT THE
POOR GIRL WAS GOING TO
SAY BEFORE SHE SAID IT...

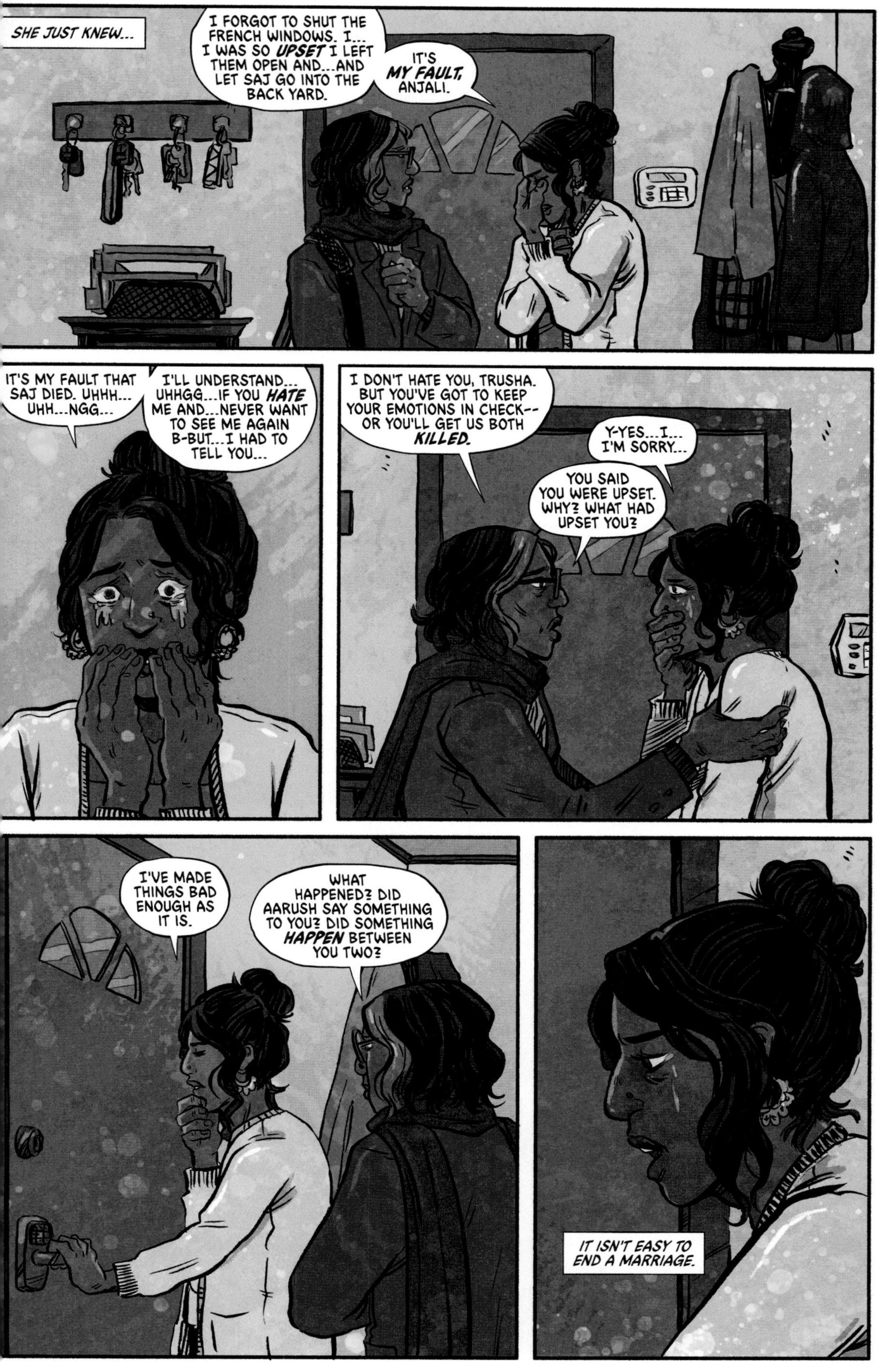
SHE JUST KNEW...
I FORGOT TO SHUT THE FRENCH WINDOWS. I... I WAS SO UPSET I LEFT THEM OPEN AND...AND LET SAJ GO INTO THE BACK YARD.
IT'S MY FAULT, ANJALI.
IT'S MY FAULT THAT SAJ DIED. UHHH... UHH...NGG...
I'LL UNDERSTAND... UHHGG...IF YOU HATE ME AND...NEVER WANT TO SEE ME AGAIN B-BUT...I HAD TO TELL YOU...
I DON'T HATE YOU, TRUSHA. BUT YOU'VE GOT TO KEEP YOUR EMOTIONS IN CHECK--OR YOU'LL GET US BOTH KILLED.
Y-YES...I... I'M SORRY...
YOU SAID YOU WERE UPSET. WHY? WHAT HAD UPSET YOU?
I'VE MADE THINGS BAD ENOUGH AS IT IS.
WHAT HAPPENED? DID AARUSH SAY SOMETHING TO YOU? DID SOMETHING HAPPEN BETWEEN YOU TWO?
IT ISN'T EASY TO END A MARRIAGE.

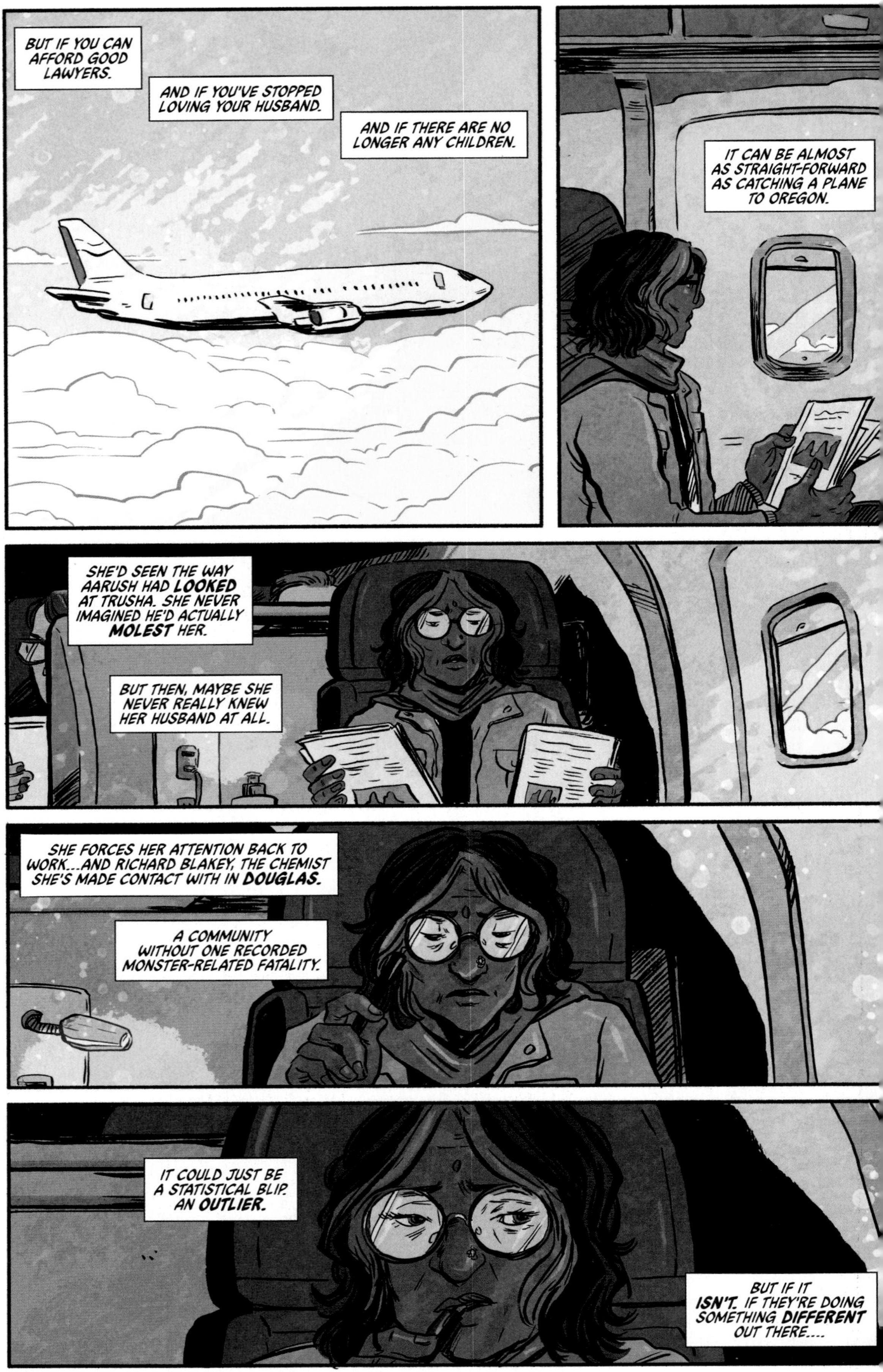
BUT IF YOU CAN AFFORD GOOD LAWYERS.
AND IF YOU'VE STOPPED LOVING YOUR HUSBAND.
AND IF THERE ARE NO LONGER ANY CHILDREN.
IT CAN BE ALMOST AS STRAIGHT-FORWARD AS CATCHING A PLANE TO OREGON.
SHE'D SEEN THE WAY AARUSH HAD LOOKED AT TRUSHA. SHE NEVER IMAGINED HE'D ACTUALLY MOLEST HER.
BUT THEN, MAYBE SHE NEVER REALLY KNEW HER HUSBAND AT ALL.
SHE FORCES HER ATTENTION BACK TO WORK...AND RICHARD BLAKEY, THE CHEMIST SHE'S MADE CONTACT WITH IN DOUGLAS.
A COMMUNITY WITHOUT ONE RECORDED MONSTER-RELATED FATALITY.
IT COULD JUST BE A STATISTICAL BLIP. AN OUTLIER.
BUT IF IT ISN'T. IF THEY'RE DOING SOMETHING DIFFERENT OUT THERE....

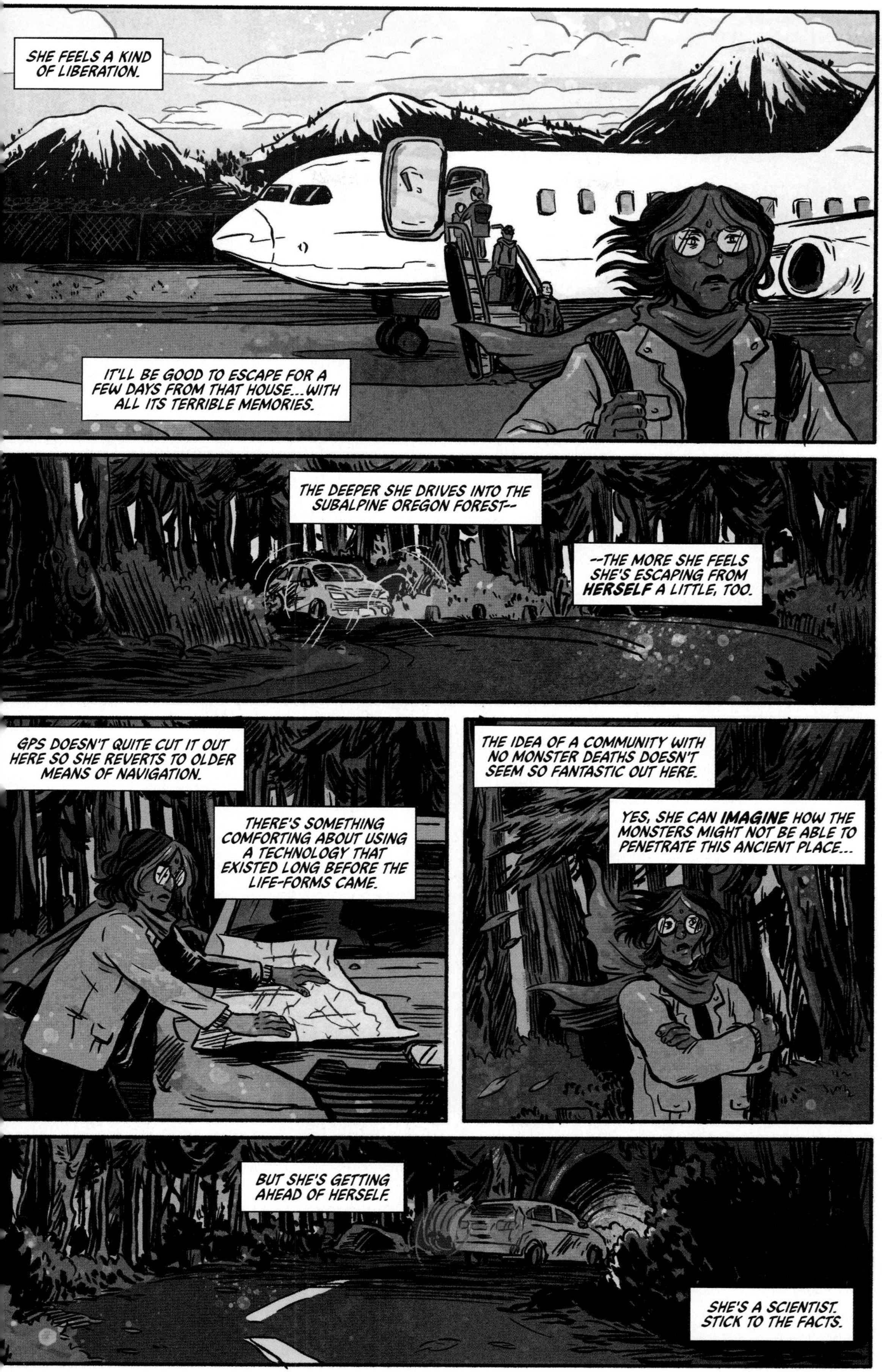
SHE FEELS A KIND OF LIBERATION.
IT'LL BE GOOD TO ESCAPE FOR A FEW DAYS FROM THAT HOUSE...WITH ALL ITS TERRIBLE MEMORIES.
THE DEEPER SHE DRIVES INTO THE SUBALPINE OREGON FOREST--
--THE MORE SHE FEELS SHE'S ESCAPING FROM HERSELF A LITTLE, TOO.
GPS DOESN'T QUITE CUT IT OUT HERE SO SHE REVERTS TO OLDER MEANS OF NAVIGATION.
THERE'S SOMETHING COMFORTING ABOUT USING A TECHNOLOGY THAT EXISTED LONG BEFORE THE LIFE-FORMS CAME.
THE IDEA OF A COMMUNITY WITH NO MONSTER DEATHS DOESN'T SEEM SO FANTASTIC OUT HERE.
YES, SHE CAN IMAGINE HOW THE MONSTERS MIGHT NOT BE ABLE TO PENETRATE THIS ANCIENT PLACE...
BUT SHE'S GETTING AHEAD OF HERSELF.
SHE'S A SCIENTIST. STICK TO THE FACTS.

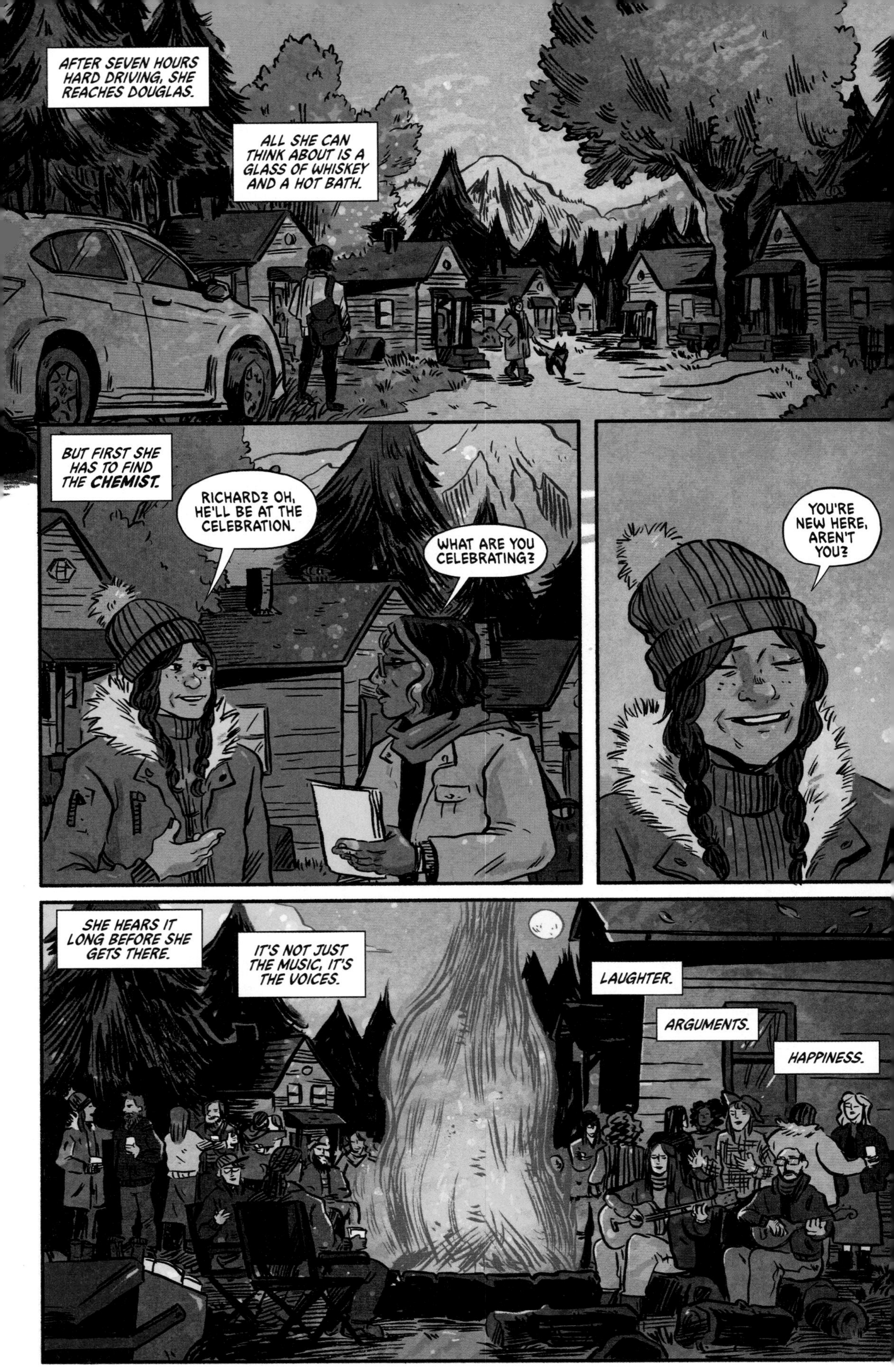
AFTER SEVEN HOURS HARD DRIVING, SHE REACHES DOUGLAS.
ALL SHE CAN THINK ABOUT IS A GLASS OF WHISKEY AND A HOT BATH.
BUT FIRST SHE HAS TO FIND THE CHEMIST.
RICHARD? OH, HE'LL BE AT THE CELEBRATION.
WHAT ARE YOU CELEBRATING?
YOU'RE NEW HERE, AREN'T YOU?
SHE HEARS IT LONG BEFORE SHE GETS THERE.
IT'S NOT JUST THE MUSIC, IT'S THE VOICES.
LAUGHTER.
ARGUMENTS.
HAPPINESS.

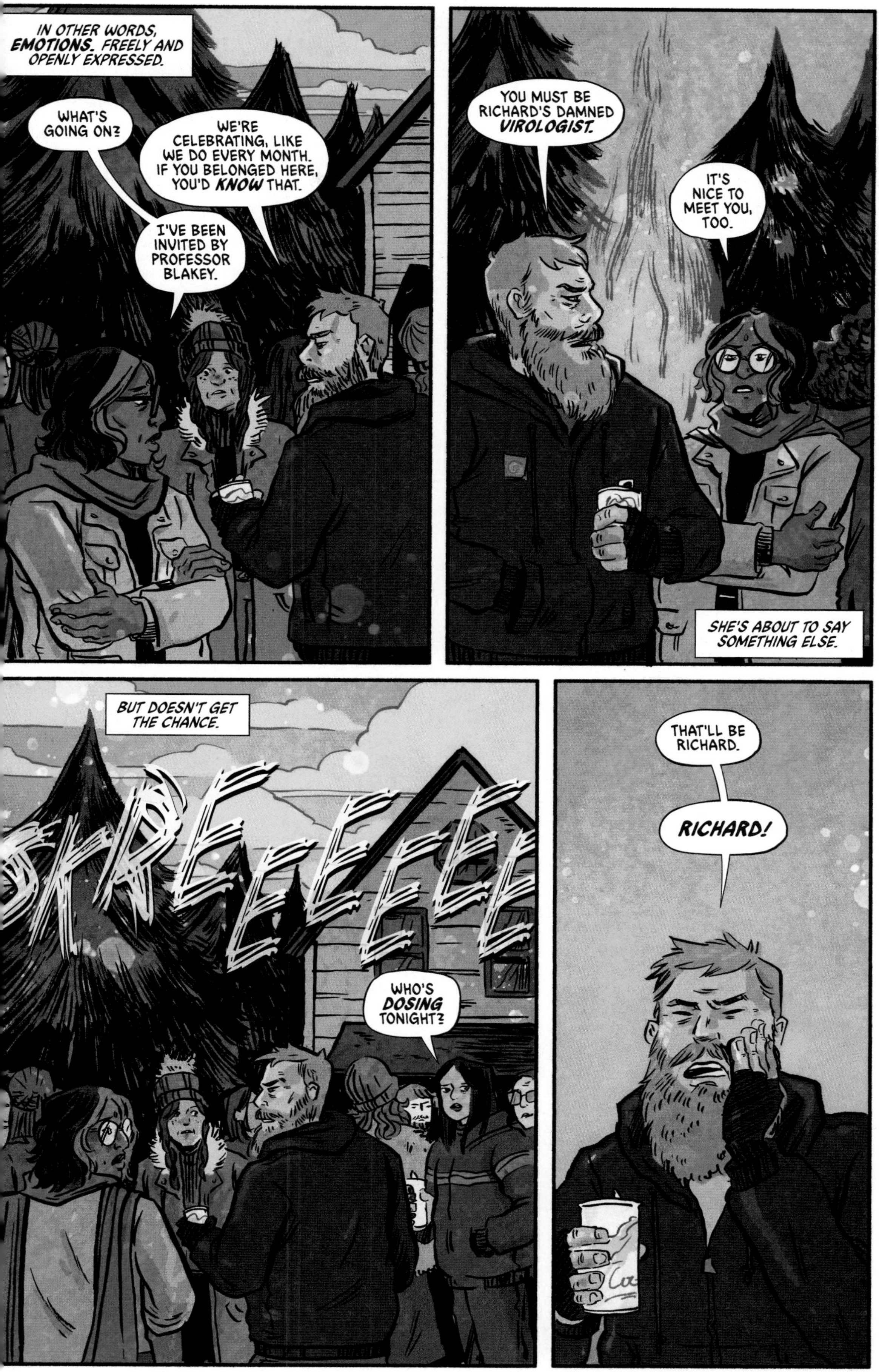
IN OTHER WORDS, EMOTIONS. FREELY AND OPENLY EXPRESSED.
WHAT'S GOING ON?
WE'RE CELEBRATING, LIKE WE DO EVERY MONTH. IF YOU BELONGED HERE, YOU'D KNOW THAT.
I'VE BEEN INVITED BY PROFESSOR BLAKEY.
YOU MUST BE RICHARD'S DAMNED VIROLOGIST.
IT'S NICE TO MEET YOU, TOO.
SHE'S ABOUT TO SAY SOMETHING ELSE.
BUT DOESN'T GET THE CHANCE.
SKREEEEEEE
WHO'S DOSING TONIGHT?
THAT'LL BE RICHARD.
RICHARD!

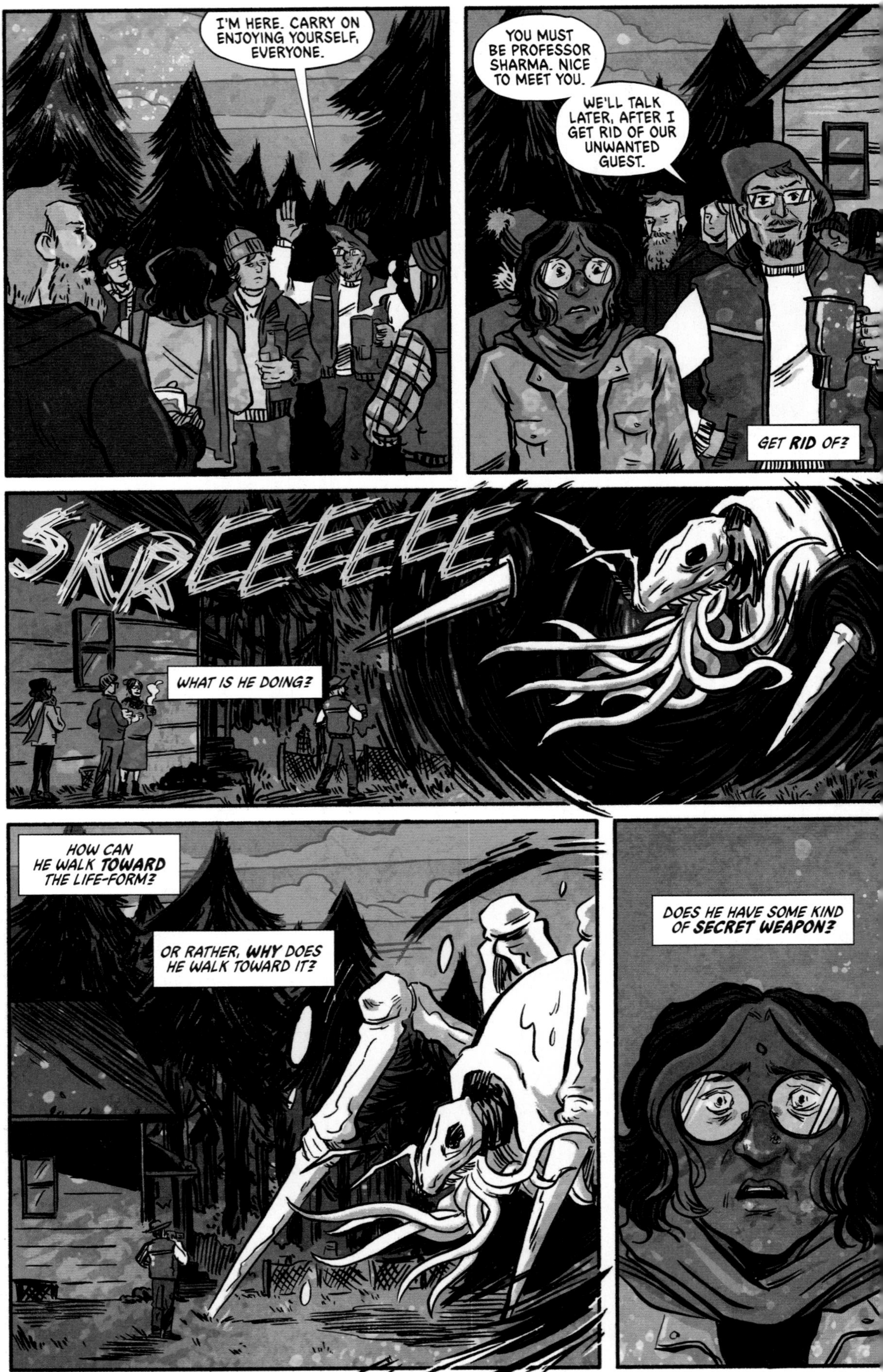

I'M HERE. CARRY ON ENJOYING YOURSELF, EVERYONE.
YOU MUST BE PROFESSOR SHARMA. NICE TO MEET YOU.
WE'LL TALK LATER, AFTER I GET RID OF OUR UNWANTED GUEST.
GET RID OF?
SKREEEEEEE
WHAT IS HE DOING?
HOW CAN HE WALK TOWARD THE LIFE-FORM?
OR RATHER, WHY DOES HE WALK TOWARD IT?
DOES HE HAVE SOME KIND OF SECRET WEAPON?

SKREEEEEE

ALL HER SENSES TELL HER TO TURN AND RUN. BUT SHE'S TRANSFIXED.

SKREEEE

BECAUSE THIS MAKES NO SENSE. THAT AWFUL NOISE, HARBINGER OF HORROR AND DEATH.

YET EVERYONE'S CONTINUING...AS THOUGH EVERYTHING WERE NORMAL.

SKREEEE

ALL RICHARD DOES IS STAND THERE AND LOOK AT IT.

THAT'S IT. HE LOOKS AT IT.

HE KEEPS LOOKING AT IT.

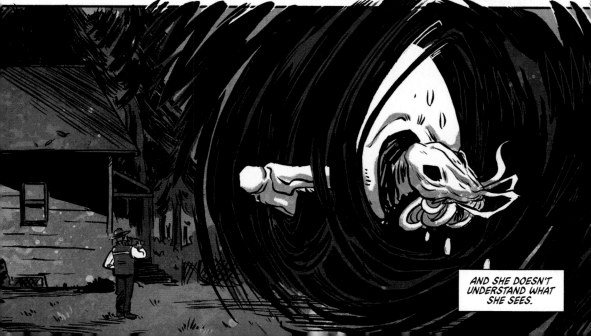

AND SHE DOESN'T UNDERSTAND WHAT SHE SEES.

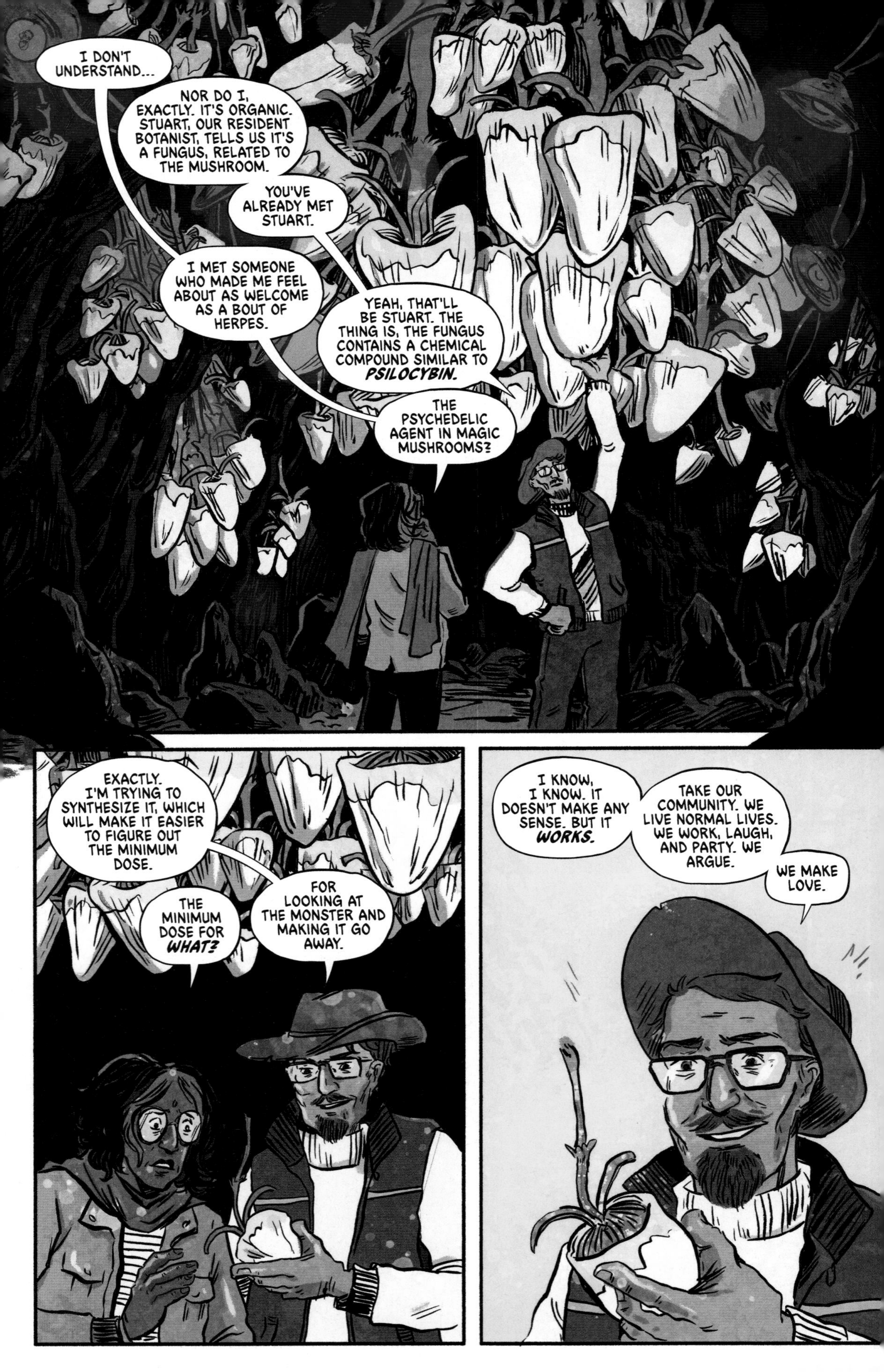
I DON'T UNDERSTAND...
NOR DO I, EXACTLY. IT'S ORGANIC. STUART, OUR RESIDENT BOTANIST, TELLS US IT'S A FUNGUS, RELATED TO THE MUSHROOM.
YOU'VE ALREADY MET STUART.
I MET SOMEONE WHO MADE ME FEEL ABOUT AS WELCOME AS A BOUT OF HERPES.
YEAH, THAT'LL BE STUART. THE THING IS, THE FUNGUS CONTAINS A CHEMICAL COMPOUND SIMILAR TO PSILOCYBIN.
THE PSYCHEDELIC AGENT IN MAGIC MUSHROOMS?
EXACTLY. I'M TRYING TO SYNTHESIZE IT, WHICH WILL MAKE IT EASIER TO FIGURE OUT THE MINIMUM DOSE.
THE MINIMUM DOSE FOR WHAT?
FOR LOOKING AT THE MONSTER AND MAKING IT GO AWAY.
I KNOW, I KNOW. IT DOESN'T MAKE ANY SENSE. BUT IT WORKS.
TAKE OUR COMMUNITY. WE LIVE NORMAL LIVES. WE WORK, LAUGH, AND PARTY. WE ARGUE.
WE MAKE LOVE.

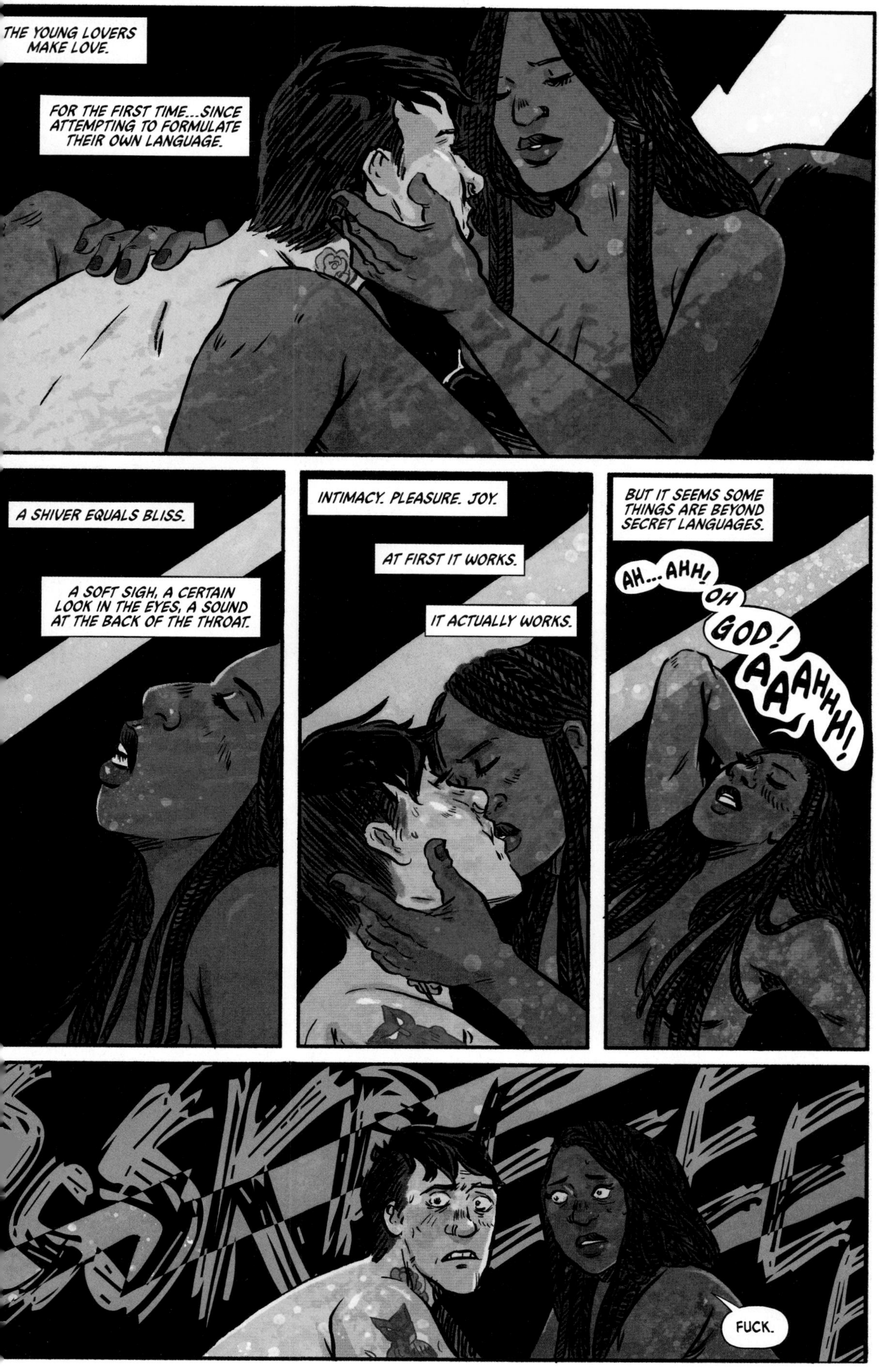
THE YOUNG LOVERS MAKE LOVE.
FOR THE FIRST TIME...SINCE ATTEMPTING TO FORMULATE THEIR OWN LANGUAGE.
A SHIVER EQUALS BLISS.
A SOFT SIGH, A CERTAIN LOOK IN THE EYES, A SOUND AT THE BACK OF THE THROAT.
INTIMACY. PLEASURE. JOY.
AT FIRST IT WORKS.
IT ACTUALLY WORKS.
BUT IT SEEMS SOME THINGS ARE BEYOND SECRET LANGUAGES.
AH...AHH! OH GOD! AAAHHH!
FUCK.

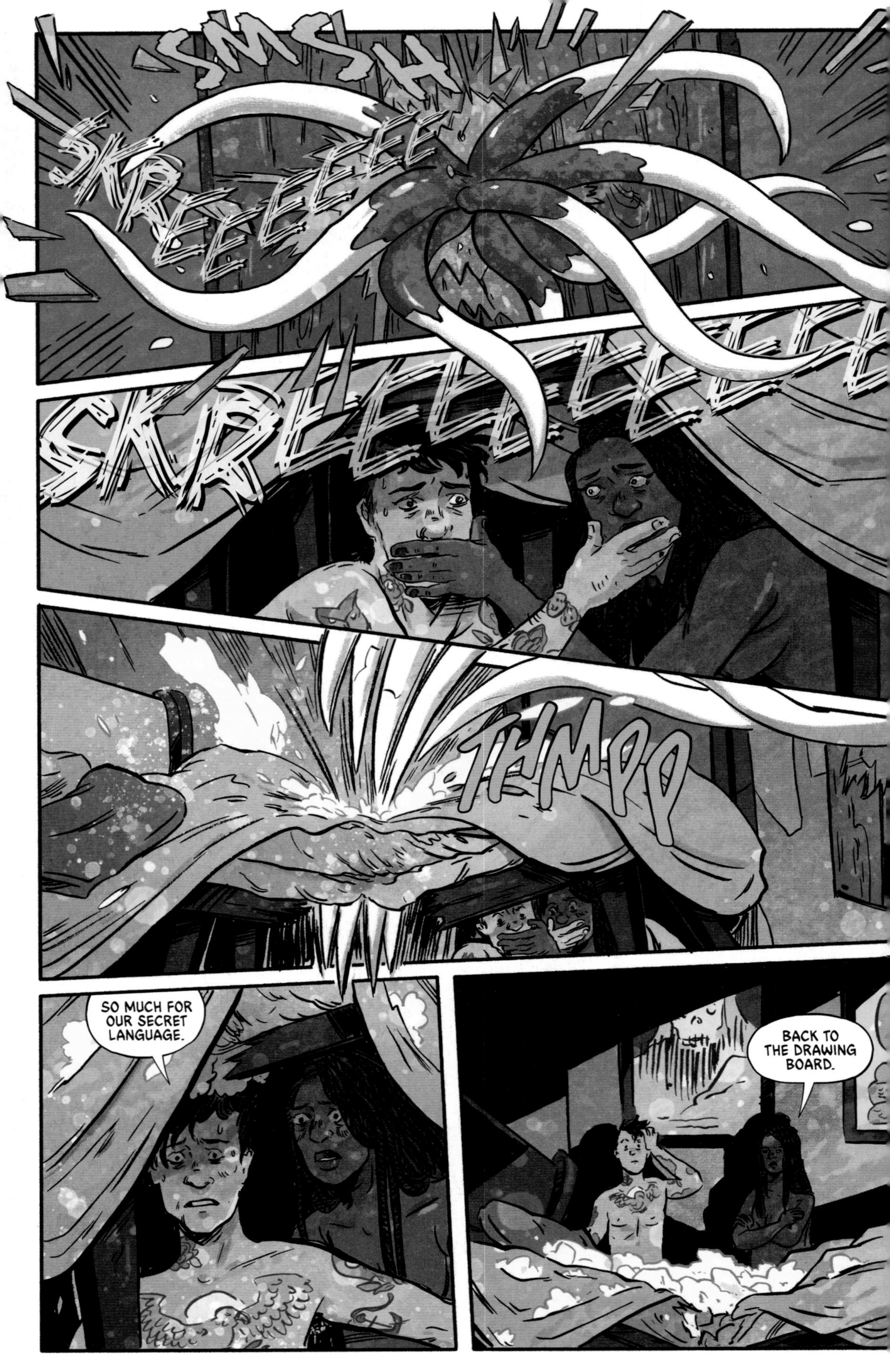
SMSH
SKREEEEEEE
SKREEEEEEEEE
THMPD
SO MUCH FOR OUR SECRET LANGUAGE.
BACK TO THE DRAWING BOARD.

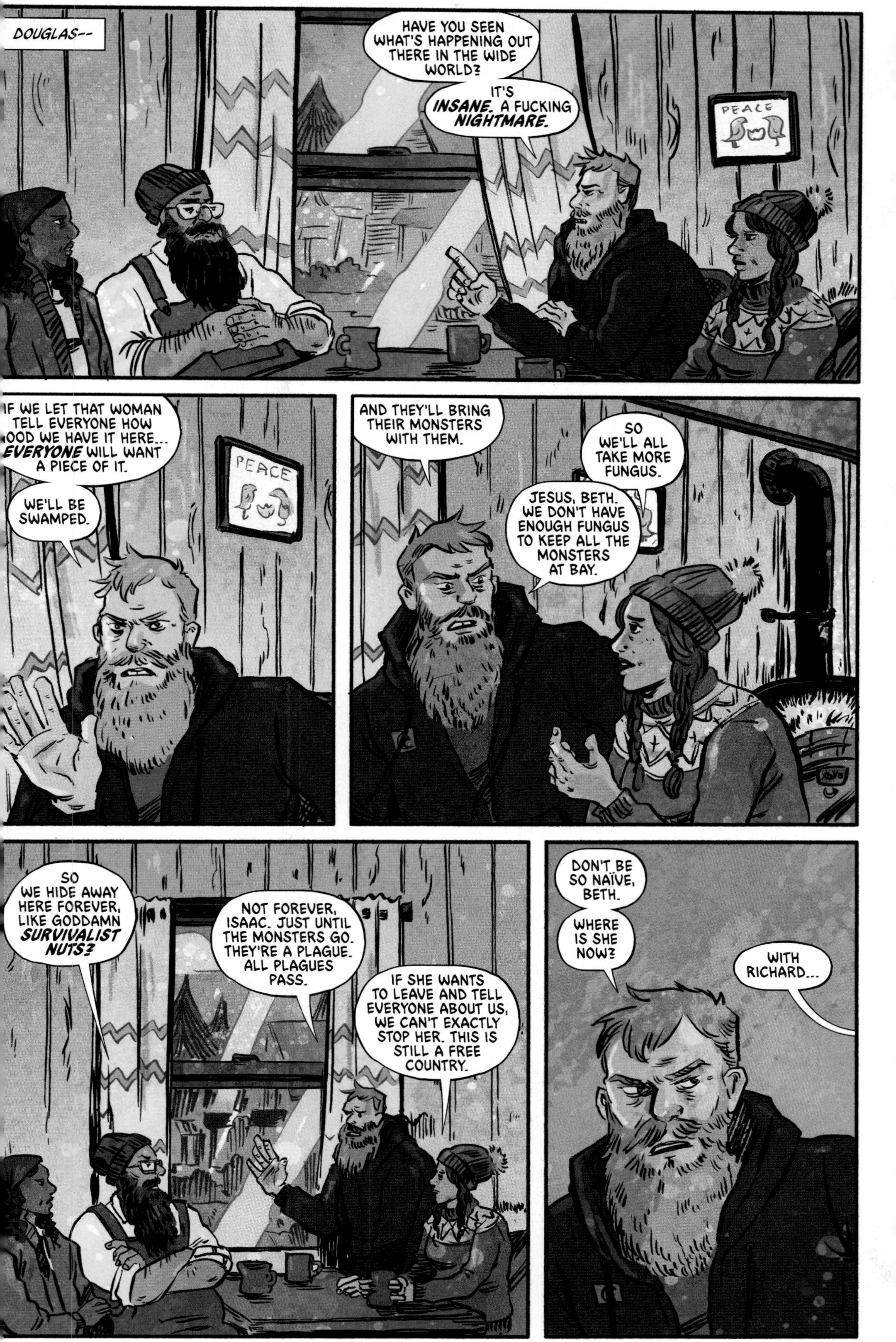
DOUGLAS--
HAVE YOU SEEN WHAT'S HAPPENING OUT THERE IN THE WIDE WORLD?
IT'S ***INSANE.*** A FUCKING ***NIGHTMARE.***
PEACE
IF WE LET THAT WOMAN TELL EVERYONE HOW OOD WE HAVE IT HERE... ***EVERYONE*** WILL WANT A PIECE OF IT.
WE'LL BE SWAMPED.
PEACE
AND THEY'LL BRING THEIR MONSTERS WITH THEM.
SO WE'LL ALL TAKE MORE FUNGUS.
JESUS, BETH. WE DON'T HAVE ENOUGH FUNGUS TO KEEP ALL THE MONSTERS AT BAY.
SO WE HIDE AWAY HERE FOREVER, LIKE GODDAMN ***SURVIVALIST NUTS?***
NOT FOREVER, ISAAC. JUST UNTIL THE MONSTERS GO. THEY'RE A PLAGUE. ALL PLAGUES PASS.
IF SHE WANTS TO LEAVE AND TELL EVERYONE ABOUT US, WE CAN'T EXACTLY STOP HER. THIS IS STILL A FREE COUNTRY.
DON'T BE SO NAÏVE, BETH.
WHERE IS SHE NOW?
WITH RICHARD...

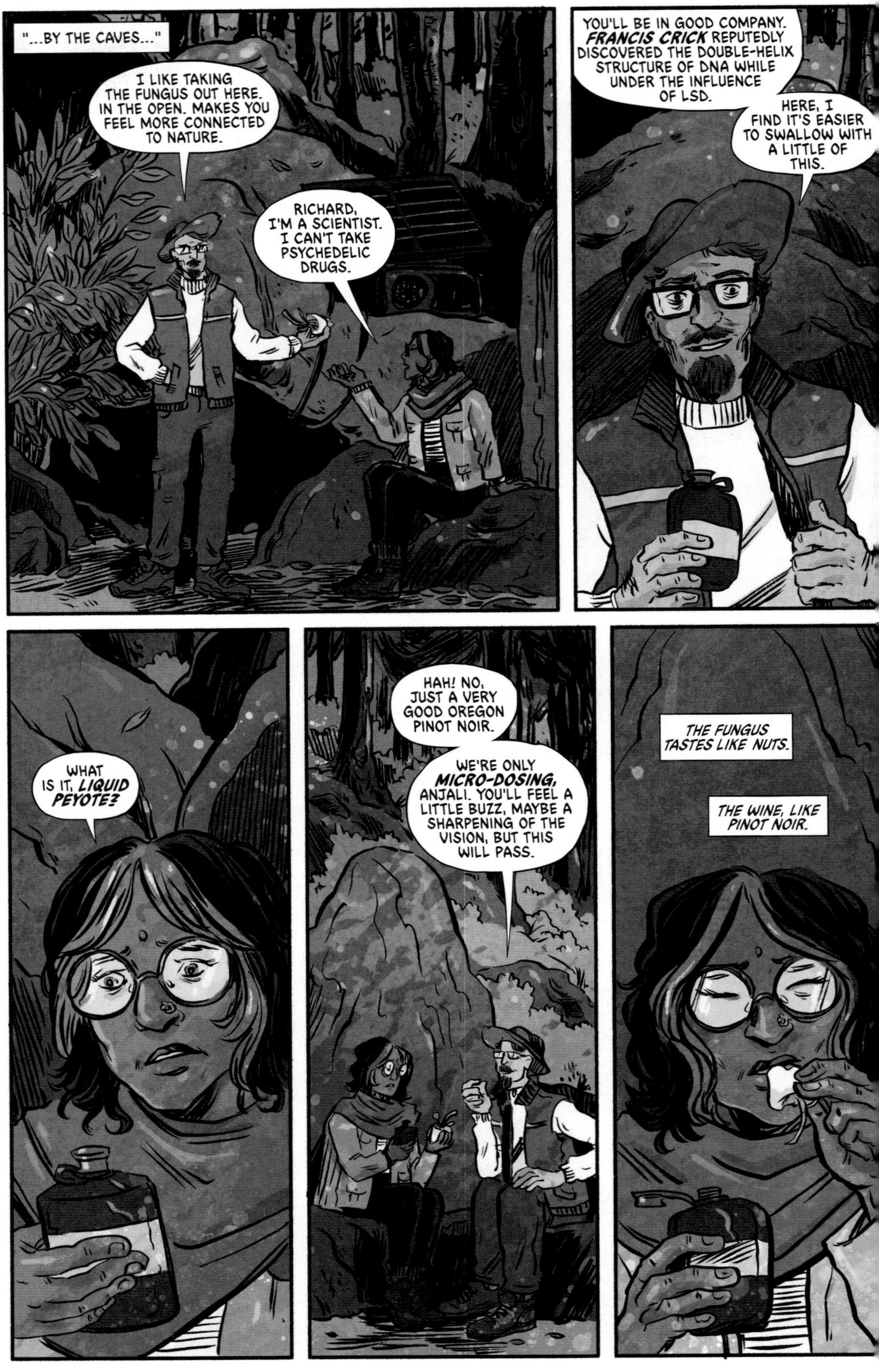
"...BY THE CAVES..."
I LIKE TAKING THE FUNGUS OUT HERE. IN THE OPEN. MAKES YOU FEEL MORE CONNECTED TO NATURE.
RICHARD, I'M A SCIENTIST. I CAN'T TAKE PSYCHEDELIC DRUGS.
YOU'LL BE IN GOOD COMPANY. *FRANCIS CRICK* REPUTEDLY DISCOVERED THE DOUBLE-HELIX STRUCTURE OF DNA WHILE UNDER THE INFLUENCE OF LSD.
HERE, I FIND IT'S EASIER TO SWALLOW WITH A LITTLE OF THIS.
WHAT IS IT, *LIQUID PEYOTE?*
HAH! NO, JUST A VERY GOOD OREGON PINOT NOIR.
WE'RE ONLY *MICRO-DOSING,* ANJALI. YOU'LL FEEL A LITTLE BUZZ, MAYBE A SHARPENING OF THE VISION, BUT THIS WILL PASS.
THE FUNGUS TASTES LIKE NUTS.
THE WINE, LIKE PINOT NOIR.

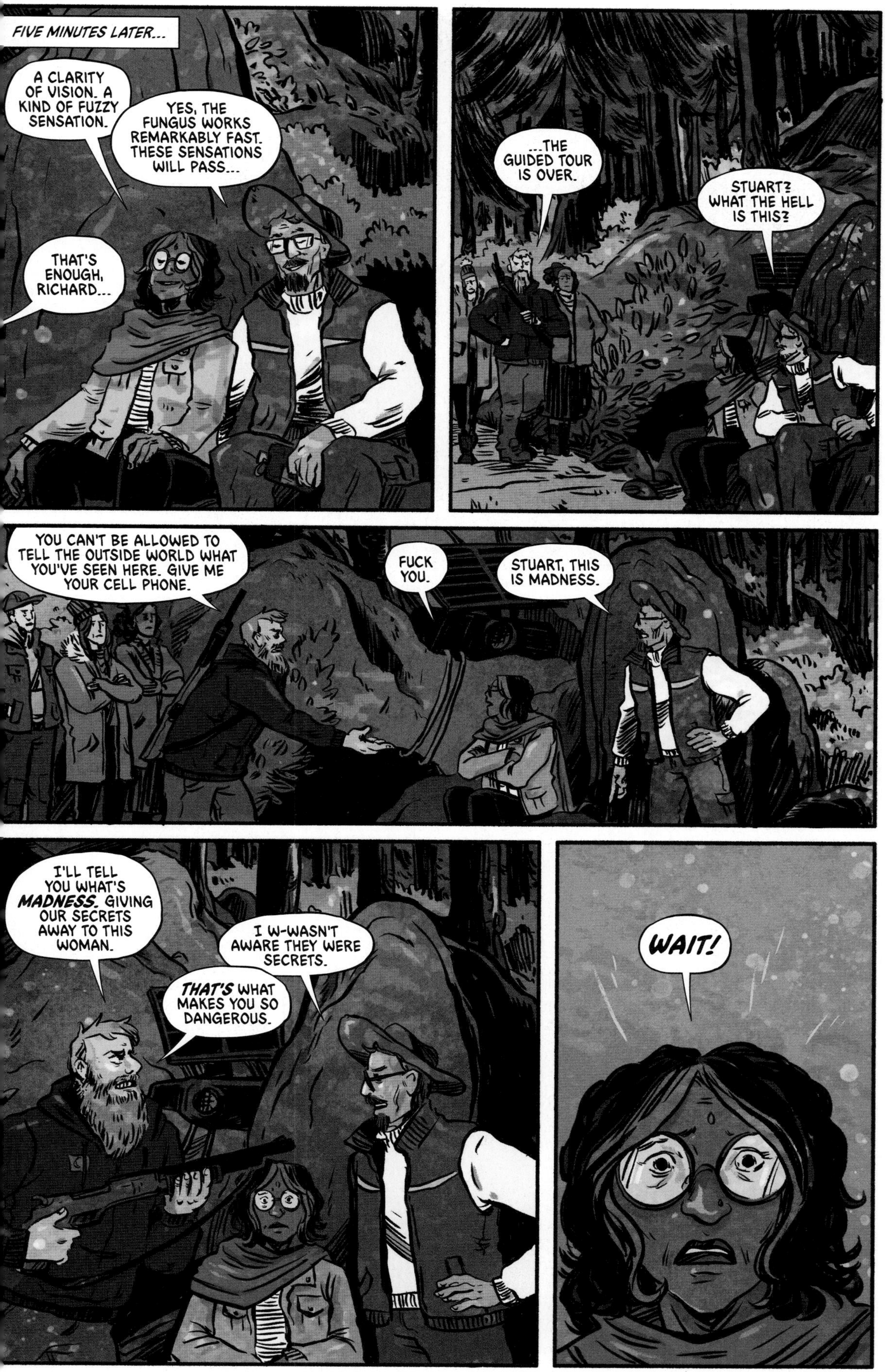
FIVE MINUTES LATER...
A CLARITY OF VISION. A KIND OF FUZZY SENSATION.
YES, THE FUNGUS WORKS REMARKABLY FAST. THESE SENSATIONS WILL PASS...
THAT'S ENOUGH, RICHARD...
...THE GUIDED TOUR IS OVER.
STUART? WHAT THE HELL IS THIS?
YOU CAN'T BE ALLOWED TO TELL THE OUTSIDE WORLD WHAT YOU'VE SEEN HERE. GIVE ME YOUR CELL PHONE.
FUCK YOU.
STUART, THIS IS MADNESS.
I'LL TELL YOU WHAT'S MADNESS. GIVING OUR SECRETS AWAY TO THIS WOMAN.
I W-WASN'T AWARE THEY WERE SECRETS.
THAT'S WHAT MAKES YOU SO DANGEROUS.
WAIT!

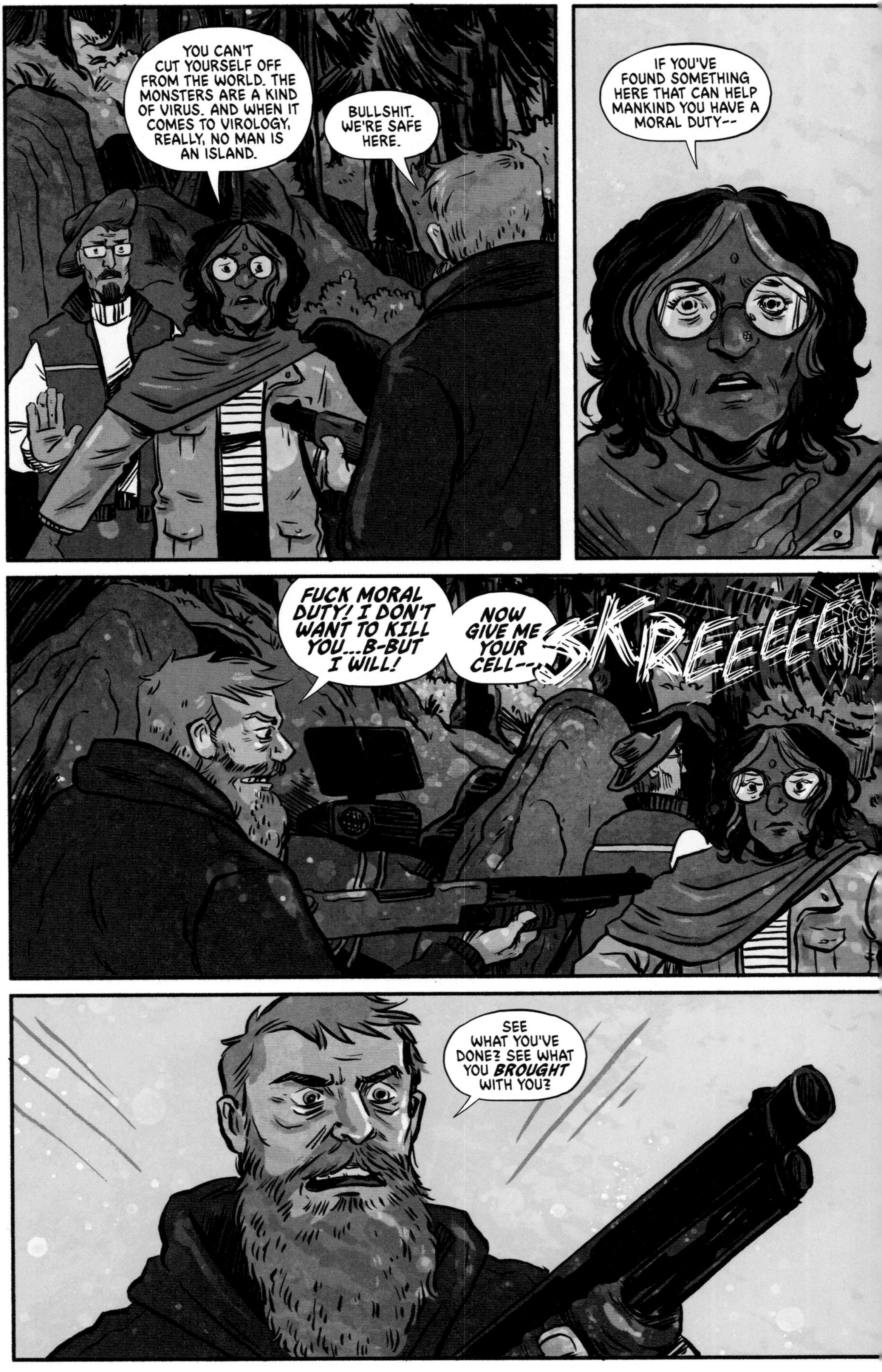
YOU CAN'T CUT YOURSELF OFF FROM THE WORLD. THE MONSTERS ARE A KIND OF VIRUS. AND WHEN IT COMES TO VIROLOGY, REALLY, NO MAN IS AN ISLAND.
BULLSHIT. WE'RE SAFE HERE.
IF YOU'VE FOUND SOMETHING HERE THAT CAN HELP MANKIND YOU HAVE A MORAL DUTY--
FUCK MORAL DUTY! I DON'T WANT TO KILL YOU...B-BUT I WILL!
NOW GIVE ME YOUR CELL--
SKREEEEE
SEE WHAT YOU'VE DONE? SEE WHAT YOU BROUGHT WITH YOU?

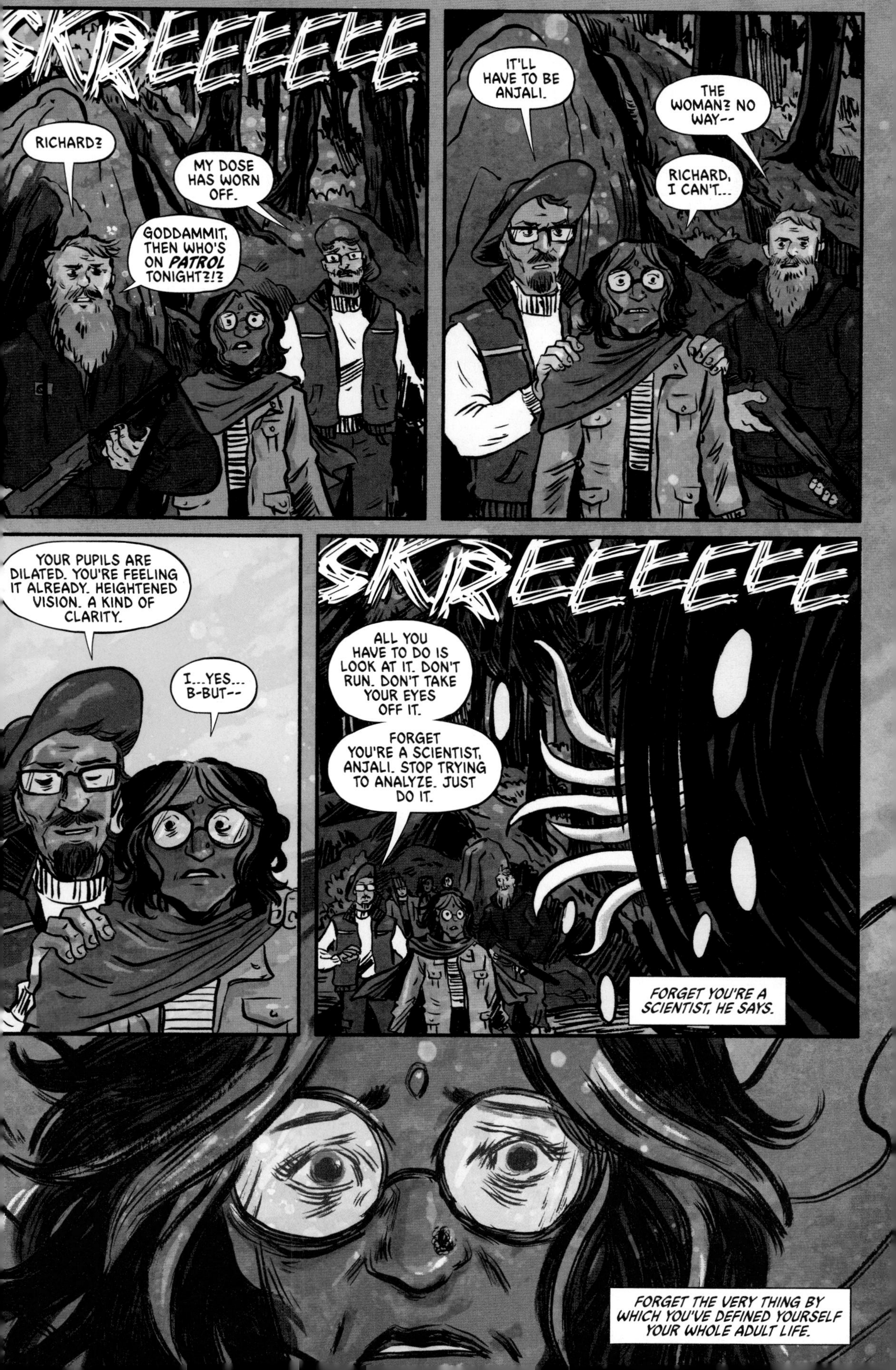
SKREEEEEE
RICHARD?
MY DOSE HAS WORN OFF.
GODDAMMIT, THEN WHO'S ON PATROL TONIGHT?!?
IT'LL HAVE TO BE ANJALI.
THE WOMAN? NO WAY--
RICHARD, I CAN'T...
YOUR PUPILS ARE DILATED. YOU'RE FEELING IT ALREADY. HEIGHTENED VISION. A KIND OF CLARITY.
I...YES... B-BUT--
SKREEEEEE
ALL YOU HAVE TO DO IS LOOK AT IT. DON'T RUN. DON'T TAKE YOUR EYES OFF IT.
FORGET YOU'RE A SCIENTIST, ANJALI. STOP TRYING TO ANALYZE. JUST DO IT.
FORGET YOU'RE A SCIENTIST, HE SAYS.
FORGET THE VERY THING BY WHICH YOU'VE DEFINED YOURSELF YOUR WHOLE ADULT LIFE.

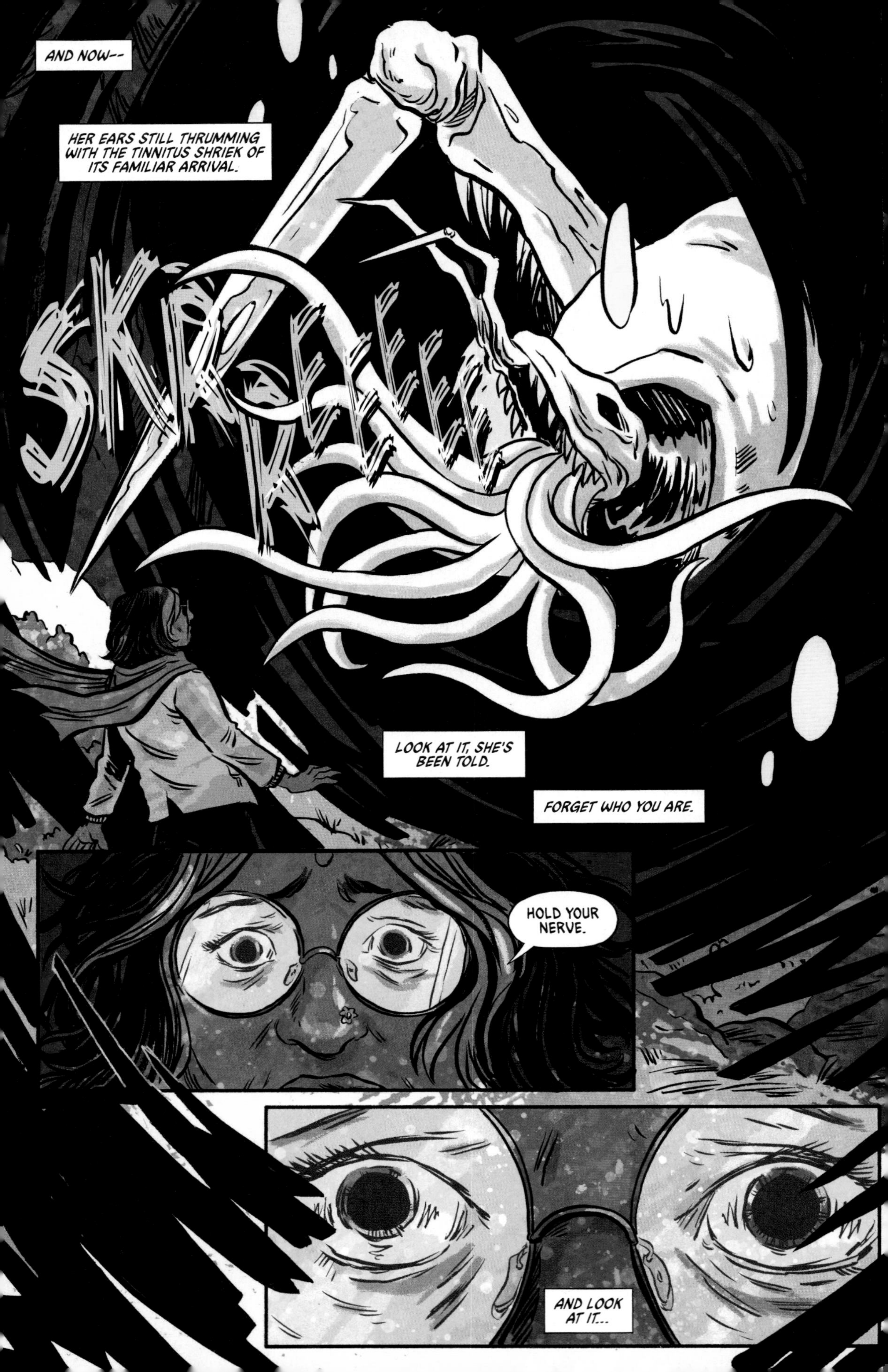
AND NOW--
HER EARS STILL THRUMMING WITH THE TINNITUS SHRIEK OF ITS FAMILIAR ARRIVAL.
SKREEEEEE
LOOK AT IT, SHE'S BEEN TOLD.
FORGET WHO YOU ARE.
HOLD YOUR NERVE.
AND LOOK AT IT...

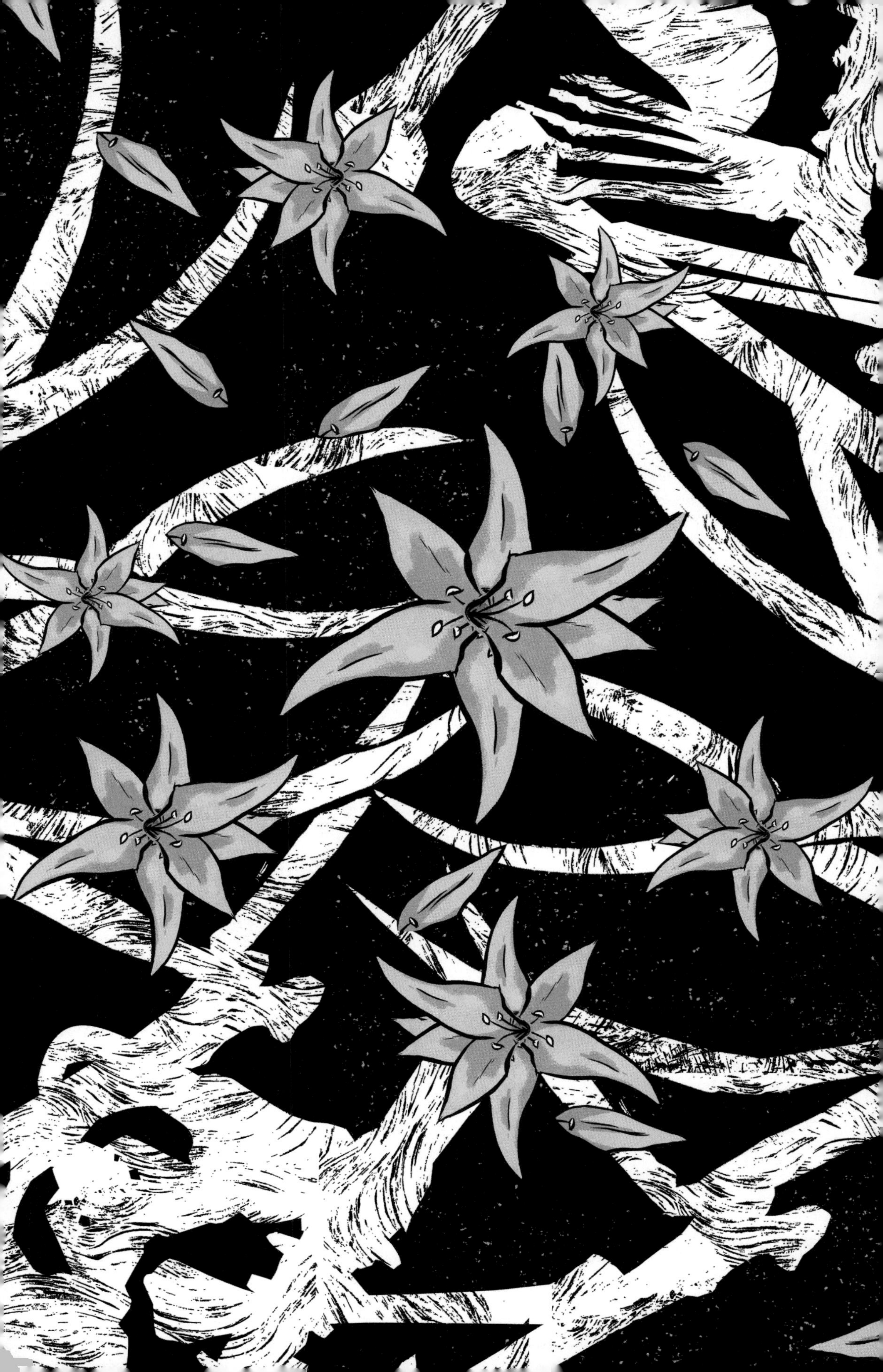

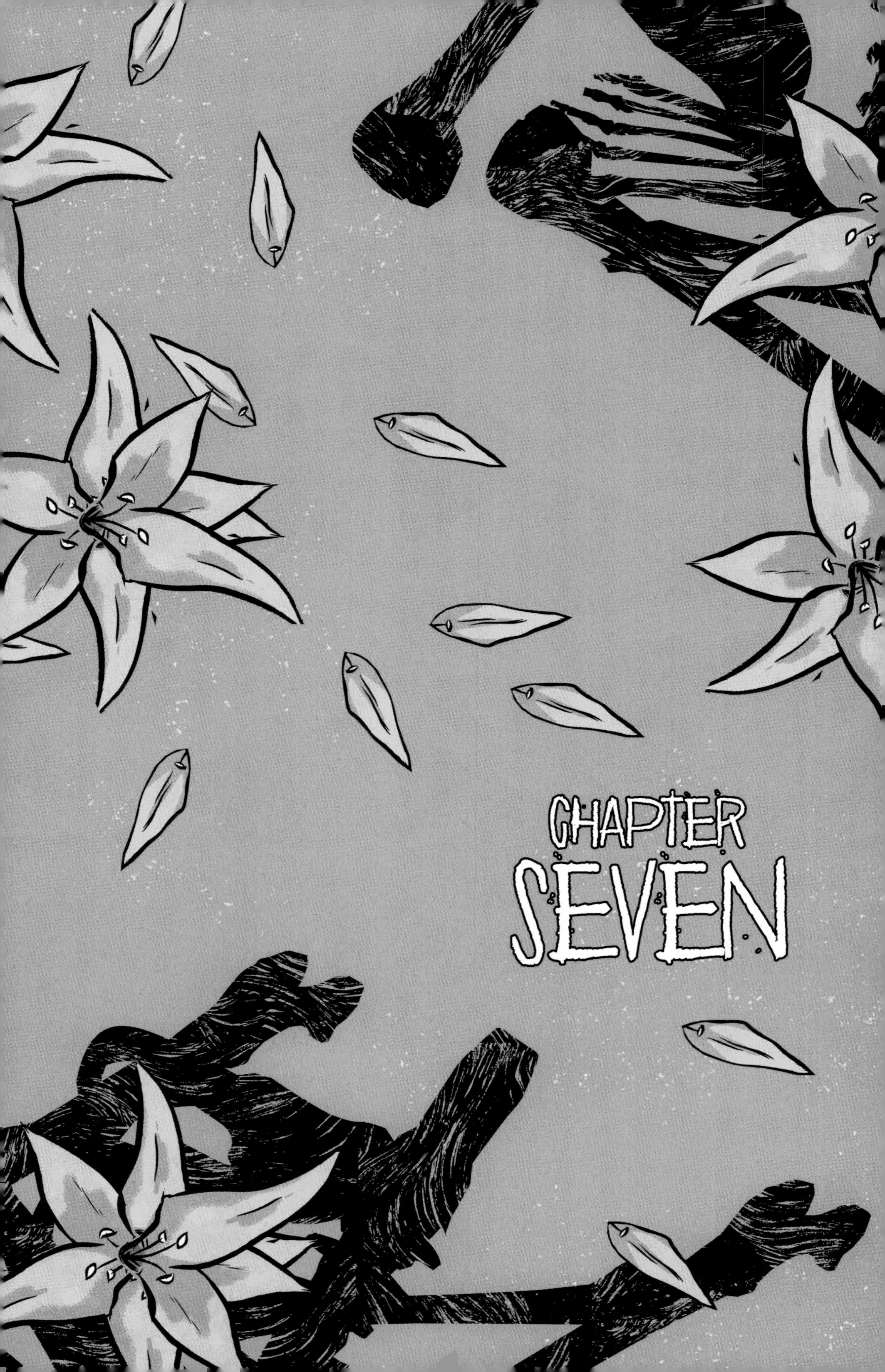
CHAPTER
SEVEN

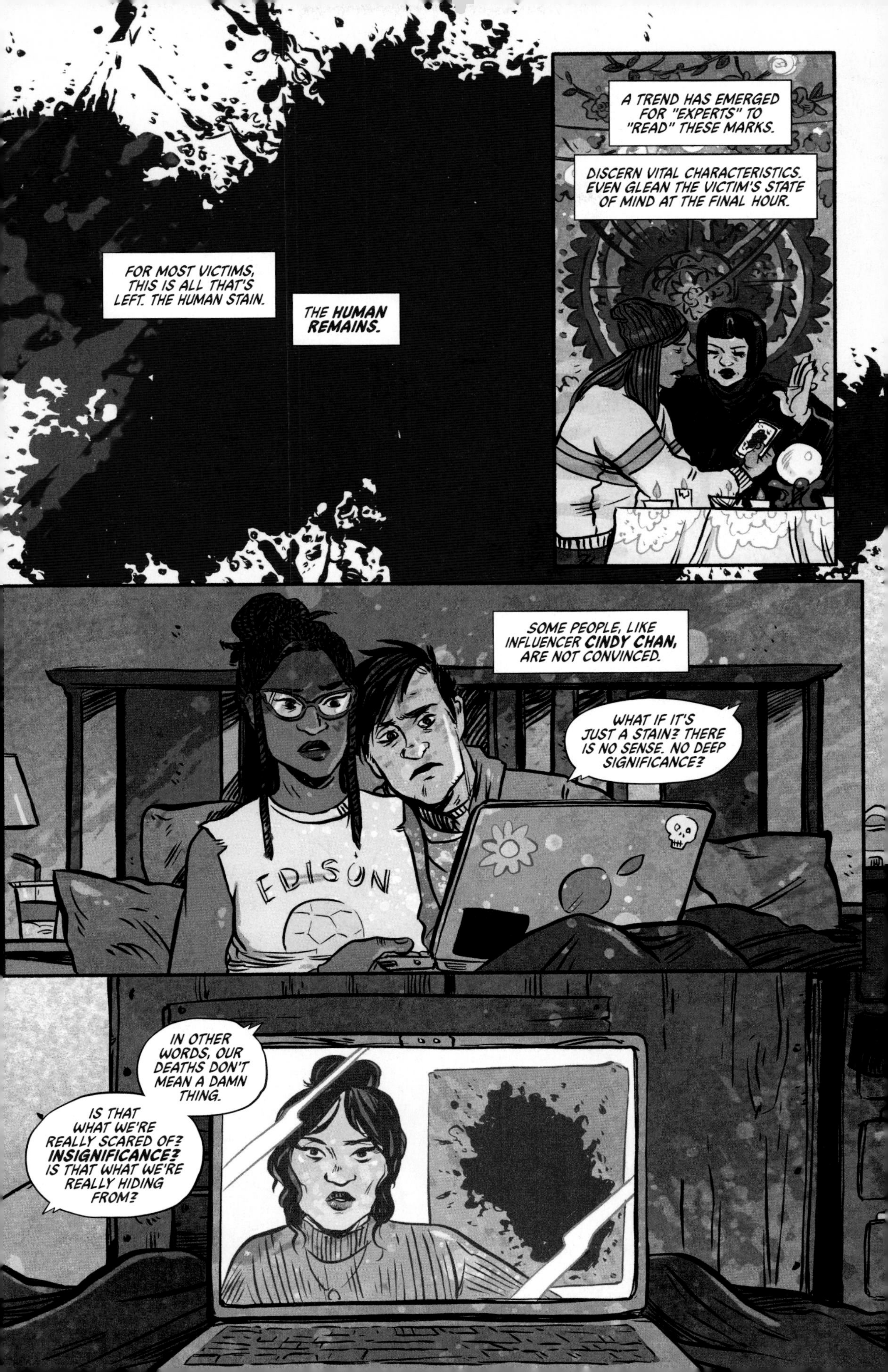
FOR MOST VICTIMS, THIS IS ALL THAT'S LEFT. THE HUMAN STAIN.
THE HUMAN REMAINS.
A TREND HAS EMERGED FOR "EXPERTS" TO "READ" THESE MARKS.
DISCERN VITAL CHARACTERISTICS. EVEN GLEAN THE VICTIM'S STATE OF MIND AT THE FINAL HOUR.
SOME PEOPLE, LIKE INFLUENCER CINDY CHAN, ARE NOT CONVINCED.
WHAT IF IT'S JUST A STAIN? THERE IS NO SENSE. NO DEEP SIGNIFICANCE?
EDISON
IN OTHER WORDS, OUR DEATHS DON'T MEAN A DAMN THING.
IS THAT WHAT WE'RE REALLY SCARED OF? INSIGNIFICANCE? IS THAT WHAT WE'RE REALLY HIDING FROM?

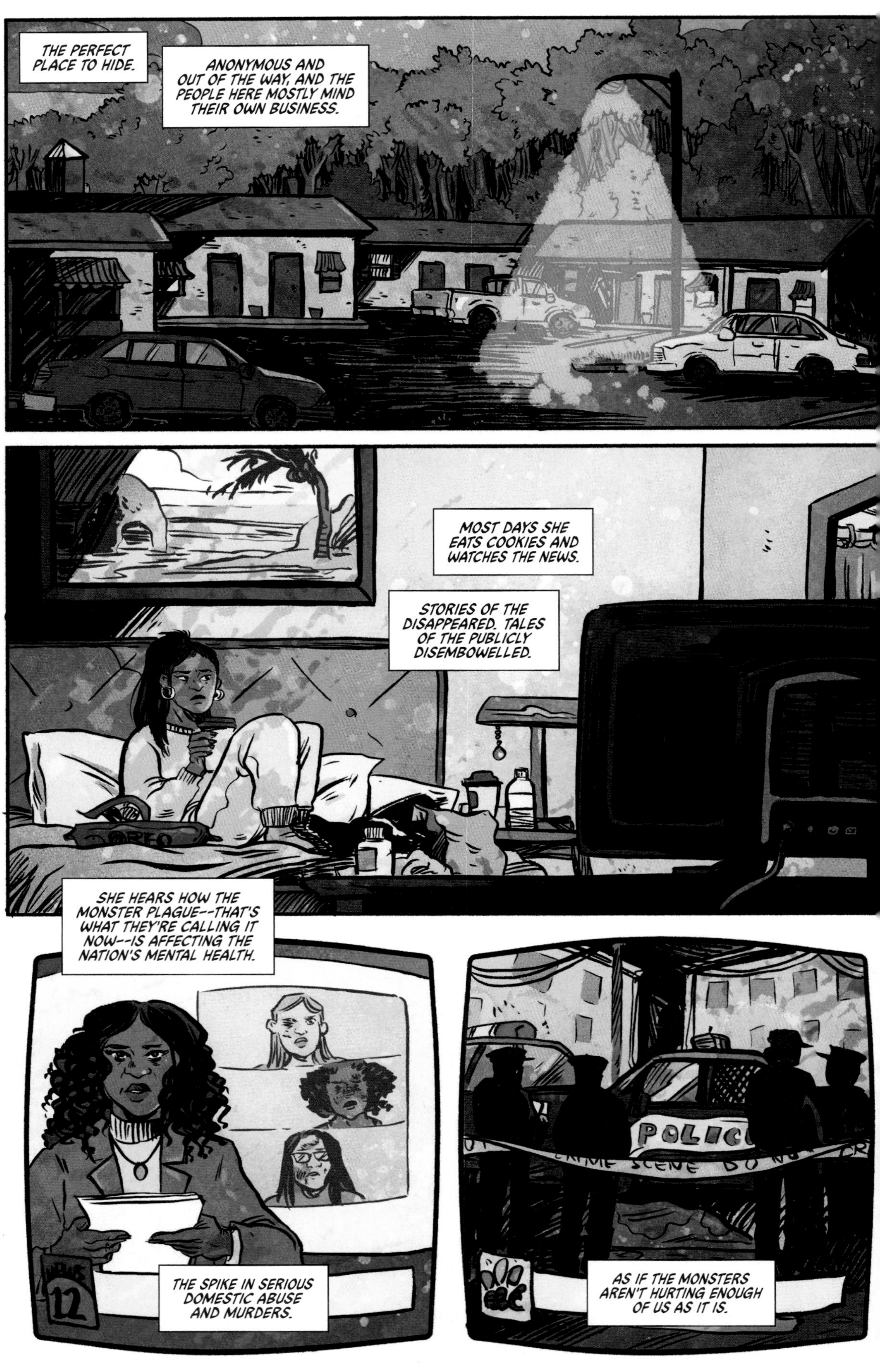
THE PERFECT PLACE TO HIDE.
ANONYMOUS AND OUT OF THE WAY, AND THE PEOPLE HERE MOSTLY MIND THEIR OWN BUSINESS.
MOST DAYS SHE EATS COOKIES AND WATCHES THE NEWS.
STORIES OF THE DISAPPEARED. TALES OF THE PUBLICLY DISEMBOWELLED.
SHE HEARS HOW THE MONSTER PLAGUE--THAT'S WHAT THEY'RE CALLING IT NOW--IS AFFECTING THE NATION'S MENTAL HEALTH.
NEWS 12
THE SPIKE IN SERIOUS DOMESTIC ABUSE AND MURDERS.
AS IF THE MONSTERS AREN'T HURTING ENOUGH OF US AS IT IS.

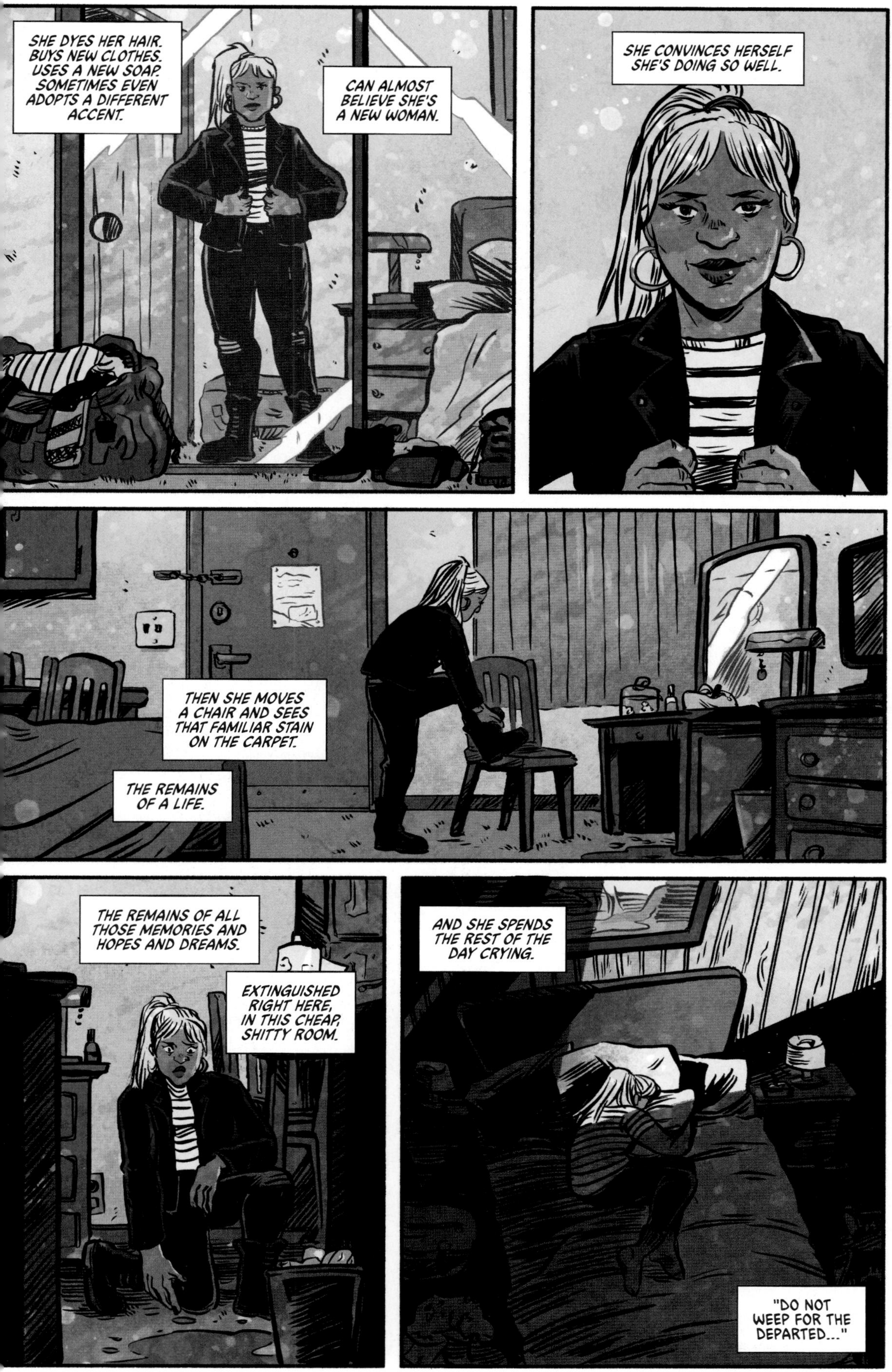
SHE DYES HER HAIR. BUYS NEW CLOTHES. USES A NEW SOAP. SOMETIMES EVEN ADOPTS A DIFFERENT ACCENT.
CAN ALMOST BELIEVE SHE'S A NEW WOMAN.
SHE CONVINCES HERSELF SHE'S DOING SO WELL.
THEN SHE MOVES A CHAIR AND SEES THAT FAMILIAR STAIN ON THE CARPET.
THE REMAINS OF A LIFE.
THE REMAINS OF ALL THOSE MEMORIES AND HOPES AND DREAMS.
EXTINGUISHED RIGHT HERE, IN THIS CHEAP, SHITTY ROOM.
AND SHE SPENDS THE REST OF THE DAY CRYING.
"DO NOT WEEP FOR THE DEPARTED..."

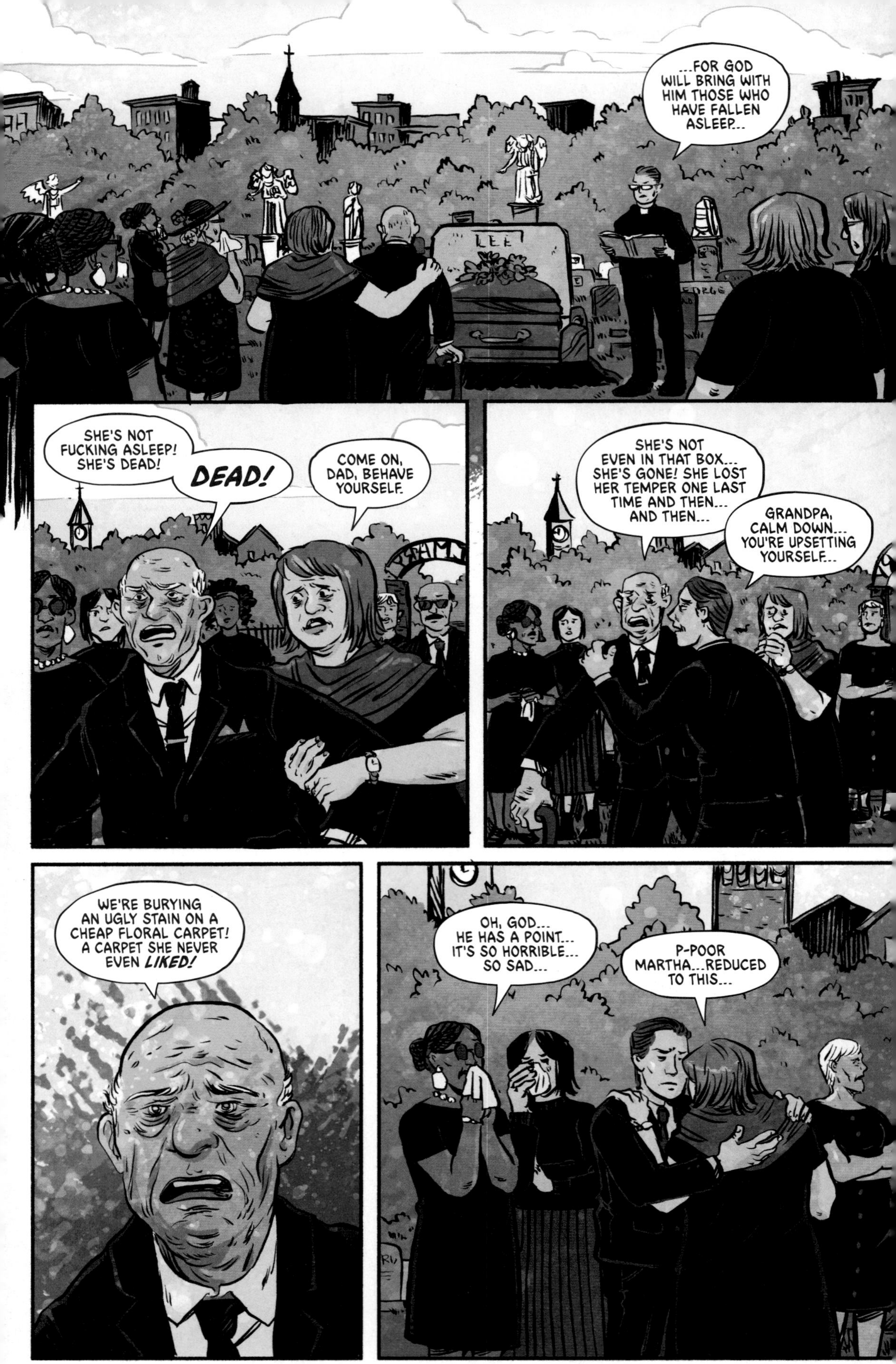
...FOR GOD WILL BRING WITH HIM THOSE WHO HAVE FALLEN ASLEEP...
LEE
SHE'S NOT FUCKING ASLEEP! SHE'S DEAD!
DEAD!
COME ON, DAD, BEHAVE YOURSELF.
SHE'S NOT EVEN IN THAT BOX... SHE'S GONE! SHE LOST HER TEMPER ONE LAST TIME AND THEN... AND THEN...
GRANDPA, CALM DOWN... YOU'RE UPSETTING YOURSELF...
WE'RE BURYING AN UGLY STAIN ON A CHEAP FLORAL CARPET! A CARPET SHE NEVER EVEN LIKED!
OH, GOD... HE HAS A POINT... IT'S SO HORRIBLE... SO SAD...
P-POOR MARTHA...REDUCED TO THIS...

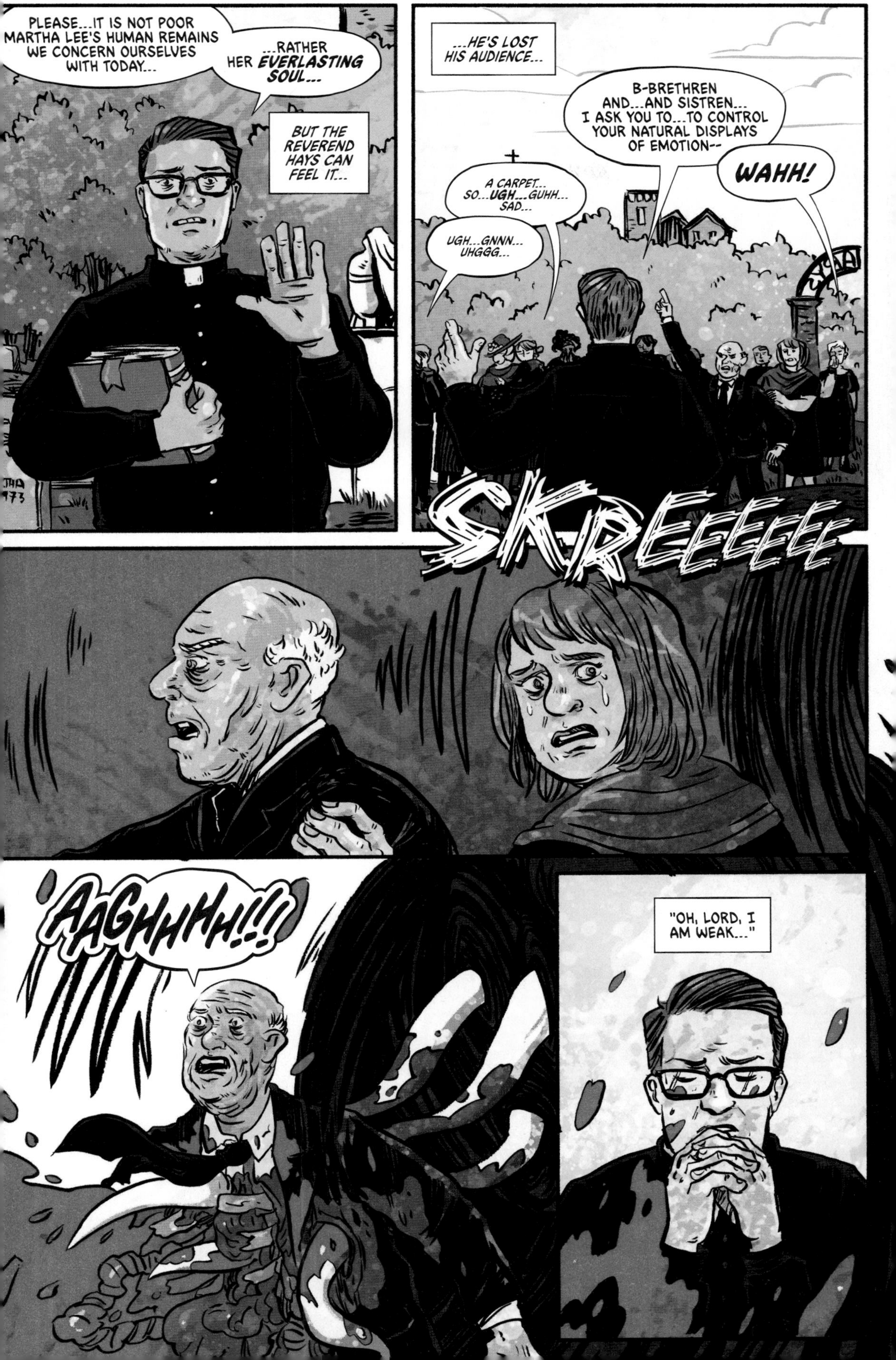
PLEASE...IT IS NOT POOR MARTHA LEE'S HUMAN REMAINS WE CONCERN OURSELVES WITH TODAY...
...RATHER HER EVERLASTING SOUL...
BUT THE REVEREND HAYS CAN FEEL IT...
...HE'S LOST HIS AUDIENCE...
B-BRETHREN AND...AND SISTREN... I ASK YOU TO...TO CONTROL YOUR NATURAL DISPLAYS OF EMOTION--
WAHH!
A CARPET... SO...UGH...GUHH... SAD...
UGH...GNNN... UHGGG...
SKREEEEEE
AAGHHHHH!!!
"OH, LORD, I AM WEAK..."

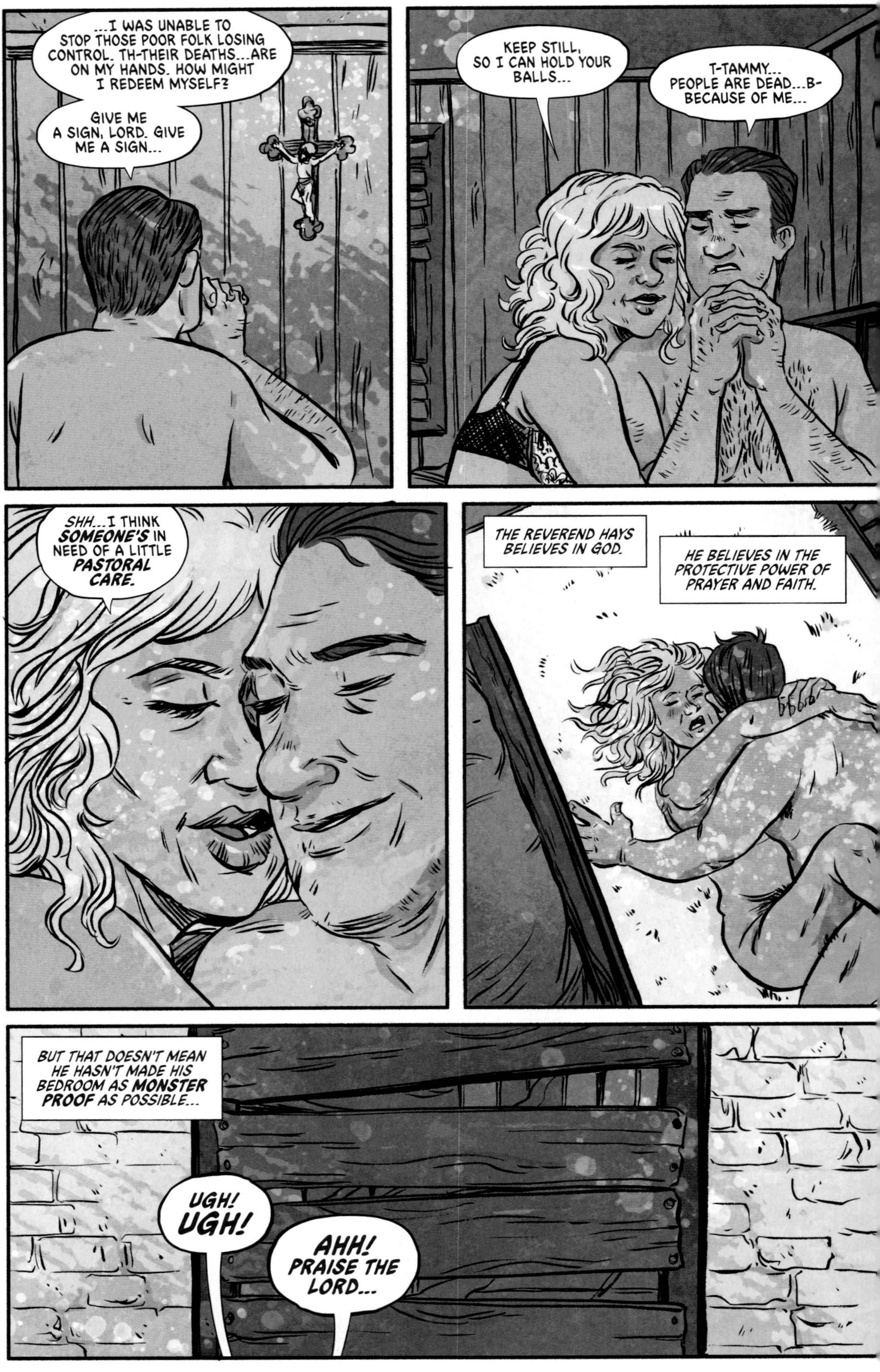
...I WAS UNABLE TO STOP THOSE POOR FOLK LOSING CONTROL. TH-THEIR DEATHS...ARE ON MY HANDS. HOW MIGHT I REDEEM MYSELF?
GIVE ME A SIGN, LORD. GIVE ME A SIGN...
KEEP STILL, SO I CAN HOLD YOUR BALLS...
T-TAMMY... PEOPLE ARE DEAD...B-BECAUSE OF ME...
SHH...I THINK SOMEONE'S IN NEED OF A LITTLE PASTORAL CARE.
THE REVEREND HAYS BELIEVES IN GOD.
HE BELIEVES IN THE PROTECTIVE POWER OF PRAYER AND FAITH.
BUT THAT DOESN'T MEAN HE HASN'T MADE HIS BEDROOM AS MONSTER PROOF AS POSSIBLE...
UGH! UGH!
AHH! PRAISE THE LORD...

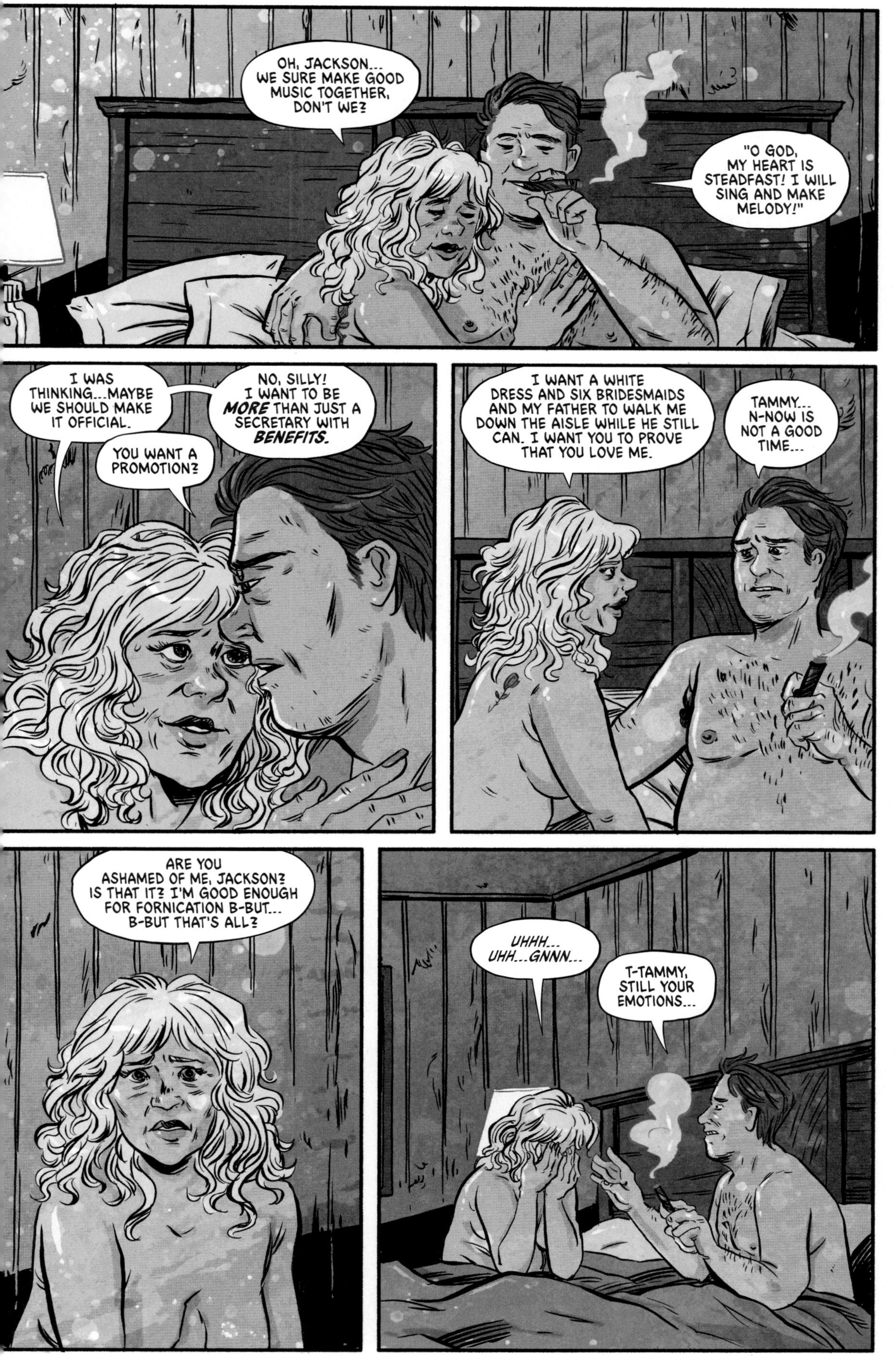
OH, JACKSON...
WE SURE MAKE GOOD
MUSIC TOGETHER,
DON'T WE?
"O GOD,
MY HEART IS
STEADFAST! I WILL
SING AND MAKE
MELODY!"
I WAS
THINKING...MAYBE
WE SHOULD MAKE
IT OFFICIAL.
YOU WANT A
PROMOTION?
NO, SILLY!
I WANT TO BE
MORE THAN JUST A
SECRETARY WITH
BENEFITS.
I WANT A WHITE
DRESS AND SIX BRIDESMAIDS
AND MY FATHER TO WALK ME
DOWN THE AISLE WHILE HE STILL
CAN. I WANT YOU TO PROVE
THAT YOU LOVE ME.
TAMMY...
N-NOW IS
NOT A GOOD
TIME...
ARE YOU
ASHAMED OF ME, JACKSON?
IS THAT IT? I'M GOOD ENOUGH
FOR FORNICATION B-BUT...
B-BUT THAT'S ALL?
UHHH...
UHH...GNNN...
T-TAMMY,
STILL YOUR
EMOTIONS...

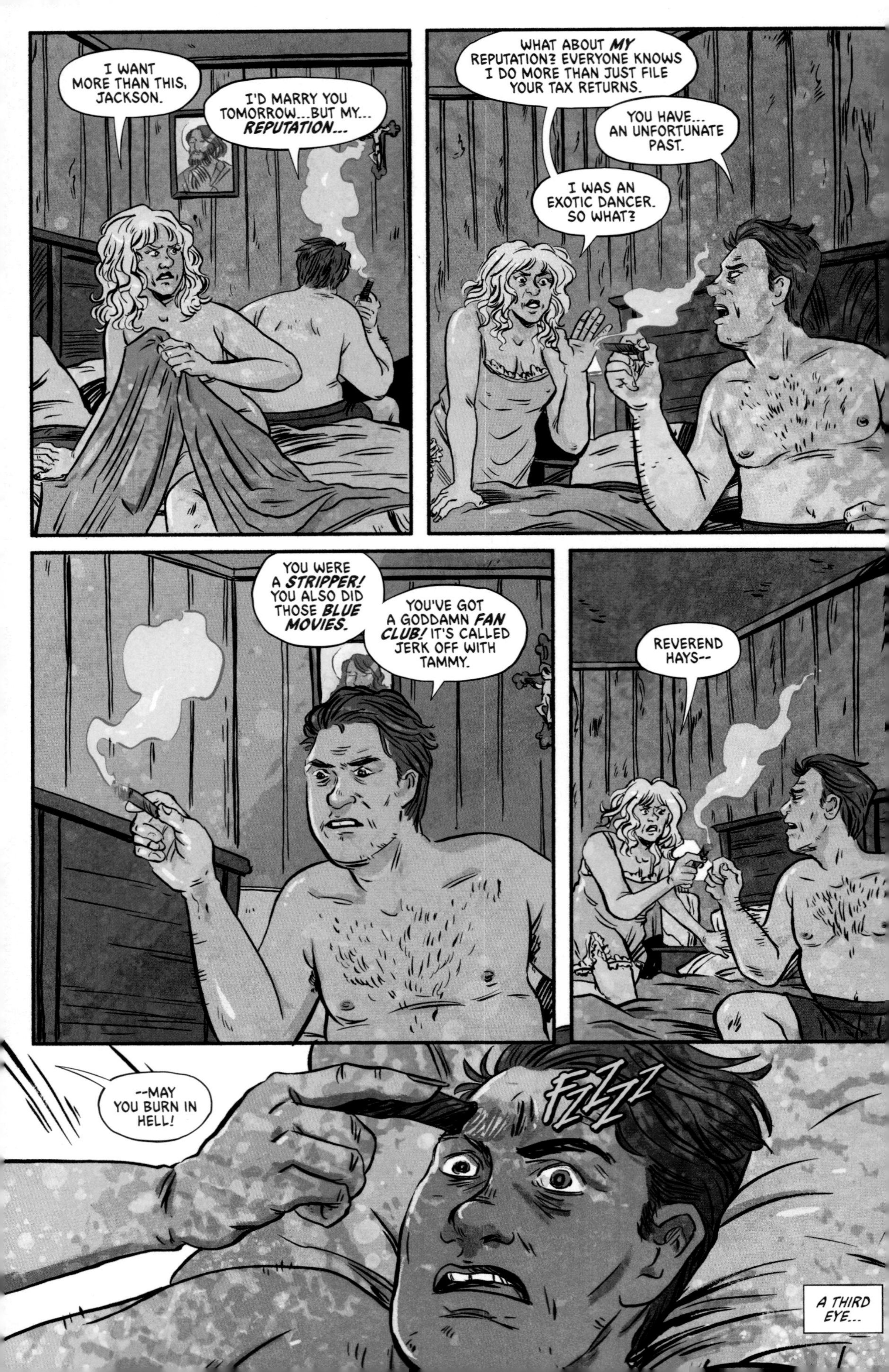
I WANT MORE THAN THIS, JACKSON.
I'D MARRY YOU TOMORROW...BUT MY... *REPUTATION...*
WHAT ABOUT *MY* REPUTATION? EVERYONE KNOWS I DO MORE THAN JUST FILE YOUR TAX RETURNS.
YOU HAVE... AN UNFORTUNATE PAST.
I WAS AN EXOTIC DANCER. SO WHAT?
YOU WERE A *STRIPPER!* YOU ALSO DID THOSE *BLUE MOVIES.*
YOU'VE GOT A GODDAMN *FAN CLUB!* IT'S CALLED JERK OFF WITH TAMMY.
REVEREND HAYS--
--MAY YOU BURN IN HELL!
FZZZZ
A THIRD EYE...

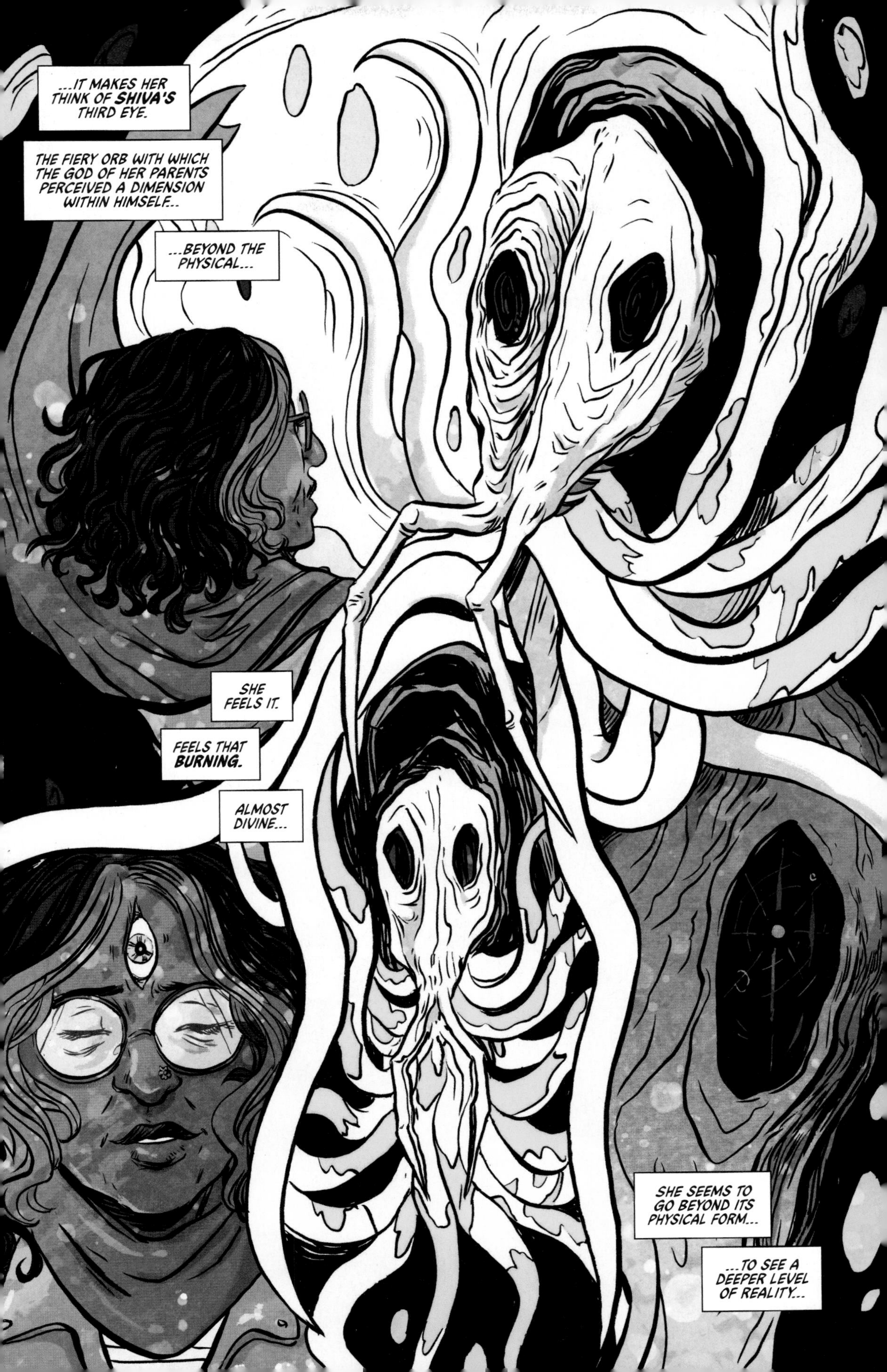
...IT MAKES HER THINK OF SHIVA'S THIRD EYE.
THE FIERY ORB WITH WHICH THE GOD OF HER PARENTS PERCEIVED A DIMENSION WITHIN HIMSELF...
...BEYOND THE PHYSICAL...
SHE FEELS IT.
FEELS THAT BURNING.
ALMOST DIVINE...
SHE SEEMS TO GO BEYOND ITS PHYSICAL FORM...
...TO SEE A DEEPER LEVEL OF REALITY...

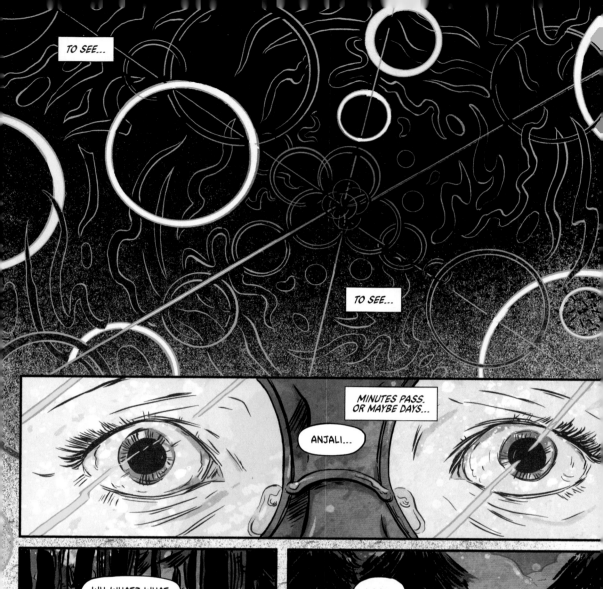

TO SEE...

TO SEE...

MINUTES PASS. OR MAYBE DAYS...

ANJALI...

WH-WHAT? WHAT HAPPENED?

YOU DID IT.

I DID... WHAT?

LOOK.

MY GOD...

SHE TRIES TO MAKE SENSE OF WHAT'S JUST HAPPENED.

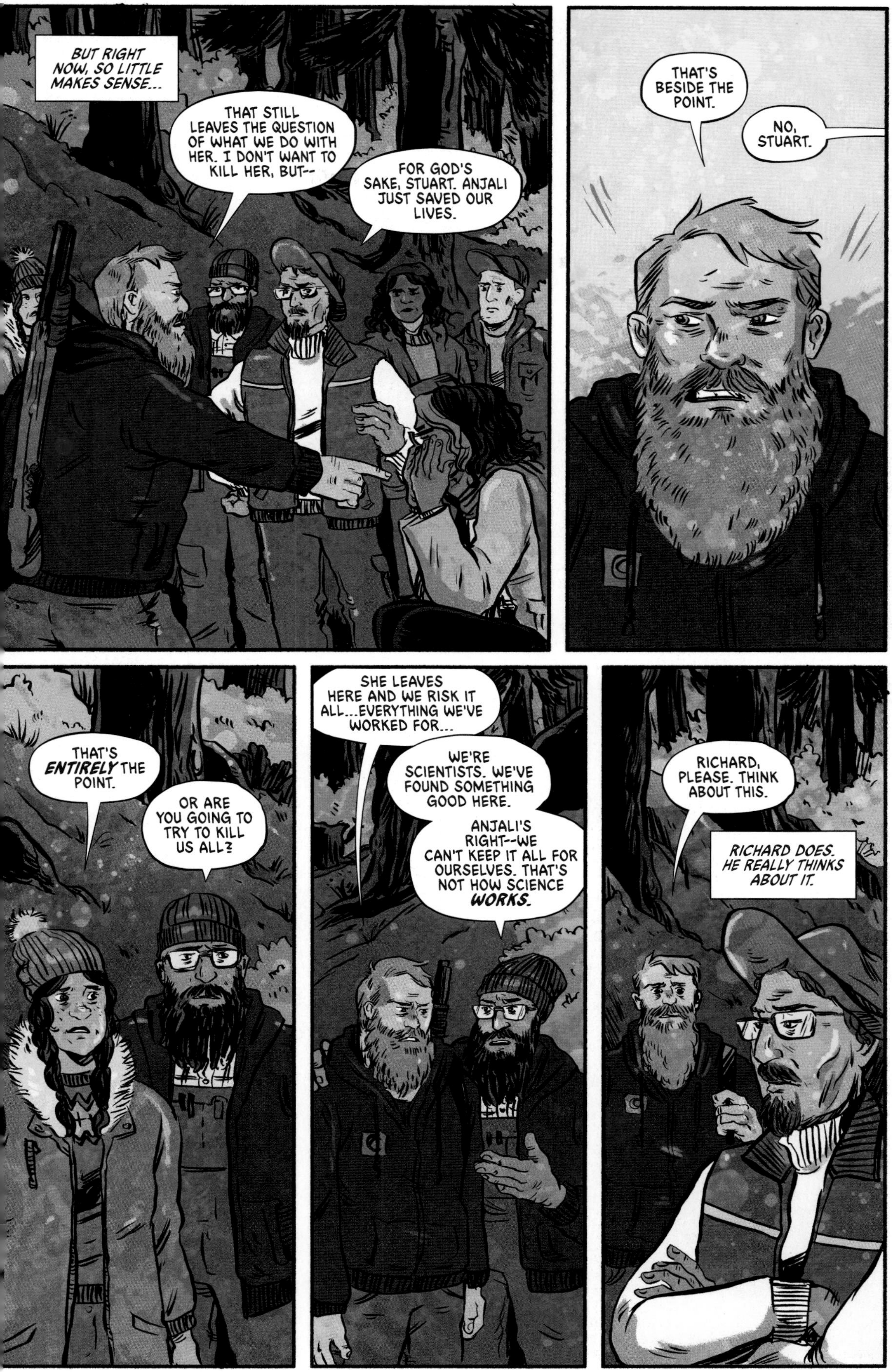

BUT RIGHT NOW, SO LITTLE MAKES SENSE...
THAT STILL LEAVES THE QUESTION OF WHAT WE DO WITH HER. I DON'T WANT TO KILL HER, BUT--
FOR GOD'S SAKE, STUART. ANJALI JUST SAVED OUR LIVES.
THAT'S BESIDE THE POINT.
NO, STUART.
THAT'S ENTIRELY THE POINT.
OR ARE YOU GOING TO TRY TO KILL US ALL?
SHE LEAVES HERE AND WE RISK IT ALL...EVERYTHING WE'VE WORKED FOR...
WE'RE SCIENTISTS. WE'VE FOUND SOMETHING GOOD HERE.
ANJALI'S RIGHT--WE CAN'T KEEP IT ALL FOR OURSELVES. THAT'S NOT HOW SCIENCE WORKS.
RICHARD, PLEASE. THINK ABOUT THIS.
RICHARD DOES. HE REALLY THINKS ABOUT IT.

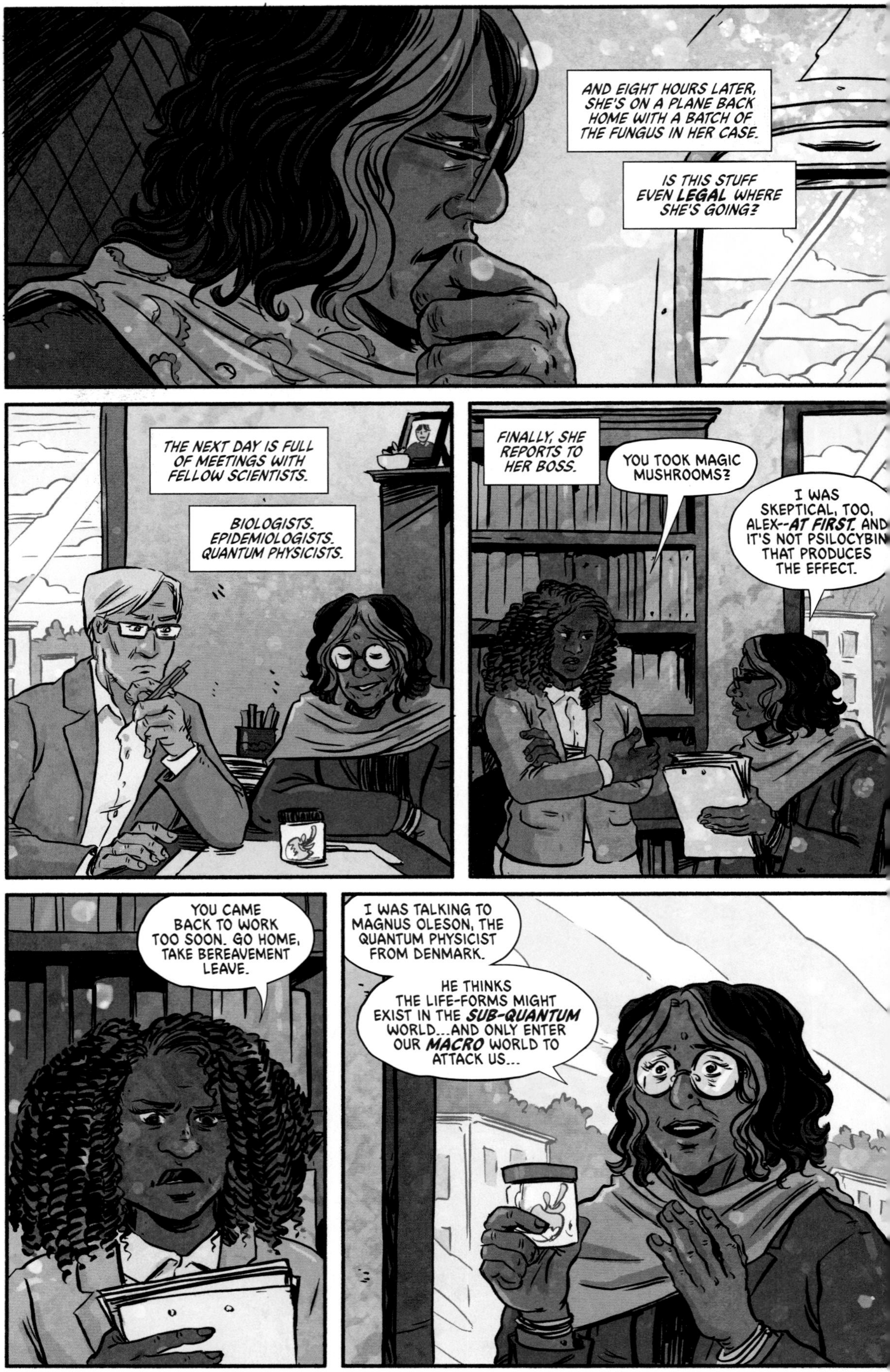
AND EIGHT HOURS LATER, SHE'S ON A PLANE BACK HOME WITH A BATCH OF THE FUNGUS IN HER CASE.
IS THIS STUFF EVEN LEGAL WHERE SHE'S GOING?
THE NEXT DAY IS FULL OF MEETINGS WITH FELLOW SCIENTISTS.
BIOLOGISTS. EPIDEMIOLOGISTS. QUANTUM PHYSICISTS.
FINALLY, SHE REPORTS TO HER BOSS.
YOU TOOK MAGIC MUSHROOMS?
I WAS SKEPTICAL, TOO, ALEX--AT FIRST. AND IT'S NOT PSILOCYBIN THAT PRODUCES THE EFFECT.
YOU CAME BACK TO WORK TOO SOON. GO HOME, TAKE BEREAVEMENT LEAVE.
I WAS TALKING TO MAGNUS OLESON, THE QUANTUM PHYSICIST FROM DENMARK.
HE THINKS THE LIFE-FORMS MIGHT EXIST IN THE SUB-QUANTUM WORLD...AND ONLY ENTER OUR MACRO WORLD TO ATTACK US...

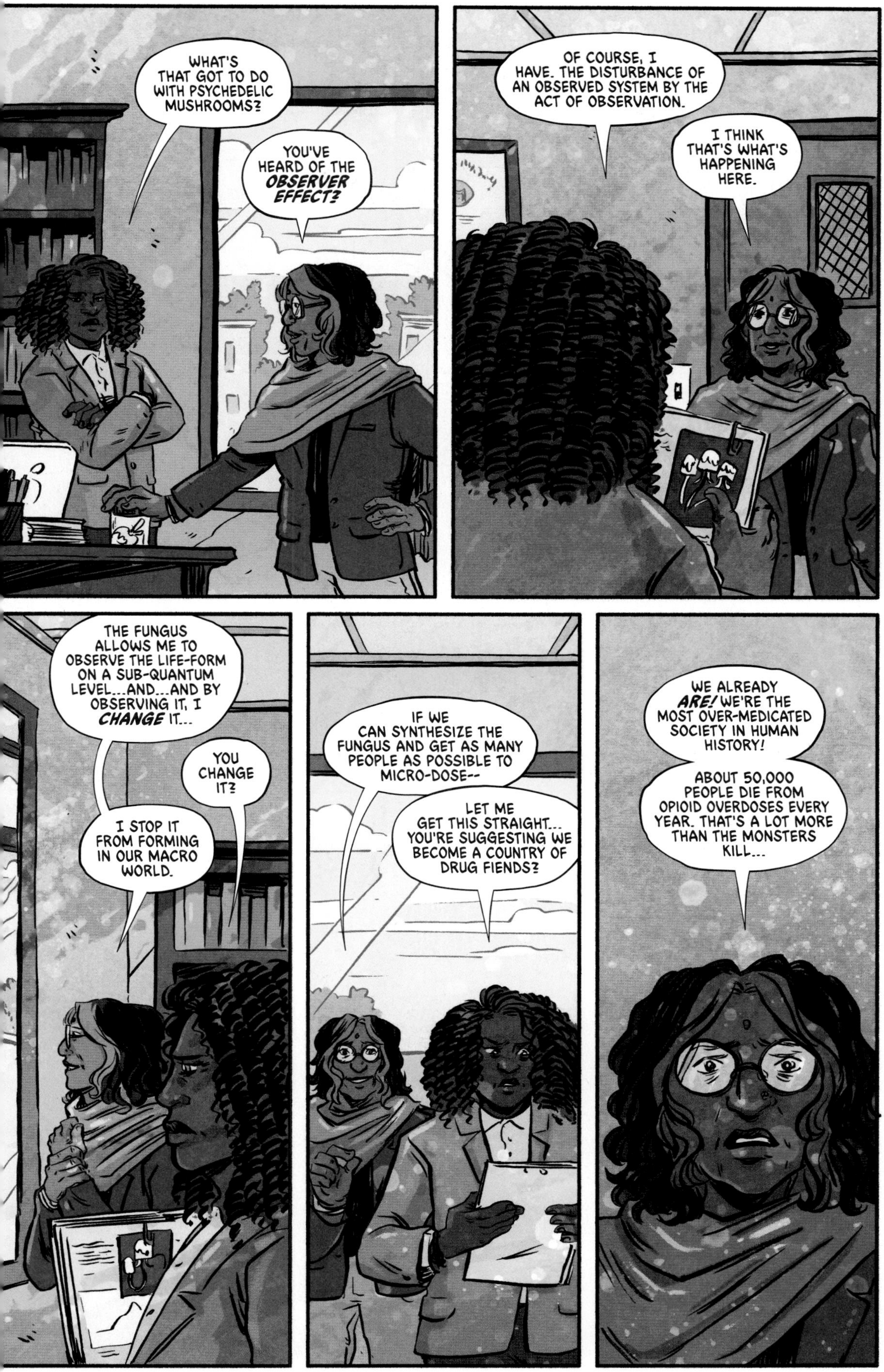
WHAT'S THAT GOT TO DO WITH PSYCHEDELIC MUSHROOMS?
YOU'VE HEARD OF THE *OBSERVER EFFECT?*
OF COURSE, I HAVE. THE DISTURBANCE OF AN OBSERVED SYSTEM BY THE ACT OF OBSERVATION.
I THINK THAT'S WHAT'S HAPPENING HERE.
THE FUNGUS ALLOWS ME TO OBSERVE THE LIFE-FORM ON A SUB-QUANTUM LEVEL...AND...AND BY OBSERVING IT, I *CHANGE* IT...
YOU CHANGE IT?
I STOP IT FROM FORMING IN OUR MACRO WORLD.
IF WE CAN SYNTHESIZE THE FUNGUS AND GET AS MANY PEOPLE AS POSSIBLE TO MICRO-DOSE--
LET ME GET THIS STRAIGHT... YOU'RE SUGGESTING WE BECOME A COUNTRY OF DRUG FIENDS?
WE ALREADY *ARE!* WE'RE THE MOST OVER-MEDICATED SOCIETY IN HUMAN HISTORY!
ABOUT 50,000 PEOPLE DIE FROM OPIOID OVERDOSES EVERY YEAR. THAT'S A LOT MORE THAN THE MONSTERS KILL...

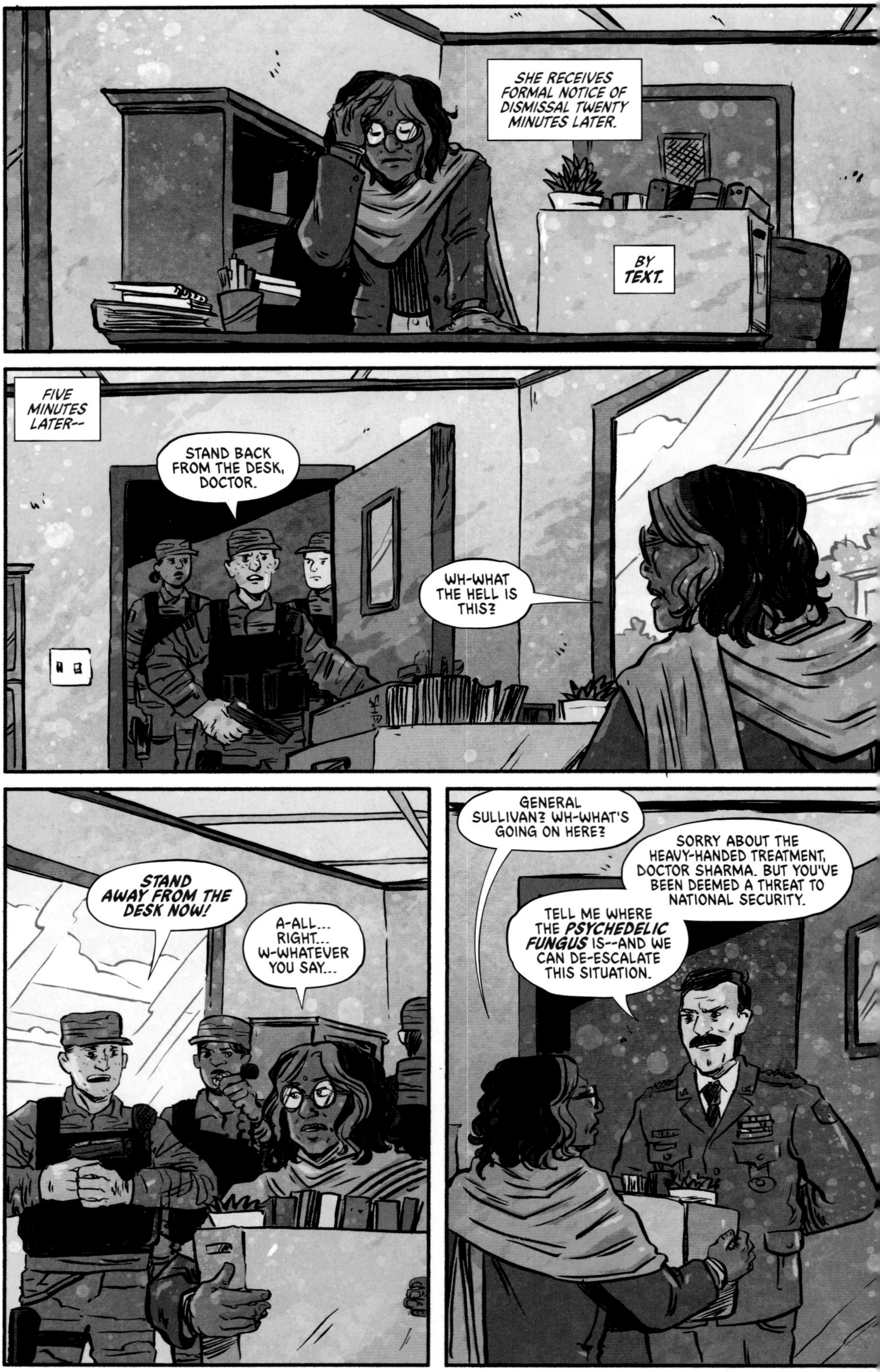
SHE RECEIVES FORMAL NOTICE OF DISMISSAL TWENTY MINUTES LATER.
BY TEXT.
FIVE MINUTES LATER--
STAND BACK FROM THE DESK, DOCTOR.
WH-WHAT THE HELL IS THIS?
STAND AWAY FROM THE DESK NOW!
A-ALL... RIGHT... W-WHATEVER YOU SAY...
GENERAL SULLIVAN? WH-WHAT'S GOING ON HERE?
SORRY ABOUT THE HEAVY-HANDED TREATMENT, DOCTOR SHARMA. BUT YOU'VE BEEN DEEMED A THREAT TO NATIONAL SECURITY.
TELL ME WHERE THE PSYCHEDELIC FUNGUS IS--AND WE CAN DE-ESCALATE THIS SITUATION.

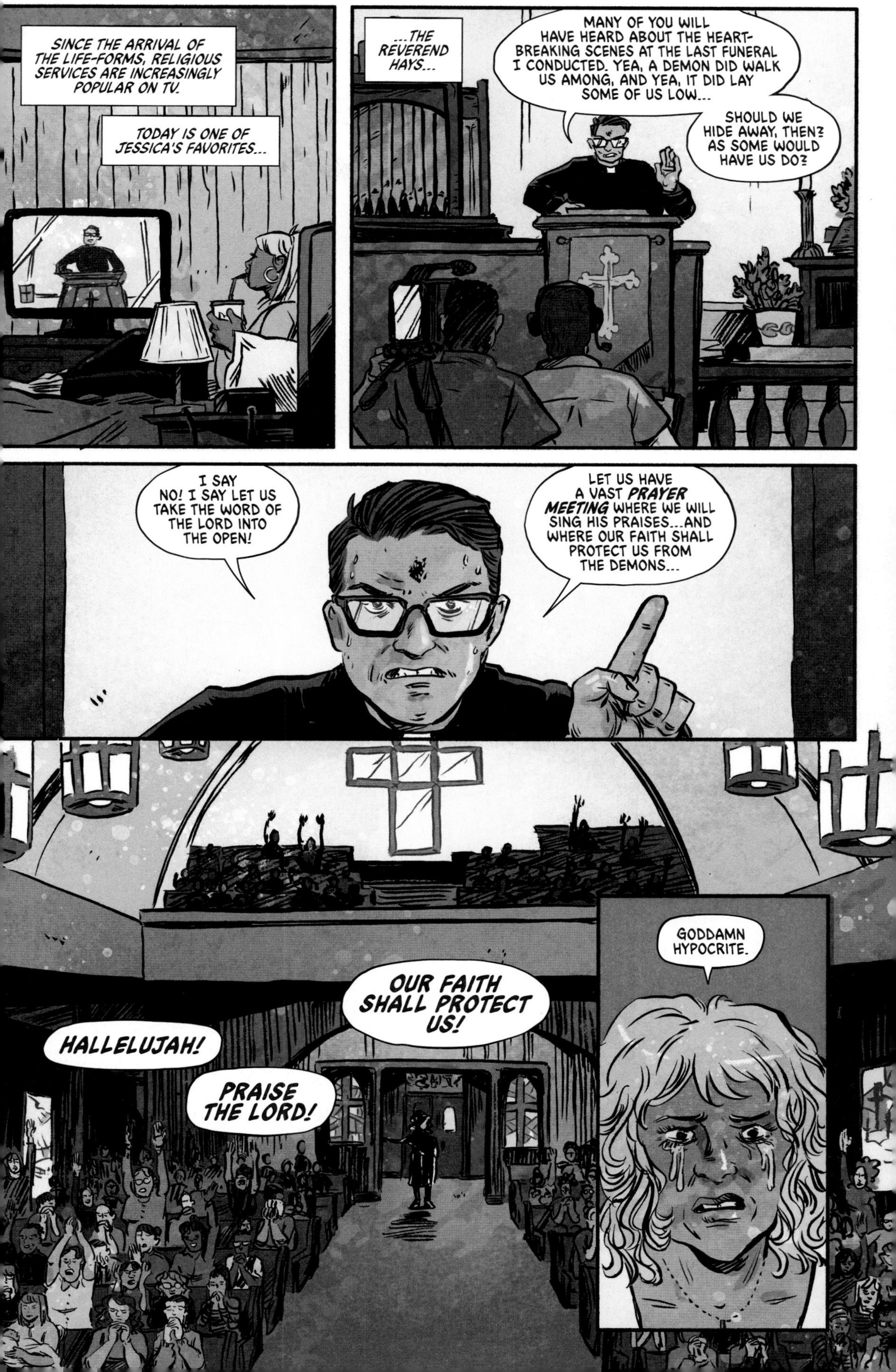
SINCE THE ARRIVAL OF THE LIFE-FORMS, RELIGIOUS SERVICES ARE INCREASINGLY POPULAR ON TV.
TODAY IS ONE OF JESSICA'S FAVORITES...
...THE REVEREND HAYS...
MANY OF YOU WILL HAVE HEARD ABOUT THE HEART-BREAKING SCENES AT THE LAST FUNERAL I CONDUCTED. YEA, A DEMON DID WALK US AMONG, AND YEA, IT DID LAY SOME OF US LOW...
SHOULD WE HIDE AWAY, THEN? AS SOME WOULD HAVE US DO?
I SAY NO! I SAY LET US TAKE THE WORD OF THE LORD INTO THE OPEN!
LET US HAVE A VAST PRAYER MEETING WHERE WE WILL SING HIS PRAISES...AND WHERE OUR FAITH SHALL PROTECT US FROM THE DEMONS...
OUR FAITH SHALL PROTECT US!
HALLELUJAH!
PRAISE THE LORD!
GODDAMN HYPOCRITE.

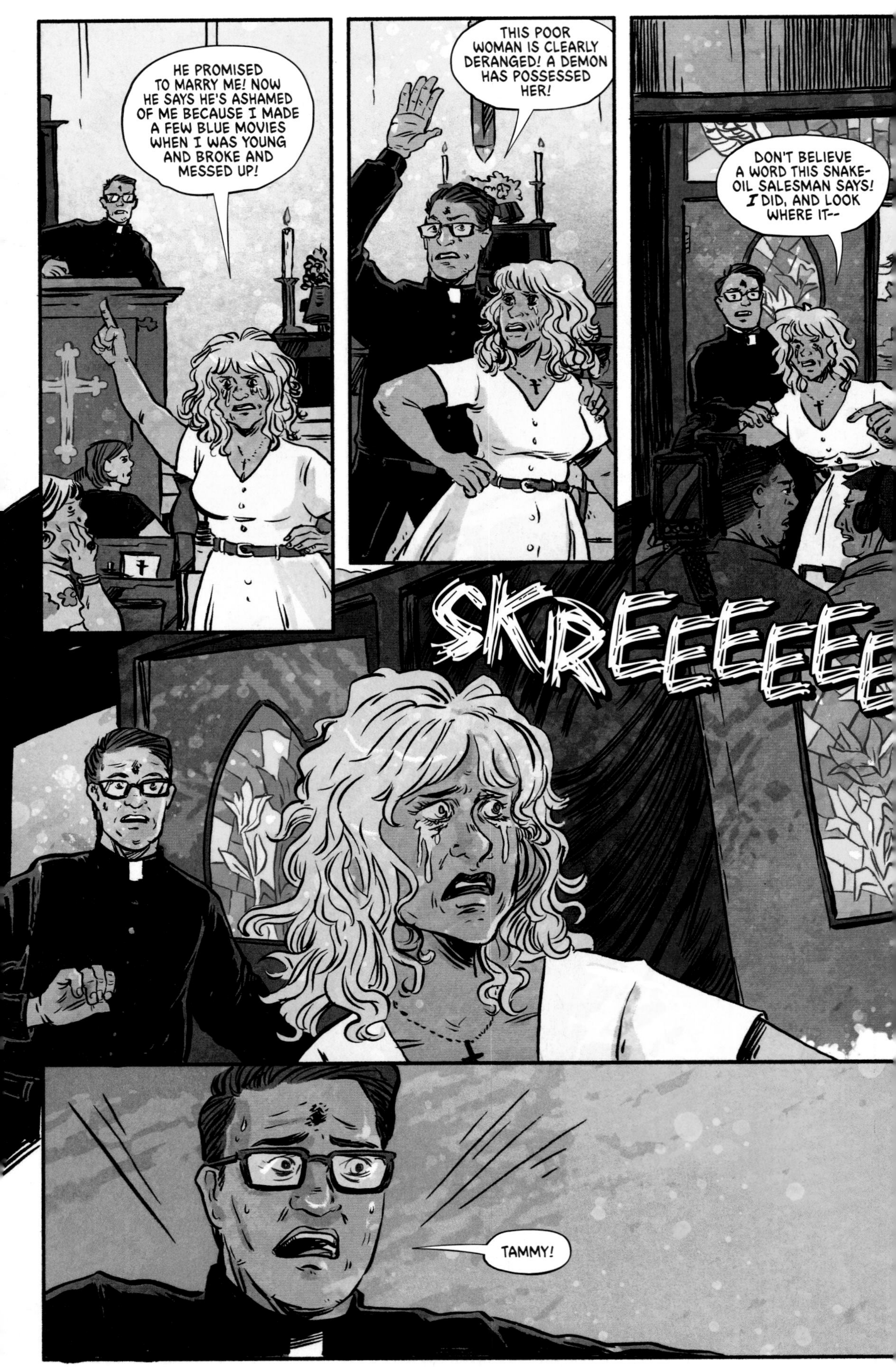
HE PROMISED TO MARRY ME! NOW HE SAYS HE'S ASHAMED OF ME BECAUSE I MADE A FEW BLUE MOVIES WHEN I WAS YOUNG AND BROKE AND MESSED UP!
THIS POOR WOMAN IS CLEARLY DERANGED! A DEMON HAS POSSESSED HER!
DON'T BELIEVE A WORD THIS SNAKE-OIL SALESMAN SAYS! *I* DID, AND LOOK WHERE IT--
SKREEEEEE
TAMMY!

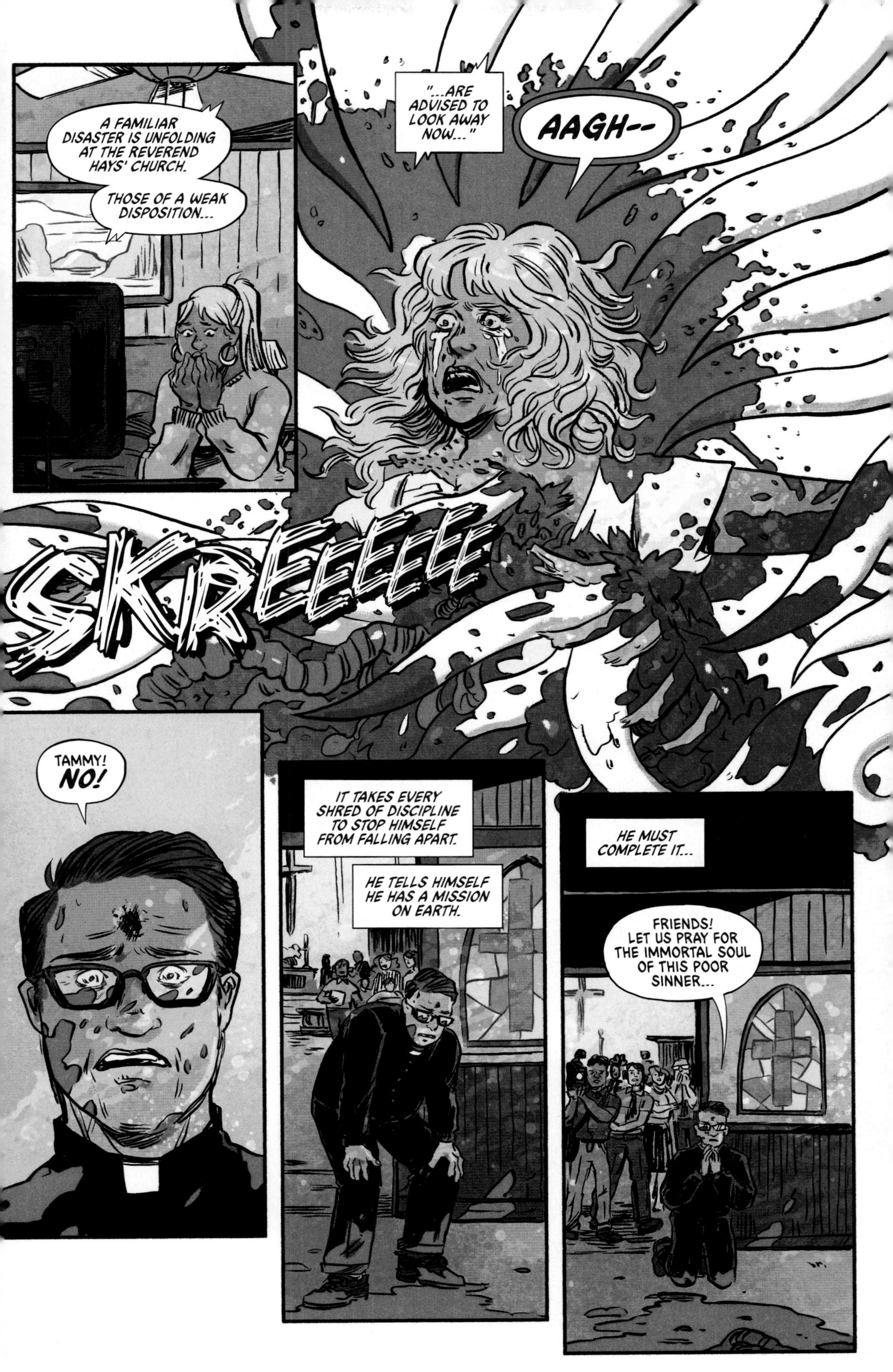
A FAMILIAR DISASTER IS UNFOLDING AT THE REVEREND HAYS' CHURCH.
THOSE OF A WEAK DISPOSITION...
"...ARE ADVISED TO LOOK AWAY NOW..."
AAGH--
SKREEEEEEE
TAMMY! NO!
IT TAKES EVERY SHRED OF DISCIPLINE TO STOP HIMSELF FROM FALLING APART.
HE TELLS HIMSELF HE HAS A MISSION ON EARTH.
HE MUST COMPLETE IT...
FRIENDS! LET US PRAY FOR THE IMMORTAL SOUL OF THIS POOR SINNER...

REVEREND HAYS, AFTER THIS TRAGEDY... ARE YOU STILL DETERMINED TO HAVE AN OPEN-AIR PRAYER MEETING?

MANY VIEWERS ARE TRANSFIXED BY THE GRIPPING MIX OF RELIGION AND MONSTERS...

MORE DETERMINED THAN EVER, SON. THE OPEN AIR PRAYER MEETING GOES AHEAD.

IT'LL BE BIG. IT'LL BE LOUD...

THERE'S DOCTOR ANJALI SHARMA, AT PRESENT UNDER HOUSE ARREST...

...IT'LL BE BIG. IT'LL BE LOUD...IT WILL BE FULL OF JOY AND CELEBRATION.

LIFEFORM ATTACK CAUGHT LIVE DURING GODTV BROADCAST

IT'LL PROBABLY RESULT IN THE DEATHS OF HUNDREDS OF GULLIBLE PEOPLE....

TWO YOUNG LOVERS LEARNING A NEW LANGUAGE...

WAIT, ARE YOU WATCHING TV WHILE WE HAVE SEX?

TRUSHA JUST PINGED ME. THIS STUFF IS INSANE.

TWO PSYCHIC TWINS JUST OUT OF A COMA...

TODAY: NOV 4, 20__

YOUR NAME IS: JEH

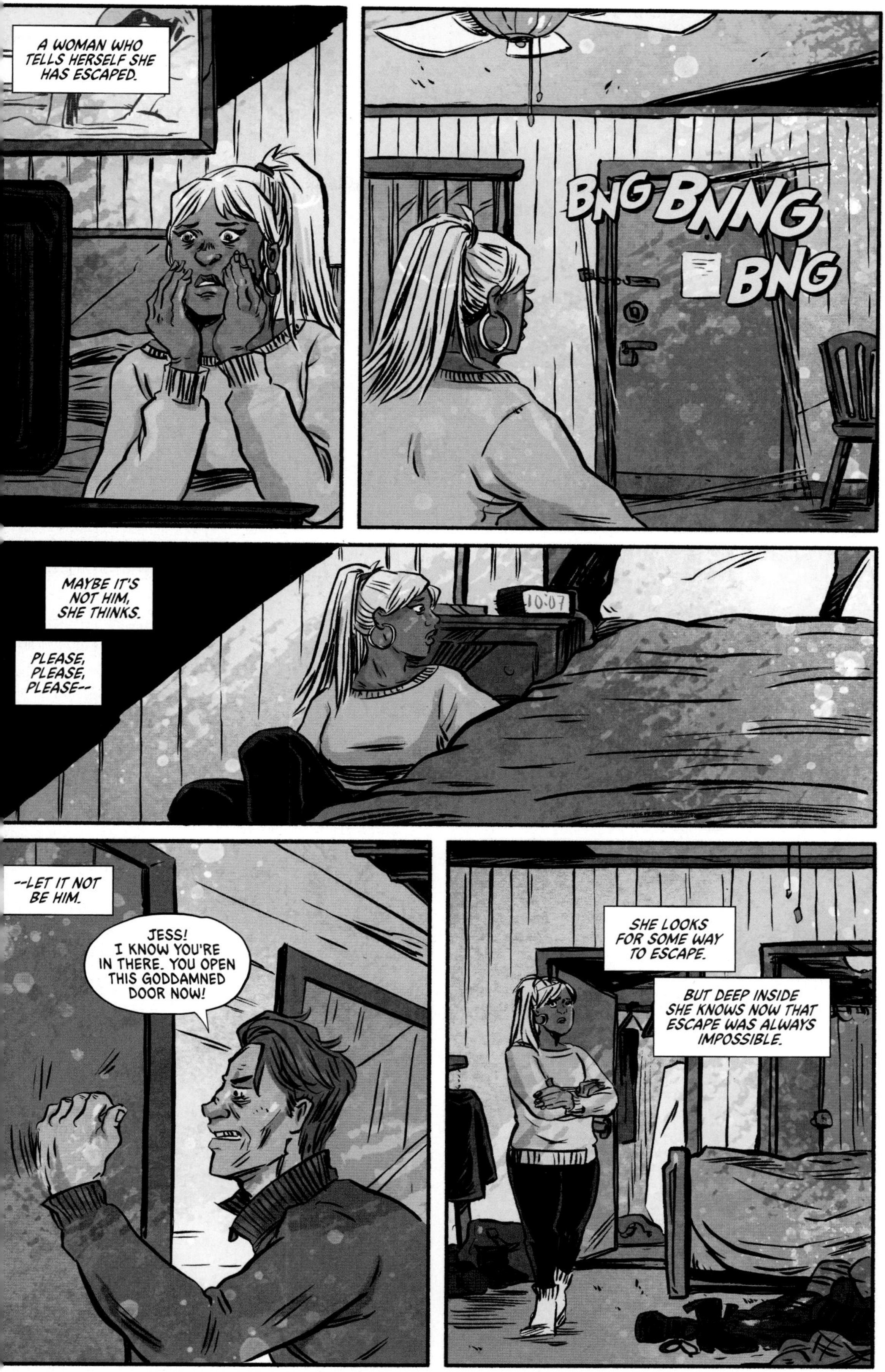
A WOMAN WHO TELLS HERSELF SHE HAS ESCAPED.
BNG BNNG BNG
MAYBE IT'S NOT HIM, SHE THINKS.
PLEASE, PLEASE, PLEASE--
10:07
--LET IT NOT BE HIM.
JESS! I KNOW YOU'RE IN THERE. YOU OPEN THIS GODDAMNED DOOR NOW!
SHE LOOKS FOR SOME WAY TO ESCAPE.
BUT DEEP INSIDE SHE KNOWS NOW THAT ESCAPE WAS ALWAYS IMPOSSIBLE.

I WON'T HURT YOU, BABY. I JUST WANT YOU TO COME HOME.

I PREFER IT HERE.

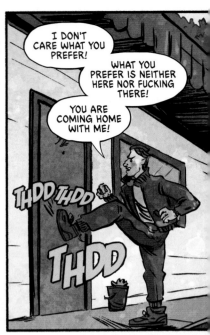

I DON'T CARE WHAT YOU PREFER!

WHAT YOU PREFER IS NEITHER HERE NOR FUCKING THERE!

YOU ARE COMING HOME WITH ME!

THDD THDD THDD

GET A HOLD OF YOURSELF--OR YOU'LL BRING DOWN A MONSTER. YOU'LL GET YOURSELF KILLED.

AND IT'LL ALL BE *YOUR FAULT*. YOU DON'T CARE WHAT HAPPENS TO ME. YOU NEVER LOVED ME.

YOU'RE COLD, JESS. KNOW THAT? YOU'RE COLD...

DON'T OPEN THE DOOR.

IF HE WANTS TO GET HIMSELF KILLED, THAT'S HIS BUSINESS.

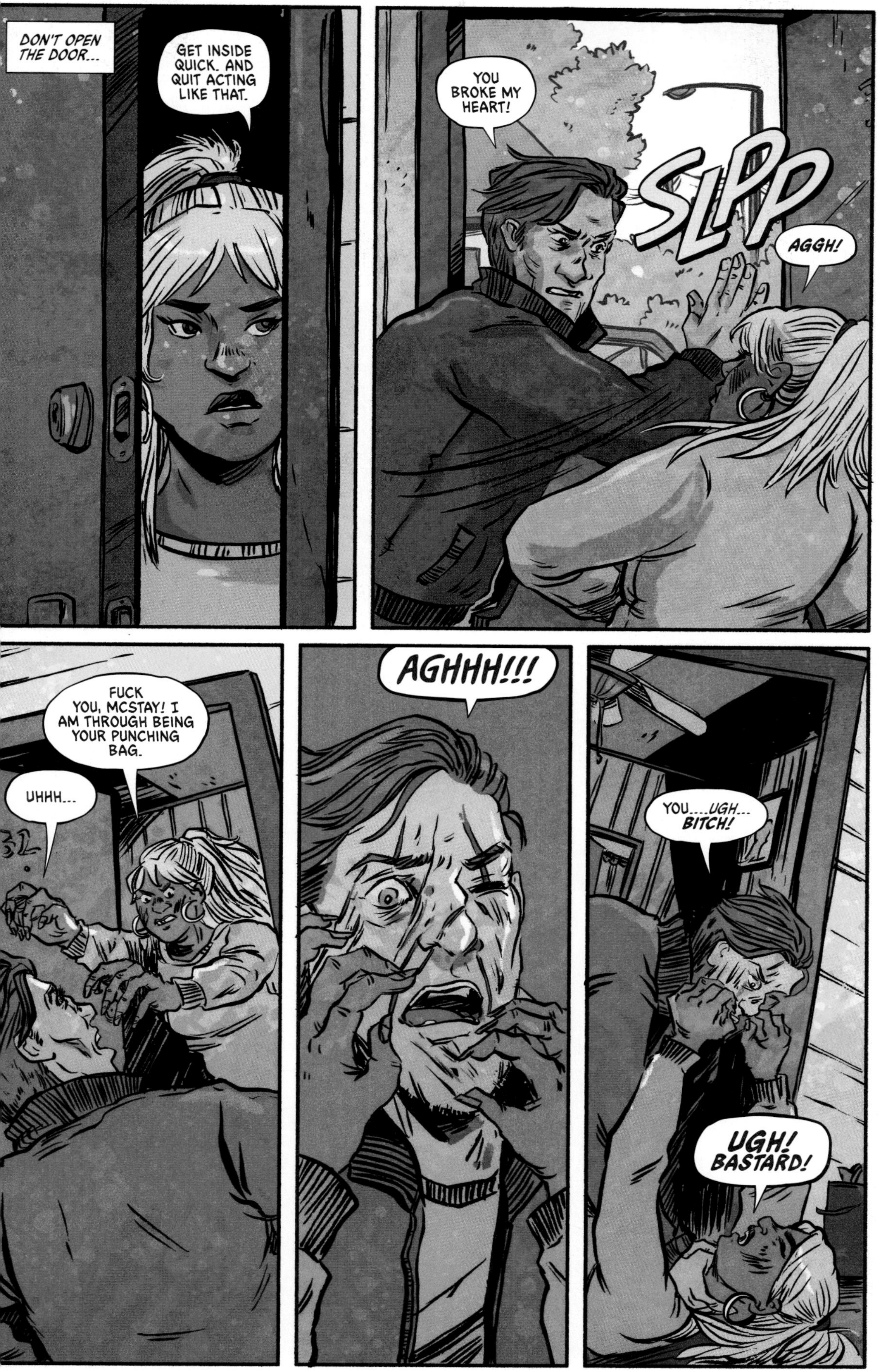
DON'T OPEN THE DOOR...
GET INSIDE QUICK. AND QUIT ACTING LIKE THAT.
YOU BROKE MY HEART!
SLPP
AGGH!
FUCK YOU, MCSTAY! I AM THROUGH BEING YOUR PUNCHING BAG.
UHHH...
AGHHH!!!
YOU....UGH... BITCH!
UGH! BASTARD!

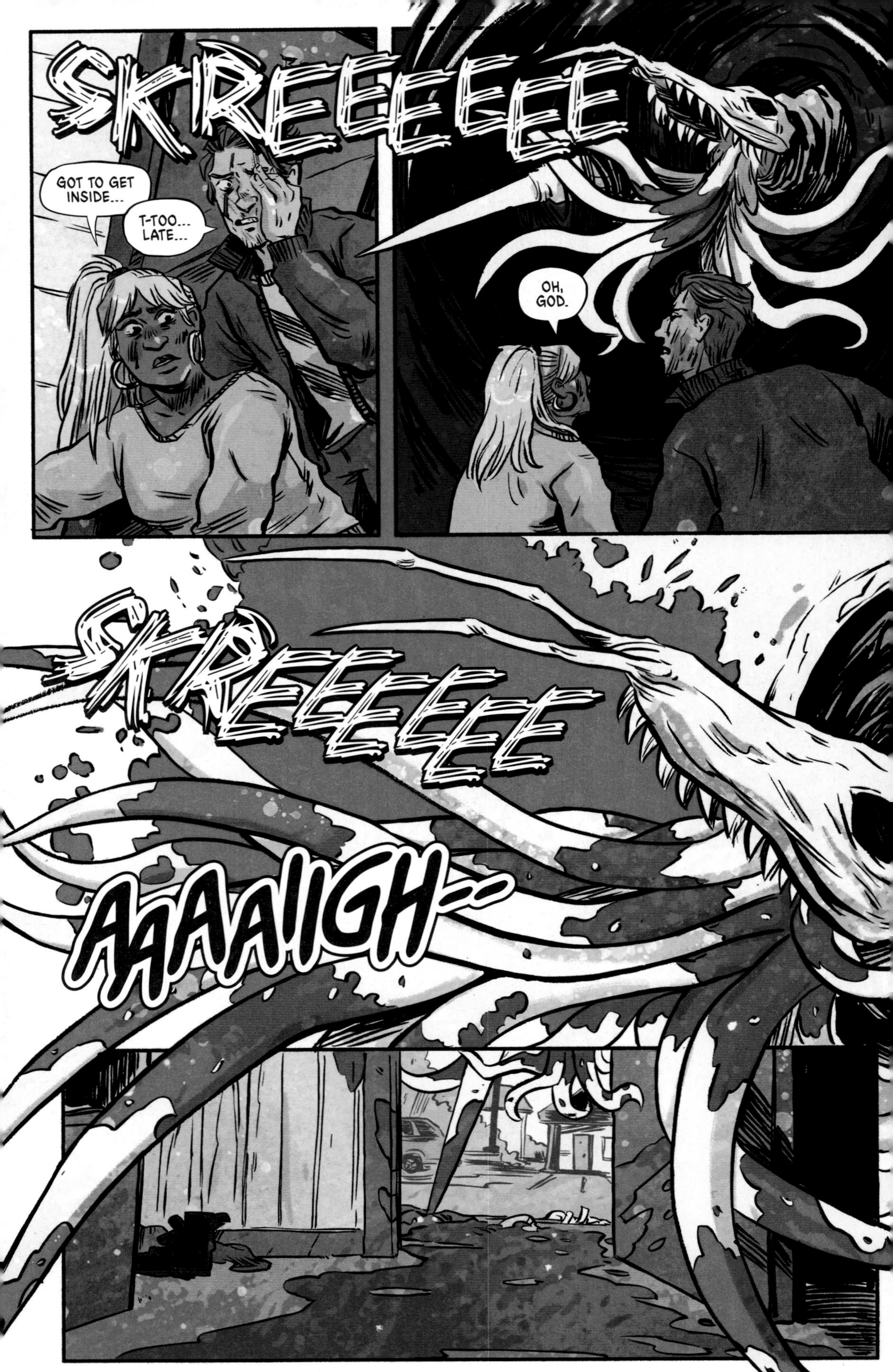
SKREEEEEE
GOT TO GET INSIDE...
T-TOO... LATE...
OH, GOD.
SKREEEEEE
AAAAIIGH--

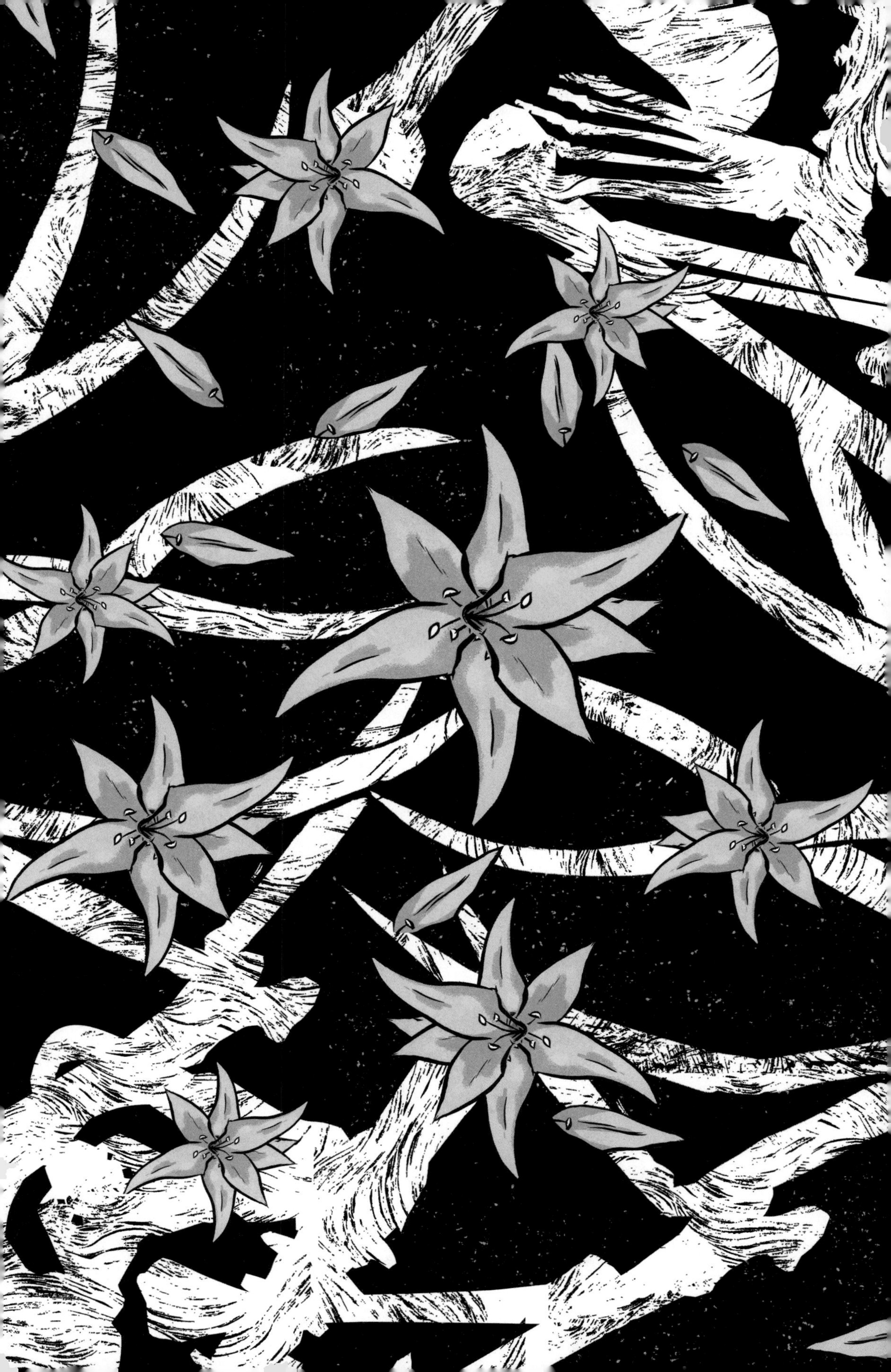

CHAPTER EIGHT

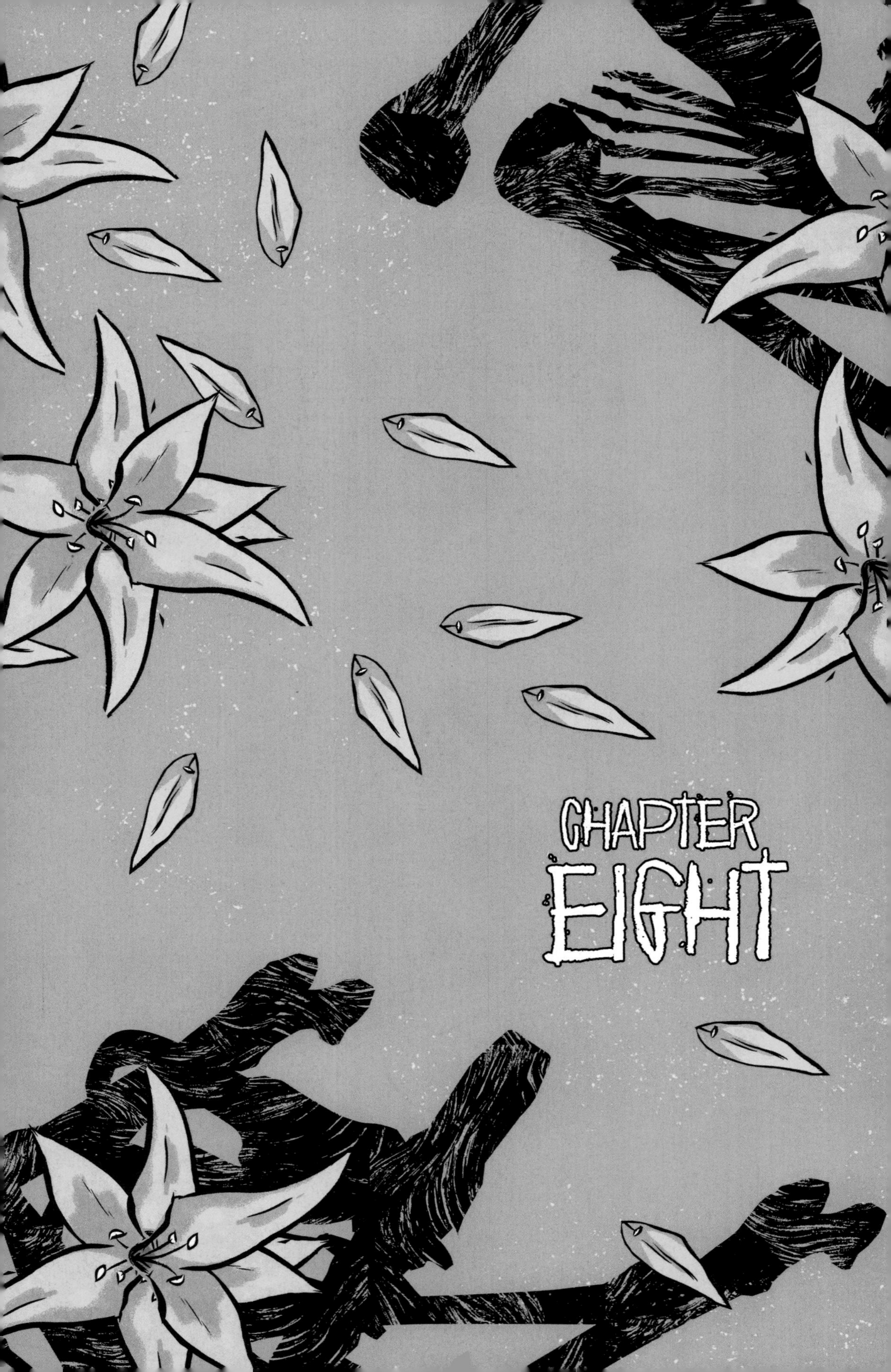

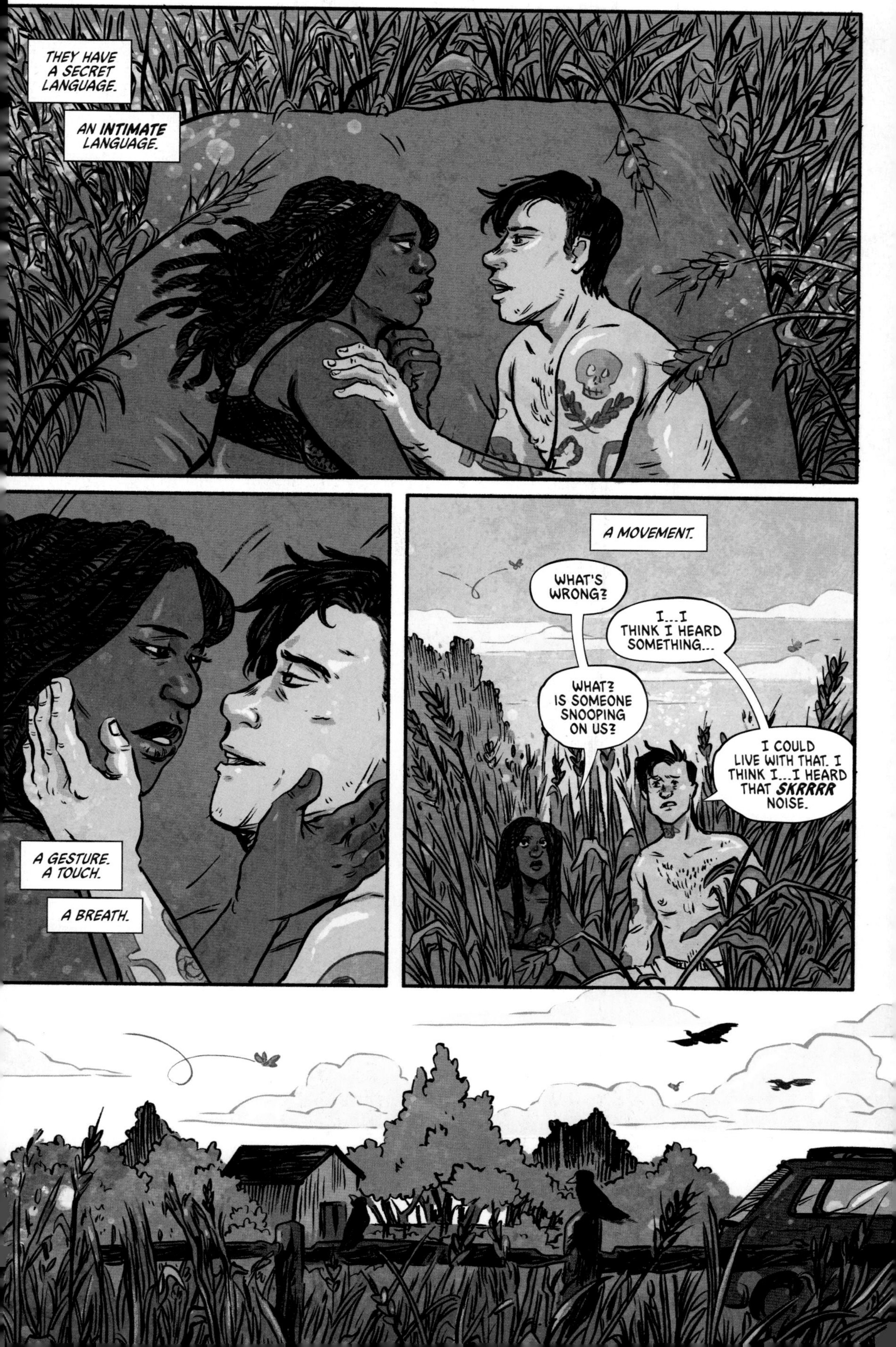
THEY HAVE A SECRET LANGUAGE.
AN INTIMATE LANGUAGE.
A GESTURE. A TOUCH.
A BREATH.
A MOVEMENT.
WHAT'S WRONG?
I...I THINK I HEARD SOMETHING...
WHAT? IS SOMEONE SNOOPING ON US?
I COULD LIVE WITH THAT. I THINK I...I HEARD THAT SKRRRR NOISE.

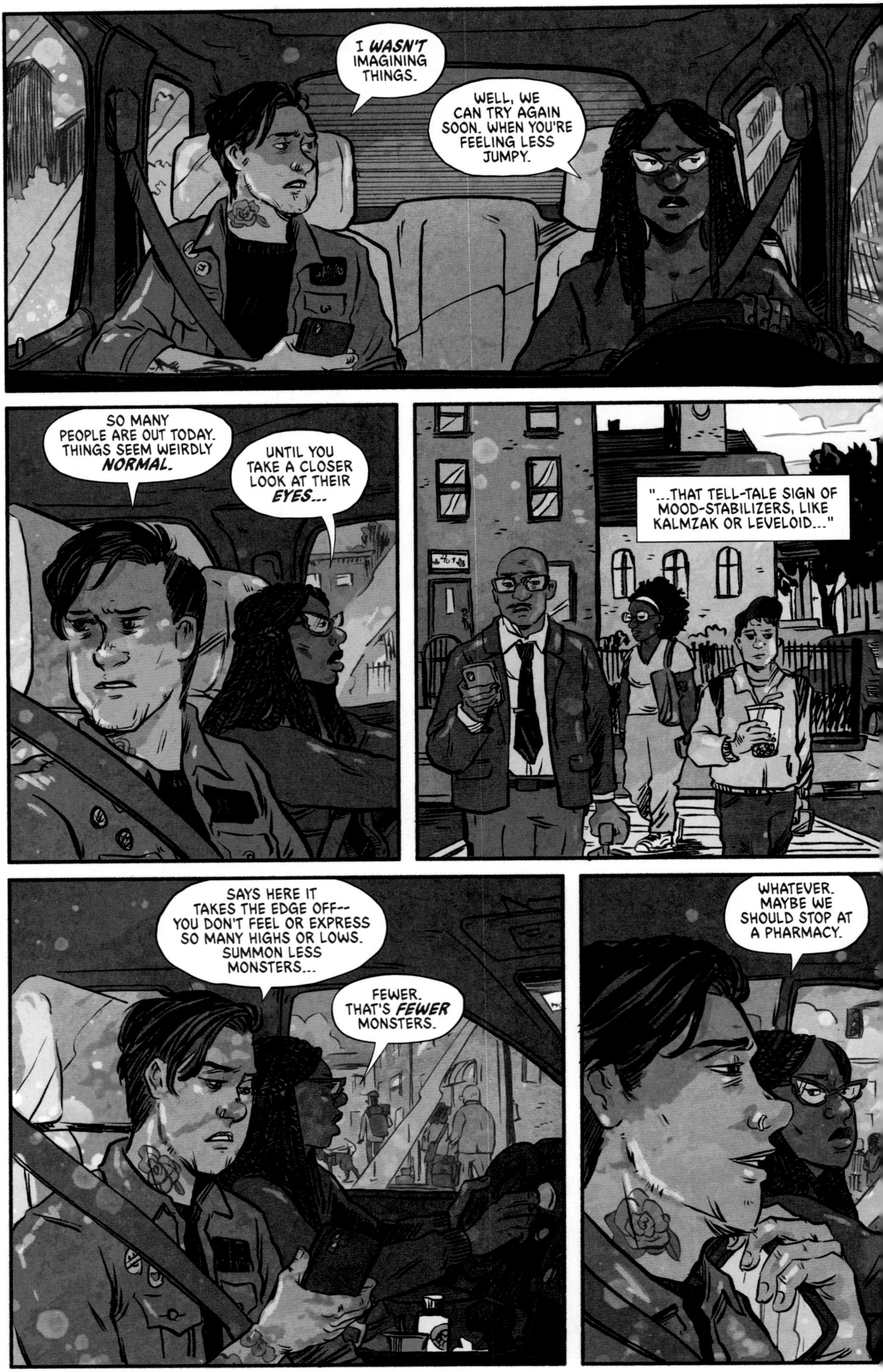
I WASN'T IMAGINING THINGS.
WELL, WE CAN TRY AGAIN SOON. WHEN YOU'RE FEELING LESS JUMPY.
SO MANY PEOPLE ARE OUT TODAY. THINGS SEEM WEIRDLY NORMAL.
UNTIL YOU TAKE A CLOSER LOOK AT THEIR EYES...
"...THAT TELL-TALE SIGN OF MOOD-STABILIZERS, LIKE KALMZAK OR LEVELOID..."
SAYS HERE IT TAKES THE EDGE OFF-- YOU DON'T FEEL OR EXPRESS SO MANY HIGHS OR LOWS. SUMMON LESS MONSTERS...
FEWER. THAT'S FEWER MONSTERS.
WHATEVER. MAYBE WE SHOULD STOP AT A PHARMACY.

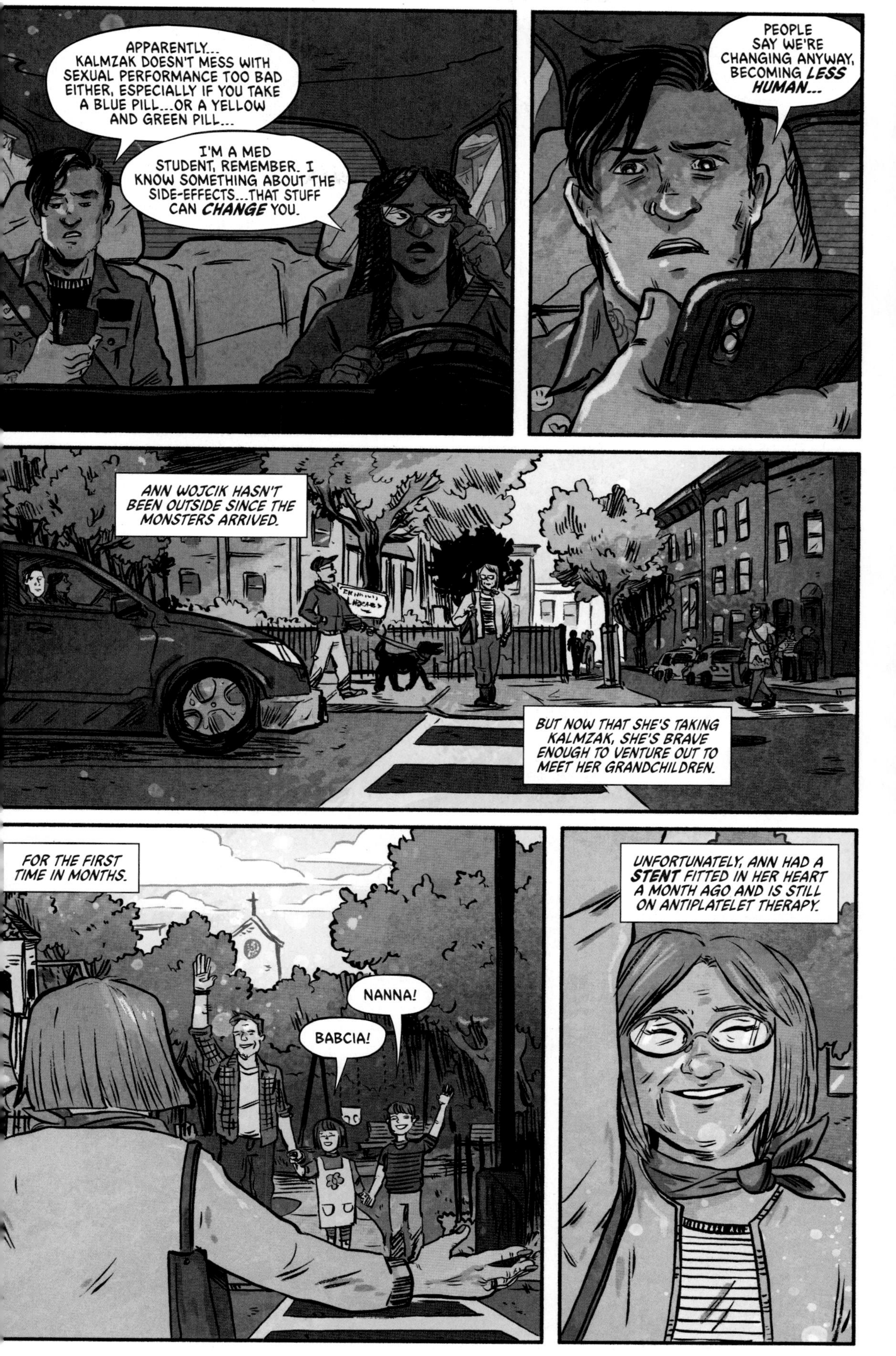
APPARENTLY... KALMZAK DOESN'T MESS WITH SEXUAL PERFORMANCE TOO BAD EITHER, ESPECIALLY IF YOU TAKE A BLUE PILL...OR A YELLOW AND GREEN PILL...
I'M A MED STUDENT, REMEMBER. I KNOW SOMETHING ABOUT THE SIDE-EFFECTS...THAT STUFF CAN CHANGE YOU.
PEOPLE SAY WE'RE CHANGING ANYWAY, BECOMING LESS HUMAN...
ANN WOJCIK HASN'T BEEN OUTSIDE SINCE THE MONSTERS ARRIVED.
BUT NOW THAT SHE'S TAKING KALMZAK, SHE'S BRAVE ENOUGH TO VENTURE OUT TO MEET HER GRANDCHILDREN.
FOR THE FIRST TIME IN MONTHS.
NANNA!
BABCIA!
UNFORTUNATELY, ANN HAD A STENT FITTED IN HER HEART A MONTH AGO AND IS STILL ON ANTIPLATELET THERAPY.

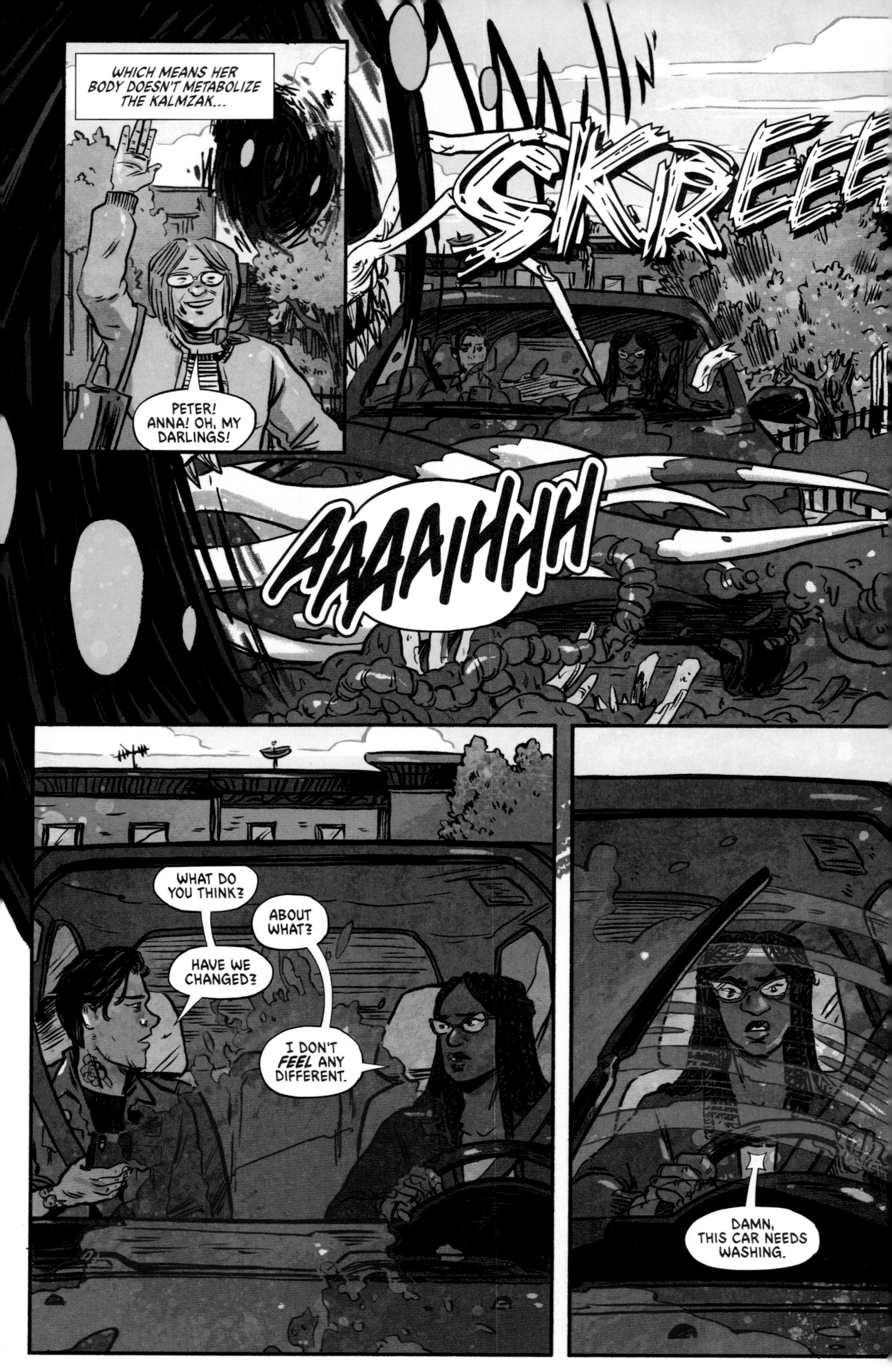
WHICH MEANS HER BODY DOESN'T METABOLIZE THE KALMZAK...
PETER! ANNA! OH, MY DARLINGS!
SKREEE
AAAAHHH
WHAT DO YOU THINK?
ABOUT WHAT?
HAVE WE CHANGED?
I DON'T *FEEL* ANY DIFFERENT.
DAMN, THIS CAR NEEDS WASHING.

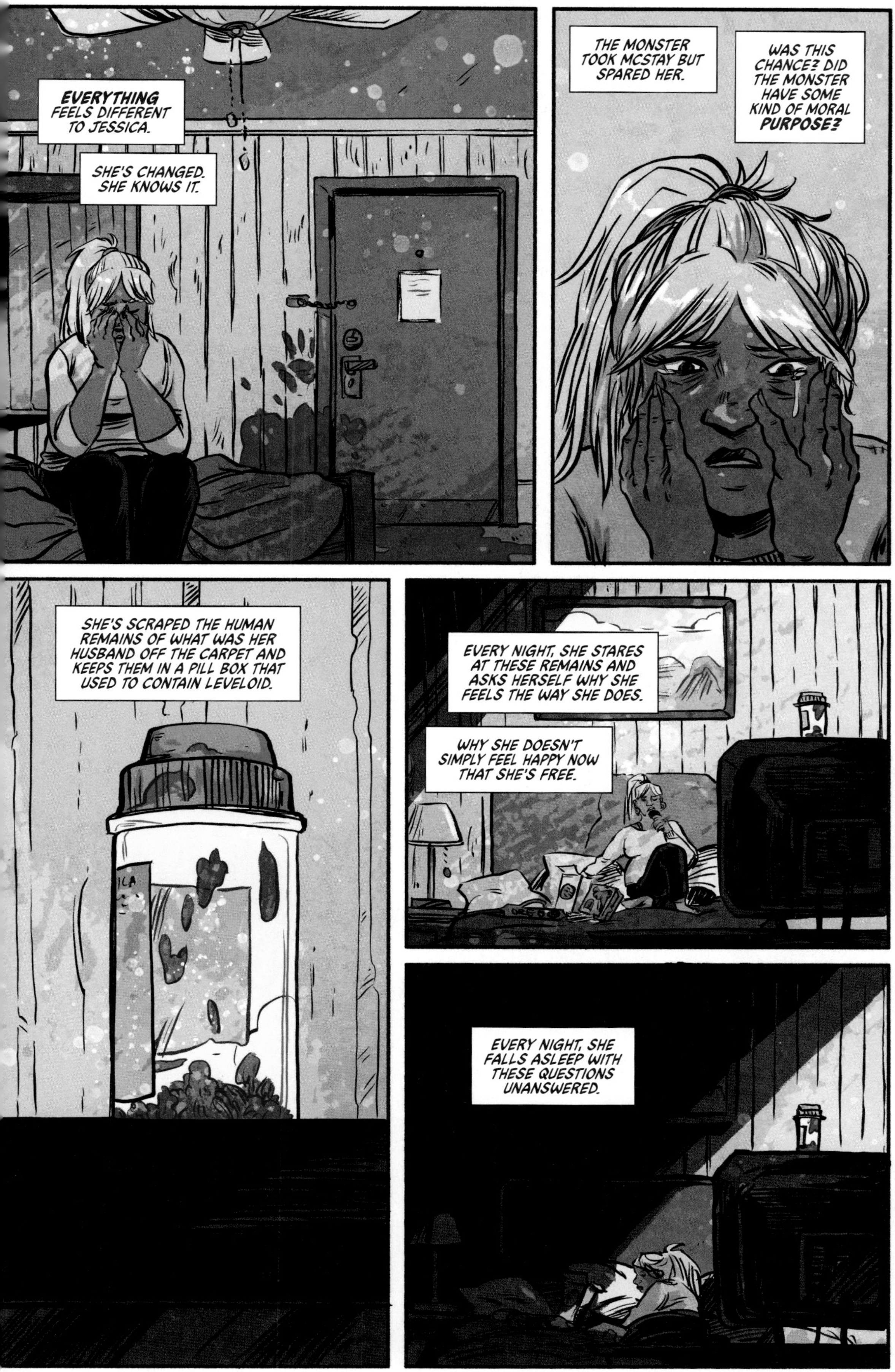
EVERYTHING FEELS DIFFERENT TO JESSICA.
SHE'S CHANGED. SHE KNOWS IT.
THE MONSTER TOOK MCSTAY BUT SPARED HER.
WAS THIS CHANCE? DID THE MONSTER HAVE SOME KIND OF MORAL PURPOSE?
SHE'S SCRAPED THE HUMAN REMAINS OF WHAT WAS HER HUSBAND OFF THE CARPET AND KEEPS THEM IN A PILL BOX THAT USED TO CONTAIN LEVELOID.
EVERY NIGHT, SHE STARES AT THESE REMAINS AND ASKS HERSELF WHY SHE FEELS THE WAY SHE DOES.
WHY SHE DOESN'T SIMPLY FEEL HAPPY NOW THAT SHE'S FREE.
EVERY NIGHT, SHE FALLS ASLEEP WITH THESE QUESTIONS UNANSWERED.

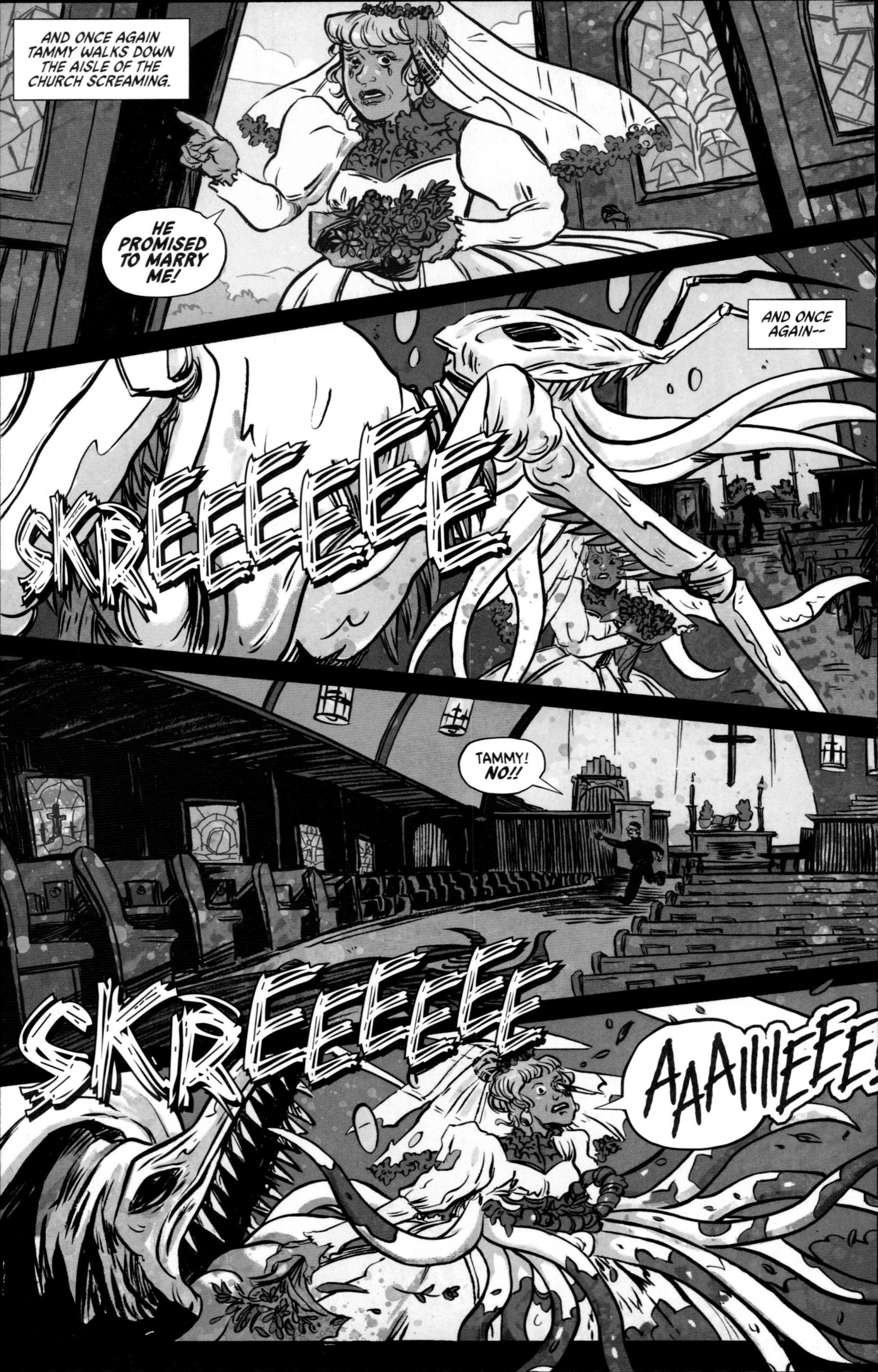
AND ONCE AGAIN TAMMY WALKS DOWN THE AISLE OF THE CHURCH SCREAMING.
HE PROMISED TO MARRY ME!
AND ONCE AGAIN--
SKREEEEEEE
TAMMY! NO!!
SKREEEEEEE
AAIIIEEE

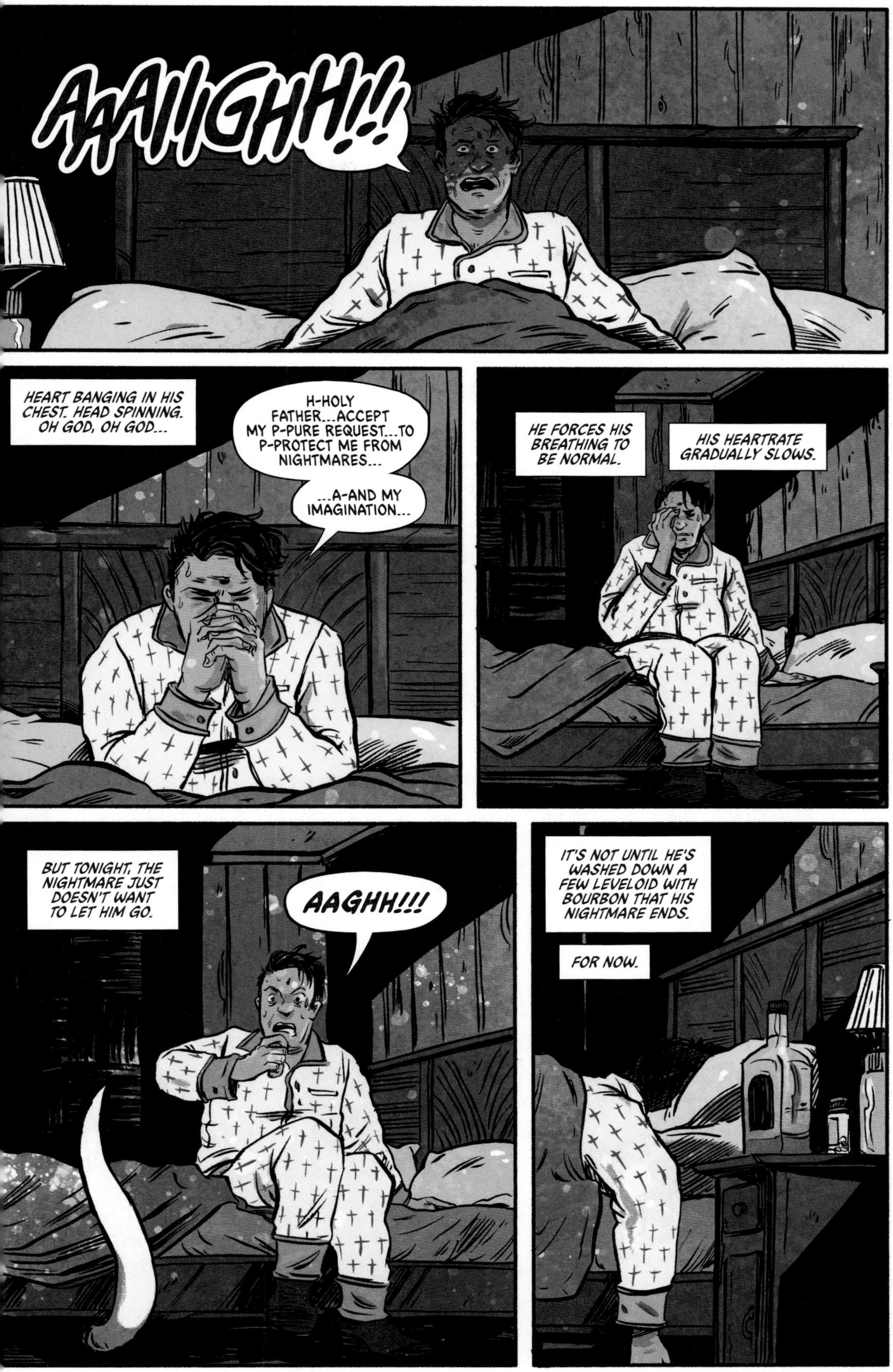
AAAIIGHH!!!
HEART BANGING IN HIS CHEST. HEAD SPINNING. OH GOD, OH GOD...
H-HOLY FATHER...ACCEPT MY P-PURE REQUEST...TO P-PROTECT ME FROM NIGHTMARES...
...A-AND MY IMAGINATION...
HE FORCES HIS BREATHING TO BE NORMAL.
HIS HEARTRATE GRADUALLY SLOWS.
BUT TONIGHT, THE NIGHTMARE JUST DOESN'T WANT TO LET HIM GO.
AAGHH!!!
IT'S NOT UNTIL HE'S WASHED DOWN A FEW LEVELOID WITH BOURBON THAT HIS NIGHTMARE ENDS.
FOR NOW.

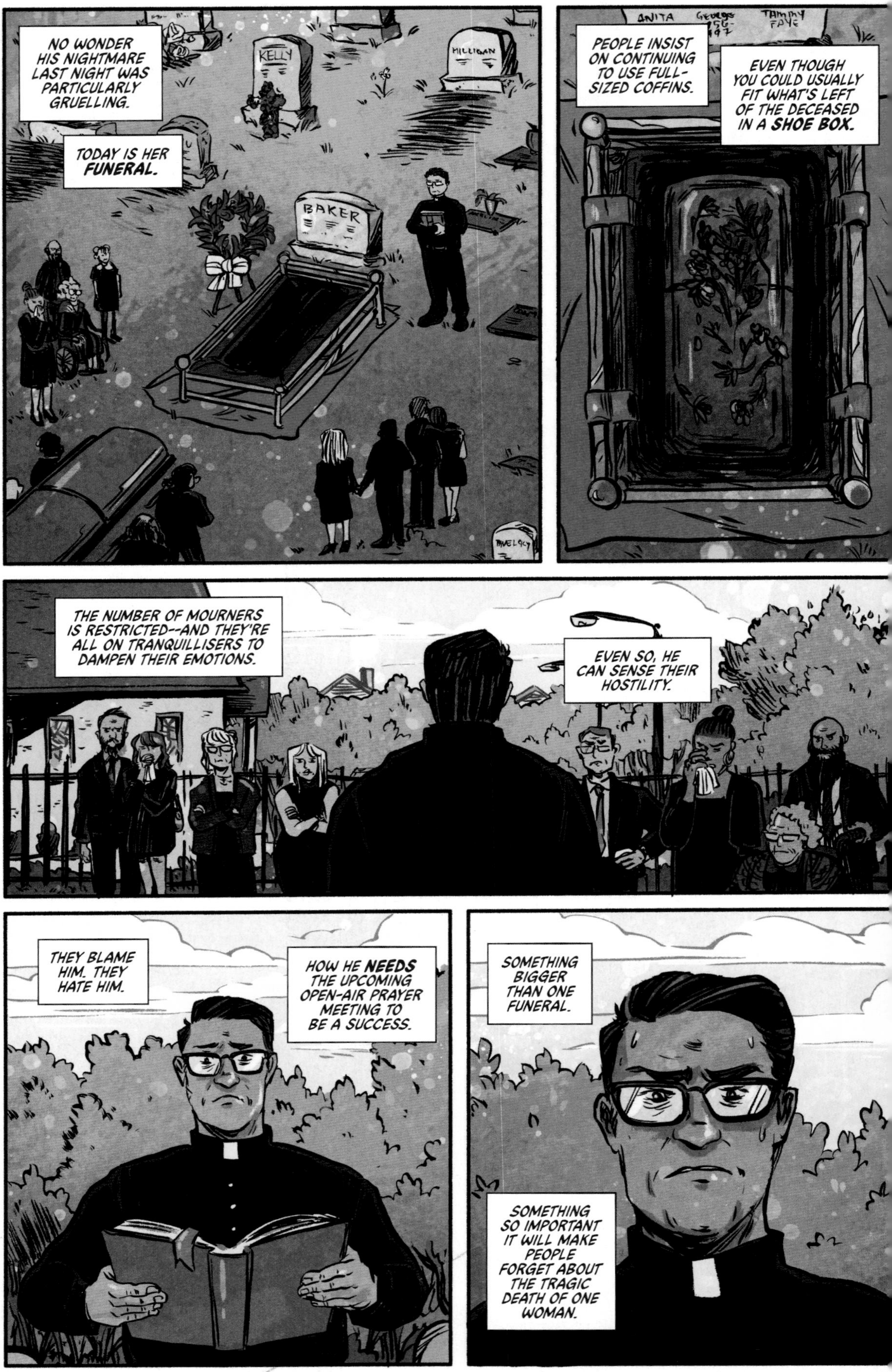
NO WONDER HIS NIGHTMARE LAST NIGHT WAS PARTICULARLY GRUELLING.
TODAY IS HER **FUNERAL.**
KELLY
MILLIGAN
BAKER
PEOPLE INSIST ON CONTINUING TO USE FULL-SIZED COFFINS.
EVEN THOUGH YOU COULD USUALLY FIT WHAT'S LEFT OF THE DECEASED IN A **SHOE BOX.**
THE NUMBER OF MOURNERS IS RESTRICTED--AND THEY'RE ALL ON TRANQUILLISERS TO DAMPEN THEIR EMOTIONS.
EVEN SO, HE CAN SENSE THEIR HOSTILITY.
THEY BLAME HIM. THEY HATE HIM.
HOW HE **NEEDS** THE UPCOMING OPEN-AIR PRAYER MEETING TO BE A SUCCESS.
SOMETHING BIGGER THAN ONE FUNERAL.
SOMETHING SO IMPORTANT IT WILL MAKE PEOPLE FORGET ABOUT THE TRAGIC DEATH OF ONE WOMAN.

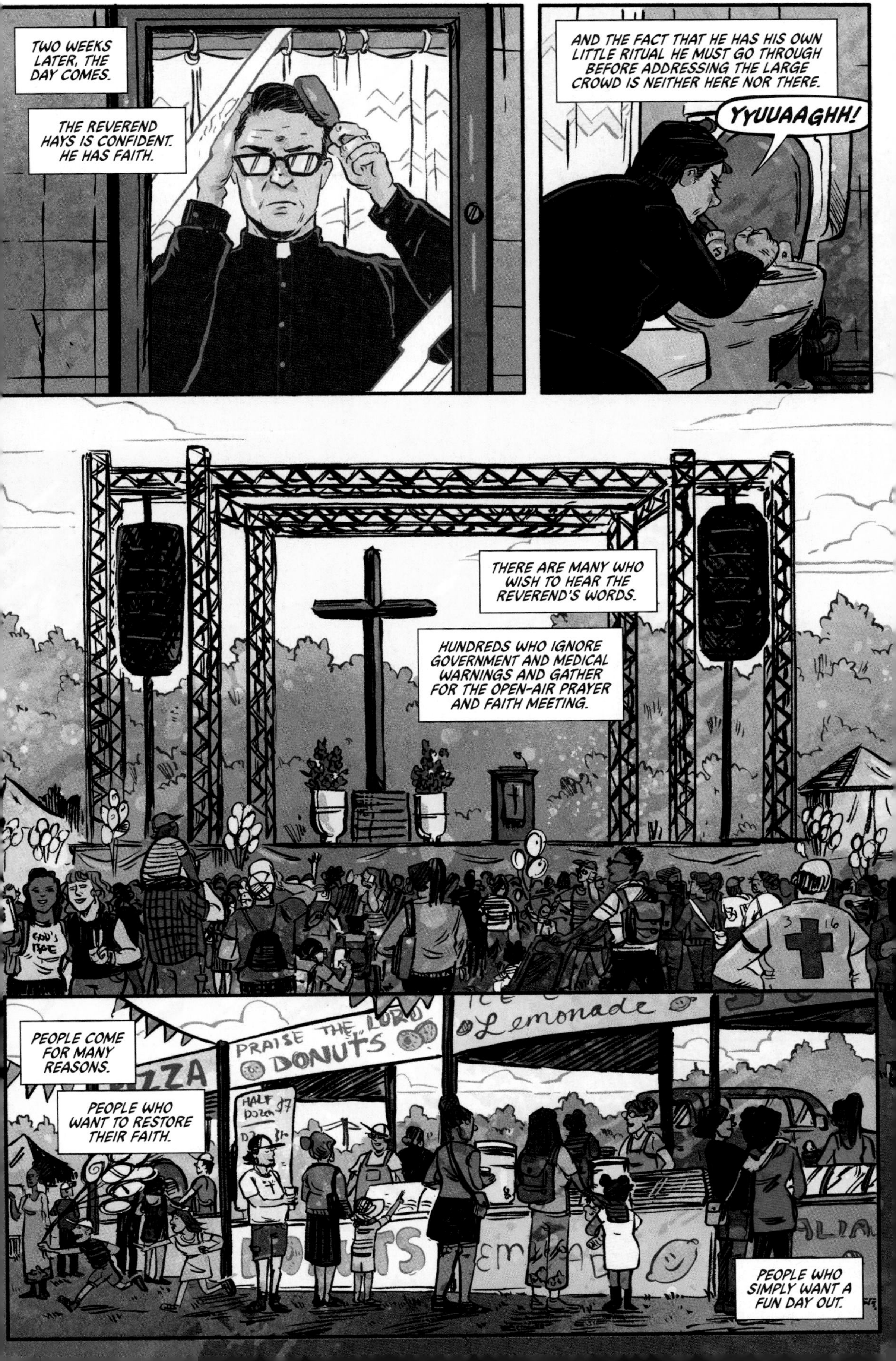
TWO WEEKS LATER, THE DAY COMES.
THE REVEREND HAYS IS CONFIDENT. HE HAS FAITH.
AND THE FACT THAT HE HAS HIS OWN LITTLE RITUAL HE MUST GO THROUGH BEFORE ADDRESSING THE LARGE CROWD IS NEITHER HERE NOR THERE.
YYUUAAGHH!
THERE ARE MANY WHO WISH TO HEAR THE REVEREND'S WORDS.
HUNDREDS WHO IGNORE GOVERNMENT AND MEDICAL WARNINGS AND GATHER FOR THE OPEN-AIR PRAYER AND FAITH MEETING.
PEOPLE COME FOR MANY REASONS.
PRAISE THE LORD DONUTS
Lemonade
PEOPLE WHO WANT TO RESTORE THEIR FAITH.
PEOPLE WHO SIMPLY WANT A FUN DAY OUT.

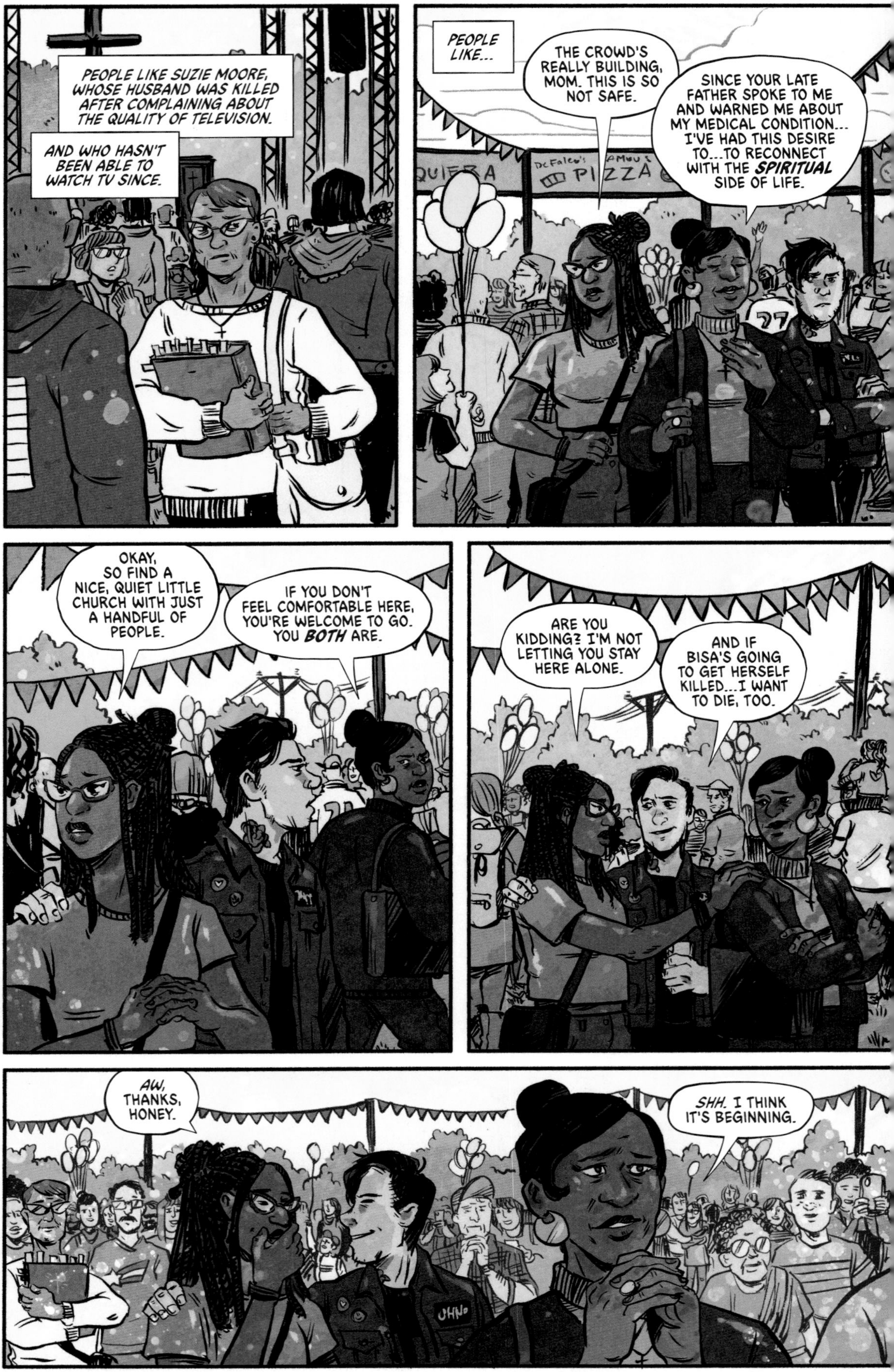
PEOPLE LIKE SUZIE MOORE, WHOSE HUSBAND WAS KILLED AFTER COMPLAINING ABOUT THE QUALITY OF TELEVISION.
AND WHO HASN'T BEEN ABLE TO WATCH TV SINCE.
PEOPLE LIKE...
THE CROWD'S REALLY BUILDING, MOM. THIS IS SO NOT SAFE.
SINCE YOUR LATE FATHER SPOKE TO ME AND WARNED ME ABOUT MY MEDICAL CONDITION... I'VE HAD THIS DESIRE TO...TO RECONNECT WITH THE *SPIRITUAL* SIDE OF LIFE.
DeFalco's PIZZA
OKAY, SO FIND A NICE, QUIET LITTLE CHURCH WITH JUST A HANDFUL OF PEOPLE.
IF YOU DON'T FEEL COMFORTABLE HERE, YOU'RE WELCOME TO GO. YOU *BOTH* ARE.
ARE YOU KIDDING? I'M NOT LETTING YOU STAY HERE ALONE.
AND IF BISA'S GOING TO GET HERSELF KILLED...I WANT TO DIE, TOO.
AW, THANKS, HONEY.
SHH. I THINK IT'S BEGINNING.

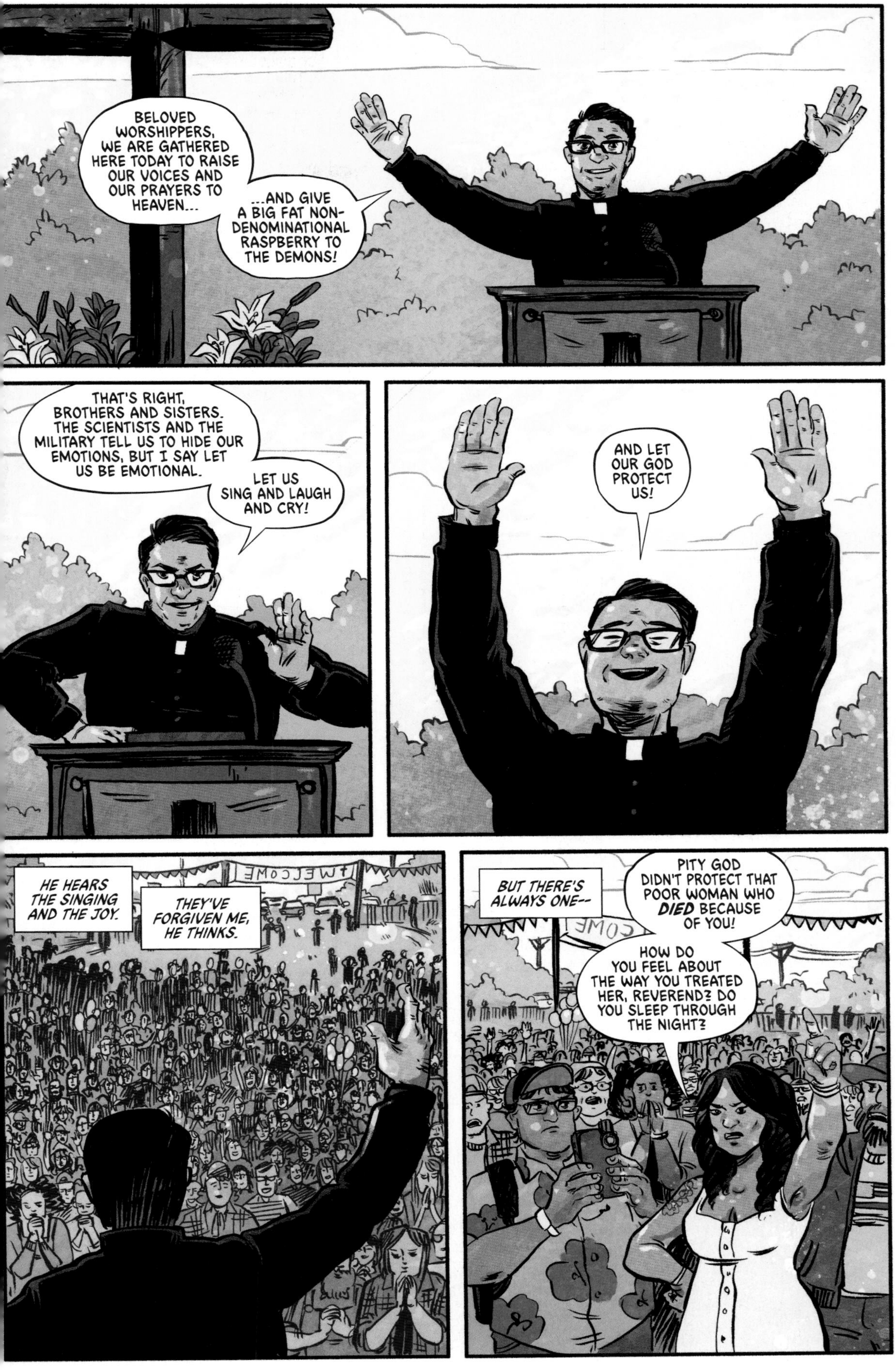
BELOVED WORSHIPPERS, WE ARE GATHERED HERE TODAY TO RAISE OUR VOICES AND OUR PRAYERS TO HEAVEN...
...AND GIVE A BIG FAT NON-DENOMINATIONAL RASPBERRY TO THE DEMONS!
THAT'S RIGHT, BROTHERS AND SISTERS. THE SCIENTISTS AND THE MILITARY TELL US TO HIDE OUR EMOTIONS, BUT I SAY LET US BE EMOTIONAL.
LET US SING AND LAUGH AND CRY!
AND LET OUR GOD PROTECT US!
WELCOME
HE HEARS THE SINGING AND THE JOY.
THEY'VE FORGIVEN ME, HE THINKS.
BUT THERE'S ALWAYS ONE--
PITY GOD DIDN'T PROTECT THAT POOR WOMAN WHO ***DIED*** BECAUSE OF YOU!
HOW DO YOU FEEL ABOUT THE WAY YOU TREATED HER, REVEREND? DO YOU SLEEP THROUGH THE NIGHT?

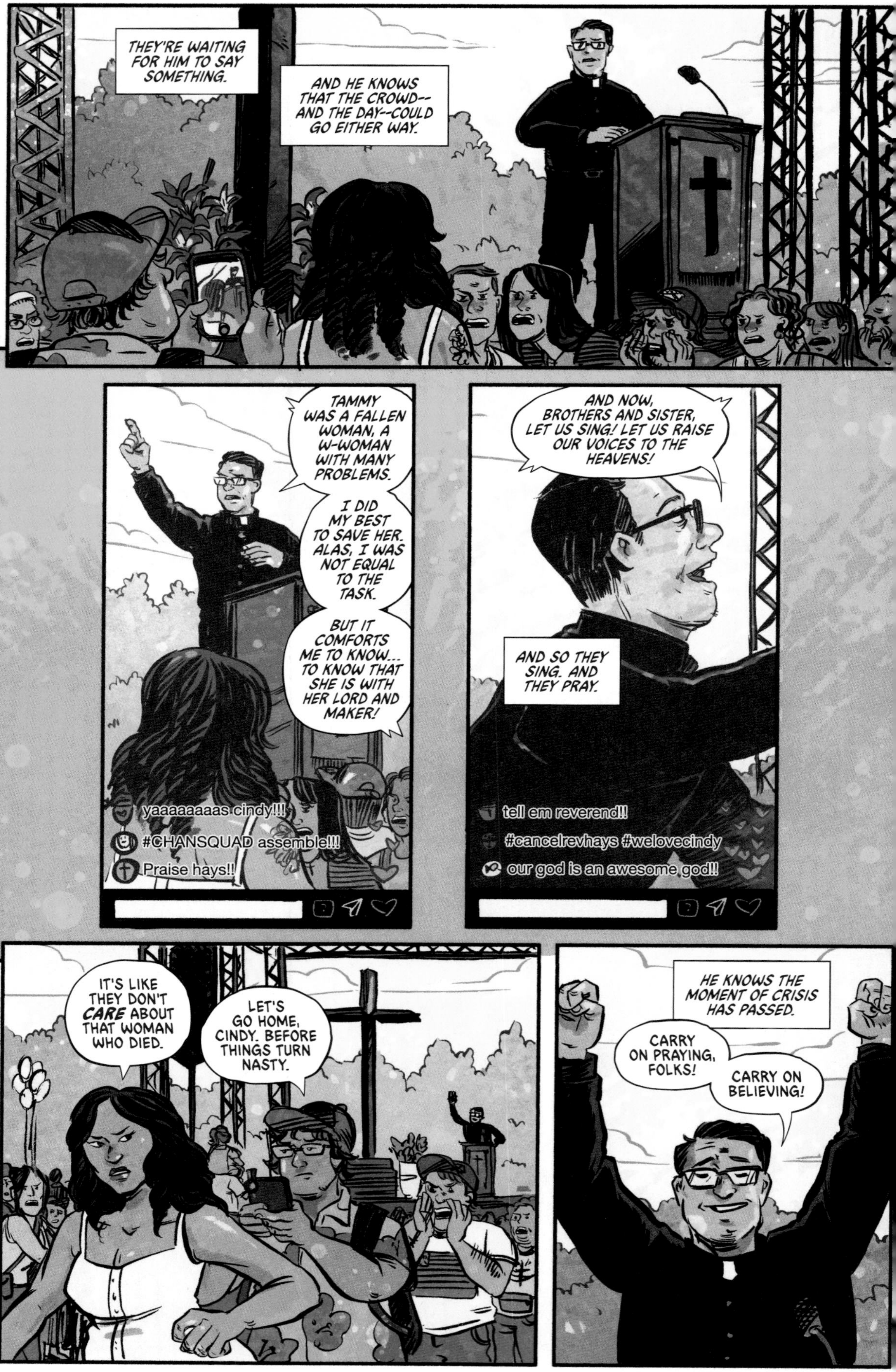
THEY'RE WAITING FOR HIM TO SAY SOMETHING.
AND HE KNOWS THAT THE CROWD-- AND THE DAY--COULD GO EITHER WAY.
TAMMY WAS A FALLEN WOMAN, A W-WOMAN WITH MANY PROBLEMS.
I DID MY BEST TO SAVE HER. ALAS, I WAS NOT EQUAL TO THE TASK.
BUT IT COMFORTS ME TO KNOW... TO KNOW THAT SHE IS WITH HER LORD AND MAKER!
yaaaaaaaas cindy!!!
#CHANSQUAD assemble!!!
Praise hays!!
AND NOW, BROTHERS AND SISTER, LET US SING! LET US RAISE OUR VOICES TO THE HEAVENS!
AND SO THEY SING. AND THEY PRAY.
tell em reverend!!
#cancelrevhays #welovecindy
our god is an awesome god!!
IT'S LIKE THEY DON'T CARE ABOUT THAT WOMAN WHO DIED.
LET'S GO HOME, CINDY. BEFORE THINGS TURN NASTY.
HE KNOWS THE MOMENT OF CRISIS HAS PASSED.
CARRY ON PRAYING, FOLKS!
CARRY ON BELIEVING!

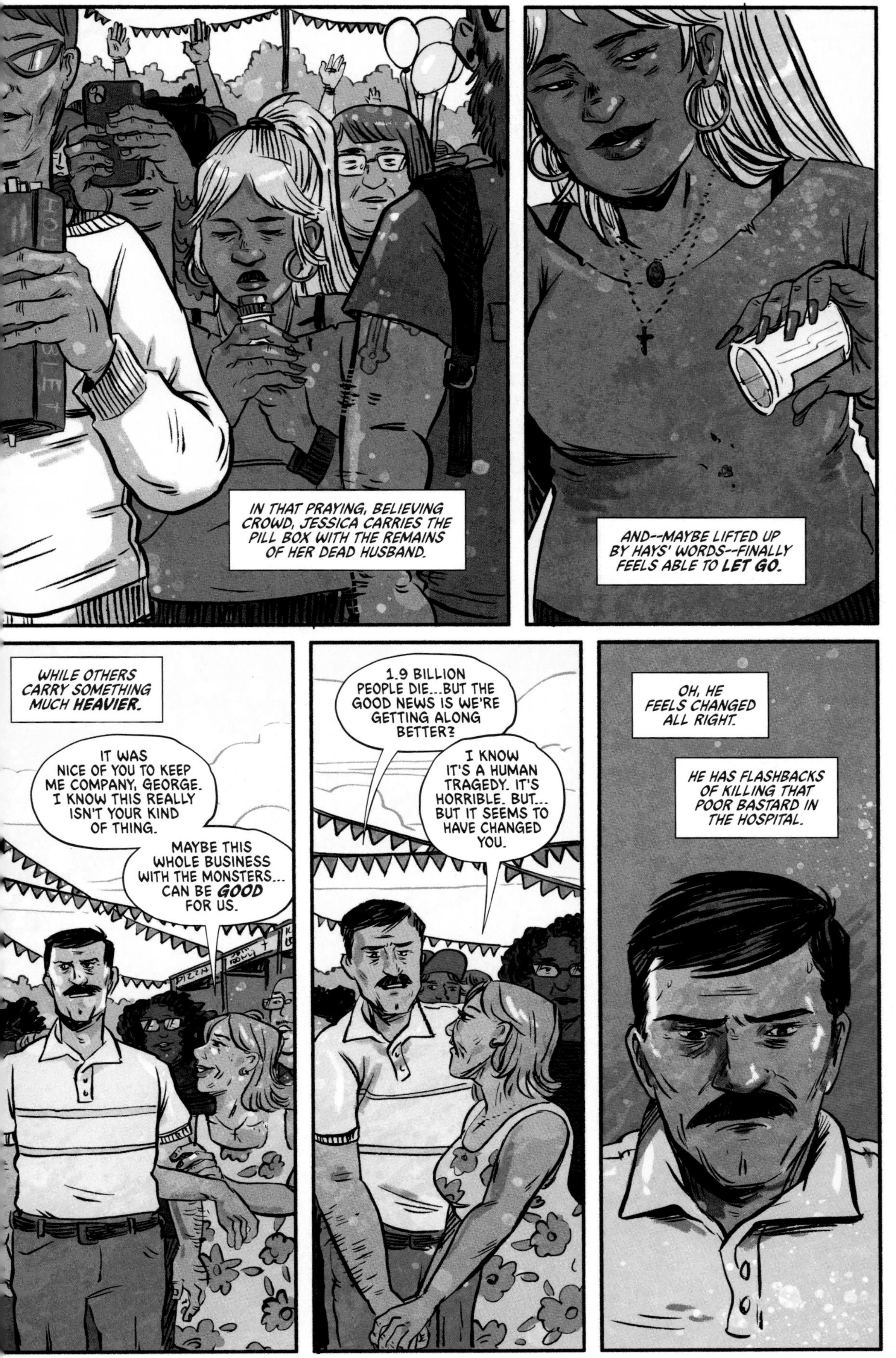
IN THAT PRAYING, BELIEVING CROWD, JESSICA CARRIES THE PILL BOX WITH THE REMAINS OF HER DEAD HUSBAND.
AND--MAYBE LIFTED UP BY HAYS' WORDS--FINALLY FEELS ABLE TO LET GO.
WHILE OTHERS CARRY SOMETHING MUCH HEAVIER.
IT WAS NICE OF YOU TO KEEP ME COMPANY, GEORGE. I KNOW THIS REALLY ISN'T YOUR KIND OF THING.
MAYBE THIS WHOLE BUSINESS WITH THE MONSTERS... CAN BE GOOD FOR US.
1.9 BILLION PEOPLE DIE...BUT THE GOOD NEWS IS WE'RE GETTING ALONG BETTER?
I KNOW IT'S A HUMAN TRAGEDY. IT'S HORRIBLE. BUT... BUT IT SEEMS TO HAVE CHANGED YOU.
OH, HE FEELS CHANGED ALL RIGHT.
HE HAS FLASHBACKS OF KILLING THAT POOR BASTARD IN THE HOSPITAL.

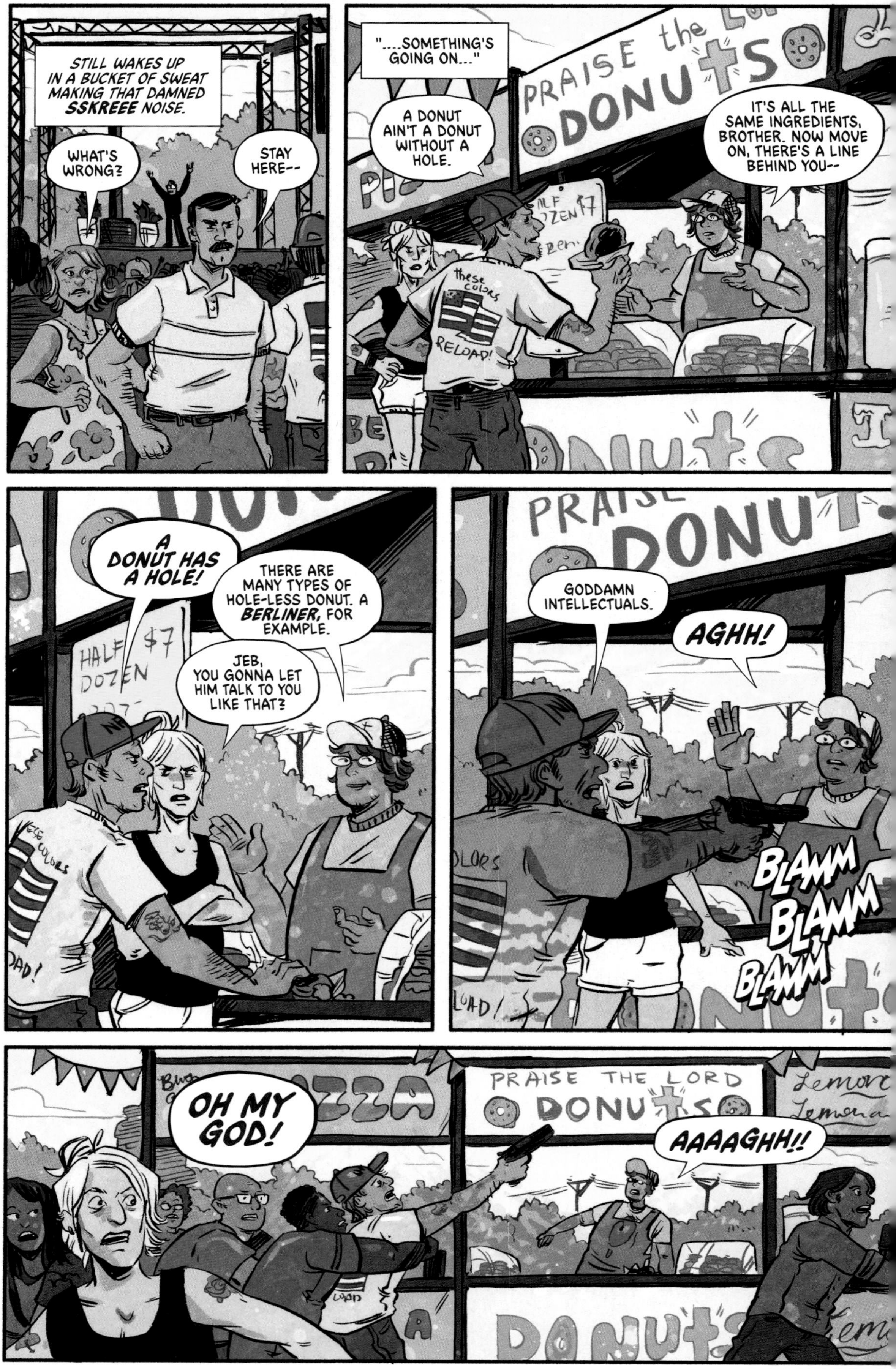
STILL WAKES UP IN A BUCKET OF SWEAT MAKING THAT DAMNED SSKREEE NOISE.
WHAT'S WRONG?
STAY HERE--
"....SOMETHING'S GOING ON..."
PRAISE the LORD DONUTS
A DONUT AIN'T A DONUT WITHOUT A HOLE.
IT'S ALL THE SAME INGREDIENTS, BROTHER. NOW MOVE ON, THERE'S A LINE BEHIND YOU--
these colors RELOAD!
A DONUT HAS A HOLE!
THERE ARE MANY TYPES OF HOLE-LESS DONUT. A BERLINER, FOR EXAMPLE.
JEB, YOU GONNA LET HIM TALK TO YOU LIKE THAT?
HALF DOZEN $7
PRAISE DONU
GODDAMN INTELLECTUALS.
AGHH!
BLAMM BLAMM BLAMM
OH MY GOD!
PRAISE THE LORD DONUTS
AAAAGHH!!

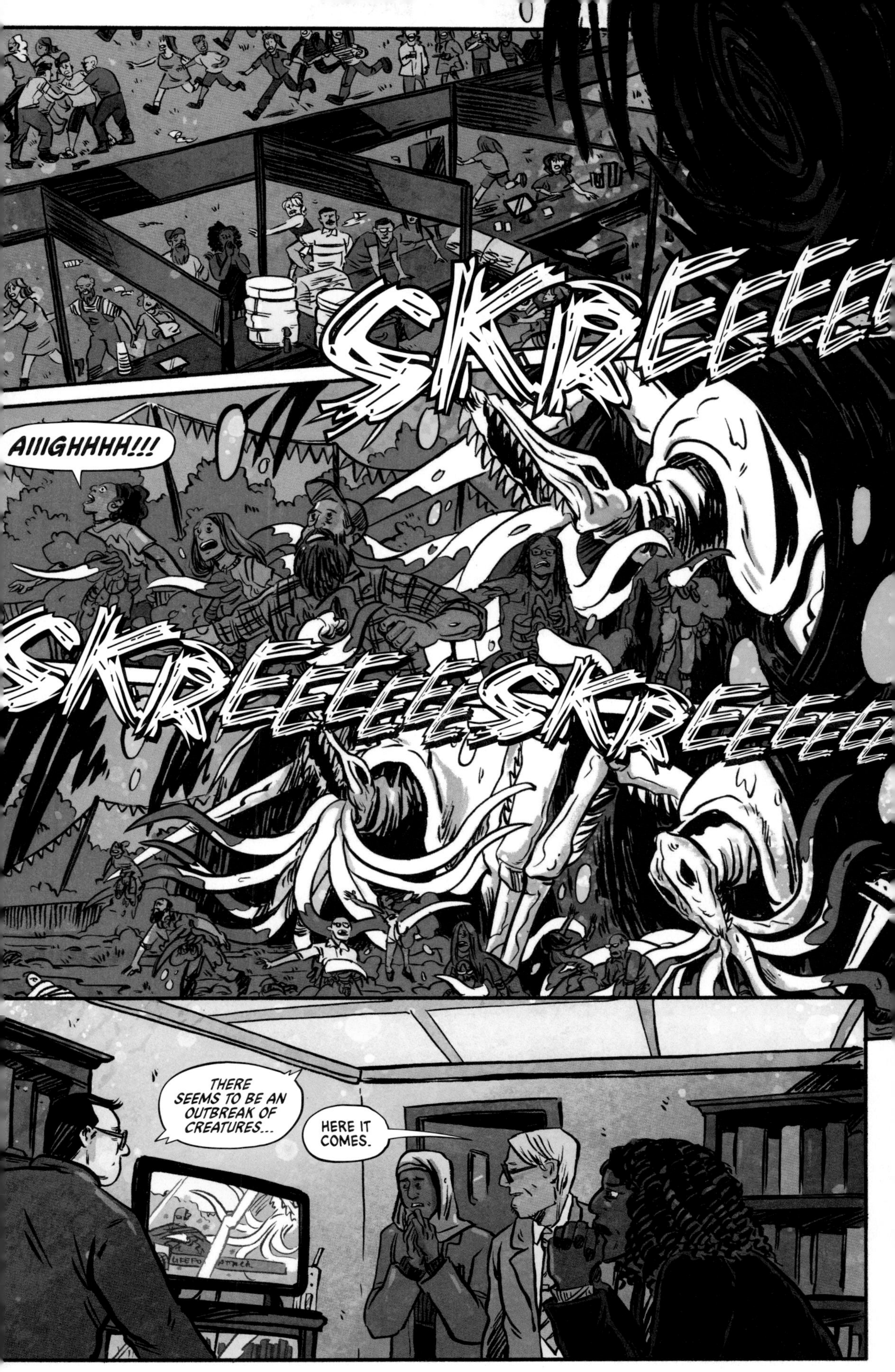
SKREEEEE
AIIIGHHHH!!!
SKREEEEEESKREEEEE
THERE SEEMS TO BE AN OUTBREAK OF CREATURES...
HERE IT COMES.

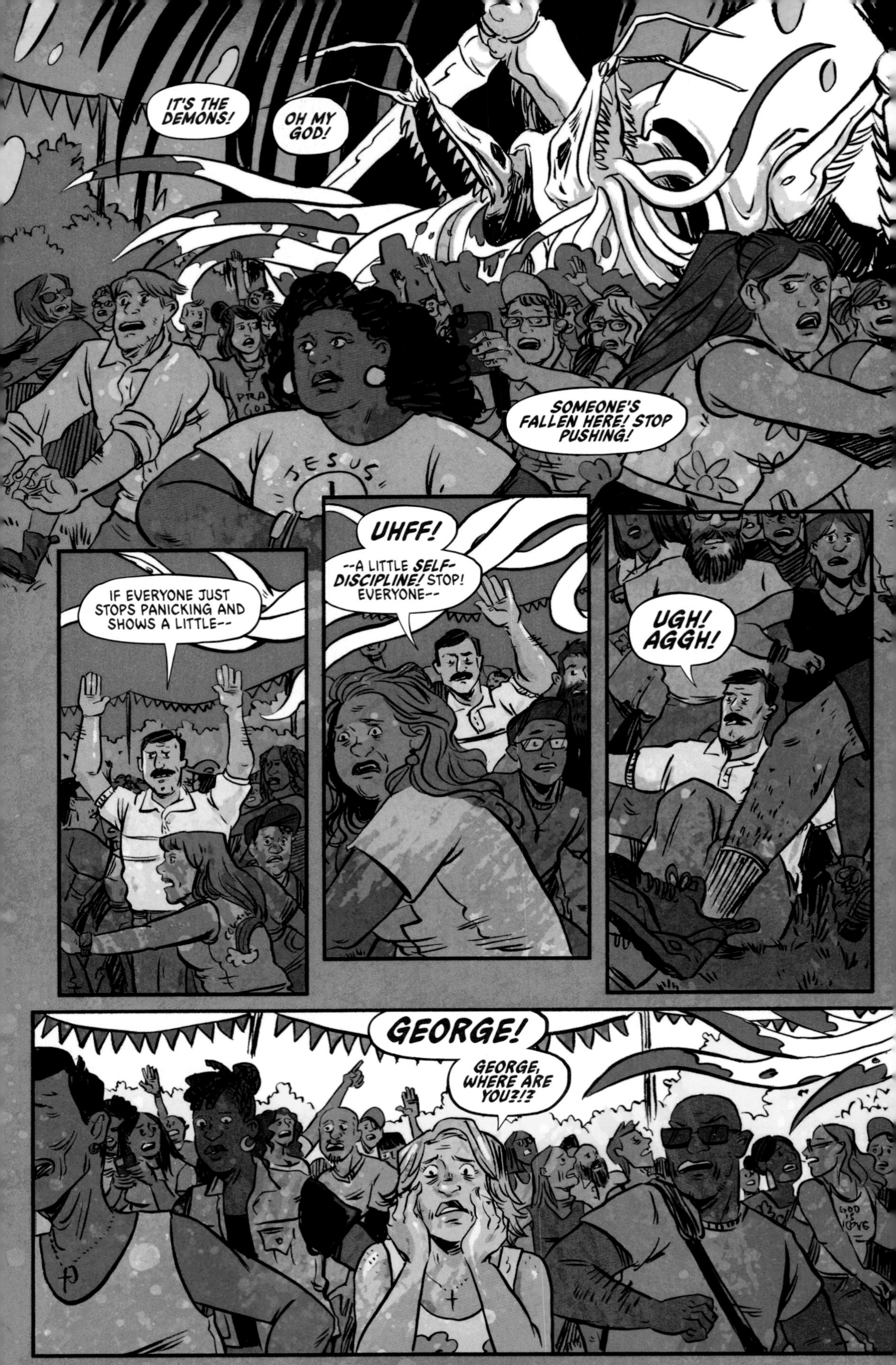
IT'S THE DEMONS!
OH MY GOD!
SOMEONE'S FALLEN HERE! STOP PUSHING!
IF EVERYONE JUST STOPS PANICKING AND SHOWS A LITTLE--
UHFF!
--A LITTLE SELF-DISCIPLINE! STOP! EVERYONE--
UGH! AGGH!
GEORGE!
GEORGE, WHERE ARE YOU?!?

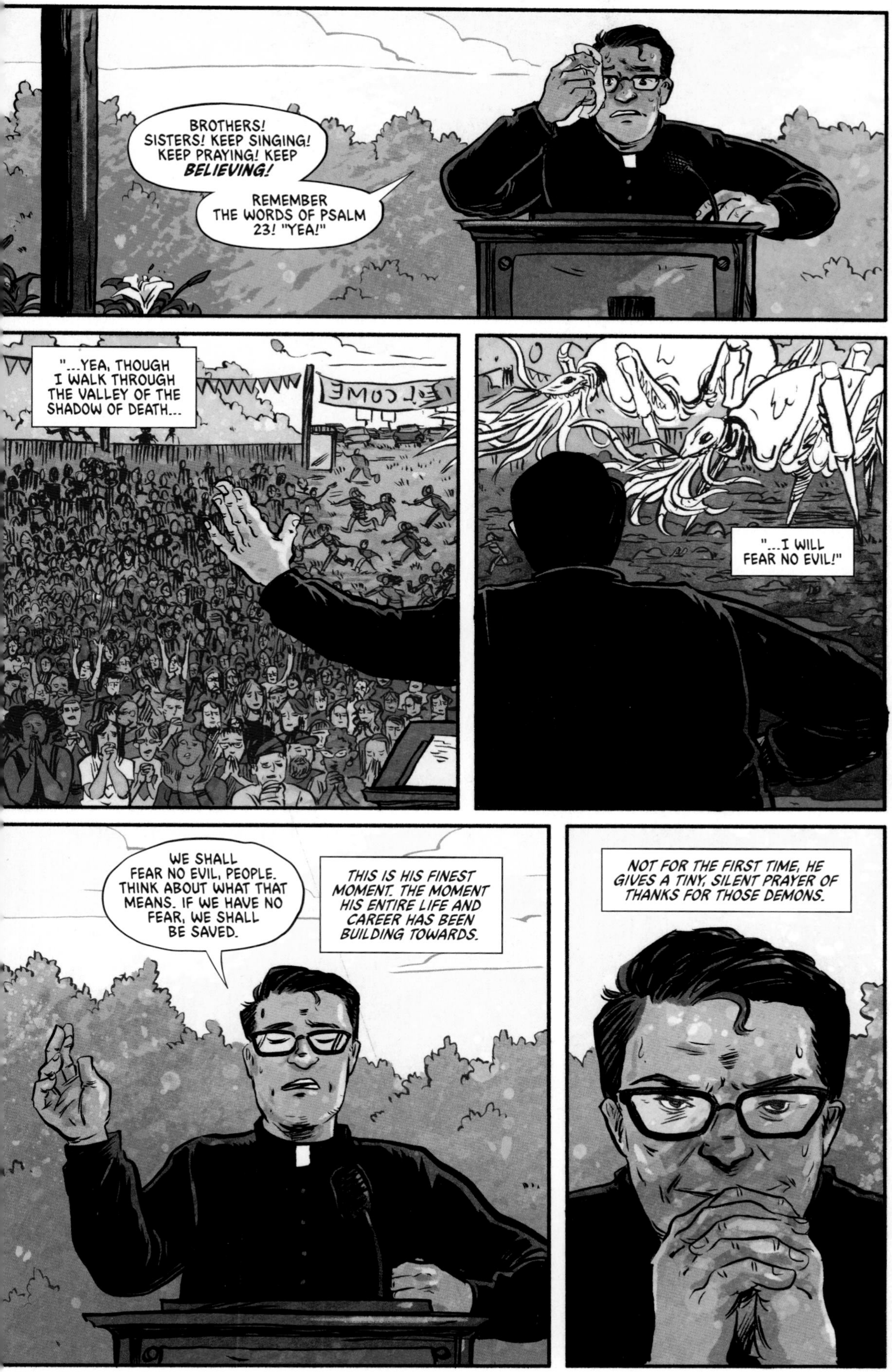
BROTHERS! SISTERS! KEEP SINGING! KEEP PRAYING! KEEP ***BELIEVING!***
REMEMBER THE WORDS OF PSALM 23! "YEA!"
"...YEA, THOUGH I WALK THROUGH THE VALLEY OF THE SHADOW OF DEATH...
WELCOME
"...I WILL FEAR NO EVIL!"
WE SHALL FEAR NO EVIL, PEOPLE. THINK ABOUT WHAT THAT MEANS. IF WE HAVE NO FEAR, WE SHALL BE SAVED.
THIS IS HIS FINEST MOMENT. THE MOMENT HIS ENTIRE LIFE AND CAREER HAS BEEN BUILDING TOWARDS.
NOT FOR THE FIRST TIME, HE GIVES A TINY, SILENT PRAYER OF THANKS FOR THOSE DEMONS.

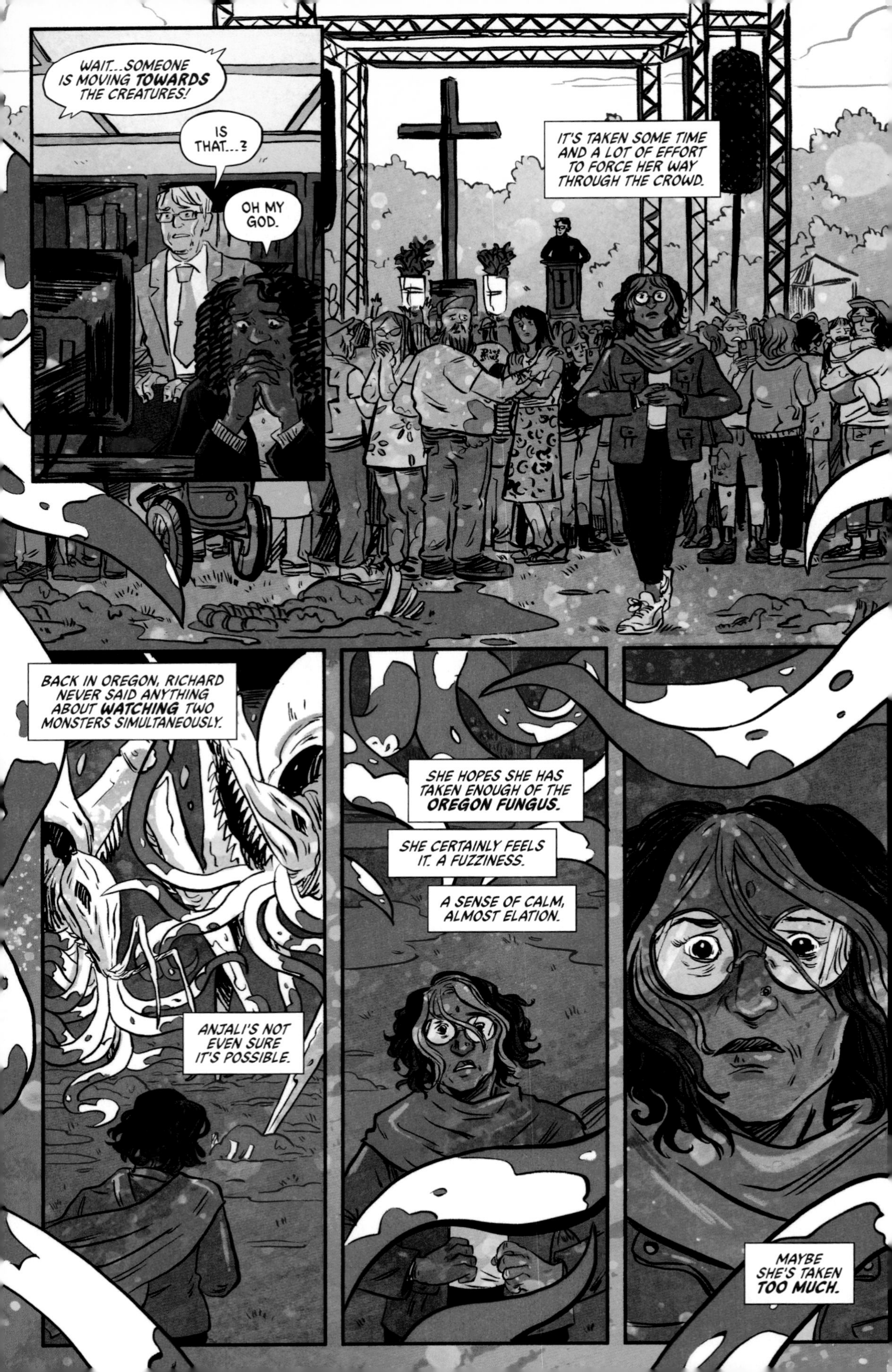
WAIT...SOMEONE IS MOVING TOWARDS THE CREATURES!
IS THAT...?
OH MY GOD.
IT'S TAKEN SOME TIME AND A LOT OF EFFORT TO FORCE HER WAY THROUGH THE CROWD.
BACK IN OREGON, RICHARD NEVER SAID ANYTHING ABOUT WATCHING TWO MONSTERS SIMULTANEOUSLY.
ANJALI'S NOT EVEN SURE IT'S POSSIBLE.
SHE HOPES SHE HAS TAKEN ENOUGH OF THE OREGON FUNGUS.
SHE CERTAINLY FEELS IT. A FUZZINESS.
A SENSE OF CALM, ALMOST ELATION.
MAYBE SHE'S TAKEN TOO MUCH.

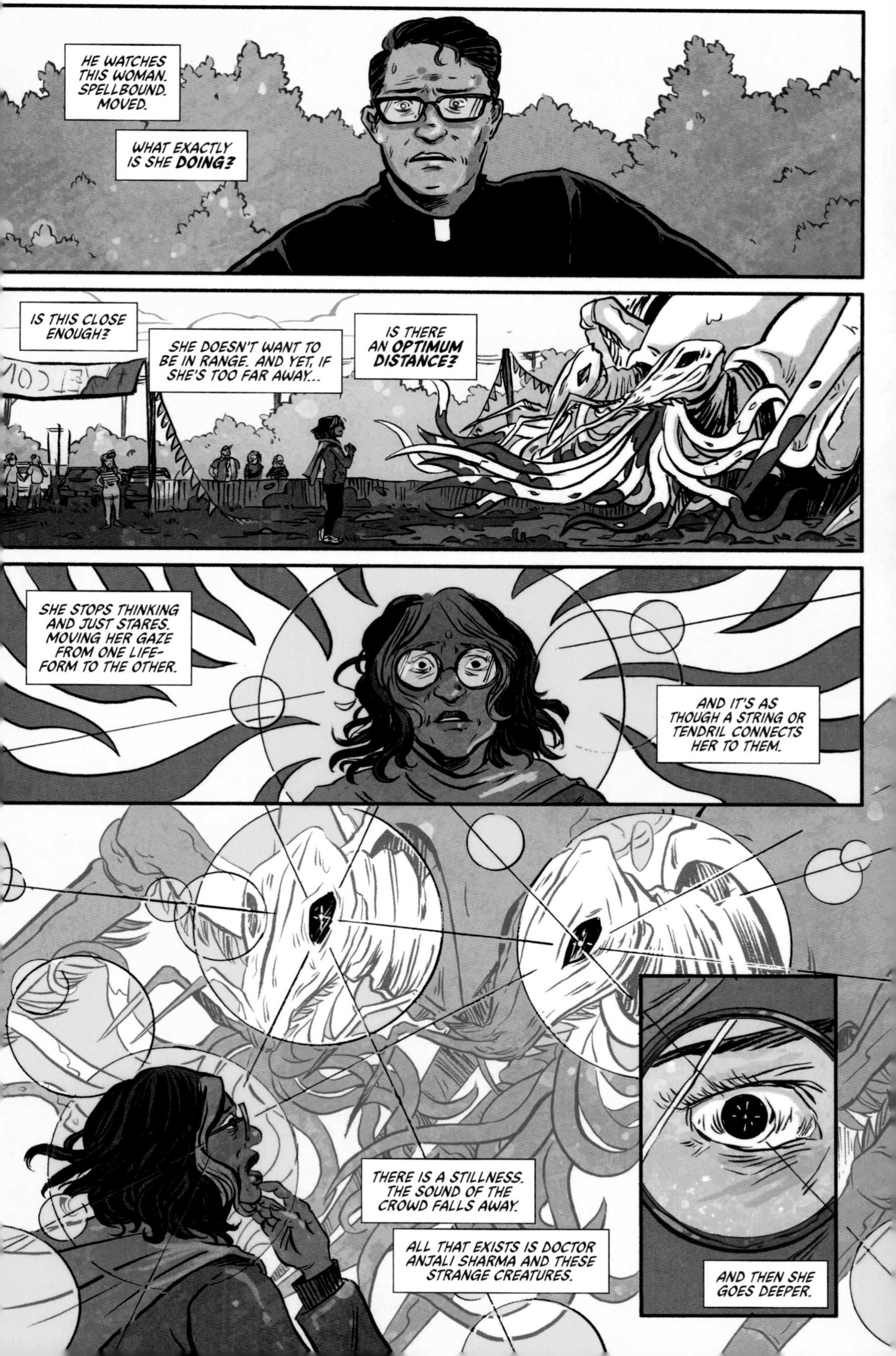
HE WATCHES THIS WOMAN. SPELLBOUND. MOVED.
WHAT EXACTLY IS SHE **DOING?**
IS THIS CLOSE ENOUGH?
SHE DOESN'T WANT TO BE IN RANGE. AND YET, IF SHE'S TOO FAR AWAY...
IS THERE AN **OPTIMUM DISTANCE?**
SHE STOPS THINKING AND JUST STARES. MOVING HER GAZE FROM ONE LIFE-FORM TO THE OTHER.
AND IT'S AS THOUGH A STRING OR TENDRIL CONNECTS HER TO THEM.
THERE IS A STILLNESS. THE SOUND OF THE CROWD FALLS AWAY.
ALL THAT EXISTS IS DOCTOR ANJALI SHARMA AND THESE STRANGE CREATURES.
AND THEN SHE GOES DEEPER.

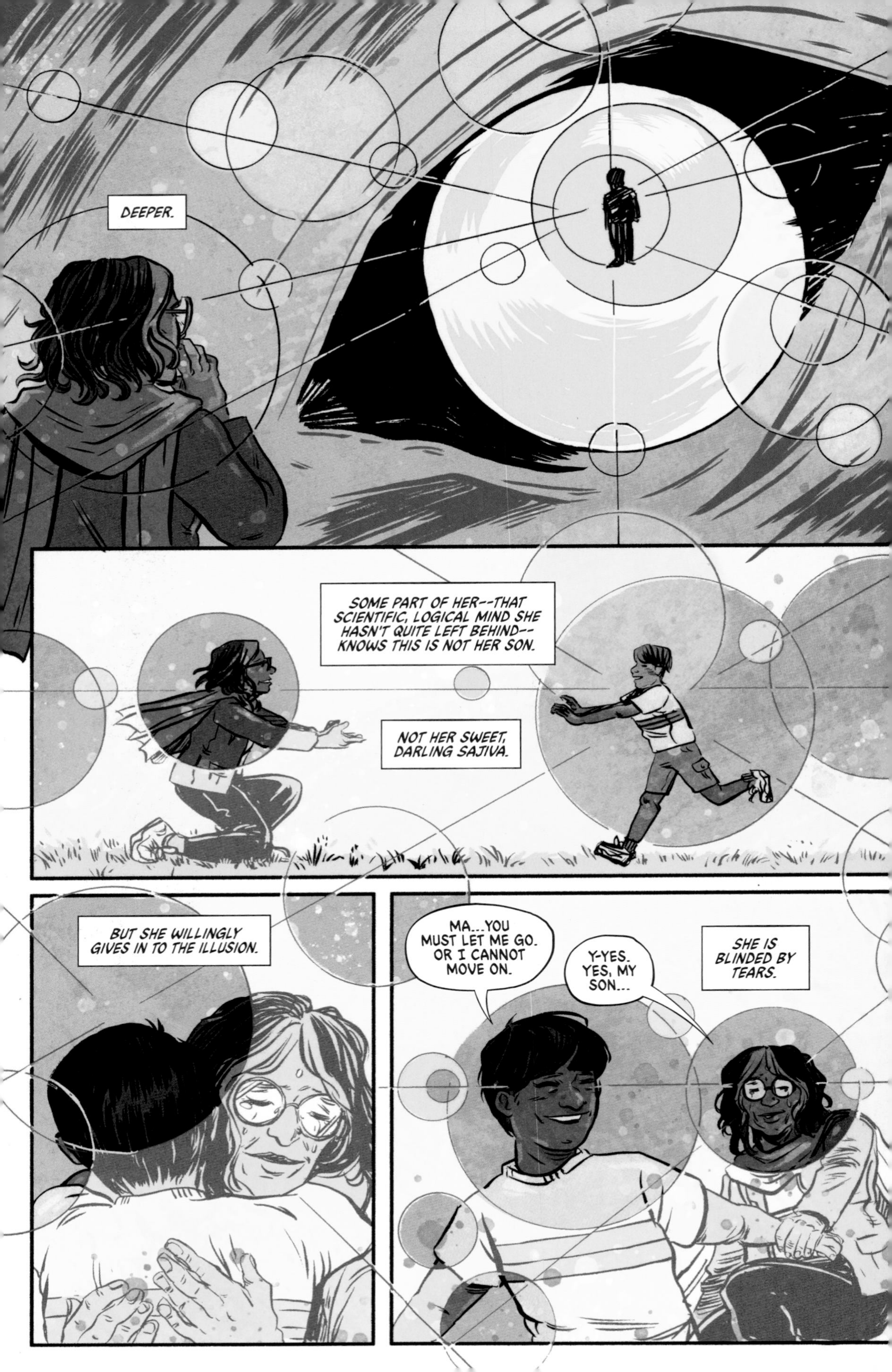
DEEPER.
SOME PART OF HER--THAT SCIENTIFIC, LOGICAL MIND SHE HASN'T QUITE LEFT BEHIND--KNOWS THIS IS NOT HER SON.
NOT HER SWEET, DARLING SAJIVA.
BUT SHE WILLINGLY GIVES IN TO THE ILLUSION.
MA...YOU MUST LET ME GO. OR I CANNOT MOVE ON.
Y-YES. YES, MY SON...
SHE IS BLINDED BY TEARS.

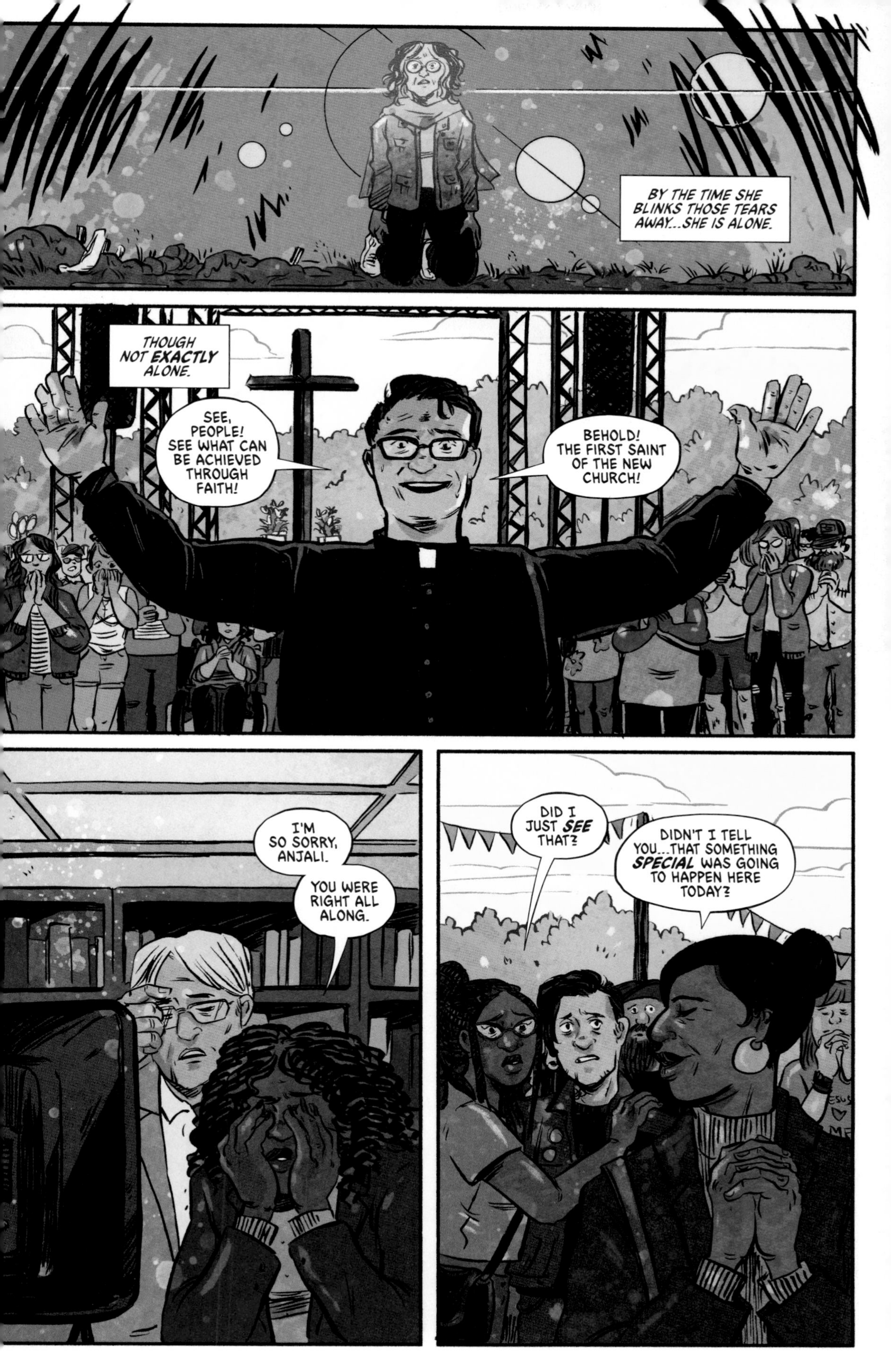
BY THE TIME SHE BLINKS THOSE TEARS AWAY...SHE IS ALONE.
THOUGH NOT **EXACTLY** ALONE.
SEE, PEOPLE! SEE WHAT CAN BE ACHIEVED THROUGH FAITH!
BEHOLD! THE FIRST SAINT OF THE NEW CHURCH!
I'M SO SORRY, ANJALI.
YOU WERE RIGHT ALL ALONG.
DID I JUST **SEE** THAT?
DIDN'T I TELL YOU...THAT SOMETHING **SPECIAL** WAS GOING TO HAPPEN HERE TODAY?

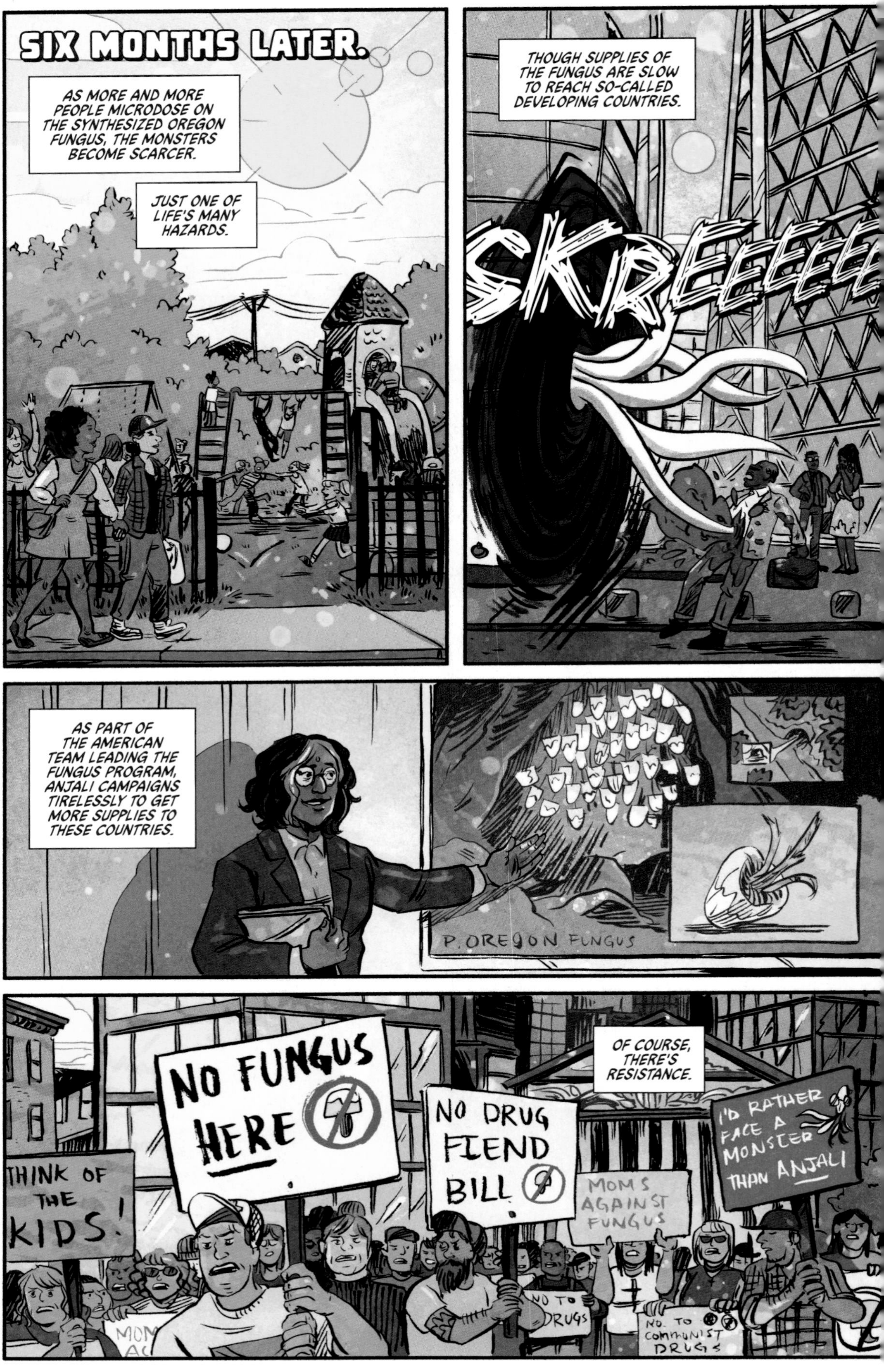
SIX MONTHS LATER.
AS MORE AND MORE PEOPLE MICRODOSE ON THE SYNTHESIZED OREGON FUNGUS, THE MONSTERS BECOME SCARCER.
JUST ONE OF LIFE'S MANY HAZARDS.
THOUGH SUPPLIES OF THE FUNGUS ARE SLOW TO REACH SO-CALLED DEVELOPING COUNTRIES.
SKREEEEEE
AS PART OF THE AMERICAN TEAM LEADING THE FUNGUS PROGRAM, ANJALI CAMPAIGNS TIRELESSLY TO GET MORE SUPPLIES TO THESE COUNTRIES.
P. OREGON FUNGUS
OF COURSE, THERE'S RESISTANCE.
THINK OF THE KIDS!
NO FUNGUS HERE
NO DRUG FIEND BILL
MOMS AGAINST FUNGUS
I'D RATHER FACE A MONSTER THAN ANJALI
NO TO DRUGS
NO TO COMMUNIST DRUGS

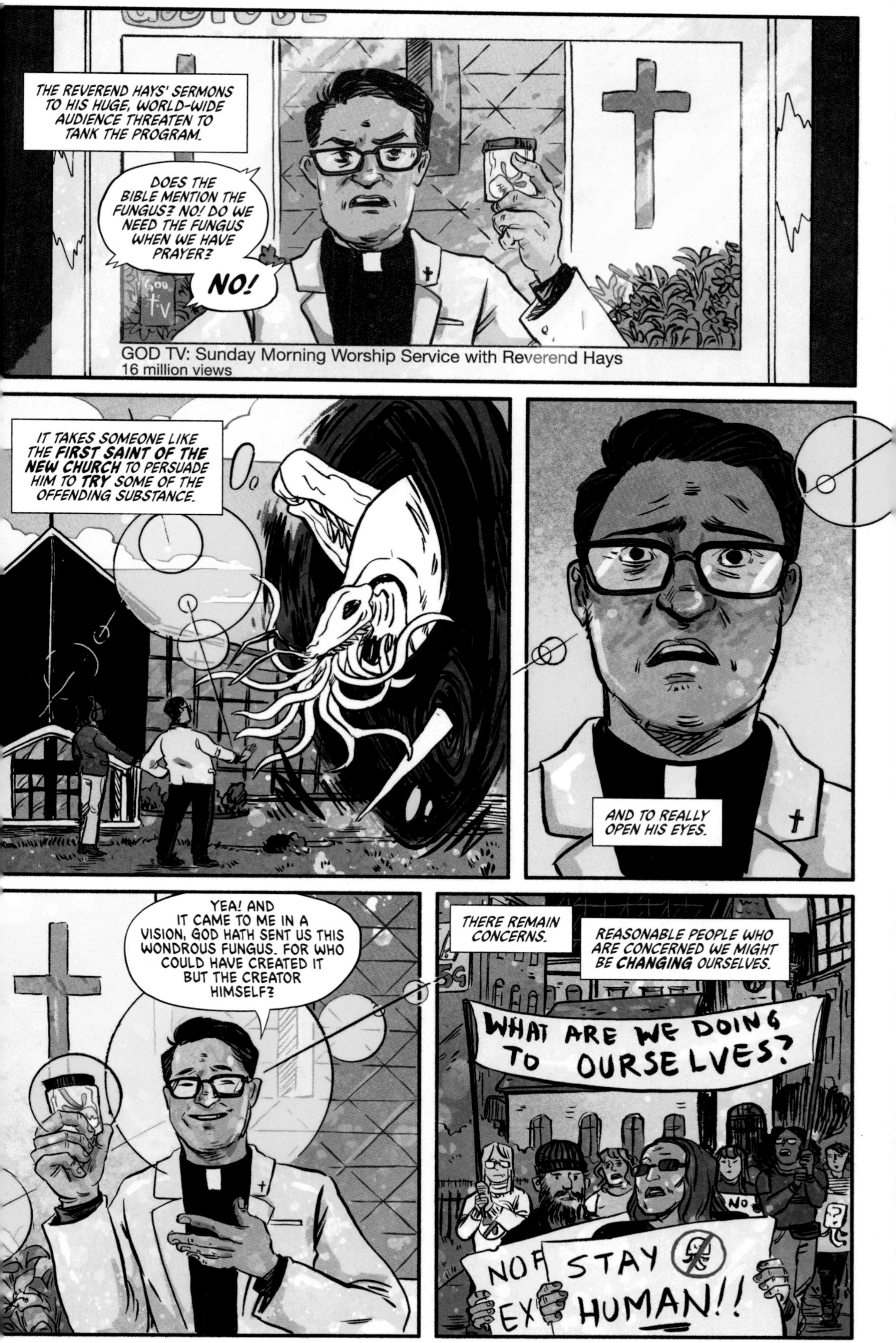

THE REVEREND HAYS' SERMONS TO HIS HUGE, WORLD-WIDE AUDIENCE THREATEN TO TANK THE PROGRAM.
DOES THE BIBLE MENTION THE FUNGUS? NO! DO WE NEED THE FUNGUS WHEN WE HAVE PRAYER?
NO!
GOD TV
GOD TV: Sunday Morning Worship Service with Reverend Hays
16 million views
IT TAKES SOMEONE LIKE THE **FIRST SAINT OF THE NEW CHURCH** TO PERSUADE HIM TO **TRY** SOME OF THE OFFENDING SUBSTANCE.
AND TO REALLY OPEN HIS EYES.
YEA! AND IT CAME TO ME IN A VISION, GOD HATH SENT US THIS WONDROUS FUNGUS. FOR WHO COULD HAVE CREATED IT BUT THE CREATOR HIMSELF?
THERE REMAIN CONCERNS.
REASONABLE PEOPLE WHO ARE CONCERNED WE MIGHT BE **CHANGING** OURSELVES.
WHAT ARE WE DOING TO OURSELVES?
NO
STAY HUMAN!!

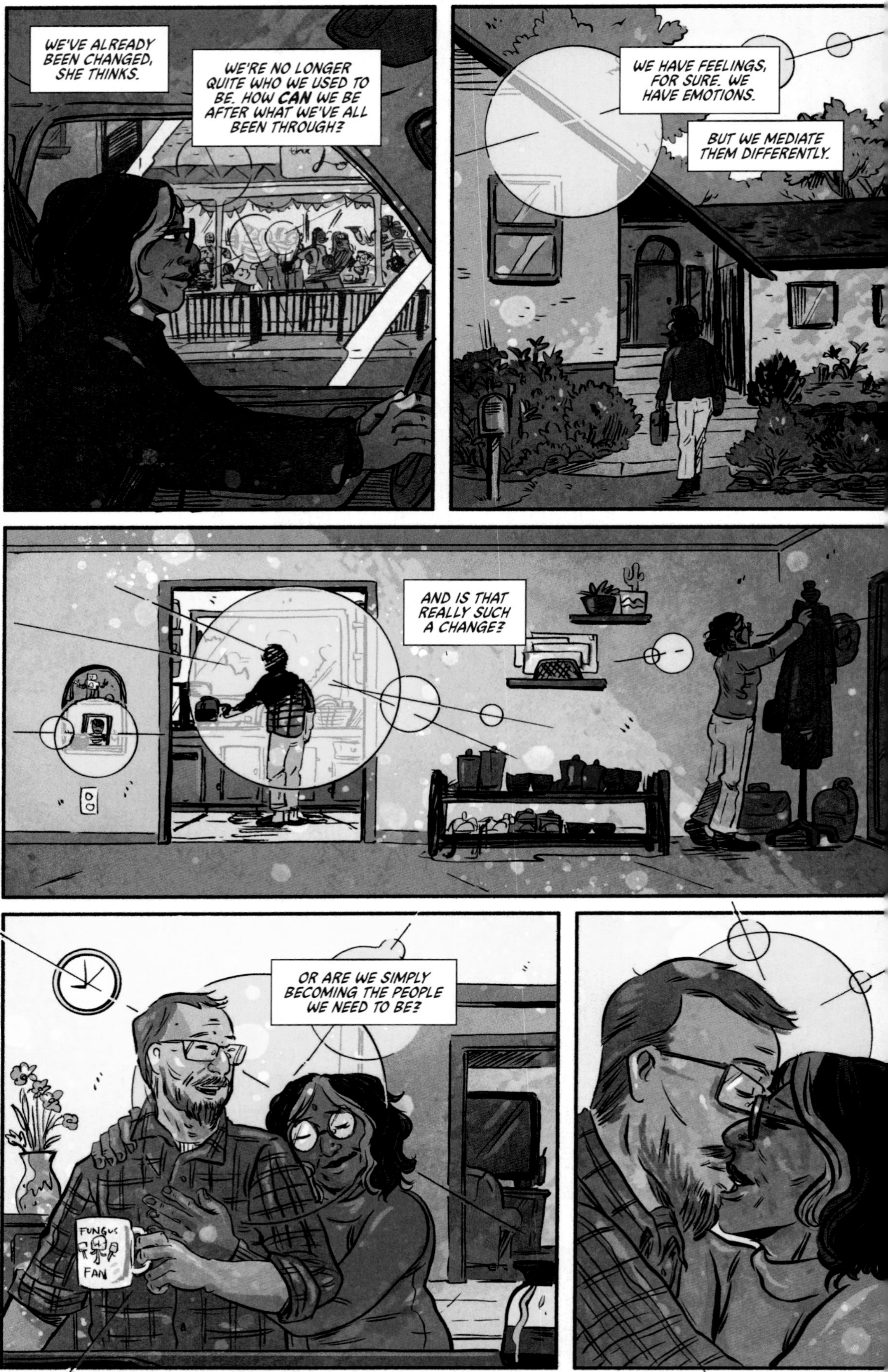
WE'VE ALREADY BEEN CHANGED, SHE THINKS.
WE'RE NO LONGER QUITE WHO WE USED TO BE. HOW CAN WE BE AFTER WHAT WE'VE ALL BEEN THROUGH?
WE HAVE FEELINGS, FOR SURE. WE HAVE EMOTIONS.
BUT WE MEDIATE THEM DIFFERENTLY.
AND IS THAT REALLY SUCH A CHANGE?
OR ARE WE SIMPLY BECOMING THE PEOPLE WE NEED TO BE?
FUNGUS FAN

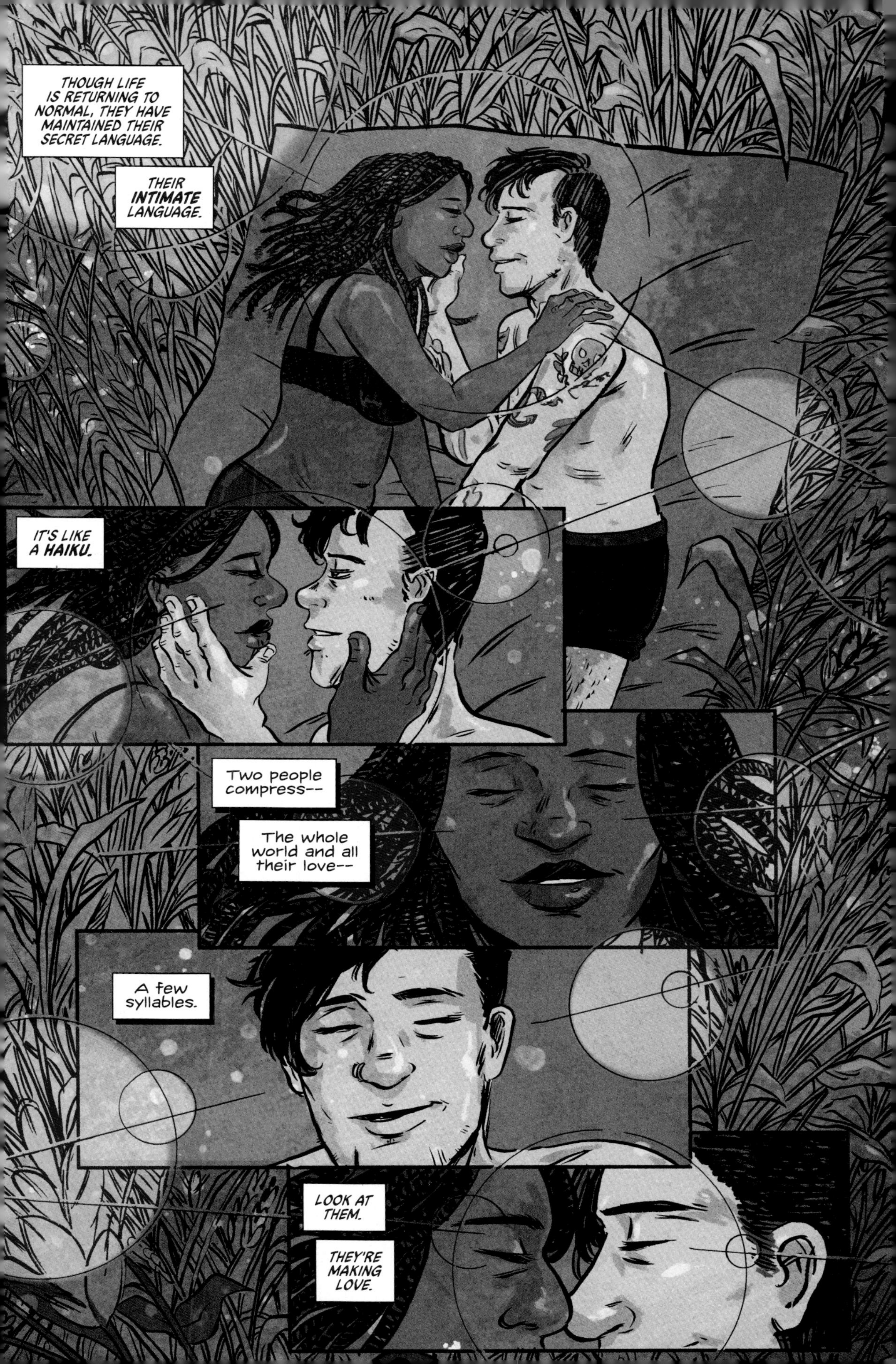
THOUGH LIFE IS RETURNING TO NORMAL, THEY HAVE MAINTAINED THEIR SECRET LANGUAGE.
THEIR **INTIMATE** LANGUAGE.
IT'S LIKE A **HAIKU.**
Two people compress--
The whole world and all their love--
A few syllables.
LOOK AT THEM.
THEY'RE MAKING LOVE.

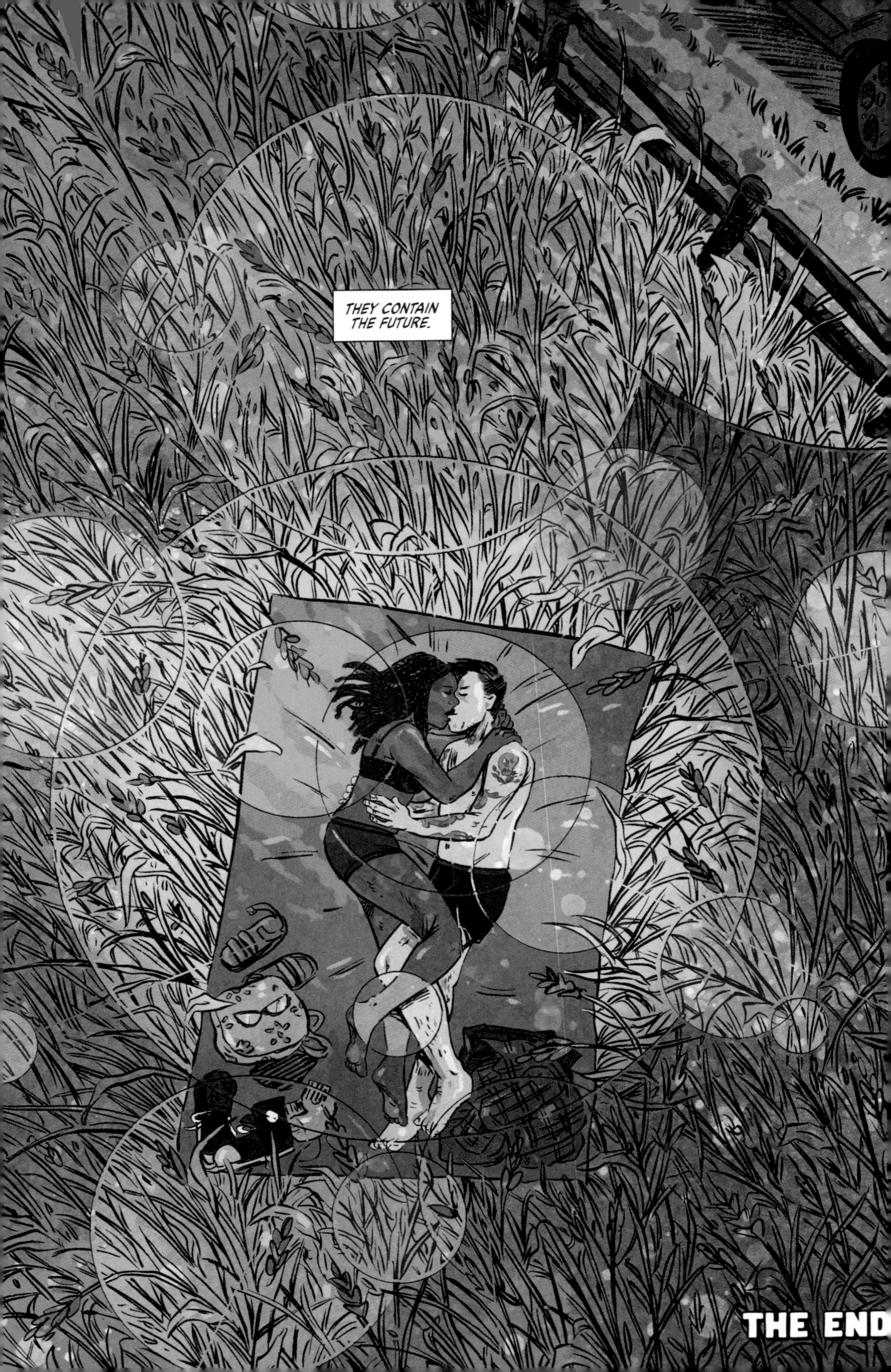
THEY CONTAIN THE FUTURE.
THE END

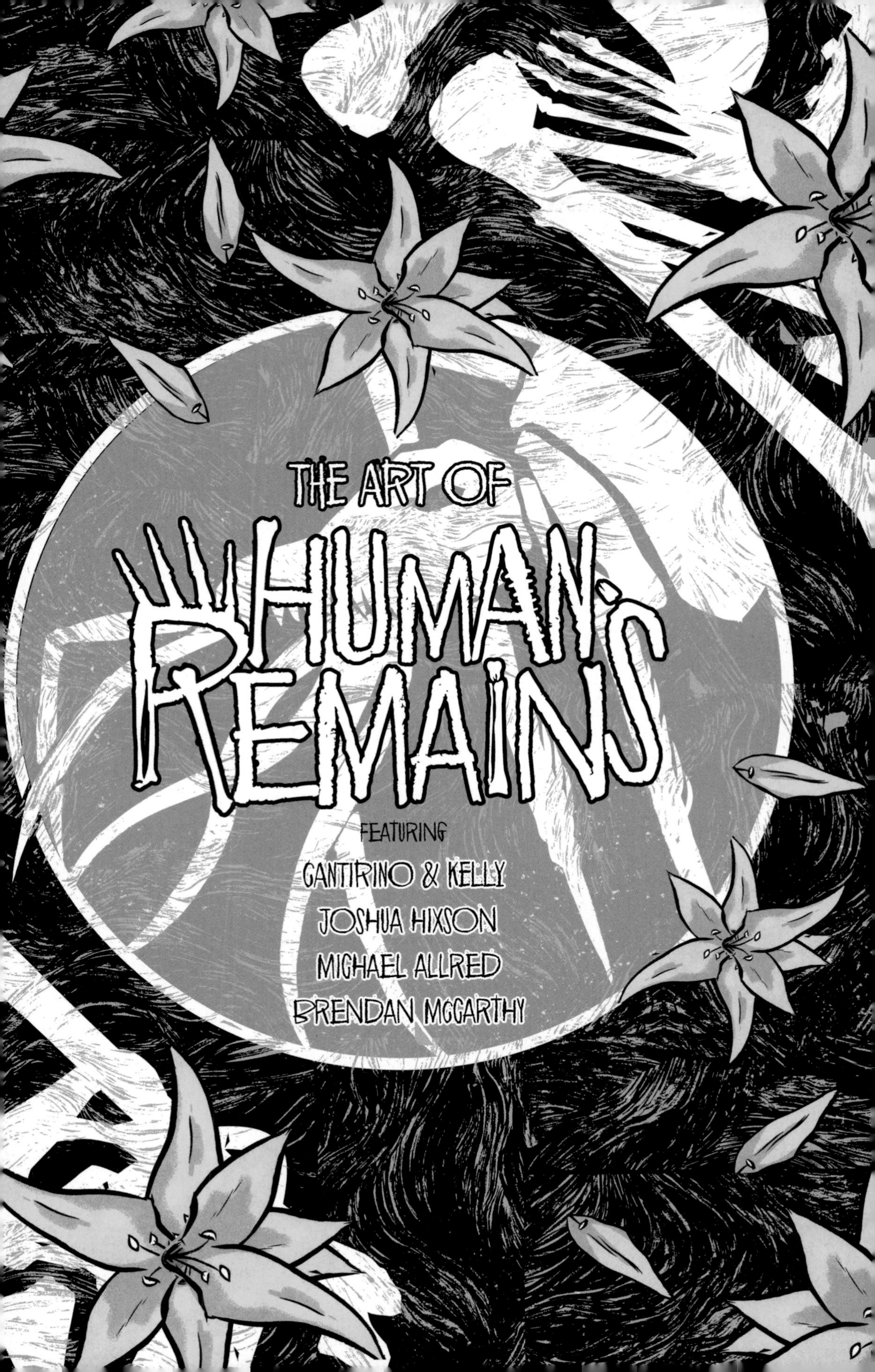
THE ART OF
HUMAN'S REMAINS
FEATURING
CANTIRINO & KELLY
JOSHUA HIXSON
MICHAEL ALLRED
BRENDAN MCCARTHY

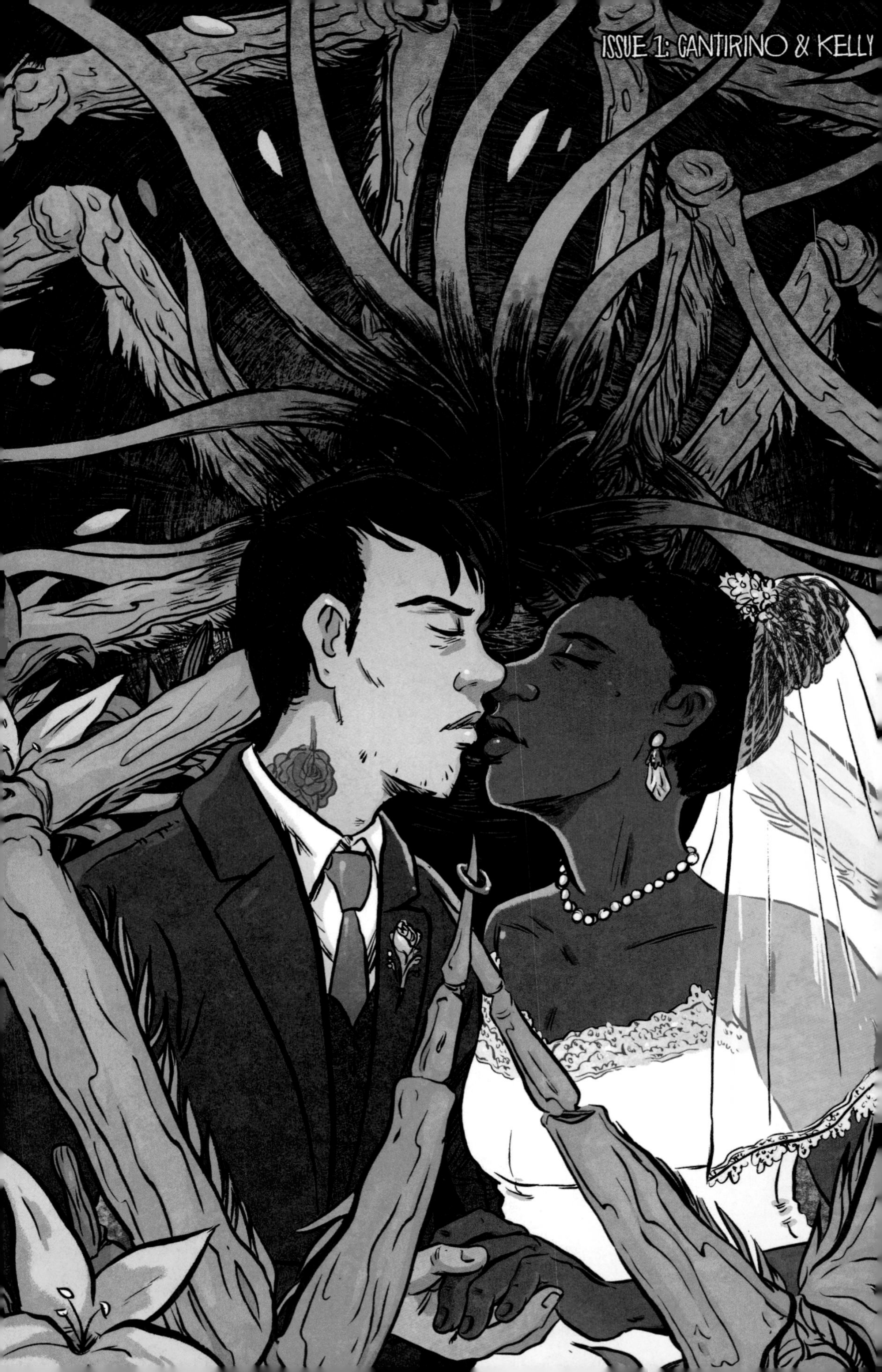
ISSUE 1: GANTIRINO & KELLY

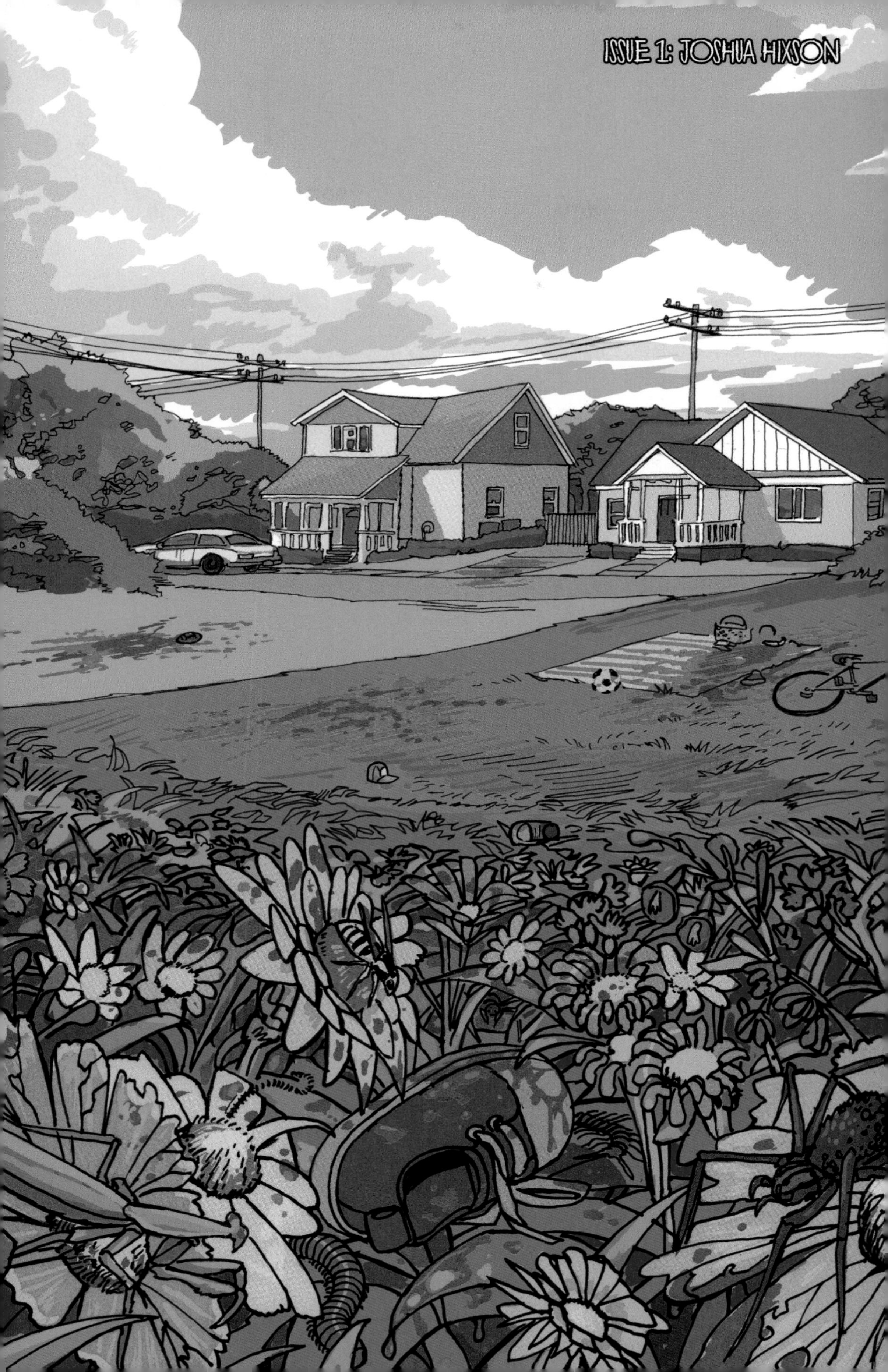
ISSUE 1: JOSHUA HIXSON

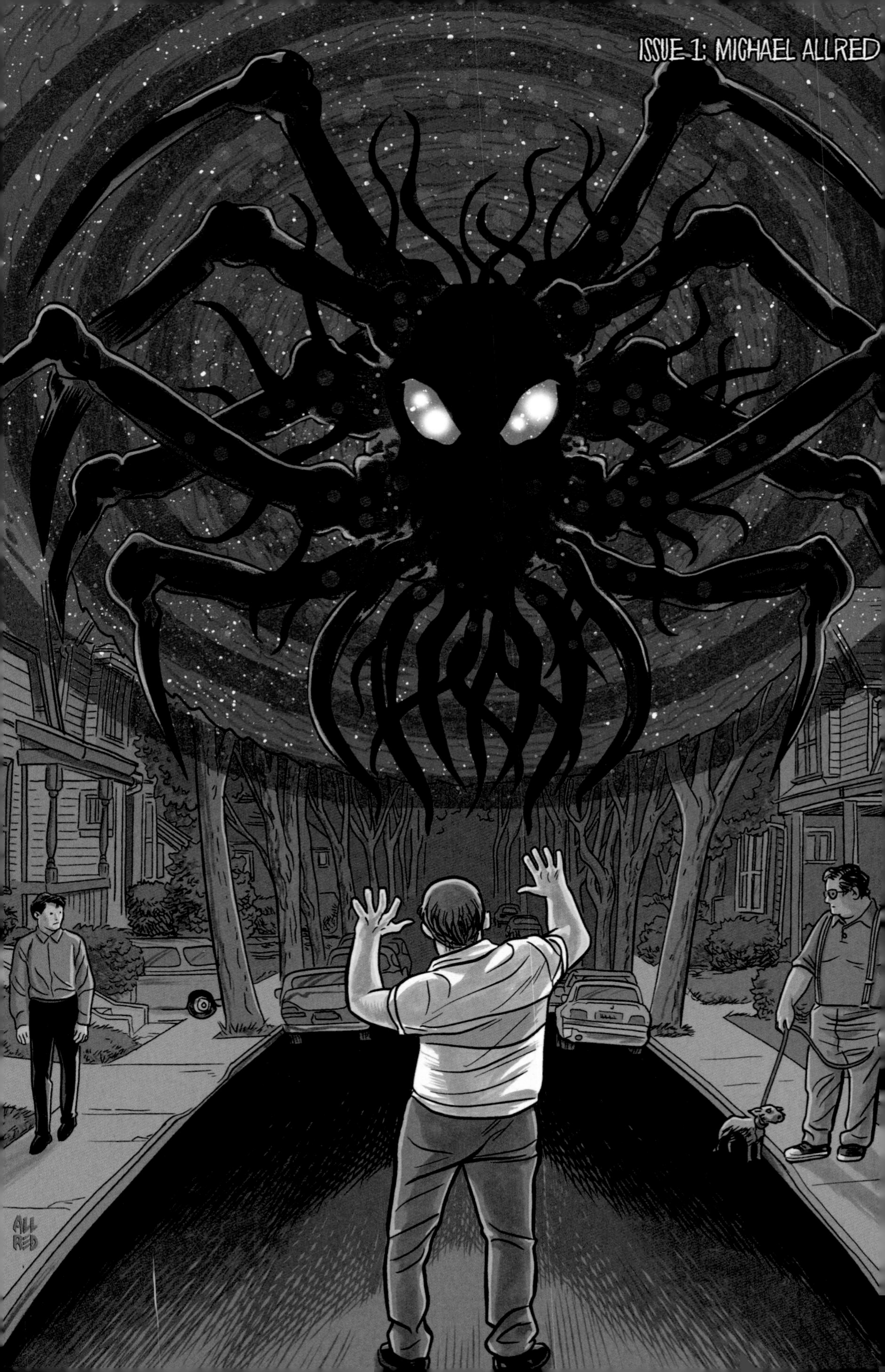

ISSUE 1: MICHAEL ALLRED

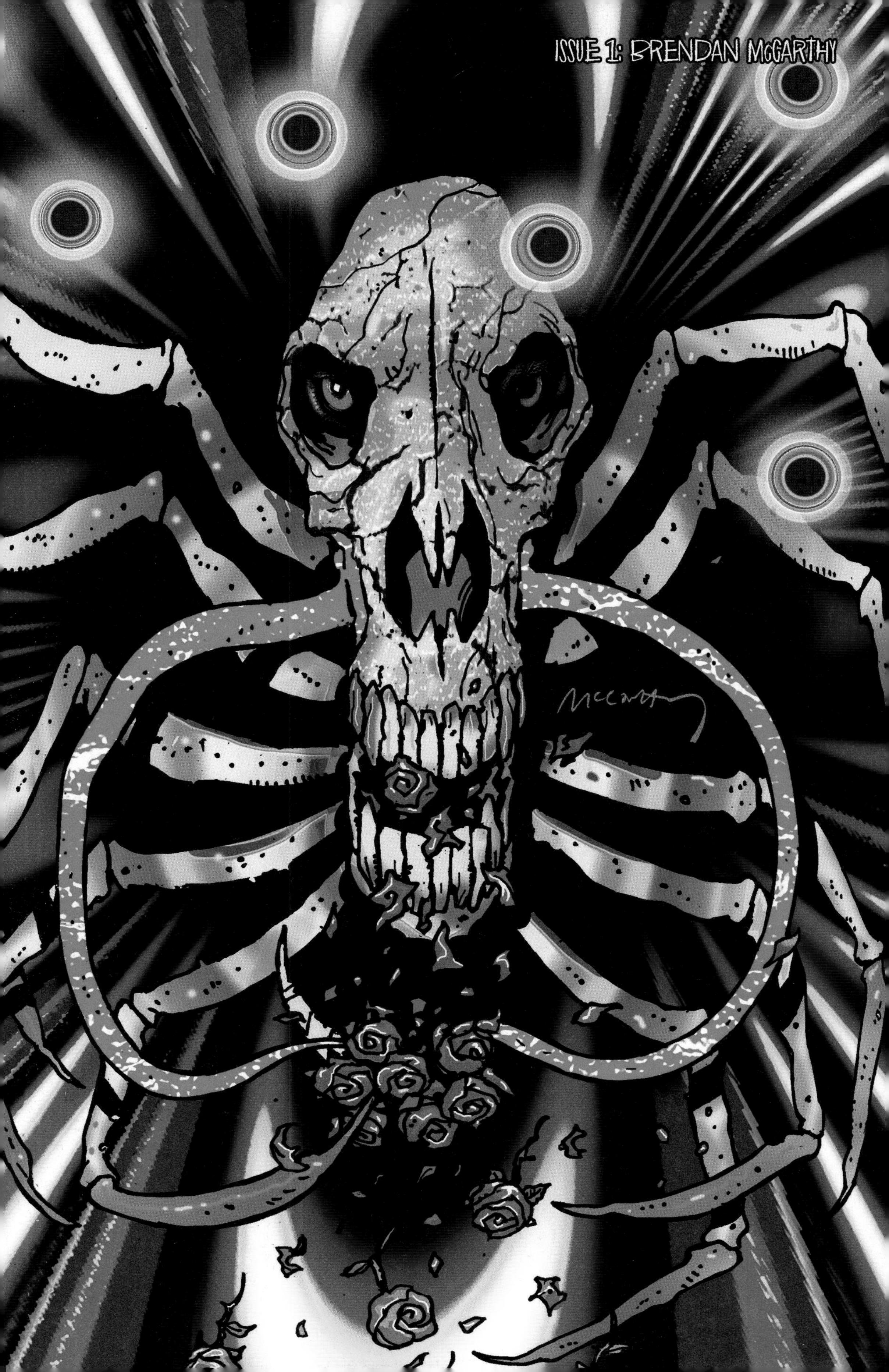
ISSUE 1: BRENDAN McCARTHY

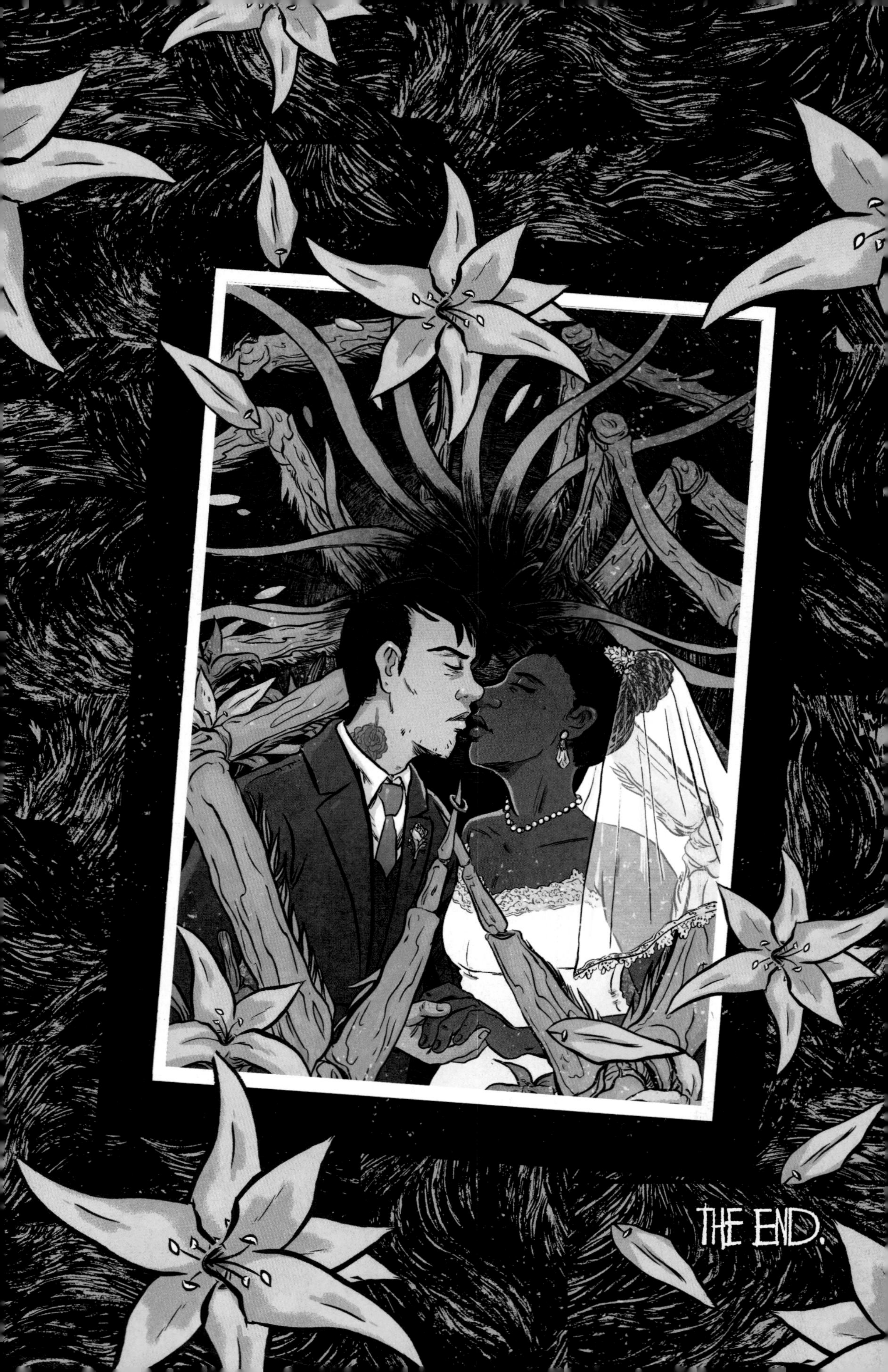
THE END.